# The Economics of Agricultural Technology
in Semiarid Sub-Saharan Africa

## The Johns Hopkins Studies in Development

Vernon W. Ruttan and T. Paul Schultz, Consulting Editors

# The Economics of Agricultural Technology in Semiarid Sub-Saharan Africa

John H. Sanders,
Barry I. Shapiro, and
Sunder Ramaswamy

The Johns Hopkins University Press
Baltimore and London

The Johns Hopkins University Press
2715 North Charles Street
Baltimore, Maryland 21218-4319
The Johns Hopkins Press Ltd., London

Library of Congress Cataloging-in-Publication Data
will be found at the end of this book. A catalog record for
this book is available from the British Library.

Permissions to reproduce previously published
material appear on page 296.

ISBN 0-8018-5139-4

# Contents

# Figures

# Tables

# Foreword

**A**FTER THE GREEN REVOLUTION in Asia, there was great enthusiasm about applying that experience to solving food production problems of the Sub-Saharan agriculture sector. Now almost thirty years have passed, and low-income farmers and consumers are still faced with chronic and acute food crises and poverty caused by population growth and environmental degradation resulting from political insecurity, severe droughts, and poor management of the natural resource base.

Population growth and environmental degradation are on a collision course. Many do not understand the fundamental relation between agriculture and the environment and do not see the role of agricultural science in searching for solutions for change. As per capita grain production has declined in Africa, so has per capita income. Many fear that unless these trends can be reversed, famine may become chronic in Africa, a fact of life to be lived with.

Donors have funded many programs, with the goal of reversing declining agricultural production trends. There have been many successes, but the economic and institutional base for maintaining these advances has not paralleled the advances in technology introduction. There has not been consistent commitment to empowerment of national institutions to address their own problems.

The authors of this book, however, believe that things are not as bleak as we have been led to believe. They suggest that there have been some notable successes and that agricultural technology is the key to success in our learning to manage dryland environments. They put forth a strategy for increasing the impact of new technologies. Their studies indicate that there are cost-effective ways of managing fertilizer and water-conserving technologies that will raise the productivity of the poor so that their incomes can rise and contribute to the base of economic growth of their countries.

This book is an important contribution to the knowledge base for international agricultural improvement.

John Yohe
INTSORMIL, University of Nebraska

# Preface

IN THE SPRING OF 1983, upon returning to the United States after twelve years in Latin America and Portugal, I was drafted as technical adviser to a project in Burkina Faso. After several intensive struggles with French and repeated trips to Burkina Faso and Niger, I focused my research program on the economic impact of new cereal technologies, principally in the Sahel and the Sudan.

Since that first trip in June 1983, I have been challenged by the puzzle of Sub-Saharan African agricultural stagnation: Why have massive infusions of aid into agricultural development and research following the droughts of 1968–73 had so little apparent impact on agricultural output growth and economic performance? This book is meant to provide some insight into this puzzle.

This book is a combined product of the analysis from fieldwork in Burkina Faso during the early 1980s and from fieldwork through the second half of the eighties and nineties, supported by the International Sorghum and Millet Improvement Program (INTSORMIL), in Burkina Faso, Mali, Niger, and the Sudan. The fieldwork and analysis are from these four countries. With appropriate adaptation for other economic, technological, and institutional environments, the analysis is expected to be useful for the rest of semiarid Sub-Saharan Africa.

Sunder Ramaswamy and Barry Shapiro were my graduate students. Both survived my advising and are now successfully engaged in teaching and doing research on development economics at Middlebury College and the International Livestock Research Institute, respectively. Both substantially expanded the scope of this research project in their dissertations and in this book.

Several others contributed to specific chapters. Mohamed M. Ahmed and I worked together on fieldwork in Sudan on the diffusion of a new hybrid sorghum, and we then collaborated on chapter 6. Pareena Lawrence extends the analytical work of Sunder Ramaswamy in the first half of her Ph.D. thesis, and this is incorporated in chapter 9. Della McMillan and Kimseyinga Savadogo report in chapter 10 on their long involvement in Burkina agriculture.

Many students, farmers, and public officials contributed to the evolution of ideas presented here. Meriting special acknowledgement are Dr. John L. Dillon and Dr. Lowell S. Hardin, for seminal ideas, insightful suggestions, and encouragement. Dr. Charles Rhykerd continually encouraged me during the writing process and for at least a year before we started. Katy Ibrahim was also in this vanguard, and I thank her. We are grateful for the diligence, editorial help, and word processing support of Mary Rice and Azeb Bekele and Jeurene Falck's assistance in drawing the maps. The book is dedicated to the intellectual stimulation and motivation received from my adviser at the University of Minnesota, Dr. Vernon W. Ruttan, and to the memory of the induction official for Africa at Purdue, Dr. D. Woods Thomas.

John H. Sanders

# Introduction

THE PERFORMANCE of agriculture and the economy in most of Sub-Saharan Africa during the last two decades is disappointing, despite a substantial flow of resources from industrialized countries. Poor performance in agriculture led to disillusionment with the ability of agricultural science to resolve Africa's food crises. This attitude is in sharp contrast with the early seventies. Then, an optimistic belief existed that agricultural research institutions could diagnose agricultural problems of the region and turn out yield-increasing technologies.

After the Sahelian drought of 1968–73, large-scale donor financing for agriculture was provided to this region and much of Sub-Saharan Africa. Filled with enthusiasm from the Green Revolution successes in Asia in the late sixties and seventies, development agencies applied the same concepts, institutions, and resources to Sub-Saharan African agriculture. Donors supported international agricultural research centers with long-term funding of multidisciplinary commodity programs and also strengthened national agricultural research centers. Now after almost two decades of substantial developmental assistance,[1] African agricultural output per capita continues to stagnate. Why? This continuing decline in per capita agricultural output is the developmental dilemma of African agriculture.

A pessimistic outlook gradually replaced the initial enthusiasm of technology proponents. The resource limitations of African agriculture are aggravated by continuing environmental degradation, natural and man-made disasters, and high population growth. Where there are no wars or ethnic violence to dissipate resources, public mismanagement often hinders developmental activities. Pessimistic extrapolations of the future have become the method used to emphasize the urgency of the problems and thus attract more funding. Unfortunately, external funders and voters in developed countries tire of hearing about seemingly hopeless situations. As Western donors turn their attention in the nineties to the former Communist countries, less attention is being paid to Sub-Saharan African agriculture.

In this book, we analyze the past and potential performance of new agricultural technologies for Sub-Saharan Africa, concentrating on four problems:

- Have there been successes of agricultural technology introduction in the region?
- Are there any common patterns of technology successes or failures that lead to a new strategy for technology development?
- How does this strategy hold up in the evolution of past experience and the potential experience with new technologies?
- What have been the roles of the public and private sectors in the introduction of new technologies, and what changes in these roles are indicated?

There is a wide range in the definition of semiarid in the literature. The International Center for Research on the Semi-Arid Tropics (ICRISAT) defines the semiarid tropics as the area with mean rainfall of 250 to 1,300 millimeters (Debrah, 1993, p. 20). This is a wide area, starting in the Sahelian zone, where crop production is probably not appropriate, and extending far into what most geographers would consider subhumid zones. A much narrower definition of dry semiarid was made by the Food and Agriculture Organization of the United Nations (FAO) of mean rainfall of 400 to 600 millimeters (FAO, 1986, pp. 46, 49). This FAO distinction was apparently made to emphasize the production potential of the moist semiarid zone of 600 to 1,200 millimeters of rainfall to discourage the categorization of moist semiarid as a marginal area. This separation of the two types of semiarid zones also roughly divides the millet-cowpea zone from the sorghum-millet-maize zone. In the areas of 1,000 to 1,200 millimeters of rainfall, we are already moving into the higher-rainfall regions, where cotton and commercial maize production become much more important. This region is usually considered as part of the subhumid zone.

One preferred definition would contain the major crop areas where seasonal water stress reduces yields and the drought-tolerant crops, sorghum and millet, are the principal components in the crop mix. Following Winrock (1992, pp. 16, 17), our definition of semiarid is the rainfall range from 500 to 1,000 millimeters or 90 to 179 plant growth days (fig. I-1). We further subdivide semiarid into the Sahelo-Sudanian and the Sudanian zones, using the World Bank convention of rainfall at 90 percent probability levels rather than mean rainfall (see chapter 2 for further detail on these agroecological zones; see chapters 4 and 5 for the analysis of technology introduction into these two semiarid zones).

This semiarid region includes most of the Sahelian countries and significant areas in Benin, Nigeria, Cameroon, Sudan, Kenya, Tanzania, Zimbabwe, Mozambique, Namibia, and Angola (fig. I-1). Semiarid includes 4

Figure I-1. Agroecological Zones in Semiarid and Subhumid Sub-Saharan
Africa

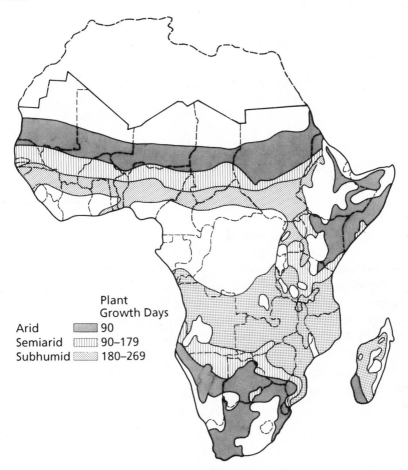

Plant
Growth Days
Arid          90
Semiarid    90–179
Subhumid   180–269

*Source:* Winrock International (1992, p. 16). Reprinted with permission of Winrock International Institute for Agricultural Development, Morrilton, Ark.
*Note:* According to this map, there is almost no semiarid zone in Niger. As seen in figure 5-1, there is an important strip of the Sahelo-Sudanian zone across Niger; this is the main crop production zone of Niger, a region of millet and cowpea.

million hectares, or 19 percent of the area of Sub-Saharan Africa. In southern Africa, this would be 34 percent and in West Africa, 20 percent, of the total area. One-fourth of both the human and the ruminant livestock populations are found in the semiarid region (Winrock International, 1992, p. 18). The incidence of human disease is lower here than in the higher-rainfall zones, so rural population generally has been higher here than in the subhumid and humid zones in West Africa. With the absence of trypanosomiasis and with the higher quality of pasture found in these lower-rainfall regions, the semiarid zone also has had a regional comparative advantage in livestock production.

Most countries in Sub-Saharan Africa with regions of drought stress also have subhumid regions (rainfall of 1,000 to 1,500 millimeters or plant growth days of 180 to 269). The same conceptual framework for technology development in the semiarid zone also turns out to be useful in this subhumid zone. Another 25 percent of the population of Sub-Saharan Africa lives in the subhumid zones (fig. I-1).[2] Moreover, the importance of the northern region of the subhumid zone in livestock production is increasing as the bush is cut, thereby pushing back the tsetse fly. Pastoralists are shifting from migratory herders grazing in the subhumid zone during the dry season to permanent settlement (Winrock International, 1992, p. 19; see also chapter 3).

This book focuses on technology development for the semiarid zone, with some attention also to the subhumid region (see chapters 3 and 10 for an evaluation of the technology performance and development in the subhumid region). These agroecological zones of semiarid and subhumid also approximately correspond with the vegetation types of the dry and moist savannas (fig. I-2). In this book there is minimal attention to the Sahelian region (mean rainfall of 350 to 500 millimeters), except for some mention in chapters 5 and 11. This Sahelian agroecological region is a marginal crop area and is most appropriately used for seasonal pasture. Recently, with higher population

Figure I-2. Moist and Dry Savannas of West Africa

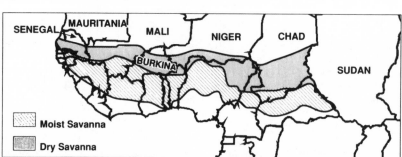

*Source:* Adapted from SAFGRAD (1992, p. 12).

pressure in higher-rainfall regions, crop production has been extending into this zone, threatening the future sustainability of the nomadic livestock production.

In this book, we do not treat the humid or rainforest zones. Here, rainfall is so high that soil leaching, insect, and disease problems are all formidable, technical problems. Root crops, maize, rice, and tree crops are important in the humid tropics for Sub-Saharan food consumption and exports,[3] but most of the food staples for Sub-Saharan Africa are produced in the two savannas. Substantial social gains are expected to come from maintaining the remaining forests. A faster rate of technological change in semiarid and subhumid zones would enable a slowdown of the forest clearing and a retreat of crop production from the Sahelian agroecological zone.

Technological change recommendations vary with rainfall, soils, and economic environments. We have already laid out the two agroecological or rainfall zones of concern here, the semiarid and the subhumid. Most food crop production, of both cereals and legumes, comes from these two regions. These are the primary production areas for maize, sorghum, millet, cowpeas, cotton, and peanuts and for the irrigated production of rice. There are also important soil differences in the region (fig. I-3). We are concerned with three different soil types in our chapters analyzing the impacts of past and potential technological changes (chapters 3 to 6). Finally, the effects of different economic environments on technology introduction and farmers' incomes will be considered throughout the book.

Most of the fieldwork and the modeling reported in this book were undertaken in Burkina Faso, Mali, Niger, and Sudan. But we believe that our conceptual approach, strategy, and policy implications are relevant, with some region-specific adaptation, to the two agroecological zones in all of Sub-Saharan Africa. This analysis also may give some insight for other semiarid and subhumid regions outside Africa.

Our field research in the early eighties began with an emphasis on the semiarid region, because that region was the principal governmental concern in Burkina Faso and Niger due to high population densities in both countries. Niger has no subhumid zone. In Burkina, previous French colonial agricultural research concentrated on the subhumid zone and achieved high payoffs in yield and output increases (chapter 3). In the eighties, the governmental objective in Burkina Faso was to obtain a similar payoff for the semiarid zone.

We begin by reviewing African economic and agricultural trends the last three decades (chapter 1) to evaluate why there is such a pessimistic outlook on African agricultural growth potential. We then present a strategy of ag-

Figure I-3. Principal Soil Associations in Semiarid and Subhumid Sub-Saharan Africa

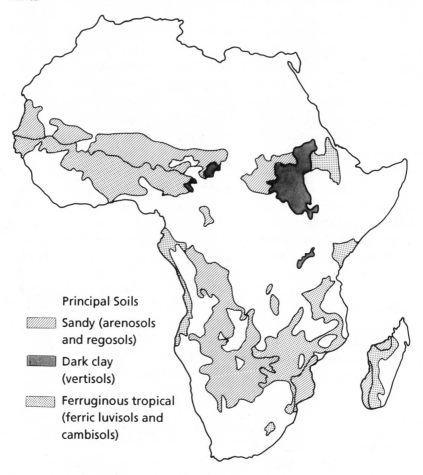

Principal Soils

Sandy (arenosols and regosols)

Dark clay (vertisols)

Ferruginous tropical (ferric luvisols and cambisols)

*Source:* Adapted from FAO, *African Agriculture* (1986, vol. 1, p. 44).

ricultural technology development for the semiarid zone based on our field research in the region over a decade (chapter 2). Detailed case studies from four regions are used to evaluate our hypotheses by identifying the characteristics of new and potential technologies for these regions (chapters 3 to 6). While our principal focus is on the semiarid zone, this strategy, with some adaptation, also is treated for the northern part of the subhumid zone. These case studies include the principal agroecological zones in the semiarid and subhumid zones plus the contrast in the introduction of a new hybrid in the irrigated and semiarid zones of the Sudan (chapter 6).

We then respond to three main criticisms of the introduction of yield-increasing technologies into these two climatic zones. The first is the riskiness of higher purchased-input used (chapter 7). Many argue that small farmers in semiarid regions find new technologies associated with purchased inputs too risky. A second critique is the sustainability of new practices based on purchased, imported chemical inputs (chapter 8). Third, the literature on women in development raises a question about whether women (and children) benefit from the introduction of new intensive technologies.[4] Since women have been the principal labor source in African agriculture and also perform household tasks and off-farm work and make critical investments of time and resources in the raising of children, any technology strategy must focus on their welfare as well as on improvements in family incomes. We evaluate family decision making, labor use, and the distribution of benefits from new technologies to respond to this concern (chapter 9).

We then consider alternative strategies, besides intensive technology development, for increasing agricultural output. We look at two principal alternatives:

- With improved disease control programs, new agricultural areas can be opened up and labor productivity increased. Are these disease-control and area-expansion programs a substitute for or a complement to the yield-increasing technologies recommended here? (chapter 10).
- Similarly, is the improved integration of mixed systems of livestock and crops an alternative to higher purchased-input levels in crop and livestock systems? Chapter 11 also evaluates the characteristics of the new intensive livestock technologies and compares these technologies with our recommendations for crop technologies.

In the conclusion (chapter 12), we review the research strategies, barriers, and alternatives to technology development.

The principal emphasis of the book is to reexamine the historic and potential performances of the semiarid and the subhumid zones to decide whether we should be optimistic or pessimistic about the future of agricultural development in Sub-Saharan Africa. This is not merely a concern of equity or income distribution for the large number of poor farmers in these regions. These regions also need to contribute to the economic growth of their countries.

**I**

# The Framework

# 1

# Economic and Agricultural Stagnation in Sub-Saharan Africa

**D**ROUGHTS and gloomy predictions about the future dominated the reports on Sub-Saharan Africa for decades. Starvation in the Horn and civil war in Rwanda were prime news stories in 1994. Malnutrition and disease, combined with declining per capita food production and stagnant economic growth over the last two decades, contributed significantly to that gloom. Of the major developing regions of the world, only in Sub-Saharan Africa has per capita food and cereal output been declining (figs. 1-1, 1-2).[1] In Asia, Africa, and Latin America, land availability has been declining as

Figure 1-1. Indexes of Per Capita Food Production in Major Developing Regions, 1961–1991

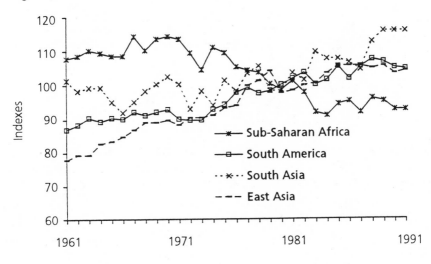

*Source:* Based on data from USDA (1993).

Figure 1-2. Cereal Production in the Developing World, 1961–1991

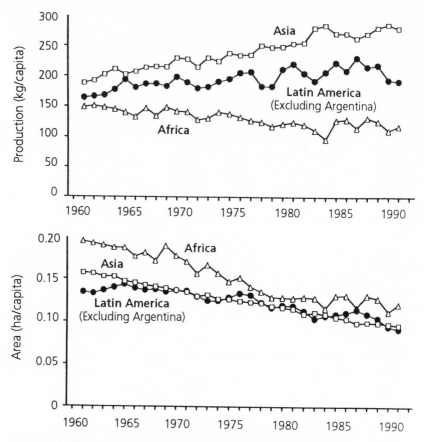

*Source:* Byerlee and Heisey (1993, p. 22). Reprinted with permission of Christopher R. Dowswell, Director for Program Coordination, Sasakawa Africa Association, Minato-ku Tokyo, Japan.

population continues to press on the available resources. However, in Africa, where there has been less productivity growth and the highest population growth, the decrease in land availability has been the most rapid.

Chronic malnutrition and poor economic growth in the region worsened with the outbreak of civil wars, as in Somalia, Sudan, Ethiopia, Mozambique, Rwanda, and Angola, or by corruption and governmental mismanagement on a large scale, as in Zaire and Nigeria. Besides the civil wars, the problems of ethnic and urban violence are increasingly pervasive phenomena in the continent.[2] With the economic declines, most people were poorer at the end of the 1980s than at the beginning. Population reproduction rates continued to be the highest in the world.

In the 1980s, fiscal deficits often arose as parastatals became larger and more inefficient. Moreover, declines in prices of primary products often sharply contracted export earnings, leading to current account deficits. Governments across Africa were pressured by the World Bank, the International Monetary Fund (IMF), and other donor agencies to reduce their public sectors and to remove various price distortions, especially in the exchange rate. The initial effects of these policies, generally referred to as structural adjustment, were decreased imports and reduced public expenditures, leading to recessions (Faini and de Melo, 1990, p. 495).[3] Another contributor to poor economic growth in the eighties was a large debt-service burden, the highest in the world relative to GDP.

Moving into the 1990s, various developing regions are competing for Western public and private funds. With the collapse of the Soviet empire, there is a large demand for capital in Russia and Eastern Europe to overhaul industry and agriculture. Many Asian countries try to imitate the successes of the newly industrialized countries (South Korea, Taiwan, Hong Kong, and Singapore). Even Latin America is regaining the confidence of investors, with reductions in the rates of inflation in most countries and more favorable economic incentives. All these opportunities for public and private investment suggest that the continuing crises and poor economic performance in Sub-Saharan Africa are unlikely to encourage greater donor involvement. Donors do not want to put funds into bottomless pits.[4]

## Economic and Agricultural Performance in Sub-Saharan Africa

Many African countries are poorer today than they were when they achieved their independence in the 1960s, despite decades of development assistance (fig. 1-3). The performance of Sub-Saharan Africa is the worst in the Third World; from 1980 to 1991, the real GDP per capita contracted by 1 percent. In contrast, East Asia and South Asia grew at rates of 6.2 percent and 3 percent respectively during the 1980s (Ayittey, 1992).

The tragedy of this slow growth in the African setting is that incomes were low to start with and access to basic services limited, leaving little or no margin for human error or natural disasters. Ten of the thirty-six African countries reported an overall economic decline over the period 1961–87. Nevertheless, even among the Sahelian countries, one-half (Burkina Faso,

Figure 1-3. Annual Per Capita Economic Growth Rates in Sub-Saharan Africa, 1961–1987

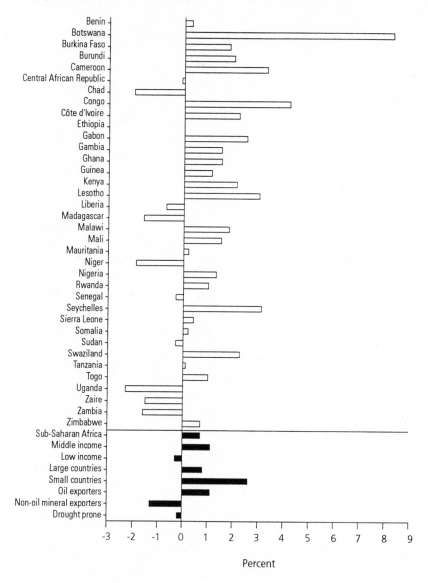

Percent

*Source:* World Bank (1989a, p. 18).

Mali, and Mauritania) had positive growth rates over the period.[5] Even for the poorest countries, there were significant differences in economic performance (Fig. 1-3).

There also were substantial differences in economic performance at different periods. First was an era of rapid growth, from 1965 to 1973. A GDP growth rate of 4 percent, excluding the Nigerian boom, is respectable (table 1-1). In this period, the growth rate of agriculture was moderate, at 1.9 percent, again omitting Nigeria. This is a reasonable growth rate in comparison with historical U.S. and Japanese growth rates in agriculture of 1.4 to 2.5 percent (Ruttan et al., 1978, p. 48). However, high population growth rates reduced substantially the economic growth per capita and turned per capita agricultural growth into a decline of −0.4 percent and −0.7 percent, with and without Nigeria, respectively, for 1965–73. So even in this relatively prosperous period, agricultural production per capita was already declining due to rapid population growth (Eicher, 1992, p. 8).

In the second period, 1973–80, reduced rainfall was an important factor in the poor agricultural performance (table 1-1; fig. 1-4). Rainfall conditions were favorable for agriculture in the fifties and sixties. This trend reversed at

Table 1-1. Economic and Agricultural Growth in Sub-Saharan Africa, 1965–1991 (percent)

|                                | 1965–1973 | 1973–1980 | 1980–1991 |
| ------------------------------ | --------- | --------- | --------- |
| GDP growth                     | 5.9       | 2.5       | 2.1       |
|                                | (4.0)     | (1.7)     |           |
| Agricultural growth            | 2.2       | − 0.3     | 1.8       |
|                                | (1.9)     | (0.7)     |           |
| Population growth              | 2.6       | 2.8       | 3.1       |
|                                | (2.6)     | (2.9)     |           |
| GDP per capita growth          | 3.3       | − 0.3     | − 1.0     |
|                                | (1.4)     | (− 1.2)   |           |
| Agricultural per capita growth | − 0.4     | − 3.1     | − 1.3     |
|                                | (− 0.7)   | (− 2.2)   |           |

*Source:* Based on data from World Bank (1989a, pp. 222, 269); World Bank (1992, pp. 241, 289); World Bank (1993).
*Note:* Calculations in parentheses exclude Nigeria. In 1990, Nigeria had 23 percent of the population of Sub-Saharan Africa.

Figure 1-4. Rainfall in the Sahel, 1921–1994

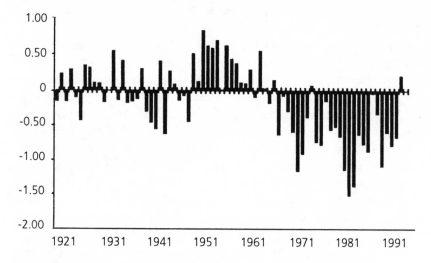

Source: FEWS (1994, p. 1). Reprinted with permission of USAID/FEWS Project, Tulane/ Pragma Group.
Note: This figure graphs the number of standard deviations from average long-term rainfall in the Sahel for each year. The base long-term mean was calculated from rainfall over the period 1951 to 1980.

the end of the 1960s, and the low-rainfall conditions continued through the early nineties. Since 1968, there have been several acute droughts, and rainfall was approximately one standard deviation below the long-term normal in West Africa. Agricultural performance in this second period, 1973–80, dragged down the rest of the economy. The first oil-price shock of 1973 also had a substantial negative effect on oil-importing economies. Growth in per capita incomes turned negative, and agricultural per capita income declines reached −2.2 percent (including Nigeria) to −3.1 percent (excluding Nigeria) for 1973–80 (table 1-1). This disastrous turn of events in the seventies motivated the Lagos conference of 1979 and two reports of the early 1980s analyzing the Sub-Saharan African agricultural dilemma.[6]

Another major drought occurred in the early eighties, along with continuing low rainfall during the decade in West Africa. However, in the second half of the 1980s, the weather was slightly more favorable for agricultural production in Sub-Saharan Africa. Agricultural output growth was then 1.8 percent in the decade (table 1-1) and 4 percent for 1985–88 (World Bank and

UNDP, 1989, p. 7). Due to the high population growth, this was still negative agricultural per capita growth for the decade, at $-1.3$ percent. Nevertheless, these total agricultural growth rates were reasonable, because there was a recovery from the seventies and then an expansion of agricultural output during the second half of the eighties.

GDP growth did not recover from the 1970s. Rather, the aggregate economic growth rates continued at low levels, especially in the 1980–91 period, with a 2.1 percent growth rate (table 1-1; also see table 1-2). Hence, per capita GDP declined over most of the seventies and eighties. This decline is in dramatic contrast to the Asian economies, where income growth and capital formation were much higher and capital formation increased in the eighties.[7] Sub-Saharan capital formation in the eighties declined 14 percent. Both structural adjustment and debt servicing reduce capital formation in the short run (Faini and de Melo, 1990, pp. 491–95), and both are considered in more

Table 1-2. Real GDP Growth, Real Per Capita GDP Growth, and Gross Capital Formation in Sub-Saharan Africa and Asia, 1974–1993 (percent)

| | 1974–83 | 1984 | 1985 | 1986 | 1987 | 1988 | 1989 | 1990 | 1991 | 1992[a] | 1993[a] |
|---|---|---|---|---|---|---|---|---|---|---|---|
| **Real GDP Growth** | | | | | | | | | | | |
| Sub-Saharan Africa | 2.3 | 2.3 | 3.6 | 3.4 | 2.0 | 2.8 | 1.7 | 1.1 | 1.4 | 2.1 | 2.2 |
| Asia | 5.8 | 8.4 | 6.7 | 6.7 | 8.1 | 8.9 | 5.3 | 5.6 | 5.8 | 5.5 | 5.7 |
| **Real per capita GDP growth** | | | | | | | | | | | |
| Sub-Saharan Africa | −0.6 | −0.7 | 0.6 | 0.4 | −1.0 | −0.2 | −1.3 | −1.9 | −1.8 | −1.1 | −1.0 |
| Asia | 3.2 | 6.6 | 5.0 | 4.9 | 6.3 | 7.1 | 3.4 | 3.8 | 4.1 | 3.9 | 4.0 |
| **Gross capital formation (percent of GDP)** | | | | | | | | | | | |
| Sub-Saharan Africa | 20.6[b] | 15.8 | 17.3 | 18.6 | 19.7 | 18.8 | 17.6 | 17.4 | 17.4 | 17.8 | — |
| Asia | 20.4[b] | 28.2 | 29.5 | 28.8 | 28.9 | 29.7 | 29.9 | 29.2 | 29.0 | 29.3 | — |

*Source:* IMF (1992, pp. 110–12).
[a] Projections.
[b] World Bank (1986, p. 24) reports these investment rates for the period 1973–80. This one observation for Asia includes only South Asia.

detail in later sections of this chapter. This decline in investment is expected to result in poor economic performance in Sub-Saharan Africa into the nineties.

In summary, the performances of the African agricultural sectors and economies were reasonable before the 1970s. During the seventies there were chronic and acute droughts and continuing high population growth, leading to low economic growth per capita in the seventies and eighties. There was then a recovery in agricultural growth in the second half of the eighties. Finally, the economic situation is extremely diverse, with negative growth on the average in the low-income countries and substantial variability between countries (fig. 1-3).

## Welfare Levels and Agricultural Demand Growth

There are various measures of improvement in quality of life of the population. Life expectancy in Sub-Saharan Africa ranged from thirty-five to forty-five years in 1960 (see table 1-3). It increased to a range of forty-three to sixty years in 1992. Infant mortality per 1,000 in the first year of life ranged from 110 to 219 in 1960, with a mean of 172. This infant mortality statistic ranged from 59 to 160, with a mean of 103, by 1992. In contrast, high-income countries had a life expectancy of seventy-seven years and an infant mortality rate of 8 per 1,000 in 1991 (World Bank, 1992, pp. 239, 293). Despite these welfare improvements, the differences between life expectancies and infant mortality rates in Sub-Saharan Africa and those in developed countries are still shockingly large, given the existent knowledge about preventive medicine and public health. Most countries of Sub-Saharan Africa experienced decreases in per capita income and in public spending on human welfare (nutrition, education, and public health) in the last decade. A more rapid improvement in these indicators of social welfare would undoubtedly have been achieved with higher economic growth.

A principal concern of any country is its ability to feed its population. Of the 786 million people in the world with chronic undernutrition, in 1988–90 178 million were from Africa, one-third of the African population. This was not only the highest regional proportion, but Africa was also the only region in which the proportion of its population with chronic dietary energy deficiency was almost constant from 1969–71 to 1988–90. In Asia and the Pacific, there were 528 million in this condition in 1988–90, but the region had reduced the proportion from 40 to 19 percent over this period (FAO and WHO, 1992, p. 6).

Table 1-3. Indicators of Social Welfare in Sub-Saharan Africa, 1960 and 1992

| | 1960 | | | 1992 | | |
|---|---|---|---|---|---|---|
| Country | Male Life Expectancy (years) | Adult Literacy (%) | Infant Mortality (per 1,000) | Male Life Expectancy (years) | Adult Literacy (%) | Infant Mortality (per 1,000) |
| Angola | 33 | — | 208 | 46 | 43 | 126 |
| Benin | 37 | — | 185 | 46 | 25 | 88 |
| Botswana | — | — | 116 | 60 | 75 | 61 |
| Burkina Faso | 37 | — | 205 | 48 | 20 | 118 |
| Cameroon | 37 | — | 163 | 55 | 57 | 64 |
| Chad | 35 | 15 | 195 | 47 | 33 | 123 |
| Côte d'Ivoire | 37 | 5 | 166 | 52 | 56 | 91 |
| Ethiopia | 36 | 15 | 175 | 46 | 50 | 123 |
| Ghana | 40 | — | 132 | 55 | 63 | 82 |
| Guinea | 35 | 20 | 203 | 44 | 27 | 135 |
| Kenya | 41 | 45 | 124 | 59 | 71 | 67 |
| Mali | 37 | 10 | 210 | 45 | 36 | 160 |
| Malawi | 37 | — | 207 | 45 | 45 | 143 |
| Mauritania | 37 | 17 | 191 | 47 | 35 | 118 |
| Niger | 37 | 8 | 192 | 46 | 31 | 125 |
| Nigeria | 39 | — | 190 | 52 | 52 | 97 |
| Senegal | 37 | 10 | 172 | 49 | 40 | 81 |
| Sierra Leone | 37 | — | 219 | 42 | 24 | 144 |
| Sudan | 39 | 20 | 170 | 51 | 28 | 100 |
| Tanzania | 42 | 66 | 147 | 41 | 55 | 103 |
| Togo | 37 | 18 | 182 | 54 | 46 | 86 |
| Uganda | 44 | — | 133 | 43 | 51 | 104 |
| Zambia | 40 | 39 | 135 | 46 | 75 | 84 |
| Zimbabwe | 45 | — | 110 | 56 | 69 | 59 |

*Source:* World Bank, 1982, 1993; for 1992 indicators and for 1960 infant mortality rates, see UNDP (1994, pp. 130, 131, 136, 137).

At 3.1 percent, the present population growth rate in Sub-Saharan Africa makes it very difficult to maintain present food consumption levels, much less eradicate malnutrition and reduce agricultural imports. A principal component of any long-term growth program for the region is to slow down the rate of population growth. Ultimately, income growth reduces population growth rates. However, several Asian countries, including India and China, have shown that government policies and social pressures can significantly reduce population growth even in countries at very low income levels. There are now known technologies and public policies to reduce population growth, but Sub-Saharan Africa is not utilizing these public policies (World Bank, 1984, chap. 4).

With population growth at these high rates and a moderate increase in per capita income growth (to 2 percent over the next two decades), growth in the demand for food will be around 4 percent. For example, in the Sahelian countries, two rates of future demand growth are presented in table 1-4.[8] The conservative projections assume the historic rates of economic growth will continue. This pessimistic projection includes economic decline for two-thirds of the Sahelian countries. Except for Burkina Faso and Mali, food demand historically has grown slowly due to economic decline. Increasing food output in the Sahel over the next decade at an annual rate of 4 to 4.5 percent to accommodate economic growth rates of 2 percent per capita would be a substantial achievement.

Developed countries have not achieved rates of agricultural growth of 3.5 to 4.5 percent over long periods, but developing countries must do so to sustain rapidly increasing growth in food demand due to population increase

Table 1-4. Components of Growth in Food Demand in the Sahel, with Historic Economic Growth Rates and Projections (percent)

| Country | Projected Population Growth (1988–2000) | Per Capita Income Growth (1965–1988) | Projected Growth in Food Demand, 1988–2000 | |
|---|---|---|---|---|
| | | | Conservative | Optimistic |
| Chad | 2.7 | −2.0 | 1.5 | 3.9 |
| Burkina Faso | 2.9 | 1.2 | 3.6 | 4.1 |
| Mali | 3.0 | 1.6 | 4.0 | 4.2 |
| Niger | 3.3 | −2.3 | 1.9 | 4.5 |
| Mauritania | 2.7 | −0.4 | 1.5 | 3.9 |
| Senegal | 3.2 | −0.8 | 2.7 | 4.4 |

*Source:* Calculated from World Bank (1990, pp. 178, 228).
*Note:* The conservative estimate assumed that per capita income growth in the period 1988–2000 would continue at the historical annual rates for the period 1965–88. The optimistic projection of demand growth assumed that per capita annual income growth rates of 2 percent would occur over the next twelve years.

and higher economic growth. In the Sub-Saharan countries over the last two decades, the growing gap between domestic demand and domestic production has been met by importing greater amounts of cereals, especially in drought years, and by relying on food aid.[9] From 1976 to 1985, Sub-Saharan Africa moved from net exports of $3.2 billion of agricultural products to net imports of $4.5 billion (FAO *Trade Year Book,* various years). Cereal imports have required large outlays of foreign exchange and further strain these debt-burdened countries.

Traditional production systems have been able to increase agricultural output 0.5 to 1 percent, mainly through area expansion. As population pressures increase, this extensification option rapidly disappears. Historically, developed countries have benefited by increasing agricultural output to keep up with food demand growth of 1 to 2 percent (Ruttan, 1991, p. 17). Rapid technological change introduction will be necessary for the rates of agricultural output growth required in Sub-Saharan Africa.

## The Diagnosis: Sources of the Agricultural Stagnation

Two explanations for the agricultural stagnation are the internal and the external factors. The internal-factors explanation (USDA, 1981; World Bank, 1981; Christensen and Witucki, 1982) emphasizes that following the colonial period, African governments were committed to industrialization and to the political support of urban residents (Lofchie, 1987). To generate the capital for industrialization, exports from agriculture were taxed. The predominant mechanism for taxing agriculture was the use of state-owned or state-controlled agricultural-marketing organizations (parastatals), often with monopoly control of agricultural product and input marketing. While parastatal marketing organizations provided public sector employment and generated savings for other public investments and consumption (Bates, 1981), they reduced the incentives for agricultural production. Producer prices for agricultural exports in many countries were as low as 30 percent of world prices and generally between 50 and 75 percent of world prices in the early 1980s[10] (World Bank, 1986, pp. 64, 65; Lele, 1981, p. 549).

A major indirect tax on agriculture has been imposed by overvalued exchange rates (World Bank, 1986; Elbadawi, 1989). Many governments compel exporters to buy local currency at the official overvalued rate with their export earnings. This implicit tax on exports is often an important source of governmental revenues as well as a disincentive to increase exports. The protection of local industries can reduce real exchange rates, especially when the local protected industries are not efficient producers. Overvalued exchange rates not only decrease the returns on exports but also reduce the costs of imported food and other consumption goods for the urban sector. In the last three decades, there has been an increasing substitution of imported wheat and rice for locally produced sorghum, millet, and maize and, in the higher-rainfall regions, root crops.[11]

In the urban areas, overvalued exchange rates and overproduction of cereals from protective policies in developed countries led to cheap cereal imports for the urban sector. Urban residents learned to organize and respond politically to rising food prices, thereby pressing these governments to continue providing low-cost food, often adding further subsidies to the currency overvaluation. Not only do urban residents press for low food prices, but in the low-income countries they also spend 50 to 60 percent of their incomes on food (Bates, 1990). Employers also want food prices to stay low as the principal wage good. Governments are concerned about urban unrest and maintaining industrial development programs. "Political regimes that are unable to provide low-cost food are seen as dangerously incompetent and as failing to protect the interests of key elements of the social order" (ibid., p. 156).

Meanwhile, with these low agricultural prices and other distortions unfavorable to agriculture, domestic food production stagnated. Farmers retreated from commercial activities to subsistence as a response to the low and unstable domestic cereal prices. There was little incentive for these farmers to invest in new technologies or in any other agricultural investment. With the unfavorable economic environment, declining soil fertility, and increasing population pressure, many farmers became dependent on food purchases (Weber et al., 1988, p. 1046). To pay for these purchases required off-farm labor, remittances, or sales of other farm products. Seasonal and long-term out-migration often became part of family income strategies. So economic distortions in the urban areas discouraged investment in agriculture and accelerated the dependence of these agricultural systems on activities outside agriculture. Within agriculture, low profitability encouraged low-productivity, risk avoidance measures, including multiple cropping, minimal input use, and extensive agricultural activities based on human labor.

The welfare of farmers was reduced not only by direct and indirect taxes on their exports and distortions reducing prices of competing imports but also by the poor rural marketing systems for industrial goods. Prices for manufactured consumer goods in rural areas tended to be very high (Berthélemy and Morrison, 1989, pp. 12, 13).[12] With reduced agricultural output prices from the taxes and high-priced consumer goods, it is amazing that agriculture performed as well as it did in the early sixties and the late eighties.

Another popular explanation for agricultural stagnation and economic slowdown blames external factors, especially the adverse environment for exports from Sub-Saharan Africa to developed countries and the worsening debt burden.[13] When the five oil-exporting countries are excluded, the terms of trade consistently moved against the low-income countries (over two-thirds of the region qualifies under this category) after the early 1970s (World Bank and UNDP, 1989, p. 11; World Bank, 1989a, pp. 24–25; Svedberg, 1991, p. 551). In the second half of the eighties, the barter terms of trade for low-income countries was 60 percent of the 1970–73 level. Low-income countries are the least able to withstand the deleterious effects of declining terms of trade.

In the 1980s, there were substantial pressures to repay the debt acquired in the seventies (Dornbusch, 1988). Although the absolute amounts of debt accumulated in Sub-Saharan Africa were small compared with the major developing-country debtors of Latin America and Asia, the small total sizes of these economies and the previous high proportions of foreign assistance resulted in the highest debt-to-GNP ratios in the world.

In 1987, the debt-to-GNP ratio was 63 percent in Latin America and 104 percent in Sub-Saharan Africa (Nafziger, 1993, p. 16). The absolute debt was much greater for the principal debtors in Latin America, so the concentration of the international financial markets was on servicing their debt there. In Sub-Saharan Africa, debt service obligations would have taken 46 percent of export earnings in 1986, 36 percent in 1986, and 24 percent in 1990 (World Bank and UNDP, 1989, p. 17; Nafziger, 1993, p. 16). With such large pressures on their limited foreign exchange, only twelve countries serviced their debts consistently during the 1980s, while twenty-five countries rescheduled their debts 105 times from 1980 to 1988 (World Bank and UNDP, 1989, p. 17). In contrast with middle-income developing countries owing over two-thirds of their debt to the private sector, in the low-income African countries only 13 percent of debt was held by the private sector (Nafziger, 1993, pp. 17, 19). In 1990, the overall Sub-Saharan debt was divided principally between governments (bilateral lending, 51 percent) and multilateral institutions (34 percent) (Nafziger, 1993, p. 10).

Total debt increased from $6 billion in 1970 to $183 billion in 1993 (Lancaster, 1991, p. 22; "African Debt," 1993). Sub-Saharan countries refused to pay 50 percent of their debt-servicing obligations. Nevertheless, debt repayments they made were equal to 20 percent of Sub-Saharan exports in 1992 (ibid.). Repayment has taken substantial resources away from both consumption and capital formation. A key issue in debt repayment discussions is understanding why previous investments had such low returns that repayment is so difficult.

Sub-Saharan African economies are still essentially producers of primary products, especially agricultural products. Since the fifties, one popular policy recommendation for economies with external economic problems from adverse terms of trade and debt is to diversify the economy away from a dependence on primary products.[14] Should Sub-Saharan Africa, like Hong Kong and Taiwan, specialize in labor-intensive manufacturing and depend on developed countries for a higher proportion of its agricultural products? There are several major problems with this position. First, Sub-Saharan industries stagnated in the eighties. In 1987 the proportion of manufacturing in GDP of these African economies was 11 percent, compared with 9 percent in 1965.[15] Sub-Saharan Africa exports few industrial products. The educational levels of the labor force are low in Sub-Saharan Africa and, relative to much of Asia, the wage rates are high (IMF, 1994b, p. 60). So it is difficult for Sub-Saharan Africa to compete in world markets with Asia in labor-intensive manufacturing exports; however, there are undoubtedly industrial subsectors or niches in which Sub-Saharan Africa could develop a comparative advantage. Unfortunately, other costs of production besides labor, especially transportation, are generally high, so the region's comparative advantage is still firmly in primary products (Lele, 1986a). Ninety percent of African exports in 1987 were primary commodities (Lancaster, 1991, p. 2). In general, the transformation of economies from primary to industrial products has not yet occurred in most of Sub-Saharan Africa (Lall, 1992, pp. 103–10).

For employment, food self-sufficiency, and foreign exchange reasons, Sub-Saharan Africa needs to develop its agricultural sector.[16] In most Sub-Saharan African countries, one-half to two-thirds of the population and labor force are in agriculture. Population in rural areas is still growing at high rates (World Bank, 1986). Urban expansion of employment has been slow. In 1990, agriculture provided 32 percent of Africa's GDP, 66 percent of employment (for 1987), and 29 percent of its exports (World Bank, 1989a, p. 8; World Bank, 1992, pp. 223, 249, 279). Moreover, there are strong political pressures on governments to avoid dependence on purchased or concessional food imports. The prices and availabilities of both types of imports fluctuate substantially, and the response of the urban sector to food-price fluctuation can be politically destabilizing.

Hence, whether analysts appeal to external or internal factors to explain the agricultural stagnation in Sub-Saharan Africa,[17] most agree that agricultural development is critical to future economic growth and improvements in welfare. The predominant cure recommended for the agricultural and economic stagnation of the 1980s, structural adjustment programs, emphasized internal adjustments by developing countries. These structural adjustment programs then had significant effects in slowing the economic growth of the eighties.

## The Recommended Cure: Structural Adjustment in the 1980s

Until the early seventies, there were favorable terms of trade for low-income countries in Sub-Saharan Africa, and governmental revenues were expanding. Public expenditures were made on infrastructure and social welfare programs and on expanding the public sector into many new activities. Various consumer subsidies were common, especially on imported cereals, gasoline, and machinery parts.

The terms of trade declined for low-income African economies in the late seventies and for the entire region in the eighties (World Bank, 1989a, pp. 24, 25). In the late seventies, external lending continued at fairly high levels and enabled governments to maintain these expenditures (McNamara, 1985, p. 6). Unfortunately, rather than investing in productive activities in agriculture, industry, and infrastructure or raising welfare levels of the low-income sector, much of public expenditures went into consumption activities, especially

- transfers to parastatals
- oil imports
- military expenditures
- presidential and ministerial looting of the public treasury
- monuments, such as statues, stadiums, palaces, and luxury hotels

The failure to profitably invest the capital inflows in the sixties and seventies was compounded by the increasing distortions and misallocations of poor economic and agricultural policies (Lancaster, 1991, pp. 2–4, 10; Bates, 1981), including

- overvalued exchange rates and trade restrictions
- distortions or controls of prices, wages, and interest rates
- growth of stifling bureaucracies
- corrupt behavior among decision makers
- expanding black markets and smuggling

Thus, in the seventies, increasing public and private consumption of capital inflows and a series of distortions led to low returns on public expenditures and little effective public investment.

Deteriorating economic conditions in Sub-Saharan African economies became critical with the economic shocks of the early eighties. The principal shocks to most developing countries were the abrupt increases in international interest rates of the early eighties and worldwide pressures from the private banking sector to recover some of their previous investments. However, in Sub-Saharan Africa almost all the debt (85 percent) was held by bilateral donors and international institutions, so the private banking system was not as involved, and interest rates were more stable. Nevertheless, Sub-Saharan Africa had the same crises as the rest of the developing countries in the 1980s, of increasing expenditures to maintain consumer subsidies and parastatals while the export sector declined, leading to unemployment and decreased tax bases. Frequently, governments handled increasing budget deficits by printing money, and inflation accelerated. There were then International Monetary Fund (IMF) pressures to reduce spending, increase taxes, and move to a contractionary monetary policy. The IMF generally recommended reductions in consumer subsidies and in transfers to the parastatals. These parastatals, as political entities, had often substantially expanded their workforces, so that a reduction in transfers implied laying off employees.

Countries resisting these changes found reduced capital flows not only from the IMF but often from the World Bank and even bilateral donors. Previously, these capital flows had enabled Sub-Saharan African countries to maintain overvalued exchange rates. Now these capital flows were reduced or cut off. This is illustrated in figure 1-5, which shows the demand and supply of real foreign exchange. To maintain a price for the domestic currency that is overvalued ($R^1$), a country needs the capital inflow $CE$ to cover the deficit between the supply and the demand for foreign exchange. The advantage of the overvalued exchange rate to the country was as a hidden tax on exports and to reduce the costs of imports and thereby benefit industrialists and urban consumers. Over time this overvalued exchange rate also builds up a domestic lobby supporting it, including a state bureaucracy to ration imports and, therefore, reduce the requirements for capital inflows ($CB$ in fig. 1-5). An import-rationing bureaucracy provides employment, enables the government to focus imports toward its political objectives, and offers opportunities for rent-seeking behavior.

Export earnings had already stagnated with the adverse movements in the terms of trade. When the capital flow $(CB)$ was now reduced or eliminated,

Figure 1-5. Demand and Supply for Real Foreign Exchange

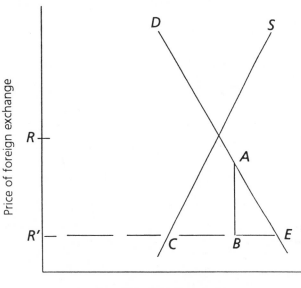

governments without reserves had no choices but to devalue. Devaluation increases the price of tradables relative to nontradables, increasing exports and decreasing imports, thereby increasing the supply of foreign exchange and reducing the demand for it as the real exchange rate moves to *R* (fig. 1-5). The IMF and the World Bank began to tie their capital movements to these devaluations.

Devaluation reduces societal welfare because it makes all tradable goods more expensive, and most African countries had been subsidizing several basic import expenditures of their urban residents, especially food and transportation expenses.[18] This welfare reduction is illustrated in figure 1-6 and explained in more detail in the appendix to this chapter. The long-term effects of devaluations are to shift resources (labor, capital, management ability) from less-productive to more-productive sectors (from the nontradable to the tradable sectors) and thereby increase the efficiency and output of the economy. The immediate consequence is a reduction in welfare of those facing higher prices and a discouraging of investment from the deflationary forces of this welfare reduction. To respond to these negative effects of fiscal reform and devaluation, these fiscal austerity and devaluation measures were com-

Figure 1-6. Impact of Devaluation on Welfare and Product Mix

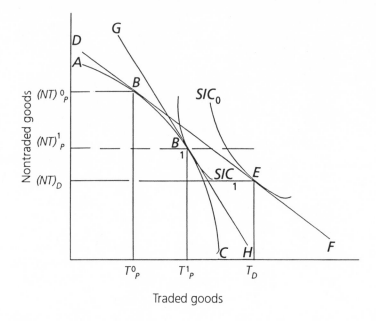

*Source:* Salter (1959).

bined with a series of other adjustments designed to increase the efficiency of the economy. The package evolved and became known as structural adjustment.

Structural adjustment began as fiscal reform to respond to overspending on parastatals and on consumer subsidies and then evolved to devaluation as the current account deficits increased.[19] As the deflationary effects of higher import prices became clear, structural adjustment also included the removal of other price distortions (subsidies and taxes), eliminating the subsidies on energy prices, increasing the efficiency or reducing the role of the parastatal organizations, and improving the regulatory environment for private entrepreneurs. These measures were aimed at improving the efficiency of resource allocation by having price signals more accurately reflect their real values to the society and by enabling private entrepreneurs to compete with and even replace parastatals.

As with most economic policies, there are losers and gainers. The losers in structural adjustment programs are civil servants, industrial workers, and other urban residents. They previously benefited from low agricultural prices, from the taxing of agricultural exports to generate a financial surplus to be spent in urban areas, and from overvalued exchange rates that made imports — including imported food — cheaper. The expected gainers from structural adjustment are farmers and new entrepreneurs. In summary, reduced employment in the parastatals and the higher urban food prices would then shift income from bureaucrats and other urban workers to farmers. Since the losers have been much more powerful politically than the gainers, strong pressures from outside donor agencies were necessary to effect these reforms (Lancaster, 1991, pp. 10, 11). Conditionality (the linking of continuing external lending to structural reform programs) became pervasive (Sachs, 1988, p. 277ff; Helleiner, 1986, pp. 63–91). In 1990, $12 billion of the $15 billion of concessional aid from the World Bank to Sub-Saharan Africa was associated with structural adjustment programs. Thirty of the forty-five Sub-Saharan African countries had implemented stabilization, structural reform programs, or both (Lancaster, 1991, p. 12).

In the eighties, the World Bank and the IMF supplemented their lending programs with policy loans[20] aimed at introducing economic reforms to shift the relative prices toward world prices and thereby enhance efficiency in resource use and improve long-run growth opportunities (Azcarate, 1986). The agricultural sector was expected to play a major role in structural reforms for various reasons. First, the sector still represented a substantial component of domestic production in most Sub-Saharan countries. Hence, the supply response in the agricultural sector became a crucial determinant of the overall response of the economy to changing economic incentives. Second, most economists and policymakers were convinced that trade and sectoral policies since the 1960s had discriminated against the agricultural sector. Redressing such a bias became an essential priority on the structural reform agenda (World Bank, 1986; Knudsen and Nash, 1991). Finally, it was argued that a healthy pattern of structural adjustment, based on exports and income expansion rather than on imports and demand contraction, would stimulate a strong performance of the agricultural sector (Faini, 1993).

Most of the countries of Sub-Saharan Africa have implemented these policies, generally with advice and financing from the IMF, the World Bank, and individual developed-country donors. The expected long-run effects of the structural adjustment programs will be

- improved incentives to farmers by increasing product prices and decreasing input costs, principally by encouraging private traders to substitute for the state trading companies
- expanded private investment

- economic efficiency gains through eliminating price distortions and input price subsidies and the control of imports
- improvements in trade balances by stimulating exports and reducing imports
- development of the appropriate energy resources and improved energy conservation by removing taxes and subsidies, thereby giving the energy sector price incentives corresponding to the value of the productive resources in the economy

Gains from structural adjustment come from the reallocation of resources into more productive activities in response to changing relative prices, including realignment of the exchange rate. With a decreased and more efficient public sector, incentives and investment efficiency are both increased for private entrepreneurs. However, in an atmosphere of pessimism and uncertainty about the future, private investors may not respond to improved price incentives. In the low-income countries, the reduction of investment by the public sector has not been offset by the growth of the private sector. Hence, the short-term effects of these policies in most low-income countries in the eighties were deflationary, reducing investment and growth and even reducing the capacity to repay the debt (Faini and de Melo, 1990).[21] Generally, the current account or trade balance problem improved with structural adjustment (table 1-5).[22]

The effects of structural adjustment on income distribution will be regressive if subsidies have been removed from basic necessities, increasing the prices of food and other basic imports. Exchange rate devaluations, especially changes such as the 50 percent devaluation of the CFA[23] in January 1994 (see the appendix to this chapter), substantially increased the prices of food, fuel imports, and machinery parts. Since undernutrition is already common in the low-income sector and this low-income sector has little capacity to adjust to relative price changes by shifting expenditure patterns, there are significant welfare reductions from structural adjustment.

The predominant attack on devaluation has been that the responsiveness to price changes is so low in the economy that instead of consumption and resource allocation shifting from the nontradable to the tradable sector, there will be contraction of the economy, with increased unemployment, decreased growth, and reduced investment (Faini and de Melo, 1990). With the deflation, private investment will decline, and the shift of productive resources between sectors will slow down. Similarly, shifts by consumers will also be minimal. The Keynesian response to these rigidities impeding adjustment is

Table 1-5. Indicators of Economic Activity Before and
After Structural Adjustment

| Indicator | Primary Product Exporters in Developing Countries | | | Selected Sub-Saharan African Countries | | |
|---|---|---|---|---|---|---|
| | 1978–1981 | 1982–1986 | 1986–1988 | Before Structural Adjustment[a] | After Structural Adjustment[a] | 1986–90 |
| GDP growth (%) | 2.8 | 1.4 | 2.4 | 2.7 | 1.8 | −0.4 to 1.1[b] |
| Investment/GDP (%) | 21.0 | 18.0 | 17.0 | 20.6 | 17.1 | 16.8 |
| Debt service/exports (%) | 15.0 | 20.0 | 29.0 | 17.5 | 23.4 | 21.9 |
| Current account/GDP (%) | | | | −9.4 | −6.5 | −4.7 |
| Real exchange rate index[c] | 103.0 | 113.0 | 139.0 | | | |

Source: Data for the primary product exporters in developing countries are from Faini and de Melo (1990, p. 494); data for Sub-Saharan Africa before and after structural adjustment are from World Bank (1988, p. 27). The principal indicators were then updated with data from World Bank, World Development Reports, for 1988 through 1992. Sudan and Guinea-Bissau were deleted for lack of data. Data for Sub-Saharan Africa 1986–90 are from World Bank, World Development Reports, for 1986 through 1990.
[a] Data refer to three years prior to and three years following the structural adjustment loans.
[b] As with the Before and After cases, this is an unweighted average of the fifteen Sub-Saharan countries implementing structural adjustment before 1985 (see comments above, in Source). The range is due to the inclusion or deletion of Tanzania.
[c] 1980 = 100.

to make strategic investments. For example, investments in food processing and preparation technologies could help make the domestically produced cereals, sorghum and millet, more competitive with the imported wheat and rice, especially if the higher opportunity costs of women's time in urban areas are an important factor in the shift of consumption patterns between imported and domestically produced cereals.

Moreover, basic infrastructure investments, as in transportation, communication, education, and other human capital, appear to be a necessary component of improved mobility of the productive resources between sectors and the creation of an industrial sector. So in responding to delays of resource adjustment during structural reform in low-income countries, we are returning to the development concepts of the fifties of increasing investment in physical capital but with the addition of also raising investment in human capital.[24] Who will pay for all this?

The donors' dilemma is: Will structural adjustment really take place if it requires shifts in political power to two groups with little previous influence, namely, farmers and new entrepreneurs? Or will the traditional power holders, especially in the governmental and industrial sectors, and the urban population as a whole press governments to undermine structural reform programs so as to hold on to their political advantages from the economic distortions? The distortions became so serious in many countries that there was popular support for structural reform. How long will this continue if welfare levels of the poor do not improve soon?

## Conclusion

Public mismanagement and rapid population growth lead many to extreme pessimism about the economic growth potential in Sub-Saharan Africa. Because agriculture continues to be the most important producer and employer in most of these economies, the performance of agriculture is critical to overall economic growth. Despite an adverse climatic and economic environment for agriculture during most of the last three decades, there have been periods of reasonable agricultural output growth, in the sixties and late eighties. International and national efforts to improve economic and agricultural policies, especially the incentives offered to farmers, have been made in the last decade and should result in higher agricultural output growth in the nineties.

Few donors or economists dispute the need for structural adjustment or the short-run negative effects of this policy on growth and investment, especially for the poorest countries. Many African policymakers have been disillusioned by structural adjustment. The initial sales pitch for these policies was generally the secondary effects of the long-run improved economic efficiency and increased output. Little emphasis was given to the immediate, well-known primary effect of a sharp contraction in social welfare resulting from the decreased capital flows and the increased import prices. Economists expected devaluation to have a large contractionary effect on consumption and investment before the improved price signals could begin a reallocation of resources. Now many policymakers in developing countries are angry about the political impacts of the first contraction and the long delay for the promised beneficial secondary effects.

The structural adjustment process may need to continue for another decade in Sub-Saharan Africa, since these are large economic and political shifts with only a small sector of domestic beneficiaries at the start of the process. In the nineties, both the elimination of the monopoly power of the parastatals and the correction of the price distortions, including those from overvalued exchange rates, will contribute to agricultural and industrial profitability through higher export prices, increased export opportunities, and the shift of resources to more profitable areas. The short-run problem is how to emerge from the recessions induced by structural adjustment and other factors. The time required by low-income countries for recovery and adjustment from the adverse effects of structural reform programs is unknown. As the process continues and benefits to consumers become more apparent, the structural adjustment programs will ultimately generate domestic support.[25] Meanwhile, the continuation of structural adjustment will depend on external donor agencies.

Most low-income countries of Sub-Saharan Africa have been dependent on a few primary product exports and on the pervasive role of the state in the economy. Industrial development is constrained by poor supporting physical infrastructure, a historic distrust of the private sector, and low previous investments in the health and education of the workers. These factors lead to high production costs that limit the ability to compete for industrial exports or to rapidly shift labor, capital, and management between sectors of the economy. Attaining long-term growth will require more than the price and institutional changes of structural adjustment. Long-term growth involves sustained productivity increases in the basic industries, especially agriculture. The rest of this book is concerned principally with the technological changes in agriculture needed to take advantage of this improved economic environment resulting from structural adjustment.[26]

Structural adjustment can only set up the environment or the playing field for economic growth. Increasing efficiency in the public and private sectors by eliminating price distortions and decreasing the public sector are the central concerns of structural adjustment programs. It will also be necessary to reduce corruption and establish clear rules of the game for entrepreneurs. These latter measures will be more difficult than eliminating price distortions and obtaining an equilibrium exchange rate (McNamara, 1985, p. 9).

## Appendix: Social Welfare Reduction of a Devaluation and the CFA Franc Devaluation in 1994

For most of Sub-Saharan Africa, problems of misallocation of public resources and the various economic shocks in the early eighties created a crisis situation. In figure 1-6, an overvalued exchange rate is tangent to the frontier of production possibilities at $B$. So $(NT)^0{}_P$ and $T^0{}_P$ are the quantities indicated by the relative prices for domestic production of nontradables and tradables. With the social indifference curve $SIC_0$, the level of nontradables desired by consumers is much lower than production. Since these cannot be traded, there is idle capacity or some underemployment in this sector. For the traded goods, the price signals do not encourage sufficient production. Much higher level of consumption, $T_D$, than of production, $T^0{}_P$, results from trade and has to be financed by capital flows. So overvaluation of the exchange rate on expenditure line $DBF$ results in an underemployment situation resulting from the wrong price signals to the economy, and the maintenance of an overvalued exchange rate becomes dependent on capital flows (see fig. 1-5, Helmers, 1988, ch. 2; Salter, 1959). One contribution of an overvalued exchange rate is as an indirect export tax. Such taxes on trade have been shown to be important revenue sources in many developing countries (Edwards, 1989, p. 256). Maintaining an overvalued exchange rate ($R^1$) requires a capital flow of $CE$ (fig. 1-5). One governmental response has been to shift the demand curve for real foreign exchange $(DE)$ to $DAB$, with import restrictions, licenses, or tariffs. This reduces the capital requirements to $CB$. The foreign exchange savings, $BE$, result from the bureaucratic restrictions reducing imports (fig. 1-5).

In the eighties, the capital flow $(CB)$ was reduced in Sub-Saharan Africa by increased pressures to repay debts and changes in donors' policies, especially their decreased interest in supporting parastatals. With the export declines from shifts in primary product prices of the late seventies and eighties and with international and national agencies unwilling to provide increased capital flows, most developing countries were forced to devalue. A similar pressure to devalue results from the shift backward of the supply curve of real foreign exchange, reflecting decreased trade and service flows. This also occurred in the early eighties as the continuing recession in the developed countries led to reduced imports from developing countries.

This consequent required devaluation is reflected in the shift of the real exchange rate to the expenditure line $GB_1H$. This is a forced reduction of social welfare to $SIC_1$ in figure 1-6, because the capital flow financing higher consumption is now eliminated. The favorable potential effects result from the domestic resource reallocation, a reduction of the production of nontradables (from $NT^0{}_P$ to $NT^1{}_P$) and an increase in the production of tradables ($T^0{}_P$ to $T^1{}_P$). Note that there is a sharp welfare contraction forced by the economic shocks now preventing the developing country from maintaining an overvalued exchange rate, since the social indifference curve shifts inward from $SIC_0$

to $SIC_1$ as a consequence of the devaluation. This reduction in welfare is the primary effect of the devaluation; but this shift was required by the reduced capital flows, which had been previously utilized to cover the difference between the supply and the demand for foreign exchange.

Due to tighter fiscal and monetary policy, the French economic community of fourteen African countries had fewer problems with inflation and lower budget and current account deficits than most other African countries in the seventies and the first half of the eighties. The French government also was a funder of last resort to provide the necessary capital flow to maintain an overvalued currency.

In the mid-eighties, the CFA zone experienced significant shocks as the terms of trade for its principal primary exports (cocoa, coffee, cotton, petroleum) declined by 50 percent (IMF, 1994b, p. 60). Moreover, the competitiveness of the zone was decreased by the appreciation of the French franc with respect to the other industrial countries of Europe. Trade with Europe represents approximately 40 percent of the GDP of the countries in the CFA zone.

The consequences for the CFA countries in comparison with the non-CFA countries of Sub-Saharan Africa over the period 1986–93 were

- GDP growth of 0.1 percent, compared with 2.5 percent
- GDP per capita growth of −2.8 percent, compared with −0.3 percent
- fiscal balance of −7.4 percent of GDP, compared with −5.6 percent
- external current account (including grants) of −7.4 percent of GDP, compared with −0.8 percent
- external debt of 74 percent of GDP, compared with 57 percent (IMF, 1994a, p. 61)

The CFA countries still maintained more fiscal and monetary discipline with an average inflation rate of 1 percent as compared with 22 percent for the non-CFA countries over this period.

Then on January 11, 1994, the CFA was devalued 50 percent. Major welfare adjustments are being observed in the CFA countries presently. Many countries have been offsetting some of these adjustments with continuing subsidies because of the large impact of food and fuel prices on the welfare of the low-income sector.

# 2

# A Strategy of Agricultural Technology Development for the Semiarid and Subhumid Regions of Sub-Saharan Africa

I N THE LAST THREE DECADES, one urgent problem in Sub-Saharan Africa was the decline of per capita output growth in the agricultural sector and a rising dependence on food imports. Presently, Sub-Saharan countries are concerned with improving agricultural production, especially food crops. Area expansion has been the conventional way of increasing output, but this is becoming difficult in most regions. Yield increases have been obtained for export crops, such as cotton and peanuts, and for irrigated crops, such as rice and green beans, and recently for rain-fed maize. Intensive techniques to augment yields are expected to become more important for the other principal food crops besides maize (see Ruttan, 1991, p. 17; World Bank, 1989a, p. 99).

The historic view of Sub-Saharan agriculture held that land was abundant and seasonal labor was the principal constraint to increased agricultural output. In a land surplus environment, farmers can move on to new areas rather than improve land productivity. To expand area and overcome seasonal labor bottlenecks, animal traction programs were promoted, especially in the last two decades and even earlier in some countries.[1] Diffusion of animal traction has accelerated in the last decade. Unfortunately, increased population growth has brought on a demise of the fallow system, the disappearance of forests, and the degradation of land and water resources.

The development of higher-yielding systems was emphasized in the international and the national agricultural research systems during the last two decades. The principal orientation, especially of the international agricultural research centers (IARCs) following Green Revolution successes, was toward introduction of new cultivars. In much of the savanna, the production environment is harsh: low-fertility and fragile soils, low and irregular rainfall.

New cultivars in the dry savannas made little impact on yields. Unfortunately, in the semiarid region of Sub-Saharan Africa, there were few successes in substantially increasing land productivity with new technologies. The failure of the cultivar approach is one basic problem considered in this chapter and the rest of the book. To respond to this we develop a strategy of technology development for semiarid regions, which then turns out to be relevant with some adaptations for subhumid regions.

## The Demand for New Technologies

In the colonial period, export and plantation agricultural sectors coexisted with subsistence production farms. The subsistence sector provided labor for the export sector and produced food for its own consumption and for domestic sale. In some countries, such as Burkina and Mali, the small-farm sector directly produced the export crop, such as cotton or peanuts, with the supervision of the exporting agency. Export crops had the foreign markets and were the principal interest of the colonial governments. Subsistence production took care of itself. There was little research or policy support for food crops, with the exception of maize in East and southern Africa. A large increase in food output, resulting from technological change, favorable policy, or even good weather, was expected to lead to a collapse in food prices due to inelastic demand.

In most countries after independence, export crops have been heavily taxed directly and indirectly, through overvalued exchange rates; hence, their production and government revenues have stagnated (World Bank, 1986). With reduced prices for imported relative to domestically produced cereals caused by currency overvaluations and other factors, the domestic food production sectors have had little economic incentive to respond to rapidly increasing urban demands for cereals, thus losing their market shares to imported rice and wheat (Delgado and Reardon, 1992; Reardon, 1993).[2] Besides the foreign exchange requirements, many governments are concerned with the political consequences of substantial price fluctuations resulting from an increased dependence on imports of basic foodstuffs.

The failure of food-producing sectors to respond to increasing demands and climatic shocks during the last two decades and the stagnation of export crops pressed national governments and donors to devote more attention and resources to the agricultural sector. Donor expenditures per farmer for agricultural research were higher in Sub-Saharan Africa than in any other developing region in the world. In 1980, donors spent $360 million on agricultural research in Sub-Saharan Africa, compared with $190 million in much more populous South Asia. After commencement of the Green Revolution in the late sixties and the Sahelian drought of 1968–73, the international agricultural research centers devoted substantial human and capital investments to Sub-Saharan Africa. These international centers also helped to strengthen the national agricultural research agencies in their food-crop research programs by providing germplasm, concepts, and practical training.

There is an important ongoing debate in many countries of Sub-Saharan Africa on the development of agricultural technology. This debate can be dichotomized into two models of development: (1) the diffusion model, and (2) the adapted science (or high payoff-input) model (Hayami and Ruttan, 1985, pp. 156–62). In the diffusion model, most technological change comes from observing successful farmers. First, best-farmer practices are identified. These practices are then diffused by the extension service. Another refinement would include scientists making further modifications to best-farmer practices on the experiment station, which are then promoted by the extension services. According to the diffusion model, technological change does not require large investments in physical and human capital. Some proponents of this school denounce experiment station research as making farmers dependent on imported inputs and monoculture, whereas most low-income farmers do not purchase inputs and do practice variations of multiple cropping (Richards, 1985, p. 126).

Diffusion of best-farmer practices and scientific observation of farmer techniques are important components of agricultural development. National governments, pressured by foreign exchange constraints, often encourage researchers to develop alternatives that use local inputs rather than encourage farmers to take the risks of high levels of purchased and often imported inputs. Some of these alternatives are

- technologies practiced by local farmers, such as indigenous techniques to increase soil fertility and water retention
- better use of manure
- new cultivars, with minimal other purchased inputs
- cereal-legume rotations
- local rock phosphates

Over the last decade, there has been substantial research and promotion of these alternatives in semiarid West Africa. There are some new, improved early-cultivar introductions with small yield increases. In general, however, the yield increases with these technologies are minimal.[3]

Historically, this diffusion technique was unsuccessful in developed countries in attaining high growth rates. Successful implementation of these technologies is associated with growth rates in agricultural output of 1 to 2 percent, far below the 4 percent goal specified as necessary by the World Bank (Cleaver and Donovan, 1994, p. 1; also see Ruttan, 1991, p. 17). With a 3 percent per capita population growth, growth in agricultural output per capita would still be only 1 percent. Since an estimated one-fourth of Sub-Saharan Africa's population, or 100 million people, presently obtain only 80 percent of their recommended daily calorie supply, this still is a very slow growth rate to respond to nutritional requirements (Cleaver and Donovan, 1994, p. 3). With the renewed growth of African economies, effective growth in agricultural demand could be in the 4 to 5 percent range (see chapter 1, note 8). Rapid growth in agricultural output in both developed and developing countries, as in the Green Revolution, is associated with moderate to high levels of input purchases, including seeds (hybrids in developed countries), agricultural chemicals (especially inorganic fertilizers), and agricultural machinery (Hayami and Ruttan, 1985, chaps. 5–8).

Technological development via the adapted science model borrows inputs, processes, and concepts from other regions but recognizes that most agricultural innovations, except for some mechanical ones, have highly location-specific requirements.[4] The job of the regional and national experiment stations, then, is to test and adapt the new technologies to the farmer circumstances in various regions. The adapted science model requires the construction of regional experiment stations; high-level scientific training of a cadre of researchers (Ph.D. level); high research costs over extended periods of time (five to ten years to produce a new cultivar); improved input and output markets; development of input industries; and improved links among scientists, entrepreneurs, and farmers. Infrastructure and information requirements are also substantial. There is a backlog of technologies and research techniques in other regions of the world. Locational adaptation is expensive, but the scientific methods for doing it are well known. Sub-Saharan Africa increasingly has the human capital (Ph.D. agricultural scientists working in teams) to make rapid gains following this model.

The choice of technology direction in the adapted science model is significantly influenced by the relative scarcity of land or labor in the agricultural sector.[5] Traditionally, Sub-Saharan Africa was considered a land surplus region, with seasonal labor shortages being the principal constraint to increases in agricultural output (Norman, Newman, and Ouedraogo, 1981; Delgado and Ranade, 1987; Pingali, Bigot, and Binswanger, 1987; Matlon, 1990, pp.

26, 29–31). To resolve a labor scarcity problem, the usual response is to introduce labor-substituting inputs, such as animal traction and herbicides.

## Extensive Technology Introduction

In the mid-eighties, animal traction was employed on an estimated 15 percent of the crop area in semiarid West Africa (Matlon, 1987, p. 69). In the comprehensive study by Matlon of various villages in Burkina Faso in the early 1980s, animal traction utilization by farmers was slightly higher in the subhumid zone (15 to 24 percent) than in either of the two semiarid zones (7 to 17 percent) (cited in McIntire, Bourzat, and Pingali, 1992, p. 59).

However, these low levels of animal traction are a phenomenon either of the early 1980s or of Burkina. Since the 1970s, animal traction has been important in the peanut basin (semiarid zone) of Senegal. Presently, over 90 percent of the farmers here utilize animal traction, principally horses, seeders, and cultivation equipment (Kelly et al., 1995). In the Senegal Oriental (subhumid), the principal cotton zone, 87 percent of the farmers utilize animal traction, including oxen and plows in the heavier soils (Valerie Kelly, unpublished data). In the Gambia, a similar high proportion of animal traction is reported (DeCosse, 1992; John McIntire, personal correspondence). In southern Mali (principally subhumid), animal traction is utilized by 86 percent of the farmers, and this includes both plowing and cultivating (Brons et. al., 1994, p. 25; Coulibaly, 1995). In one region in the Maradi zone (semiarid) of Niger, 43 percent of the farmers utilize animal traction (Lowenberg-Deboer et al., 1992). Another study of the Sudanian zone of Niger (higher rainfall semiarid) reported 14 to 24 percent use of animal traction for agricultural activities (Hopkins and Berry, 1994). Aerial photography and subsequent field interviews have shown the concentration of animal traction in the semiarid and subhumid zones of Nigeria (Bourn and Wint, 1994, pp. 15, 16). Clearly, animal traction utilization has presently reached high levels in much of the semiarid and subhumid zones of West Africa, with most farmers utilizing this technique in the higher rainfall zones and where there has been a profitable crop (peanuts and cotton).

Animal traction is becoming pervasive in the more developed parts of West Africa, including Senegal, Gambia, southern Mali, southwestern Burkina Faso, and northern Nigeria. Animal traction is much less important in the drier and poorer agricultural regions such as most of Niger, Mauritania, Chad, and semiarid Burkina Faso, where it is used by fewer than 10 percent of farmers. The impacts of this technology are:

- expansion of crop area
- higher yields through more timely critical operations, improved water retention, or improvement of seeding performance
- extension of the crop area into higher-quality but heavier soils, such as vertisols, or into low-lying areas

The primary effect of animal traction in most empirical studies is a significant increase in crop area per worker. In Burkina Faso, when the number of workers was held constant, animal traction was shown to increase the area cultivated by 2 hectares per farm. This area increase occurred with a time lag after experience was gained with animal traction (Jaeger and Matlon, 1990, p. 41). In Mali, the introduction of oxen and plow increased the cultivated areas 22 percent, from 4.1 to 5 hectares (Adesina, 1992, p. 137). Another 34 percent increase was obtained with the addition of a weeder (Adesina, 1992, p. 138).

The second effect of animal traction, yield increases, was difficult to document on the farm. Yield increases for semiarid West African experiment stations from animal traction plowing range from 19 to 36 percent for groundnuts, pearl millet, sorghum, maize, cotton, and paddy rice (Nicou and Charreau, 1985, p. 20; Pingali, Bigot, and Binswanger, 1987, p. 64). One principal explanation in semiarid regions for yield increases with plowing is increased water retention from improved land preparation (Nicou and Charreau, 1985, p. 19). In southwest Mali, animal traction was associated with higher yields on farmers' fields (Adesina, 1992, p. 134). In this higher-rainfall zone, there is sufficient time to plow. In contrast, in the lower-rainfall zones, the gains from plowing can be offset by losses from the delay in sowing (Pingali, Bigot, and Binswanger, et al., 1987, p. 67). With plowing, a farmer must wait for the first hard rains and then for drying. With a planting stick, he can anticipate the rains or plant immediately after the rains. Since the rainfall season is so short, there is a high return to earlier planting. In these lower-rainfall regions, the principal mechanized operation is weeding. Yield gains from weeding can be obtained from a more timely operation; however, on-farm yield comparisons of animal and manual power are confounded by differences in labor availability and management. In summary, there are potential benefits to mechanization from improved water-holding capacity and more timely operations, even though effects of individual yields have not been separated in farm-level studies.

A third effect from animal traction, enabling the expansion onto heavier soils, is associated with Boserup (see Pingali, Bigot, and Binswanger, 1987, pp. 60–67).[6] At lower population densities, farmers first settle the middle regions of the toposequence.[7] Soils here are not difficult to prepare. At higher population densities, farmers are pressured to cultivate the heavier soils of the bottom lands. Although these soils have higher fertility, they are frequently difficult to prepare, requiring animal traction.[8] Vertisols also fall in this category; they are cultivated predominantly by animal or mechanical traction.

Consistently observed in West Africa is an approximate doubling of family size in animal traction households as compared with hand tillage households (Jaeger and Matlon, 1990). At the higher-wealth levels resulting from investment in animal traction, the household head can afford more wives, and he expands the family size (Boserup, 1970, chap. 2). A larger family size facilitates the care of animals throughout the year and the provision of additional labor for the other nonmechanized operations on a larger scale (Jaeger and Matlon, 1990, pp. 45, 47). The costs in animal care are reduced with larger family size and with the availability of more land for extended grazing. Although animal traction can resolve a seasonal labor bottleneck, it is associated with increased crop area, hence, higher total labor demand.

Animal traction is almost exclusively a male operation. Animal traction and other new technologies have been observed to shift control of farm resources and farm output away from women. Historically, in farm operations without new technologies, women provided 60 to 80 percent of the labor force (Boserup, 1970; also see chapter 10).

In summary, animal traction, like most mechanical technologies, is primarily a substitute for labor, making further land expansion possible. Generally, animal power is introduced first for transportation and then for either land preparation or weeding (Jaeger and Matlon, 1990). Rarely does animal traction substitute for human labor in both of the production operations in the initial stage, but the returns to introduction are substantially increased when both land preparation and weeding are mechanized (Jaeger and Matlon, 1990, pp. 46, 47).[9] There are yield effects from mechanization where the timely performance of certain operations can affect their productivity or where mechanized operations, especially plowing, increase water use efficiency or improve stand establishment through higher seeding rates (Jaeger and Matlon, 1990, p. 38). Nevertheless, the principal effect of mechanization is to allow area expansion, and this area expansion is generally observed with animal traction in Sub-Saharan Africa. Area expansion can take place when seasonal labor bottlenecks in weeding or planting are overcome and there is cropland available for expansion.

The predominant area of animal traction expansion in West Africa is the northern section of the moist savanna above the tsetse-fly region, such as in southwest Burkina Faso and southern Mali.[10] Animal traction is associated with the shifts to yield-increasing technologies of improved cultivars and fertilizers. Here the seasonal labor bottleneck becomes pressing when yield-increasing technologies are introduced. The explanation that animal traction is found where population density is high and market access is good (McIntire, Bourzat, and Pingali, 1992, pp. 48, 49, 56; Boserup, 1965; Pingali, Bigot, and Binswanger, 1987) is consistent with our explanation. The shift to yield-increasing technologies is associated with the disappearance of fallow, the lowering of the implicit value of labor relative to land, and the potential to sell the increased production to a market center.

Animal traction has been increasing rapidly, especially in the subhumid zone and in the higher rainfall semiarid (Sudanian) zone. Intensive, yield-increasing technologies are being introduced most rapidly in the subhumid zone; they create the demand to overcome a seasonal labor bottleneck and also increase the available capital, making it easier to purchase animals and implements. McIntire, Bourzat, and Pingali (1992, pp. 52–56, 63), argue that animal traction is concentrated in the highlands and in semiarid regions. We have observed that animal traction and now small tractors are being introduced most rapidly in subhumid zones. In these areas, rapid increases in productivity are occurring in cotton and maize production. The introduction of animal traction is associated with higher levels of fertilization, improved cultivars, improved management practices, and increased seasonal demand for labor. This last factor of increased seasonal demand for labor is critical to our strategy, as our argument is that the principal constraint in the subhumid zone is lack of quality land. Once this constraint is overcome with improvements in soil fertility and, in the semiarid case, also water availability, the demand for seasonal labor increases significantly, and farmers have the resources to purchase animals and equipment. The rapid introduction of animal traction in southwestern Burkina Faso, Mali-Sud, southern Senegal, and Gambia support our argument.

McIntire, Bourzat, and Pingali (1992, p. 68) also point out that the pure yield effects of animal traction are small and do not justify the investment. When animal traction enables an area expansion or overcomes a critical seasonal bottleneck, it is profitable to introduce it. We argue that the second effect is the most common and is associated with the intensification or introduction of technologies to increase yields. The intensive, yield-increasing technologies raise the demand for seasonal labor and increase farm incomes sufficiently that farmers can acquire animals and equipment. In other semiarid regions, farmers with abundant land area can also mechanize if they can afford the purchases. Often they cannot, so the rate of increase in animal traction is faster when the intensification is taking place.

In many semiarid regions, population growth has been so rapid that it is no longer an option to expand the cultivated areas. At higher population densities, the fallow systems of extensive agriculture are not sustainable, and soils can become degraded by overuse. Before extensive degradation in some areas, such as in southern Mali, farmers have been able to build up animal stocks and use animal traction and higher levels of manure (see chapter 3). In other areas, such as the Sudanian zone of Burkina, the potential to support large animals and thereby obtain interactions between livestock and crops is reduced with higher population densities and settlement pushed into marginal areas. Animal traction can then accelerate the land degradation process by facilitating the extension of cropland into more marginal regions.

## Failure of the Crop Yield Increase Strategies in the Sahelian Countries

In the Sahelian countries, 1950–67 was a period of above-average rainfall. With better agricultural conditions and public health programs, population growth accelerated.[11] Pasture growth with higher rainfall, improved animal health, and the well-drilling programs all facilitated an expansion of the animal population. With higher rainfall, agricultural population pushed north into more marginal land areas, and population pressure accelerated the reduction or disappearance of the traditional fallow system.

From 1968 to the present, drought was chronic, with the rainfall being one standard deviation below the long-term average (see fig. 1-4; also see Glantz, 1987; Mellor and Gavian, 1987; p. 544). Moreover, there have been two widespread acute droughts, in 1968–73 and 1982–84 (see Sen, 1981, pp. 113–30, for an account of the 1968–73 drought). During these periods, livestock died, and crops failed on a large scale. Shorter-season cultivars of both millet and sorghum were widely disseminated in the last two decades in the Sahel in response to the reduced rainfall levels (Vierich and Stoop, 1990; also see chapter 5).

As the land fertility deteriorated with the disappearance of fallow, cereal yields fell, and the more stress-tolerant millet replaced sorghum (see chapter 4; Vierich and Stoop, 1990; Ames, 1986). Farmers also attempt to maintain family cereal-consumption levels by expanding crop area onto more marginal agricultural lands. Hence, the amount of communal land for livestock is reduced, and the area available is often overgrazed. Mixed farming systems and improved rotations with legumes are systems that increase organic matter content and improve soil fertility levels. However, with cereal yields declining and soil quality deteriorating, Sahelian farmers must first devote their attention to cereal productivity. Hence, the agricultural development strategies from 1973 to the present concentrated on technologies to increase cereal yields. Plant breeding has been the predominant discipline, with other disciplines providing a supporting role. This stress on breeding results from the successes of the Green Revolution (wheat and rice in predominantly irrigated regions of Asia, South America, and North Africa) and other breeding successes in the agriculture of developed countries.

One common characteristic of regions where breeding has been successful is the moderate to high utilization of improved agronomic practices, including water control and inorganic fertilizer. In the United States, where sorghum yields tripled in thirty years from 1.2 metric tons per hectare in 1950 to more than 3.8 metric tons per hectare in 1980, the genetic contribution was estimated to be from 28 to 39 percent (Miller and Kebede, 1984, pp. 6, 11). Over 60 percent of these large yield gains in the United States were due to improved agronomy practices, especially fertilization, the use of herbicides, and water control (ibid., p. 7). The new cultivars generally respond better to higher input use, so the technological development strategy needs to include both breeding and improved agronomy (F. Miller, pers. corres.).

In the semiarid regions of West Africa, cereal breeding efforts began with the French and English colonial research organizations and were accelerated after 1973 by the international and national agricultural research agencies. Cereal breeding for the principal food grains, millet and sorghum, has been generally unsuccessful in introducing new cultivars on farmers' fields from 1973 to the present (for a detailed history of the breeding activities, see Andrews, 1986). An exception to this was the introduction of new millet cultivars in the peanut basin of Senegal. We return to this case later in this chapter. Many reasons are given for this failure of the breeding activities, most of which are now being addressed (see Matlon, 1987, pp. 11–73; 1990):

- Early sorghum breeding emphasized successful Indian material. However, the conditions in semiarid West Africa are very different from those in India. For example, extremely high soil temperatures at planting in the Sahel result in stand establishment problems for exotic material.
- In the initial stages of selection, cultivar development was concen-

trated on the experiment station with mechanized land preparation, high levels of inorganic fertilizer, and other sophisticated cultural practices. In contrast, most cereal farmers in semiarid regions use only family labor, retain seed, and do not purchase inputs such as agricultural chemicals.

• In semiarid West Africa, there is much microvariation in climate, soils, and systems of production. Hence, stress levels are not only high but variable among sites. It was difficult for scientists to anticipate the stress levels for which they should be evaluating their material.

Many of the breeding problems have now been corrected. The sorghum research programs of the Sahelian countries are using predominantly African material for their crossing. It is becoming increasingly accepted that cultivar evaluation should continue into regional trials and then onto farms, where input levels should be set closer to but not at farmers' levels of input use. Moderate improvements in purchased input levels will need to precede cultivar introduction.

The central problem of agricultural technology development in semiarid regions is that too much has been expected of the breeders. In contrast with those regions of the world where breeding activities have been successful, semiarid agriculture takes place in an extremely harsh environment, with low and irregular rainfall, multiple soil fertility problems, including very low levels of the two basic nutrients, nitrogen and phosphorus, and minimal use of purchased inputs. Asking breeders to resolve all these problems prior to basic improvements in water availability and soil fertility was unrealistic. Moderate improvements in the agronomic environment of the semiarid regions would enable breeders to concentrate on developing cultivars for an improved and less variable agronomic environment.[12]

## A Strategy of Intensive Agricultural Technology Development

In the semiarid region of Sub-Saharan Africa, the principal constraint to increases in crop output is obvious from the definition of the region — that is, soil moisture (Carr, 1989, p. xiii; Sanders, Nagy, and Ramaswamy, 1990; Matlon, 1990, p. 18).[13] Nevertheless, in the last two decades there has been little investment in irrigation in the region (Barghouti and Lallement, 1988). One principal reason is the prohibitive costs (Matlon, 1987, p. 66). Construction and rehabilitation of existing schemes were estimated to cost between

$5,000 and $20,000 per hectare in the eighties (Lele, 1981, p. 249; Matlon, 1990, p. 19; also see Morris, Thom, and Norman, 1984). Further, there is minimal potential for large-scale irrigation; most arable land is rain-fed. Another recent approach has been the promotion of smaller, cheaper, farmer-managed irrigation systems. In some of these projects, investment costs have been reduced to a range of $1,200 to $4,000 per hectare (Cleaver and Donovan, 1994, p. 7).

The effects of low and irregular rainfall on crop yields are frequently aggravated after cultivation by soil crusting, which leads to serious infiltration problems. Therefore, on heavier soils, water-retention techniques can become critical to reduce runoff and to use the available rainfall (see chapters 4 and 5 for the soil difference effects). Fortunately, there are numerous techniques for water conservation or retention besides irrigation, and many have good potential in the region (Carr, 1989, pp. 46–48; Lynam and Blackie, 1994, p. 113; Reij, Mulder, and Begeman, 1988).

Just making water available when nutrient levels in the soil are low generally results in only a small yield response (Sanders, Nagy, and Ramaswamy, 1990, p. 10). Even at slightly higher nutrient levels, cereals will quickly deplete or mine the available nutrients. Applying fertilizers (organic or inorganic) without an assured water supply is economically risky, because the response to fertilizer depends on the availability of water at the critical stages of plant development. Combined technologies to increase soil moisture and crop nutrients have been shown to raise yields 50 to 100 percent and to be highly profitable during several years of testing on both the experiment station and farmers' fields (Nagy, Sanders, and Ohm, 1988; Sanders, Nagy, and Ramaswamy, 1990, pp. 11–15). In most of the semiarid regions, the constraints of inadequate water availability and low soil fertility must be simultaneously attacked. Combining the two, increased water availability and moderate fertilizer levels, results in large and consistent increases of cereal yields (see chapters 4 to 6). These innovations are highly profitable at low levels of risk to the farmers. The combined technologies are land substituting and increase the demand for labor.

The profitability of substituting new technologies for land is strongly influenced by land and labor prices and the availability of additional labor for the labor-intensive activities to retain water. The changes in land and labor availabilities in the semiarid zone thus affect the extent to which these technologies are economically appropriate.

One of the principal phenomena in Sub-Saharan African countries is an increasing population pressure on the land, causing a breakdown of the traditional rotation system of long fallow periods of ten to fifteen years. Shorter fallow periods, without replacing soil nutrients with purchased inputs, cause crop yields to decrease over time. Farmers must increase cultivated area to maintain production levels. This pushes crop cultivation into more marginal areas, thereby decreasing communal grazing areas. As cattle are sold or entrusted to migrating herders, this source of organic fertilizer declines. In some areas of Sub-Saharan Africa, farmers can migrate or depend more on remittances. In others, there is sufficient grazing land that they can use more labor-intensive techniques to improve the quality of manure (see chapter 3).

Less heavily populated regions of semiarid Sub-Saharan Africa will experience these same problems as population growth and migration between regions continue. The principal constraint of low-quality land, with inadequate water retention capacity and low soil fertility, is the same in low-population-density as in high-population-density areas in the semiarid regions. However, most of the agronomic techniques for improving water availability are extremely labor-intensive, so farmers often have more profitable alternative activities until population pressure becomes higher or the value of crop production increases (see chapter 4 for a more systematic treatment).[14] The response to the increased relative cost of land is to introduce intensive technologies and then, as seasonal-labor availability becomes constraining, also to combine these technologies with animal traction.

Soil mining and soil depletion from poor cultural practices become widespread problems with increased population pressure. As cultivated areas are extended, wind and water erosion and soil crusting occur as farmers intensively cultivate the remaining areas and follow the traditional cultural practices of utilizing or burning crop residues. With declining soil quality, farmers must increase their labor inputs to maintain the same output levels.

At the initial unit isoquant $ACB$ and isocost I, labor utilization is $L_0$ (see fig. 2-1). As cultivation is pushed into marginal areas and the fallow system breaks down, land quality begins to deteriorate, so that more inputs are required to produce the same output, and the isoquant rotates out to $ACD$.[15] At the same relative costs of labor and land, more labor must be used ($L_1$) to offset this soil-fertility decline and reach the same production level. Rural population growth is still rapid, maintaining a high percentage of the rural population in agriculture (50 to 90 percent) and keeping the wage rates low. Relative to the growth in the labor supply, nonfarm opportunities are growing only slowly.[16] With labor productivity reduced in agriculture by falling land quality,[17] lack of capital investment in land-substituting inputs, and continuing growth of the rural labor force, a new isocost (III) reflects this deterioration in the relative value of labor. (For evidence of declining productivity of

Figure 2-1. Impact of Land Degradation and New Technology on Use of Land and Labor

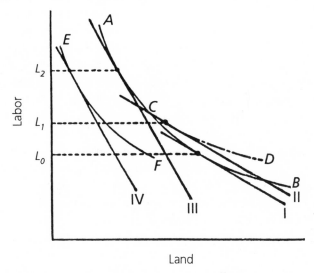

Source: Adapted from Sanders, Nagy, and Ramaswamy (1990).

labor, see Block and Timmer, 1992.) The new isocost line III then results in further increases of labor ($L_2$) to maintain output levels.

The induced innovation theory considers technological change to be responsive to the economic signals from factor and product prices (Hayami and Ruttan, 1985, pp. 84–93). In this case, the reduction in land quality and supply, together with the reduced productivity of labor, induces researchers and governments to produce and promote, and farmers to adopt, new technologies, substituting increased capital investment for land. The shift to a new isoquant, $EF$, results from the technological change. This technological change also involves higher labor use than that associated with either pre- or post-land-deterioration cases ($L_0$ and $L_1$).[18]

Critics of the more intensive water retention technologies recommended above have emphasized the large increases in labor requirements ($L_2 - L_0$) (Matlon, 1990, p. 27). This change in the use of labor is substantial. However, the soil degradation and the consequent fall in the marginal productivity of labor already required this increased amount of labor ($L_2$) to produce the same level of output with less land. Thus, it is the land degradation and the decreased value of farm-family labor with few nonfarm alternatives or little potential for further out-migration that create the increase in labor use. Technological change is a response to this demand for a technology that substitutes for land. Presently, farmers in degraded regions are using new water retention technologies that can be undertaken outside the crop season. However, the larger yield gains result from those improved water retention activities, such as tied ridges or improved land preparation, that need to be done during the crop season at critical periods in which there are already seasonal labor shortages. Hence, the yield-increasing technologies will often need to be combined with animal traction to reduce the labor required during the period of the critical seasonal labor operations, at either planting or weeding, or both.

The above new technologies are innovations to improve land quality. In the subhumid zone, these innovations are principally soil amendments and new cultivars. In the dry savanna (semiarid zone), these combined innovations are water retention techniques, soil fertility amendments, and new cultivars. The emphasis here on new technology development is principally for yield-increasing purchased inputs and water retention techniques. However, to maximize the response to improved agronomic environments, new cultivars will generally be necessary. Traditional cultivars in low-input environments can tolerate adverse conditions but generally do not respond well to moderate or high inputs. Therefore, a breeding strategy to accompany moderate increases in inorganic inputs and water availability is considered a fundamental part of the agricultural technology development strategy.

In conclusion, the principal constraint to increases in output in the subhumid and semiarid regions of Sub-Saharan African agriculture is hypothesized to be soil quality. In semiarid regions, increased water availability must be combined with soil fertility improvements. Together, these will increase incomes and often reduce the variability of these incomes. When water retention activity also involves increased labor requirements at critical periods of the crop season, use of animal traction implements, such as the adaptation of the tractor furrow diker of the Texas high plains to construct tied ridges, can be undertaken. The required changes are complicated, since there are three new inputs. However, they have been successfully introduced in farm trials. Variations of these technologies responding to the two principal constraints of water availability and soil fertility are now being observed on farmers' fields (Sanders, Nagy, and Ramaswamy, 1990).

A fundamental component for new technology introduction is that agriculture be profitable and risk levels reduced. Two years after the major drought of 1984, with the second year of predominantly good harvests of sorghum, millet, and maize in the Sahel and low international prices of rice and wheat, 1986 sorghum and millet prices collapsed in both Niger (table 2-1) and Bur-

Table 2-1. Real Cereal Prices for Millet and
Sorghum in Maradi, Niger, 1983–1987
(CFA per kilogram, 1984 base)

| Year | Millet | Sorghum |
|------|--------|---------|
| 1983 | 79 | 86 |
| 1984 | 160 | 144 |
| 1985 | 60 | 68 |
| 1986 | 36 | 36 |
| 1987 | 56 | 56 |

*Source:* Sanders (1989, p. 143). Reprinted from *Agricultural Systems* 30:139–54 with kind permission from Elsevier Science Ltd., The Boulevard, Langford Lane, Kidlington OX5 1GB, U.K.
*Note:* Nominal market prices are reported in Adesina (1988). The consumer price index used for deflation is from IMF (*International Financial Statistics,* 1988, p. 389).

kina Faso. At these low cereal prices, there is minimal interest by cereal producers in adopting new technologies and by public officials in increasing cereal productivity. Developed countries generally do not let the prices of their basic food staples collapse. The combined effects of yield risk from drought, insects, and disease and price risk from a favorable production season are expected to be too many risks for farmers to take. Water retention helps manage yield risks. Some policy measures to reduce price risk seem appropriate to encourage more rapid technology introduction.

## Recent Introduction of Intensive Technologies: A Preliminary Evaluation of the Strategy

In the previous section, the principal constraints to output increases in semiarid Sub-Saharan African agriculture are hypothesized to be water availability and soil fertility.[19] Researchers tend to consider one input change at a time, and farmers to introduce one-input changes, acquiring experience from learning-by-doing before introducing other inputs. Therefore, it is difficult both to obtain the necessary adaptive research and to successfully extend the combined inputs to farmers. Nevertheless, in the regions with higher agricultural potential, that is, the moist savanna, technology introduction was rapid.

In these better-endowed regions, there is a greater impact from each individual component. In contrast, the less-endowed regions have more pressing constraints from inadequate water availability and low soil fertility, so it becomes more critical to introduce several new inputs simultaneously to have a significant, profitable effect on yields. Even in regions with lower resource bases, where progress has been slower, there were some successes. A comprehensive evaluation of the above theory of technology development is undertaken in chapters 3 through 6.

Are the new technologies being successfully introduced in West Africa consistent with the above strategy recommendations? The region with the most rapid technological change, the Sudano-Guinean zone, has the highest rainfall (fig. 2-2). Here, the introduction of new cotton cultivars was combined with increasing levels of inorganic fertilizer (tables 2-2, 2-3). Moderately high levels of inorganic fertilizer were utilized on both cotton and the major cereal, maize. New cotton and maize cultivars with modified spacing, density, and timing recommendations then complemented the yield effects of increased inorganic fertilization. In southern Mali in the late eighties and early nineties, there has been a rapid increase in the quality and quantity of organic fertilization (for more details on all these technologies in the Sudano-Guinean zone, see chapters 3 and 10). The most pervasive and highest rates of diffusion of animal traction are found in the high-rainfall (Sudano-Guinean) region, where there are high-value cash crops and rapid introduction of new intensive technologies, including the Sudano-Guinean zones of southern Mali

Figure 2-2. Principal Climatic Zones of Semiarid West Africa

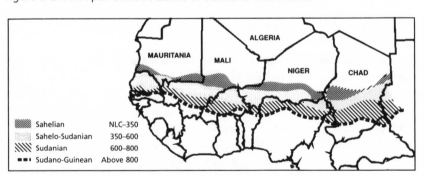

*Source:* Adapted from Gorse and Steeds (1987, appendix).
*Note:* NLC is the northern limit of cultivation. Numbers given refer to isohyets in millimeters of rainfall at 90 percent probability levels. Only the upper boundary of the Sudano-Guinean zone is shown.

Table 2-2. Characteristics of the Major Agroecological Zones in the West Africa Semiarid Tropics (WASAT)

| Zone | Rainfall[a] | Area (% of WASAT)[b] | Population (% of WASAT) | Cropping System | Population Density | Crop Technology Development Potential |
|------|------------|----------------------|-------------------------|-----------------|--------------------|---------------------------------------|
| Sudano-Guinean | 800–1,100 | 24 | 6 | Highly diversified, high-input systems; cotton, maize, peanuts, sorghum, millet, vegetables, cowpeas, rice, livestock | Low; high disease risk historically but less now | High |
| Sudanian | 600–800 | 21 | 59 | Sorghum, millet,[c] maize, cowpeas, vegetables, some cotton | High | Moderate |
| Sahelo-Sudanian | 350–600 | 30 | 19 | Same as Sudanian, but moving farther north; millet-cowpea intercropping, some sorghum, nomadic grazing | High in southern section, but declining farther north | Lower than for Sudanian sorghum system; low for millet-cowpea system |
| Sahelian | <350 | 24 | 16 | Transhumance or traditional nomad center; subsistence millet, cowpeas | Low | Minimal, except around water |

*Source:* Rainfall divisions are from Gorse and Steeds (1987, pp. 2, 42, 43). For a similar table, see Debrah (1993, p. 20). For more detail on cropping systems, technology adoption, and potential technology introduction, see Sanders (1989) and Matlon (1990). Also see Posner and Gilbert (1991).

[a] In millimeters, 90% probability.

[b] Estimates of the cultivable area in the four zones are Sudano-Guinean, 42%; Sudanian, 37%; Sahelo-Sudanian, 30%; Sahelian, 29%.

[c] The sorghum system predominates in heavier soils; millet in lighter, sandier soils; and a mix of sorghum and millet in the intermediate soils.

Table 2-3. Technologies Successfully Introduced in the Three Principal Agroecological Zones of the West Africa Semiarid Tropics

| | | Effects on Principal Constraints | |
|---|---|---|---|
| Zone | Technology | Water Availability | Soil Fertility |
| Sudano-Guinean | New cotton and maize culti-vars with inorganic fertilizer and improved agronomic practices; rapid increase in use of organic fertilizers | Rainfall adequate in most years in this zone | Fertilizer used in the combined tech-nology package |
| Sudanian | Contour dikes, zaï, and organic fertilizer; early cereal and cowpea cultivars; in Mali, ridging and in-creases in organic fertilizers | Runoff water held; drought escape with earliness | Organic fertilizer; cultivars selected for low soil fertil-ity conditions |
| Sahelo-Sudanian | Early cereal and cowpea cul-tivars and phosphorus fertil-izer; contour dikes, zaï, and organic fertilizers; supple-mentary irrigation;[a] new mil-let cultivars in peanut basin, Senegal | Drought escape with earliness; runoff water held; full water control | Recently, chemical fertilizer in Niger and Senegal; organic fertilizers; rice heavily fertilized |

[a] Only small areas of supplementary irrigation (less than one hectare) provided by government to farmers; these are a type of income stabilization for dryland farmers.

and southwestern Burkina Faso and in Gambia (Matlon, 1990, p. 37).

There is an ongoing water revolution in the region of more degraded soils of the dry savanna in the Sahel. Dikes to slow runoff have been rapidly intro-duced since the early eighties in the Sudanian and the Sahelo-Sudanian re-gions in Burkina Faso and Niger. In northern Burkina Faso alone, there were 60,000 hectares with these dikes in the mid-eighties (World Bank, 1989a, p. 98; also see chapter 4).[20] These dikes are constructed on the contour at fairly wide intervals of ten to forty meters, depending on the slope. The dikes accu-mulate soil from higher up on the toposequence for one to two meters behind them. This soil accumulation is often accompanied by the application of or-ganic fertilizer (Wright, 1985, p. 56). Many farmers dig holes all over the field *(zaï)* for water retention and plant their cereals between these holes. These combined techniques respond to both constraints (water availability and soil fertility). Dikes and zaï are constructed outside the crop season and are predominantly found in the most severely degraded regions. In the off-season, the opportunity costs of family labor in most regions are lower than during the crop season (see chapter 4 for an expanded discussion and documentation). The higher incidence of the dikes in the most degraded region is consistent with the theory presented earlier. In the most degraded regions, the available opportunities for labor are much fewer than in those areas with less population pressure and more adequate resources.

In the Sudanian zone of southern Mali, a pervasive use of animal traction has enabled farmers to construct ridges on the contour. This technique has been combined with increasing use of manure mixed with straw from the millet and sorghum residues. Covered compost heaps are also increasingly used to improve the quality as fertilizer of this manure and household wastes (see chapter 3 for details). In this environment, with improved water retention and higher soil fertility, new millet and cowpea cultivars are now being introduced. The new millet cultivars, Toroniou c1 and Benkadinion, are improved local selections. So there are effects here of organic fertilizer, seed treatment (Apron Plus), and improved quality seed. Yield gains of 200 to 300 kilograms per hectare are estimated on farmers' fields from these combined inputs, 22 to 33 percent yield increases (Maiga et al., 1994, pp. iv, 28, 31).

In the Sahelo-Sudanian region of Senegal, the French concentrated their research on the cereals and peanuts for the Sahelian countries. A millet research program was begun in Bambey in 1931. This center released the selection from farmers' cultivars, Souna III, in 1973 and, in collaboration with ICRISAT, IBV 8001 and IBV 8004 in 1983 (Leaphart 1994, pp. 3, 4). The ICRISAT material included resistance to Downey Mildew. This resistance was a critical contribution to the success of new millet cultivars, as this disease is considered to be the principal biotic constraint to increasing millet yields in both India and West Africa. In the nineties, seed sales continued for all three, with the predominant material still being Souna III. As farmers' cultivars deteriorate, the farmers replace them with the new seed of the now traditional cultivars. In the higher-rainfall regions of the peanut basin, inorganic fertilizer is increasingly being used on millet (M. Gaye, field observations). Despite concentrating most research resources on peanuts and cotton, the French system did introduce some new millet cultivars and was aided by ICRISAT in the early eighties.

For the rain-fed cereals, Senegal has concentrated since the late eighties on improving agronomy and has shifted its breeders into other activities. Senegal has long been the leader in agricultural research in the Sahel with French investments and personnel, especially in the colonial period and continuing through the 1970s. In Bambey, this institutional switch away from breeding is consistent with our hypotheses about the requirements for successful technological change in the semiarid zone and is expected to be followed by other research institutions in the semiarid zone. However, once water availability and soil fertility are improved, a substantial effect is expected from new cultivars. Those regions successfully introducing these agronomic improvements need to be concerned with obtaining new cultivars for these improved environments. Some specialization and borrowing between research institutions in semiarid West Africa seems to be an especially appropriate strategy.

Another important innovation in both the Sudanian and the Sahelo-Sudanian zones is the introduction of shorter-season cultivars of sorghum, millet, and cowpeas. There has been diffusion of new cultivars, principally between farmers (Coulibaly, 1987; Matlon, 1990, pp. 25, 26; Vierich and Stoop, 1990).[21] Since the start of the drought (1968–73), rainfall has been one standard deviation below the long-term norm in semiarid West Africa (Glantz, 1987, p. 39). Hence, the payoff from early or short-season varieties has increased since 1968. Earliness allows for drought escape. Improved farmer cultivars were selected under low soil fertility conditions. This is only a temporary strategy, as continuing crop production without improving soil fertility will exhaust the soil. This introduction of new cultivars alone gives only small income increases to farmers but raises yields in adverse rainfall seasons, thus improving food security (see chapter 5). The introduction of new cowpea cultivars is associated with yield maintenance, as cowpeas are attacked by a large number of insect and disease pests (Sanders, 1994, pp. 9, 10, 27, 28).

In the sandy dune soils of Niger, where farmers have seen the impact of phosphorus, there was a rapid increase in the use of simple superphosphate (Mokwunye and Hammond, 1992, pp. 131, 132). This is a dramatic, recent phenomenon, as these farmers are some of the poorest in the region and the zone is one of the most difficult for crop production. Yet the missing components for technology adoption were apparently farmer exposure to fertilizer response and availability of fertilizer supplies (see chapter 5). On the Nigerien border, near Maradi, inorganic fertilizer has been widely introduced in cereal production in the Sudanian zone. Here, ridging is generally done to increase water retention.

Because of high capital requirements, maintenance, and recovery costs, irrigation was not promoted in the last decade, except for small-scale and supplementary irrigation. Nevertheless, in some regions, large-scale irrigation projects were important for farmers. In Niger, irrigation projects frequently serve as an income base for dryland farmers. In one zone, each farmer was given 0.4 hectare of irrigated area; the farmers also produce on 3 to 5 hectares of dryland. On the 0.4 hectare, farmers produce irrigated rice with exotic cultivars and high levels of inorganic fertilizer. Clearly, these technologies resolve both constraints discussed (Shapiro, 1990, p. 83; chapter 5).

In the Sudan, a new sorghum hybrid was introduced into both the rain-fed and the irrigated regions in 1985. Farmer adoption is now progressing steadily in the irrigated region, where farmers use inorganic fertilizer and improved agroeconomic practices as well as irrigation water. On the drylands, after some brief experimentation with the new cultivar, farmers returned to traditional sorghum cultivars and extensive production techniques without inorganic inputs. The new sorghum cultivar has been successful where irrigation water and moderate fertilizer use were available.[22] Without these inputs, farmers have rejected the new cultivar (see chapter 6 for more details).

## Conclusion

Sub-Saharan Africa is often described as a land surplus region, with the availability of seasonal labor as the main constraint to output increase. However, the lower levels of animal traction adoption, except where intensive yield-increasing technologies were introduced, indicate the need for reevaluation of this conventional assumption. Animal traction is also being introduced in some regions with little yield-increasing technology introduction. The introduction of donkey traction in the Sudanian and Sahelo-Sudanian zones of Burkina Faso is an example. This introduction is much less rapid than in the Sudano-Guinean zone, where yield-increasing technological change has been most rapidly introduced for all the regions considered.

The period of land area expansion into new regions is gone or rapidly disappearing for most semiarid regions (Matlon, 1990, p. 38). We previously hypothesized that the principal constraints to increasing agricultural output in semiarid regions are problems with water retention and soil fertility. In broadening this to the subhumid regions, we would define the general constraint as soil quality. In the subhumid zone, this involves principally soil fertility improvements and new cultivars. In the semiarid regions, higher nutrient levels often require increased water availability at critical times of crop production.

One central problem of agricultural technology development in Sub-Saharan African agriculture was the failure to change emphasis from plant breeding. When technology development is directed toward rain-fed agriculture in areas with limited resources, the initial emphasis needs to be on improving soil fertility and, in semiarid regions, providing more water. As more water and soil nutrients become available, the local cultivars historically selected by farmers for good stress resistance will not be very responsive to these improved environments. Hence, there will be an important role for breeding of new cultivars to more efficiently use these moderately higher inputs. However, breeding alone or breeding with local technology adaptations will not be sufficient to generate substantial yield increases. In the long run, some breeding for tolerance to drought and soil nutrient deficiency stress can be as useful in semiarid Africa as on the high plains of Texas. Some new cultivars of millet, cowpea, maize, and cotton have already been introduced into Sub-Saharan Africa, but substantial yield increases were achieved only when these new cultivars were combined with higher levels of inorganic inputs.

In most semiarid regions, the fundamental and primary innovations will involve simultaneous technology introduction to make more water and more highly fertile soil available. The increased labor requirements will then require animal traction and often new implements. Once the agronomic improvements are in place, there can be a high return to the breeding program.

# II

# Technology Development for Specific Regions

# 3

## Success Stories: New Crop Technologies in the Sudano-Guinean Zone of Burkina Faso and Mali

CHAPTER 3 is the first of four chapters that evaluate two principal hypotheses of this book for four different regions. The first hypothesis is that there has been some technological change in the savannas of Sub-Saharan Africa. Our second hypothesis is that these successful technologies have included, and future technologies will need to include, improvements in resource management, that is, soil fertility and water management. In the Sudano-Guinean region, rainfall is above 800 millimeters in nine out of ten years. Thus, sufficient water is available in most years for the predominant crops of cotton, maize, sorghum, millet, cowpeas, and peanuts.

The most successful research experiences in Burkina Faso, Mali, and Senegal were in this region. New cultivar introductions of cotton and maize were very successful and were combined with crop management improvements, including increases in fertilization, density, and pest control, in each country. These regions have become surplus grain producers and exporters to the lower-rainfall regions in all three countries. With the higher rainfall in the Sudano-Guinean zone, there is more agricultural potential than in the dry savanna regions (see table 2-2).

This higher rainfall in the Sudano-Guinean region is associated with a higher incidence of human and animal diseases, especially malaria, sleeping sickness, and river blindness (see chapter 10). The pressures of human and animal disease have historically restrained settlement, as have the greater labor requirements for land clearing. More recently, improved public health and investment in infrastructure in these countries has facilitated area extension and land clearing. In-migration is now occurring at rapid rates from the lower-rainfall Sudanian and Sahelo-Sudanian regions.

There have been some technology successes in the two lower-rainfall regions, but the main accomplishments have been in the Sudano-Guinean zone. The high rates of migration into this region in the last two decades were motivated by the rapid depletion of natural resources (forests, water, soil) in the dry savanna zones; hence, a sustainable development strategy needs to be concerned with all three regions (see chapters 4, 5, and 8).

## The Cotton Success Story

In the French colonial period, the main emphasis of research and economic policies was on the export crops, cotton and peanuts, in this higher-rainfall region. From 1902 to 1952 in Burkina Faso, farmers were required to pay a tax in French currency and could raise this currency only by selling cotton. This was a very inefficient system, so farmer incentives and yields remained low. In 1952 a French cotton company, Compagnie Française pour le Developpement des Fibres Textiles (CFDT), began operation in cotton production in southwestern Burkina Faso. This company supplied inputs, provided technical recommendations, and purchased the cotton. This pattern of cotton production organized around an input-supplying, cotton-exporting company, often with governmental support, is now found all over the former French colonies of Sub-Saharan Africa (Savadogo, 1990, pp. 26, 27; CFDT, 1992).

From 1951 to 1965, Burkina cotton yields were stagnant (below 200 kilograms per hectare). In contrast, the cotton area increases were very rapid from 1951 to 1969. The cotton area leveled off from 1969 to the mid-1980s, then took off again until 1987. There were some yield increases in the late sixties, but the rapid yield increases were from 1971 through 1986. From the midsixties, cotton yields have increased from less than 200 kilograms per hectare to 1.3 metric tons per hectare in 1986–87 (fig. 3-1). These higher yield levels are associated with increased inorganic fertilizer and pesticide use, improved agronomy, and the regular introduction of new cultivars in both Burkina and Mali (Savadogo, 1990, pp. 19ff; Girdis, 1993, pp. 15–19). The yield decline after 1986 is associated with the world price collapse of cotton in that year and the elimination of the subsidies on cotton inputs. In recent years, there has been more breeding emphasis on qualitative improvements[1] as the CFDT obtained a price premium for higher-quality cotton (CFDT, 1992, pp. 76, 78).

The quantity of compound fertilizer, consumed principally by cotton and maize producers in the Sudano-Guinean regions of Burkina, increased from 3,000 tons in 1977 to 16,000 tons in 1986. On cotton, average NPK fertilizer use on cotton in southwestern Burkina in the mid-1980s ranged from 131 to 148 kilograms per hectare (Savadogo, 1990, p. 19, 29).[2] Use of inorganic

Figure 3-1. Cotton Area and Yields in Burkina Faso, 1951–1992

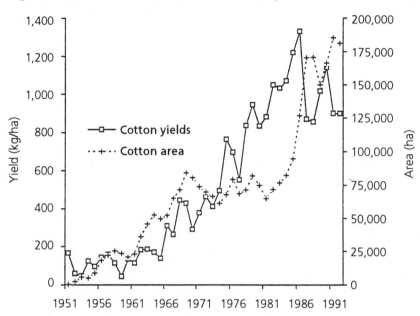

*Source:* Based on data from Savadogo (1990, pp. 30, 31) and CFDT (1992, pp. 75, 76).

fertilizer declined slightly with the elimination of the subsidies in the late eighties. In southern Mali, average use on cotton fell from 190 to 150 kilograms per hectare (Girdis, 1993, p. 15). These are still only moderate levels of inorganic nutrients compared with use in developed countries.

In both southern Mali and southwestern Burkina Faso, the more intensive cotton technologies were also associated with the rapid introduction of animal traction. In these areas the yield-increasing technologies substantially increased the demand for labor and for area expansion. In southern Mali, over 80 percent of the farmers own a plow (Dioné, 1989). In the Burkina cotton zone, 38 percent of the farmers had animal traction in 1983 (Savadogo, 1990), but a decade later animal traction approximated the Mali levels in the cotton zones (see chapter 10).

Table 3-1 indicates the relation between cotton yields and inorganic fertilizer use with a between-country comparison. Without inorganic fertilizer and pesticides, cotton yields remain in the 250–350 kilograms per hectare range. In those countries where farmers use inorganic fertilizers, however, yields are

Table 3-1. Average Cotton Yields and Use of Chemicals in Six African Countries

| | Cameroon (1986–1987) | Nigeria (1985–1986) | Senegal (1984–1985) | Kenya (1985–1986) | Malawi (1980–1981) | Tanzania (1983–1984) |
|---|---|---|---|---|---|---|
| Crop area sprayed (%) | 95 | 0 | 99 | 10–20 | 90 | 10 |
| Crop area with inorganic fertilizer (%) | 95 | 0 | 99 | 0–5 | 13 | 0 |
| Yields (kg/ha) | 1,300 | 250 | 1,012 | 350 | 700 | 400 |

*Source:* Lele, van de Walle, and Gbetibuou (1989, p. 11).

over 1 metric ton per hectare. Fertilizer use and higher cotton yields are associated with the former French colonies, such as Cameroon and Senegal. The essential components of the CFDT success have been providing farmers with fertilizer on credit, timely payment of a product price known before planting, and support of an excellent research and input services system (Lele, van de Walle, and Gbetibuou, 1989, p. 6). This combination of technological and institutional support in cotton production is a significant model of development.[3] Based on the substantially higher yields, the output in the former French colonies grew 740 percent from 1960 to 1985. In contrast, the extensive, low-yielding production system in the anglophone countries resulted in an increased production of only 60 percent over that period. Francophone cotton production increased from 11 percent of Sub-Saharan African output in 1961–62 to almost half in 1987 (Lele, van de Walle, and Gbetibuou, 1989, p. 8). Francophone cotton development organized by the CFDT has resulted in sustained increases in cotton yields with the development and dissemination of intensive seed and chemical technologies (Lele, van de Walle, and Gbetibuou, 1989, p. 31).[4]

Strong regional research and institutional support not only increased yields but also concentrated production of cotton in the Sudano-Guinean zones of southwest Burkina and southeastern Mali (Mali-Sud), where there was a natural comparative advantage due to the higher rainfall and better soils. In the early sixties, only 33 percent of total cotton production was in the southwest of Burkina Faso, but in the early eighties, 92 percent of production was in this area (Savadogo, 1990, pp. 29, 30, 31).

## The Maize Story

The introduction of new cultivars and associated technology for maize during the 1980s was another success story in the Sudano-Guinean zone (table 3-2). In the Sahel, maize is a minor crop compared to sorghum and millet.[5] In

Table 3-2. Area Planted to Improved Maize Varieties and Hybrids, Sub-Saharan Africa, 1990

| Country | Total Maize Area ($\times$ 1,000 ha) | Area Sown to Improved Open-Pollinated Varieties (%) Min.[a] | Max.[a] | Area Sown to Hybrids (%) | Maize Area Sown to Improved Germplasm (%) Min.[a] | Max.[a] | Maize Area Sown to CIMMYT Germplasm (%) |
|---|---|---|---|---|---|---|---|
| Tanzania | 1,631 | 6 | 18 | 6 | 12 | 24 | 60 |
| Nigeria | 1,500 | 22 | 87 | 2 | 24 | 89 | 59[b] |
| Kenya | 1,500 | 8 | 8 | 62 | 70 | 70 | 1 |
| Malawi | 1,344 | 3 | 3 | 11 | 14 | 14 | 1 |
| Zimbabwe | 1,150 | 0 | 0 | 96 | 96 | 96 | 0 |
| Ethiopia | 1,050 | 8 | 24 | 5 | 13 | 29 | 33 |
| Mozambique | 1,015 | 17 | 17 | 1 | 18 | 18 | 94 |
| Zambia | 763 | 5 | 5 | 72 | 77 | 77 | 6 |
| Côte d'Ivoire | 691 | 14 | 42 | 4 | 18 | 46 | 88 |
| Ghana | 465 | 16 | 48 | 0 | 16 | 48 | 91 |
| Benin | 454 | 9 | 27 | 1 | 10 | 28 | 61[b] |
| Uganda | 389 | 30 | 70 | 10 | 40 | 80 | 0 |
| Togo | 296 | 7 | 18 | 3 | 10 | 21 | 81 |
| Burkina Faso | 216 | 15 | 70 | 2 | 17 | 72 | 48 |
| Cameroon | 200 | 20 | 67 | 1 | 21 | 68 | 72[b] |
| Mali | 170 | 36 | 50 | 0 | 36 | 50 | 27 |
| Lesotho | 145 | 12 | 12 | 70 | 82 | 82 | 15 |
| Burundi | 124 | 5 | 20 | 0 | 5 | 25 | 81 |
| Senegal | 117 | 100 | 100 | 0 | 100 | 100 | 100 |
| Swaziland | 84 | 0 | 0 | 90 | 90 | 90 | 0 |
| Total[c] | 14,500 | 11 | 26 | 23 | 34 | 49 | 33 |

*Source:* Reprinted from Byerlee et al. (1994, p. 7).
[a] Min. = area usually based on seed sales; max. = area based on surveys or breeders' estimates.
[b] Germplasm from IITA (International Institute of Tropical Agriculture) that includes some CIMMYT germplasm in its background.
[c] Excludes more than one million hectares of maize in Zaire, Angola, Somalia, and Namibia not covered by the survey.

the late eighties, maize was 8 percent of cereal area in Burkina, 5 percent in Senegal, and 20 percent in Mali.[6] At the end of the decade, new cultivars were used in over one-fourth of the area in maize in Burkina Faso, over one-third of the maize area in Mali, and all of the area in maize in Senegal.

Maize yield increases in Mali were greater than those of cotton in the seventies and eighties from 600 kilograms per hectare in the early seventies to 1.75 metric tons per hectare in the late eighties (Girdis, 1993, p. 19). In the cotton zone of southern Mali, the area in improved maize cultivars combined with inorganic fertilizers increased from 6,000 to more than 75,000 hectares from 1976 to 1989 (Boughton and de Frahan, 1994, p. 22; Holtzman et al., 1991, p. 5). In all three Sahelian countries (Burkina, Senegal, and Mali), new early maize cultivars are now on a substantial proportion of their maize area. These new early cultivars increase the ability of maize to compete with the drought tolerance of sorghum and millet through drought escape. Earliness also enables maize to be planted early and then harvested in the *soudure,* or hungry season, before the principal cereals of sorghum and millet.[7]

The rapid introduction of new maize technologies of the eighties is demonstrated by the 4.8 to 6.7 percent annual growth rates of yields for Ghana, Burkina Faso, and Mali (fig. 3-2). The introduction of the new maize cultivars has been concentrated in the wet savannas, both in the Sudano-Guinean zones of Burkina Faso and Mali and in the coastal countries.[8] In 1995, 33 to 50 percent of the maize area in Sub-Saharan Africa was planted to improved varieties (Byerlee, 1994, p. 9; see also table 3-2). Maize has been an outstanding success story for the IARCs (international agricultural research centers) and the NARSs (national agricultural research systems) in Sub-Saharan Africa (Fajemisin, 1992). The increased maize productivity and concentration in the subhumid zone resulted in a real price decline, which benefited the maize importers in the semiarid regions.

The substantial maize yield variability indicates the riskiness of maize production, since maize is very sensitive to water availability. The most rapid introduction of maize technology occurred in the Sudano-Guinean zone, where there was sufficient rainfall that inorganic fertilization was less risky and more profitable than in the dry savanna (Smith et al., 1994; Dakurah et al., 1992; Marfo and Tripp, 1992, p. 62).[9] In the wet savanna, the new maize cultivars are generally combined with inorganic fertilizers. For example, a case study for the wet savanna of northern Nigeria (average rainfall of 900 to 1,200 millimeters) showed a complete replacement of local cultivars with an improved maize cultivar, with most farmers also using inorganic fertilizer.

Figure 3-2. Maize Yields in Ghana, Mali, and Burkina Faso, 1965–1992

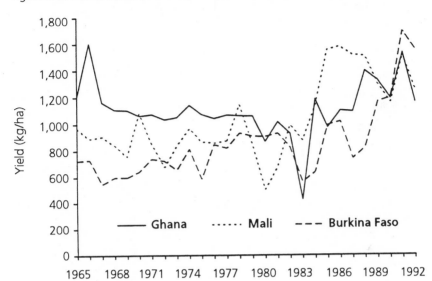

*Source:* Based on data from FAO, *FAO Production Year Book* (1986–93); FAO, *World Crop and Livestock Statistics,* 1987.
*Note:* Growth rates (in percent per annum) for the period 1965–79 were: Ghana, −1.41; Mali, 0.20; and Burkina Faso, 2.40. For 1980–92, they were: Ghana, 4.82; Mali, 6.67; and Burkina Faso, 5.69.

Since the mid-seventies, this maize technology introduction has resulted in a rapid increase in maize consumption, replacing the traditional food staples of millet and sorghum. The use of inorganic fertilizer in northern Nigeria has spread to other crops, especially sorghum (Smith et al., 1994, pp. 9, 10, 16).

In the semiarid zone, little or no inorganic fertilizer is used with maize, and the introduction of new cultivars has been less rapid (for a Kenyan example, see Byerlee and Heisey, 1993, p. 42). A between-country comparison indicates the general association between new maize cultivar adoption and use of inorganic fertilizer in Sub-Saharan African countries (table 3-3; Byerlee, 1994, pp. 15–18; Karanja, 1990; Smale and Heisey, 1994). Increasing use of fertilizer and reducing farm-level fertilizer costs are clearly important research and development priorities. The new cultivars generally are much more responsive to the higher fertility conditions than the traditional cultivars. In two of the four countries, inorganic fertilizer use was even more pervasive than the spread of new cultivars. With the risk associated with the use of

Table 3-3. Adoption of Improved Maize Cultivars and Use of Inorganic Fertilizer (percent of maize acreage)

| Country (year) | Improved Varieties or Hybrids | Inorganic Fertilizer Use |
|---|---|---|
| Malawi (1990) | 18 | 65 |
| Eastern Zambia (mid-1980s) | 29 | 56 |
| Ghana (1990) | 48 | 26 |
| Zimbabwe | 100 | 20 |

*Source:* Based on Byerlee (1993, p. 11).

Table 3-4. Annual Farm Incomes for Hand Traction and Animal Traction Households Before and After the Introduction of New Technologies in the Sudano-Guinean Zone of Burkina Faso

| Income (US$)[a] | Hand Traction Households | | Animal Traction Households | |
|---|---|---|---|---|
| | Before[b] | After[c] | Before[b] | After[c] |
| Total farm income | 704.00 | 1,111.00 | 1,140.00 | 1,813.00 |
| Per capita income[d] | 117.00 | 167.00 | 180.00 | 204.00 |
| Wages per hour | 0.24 | 0.39 | 0.38 | 0.47 |

*Source:* Data from Lawrence (1993, pp. 92, 93).
[a] Exchange rate is CFA272/US$ (IMF, *International Financial Statistics,* 1992).
[b] Includes only traditional cultivars and technologies without inorganic inputs.
[c] Includes use of fertilizers, pesticides, and high-yielding varieties of cotton and maize.
[d] Incomes are reported for six workers in the hand traction households; in the animal traction households, there were eight workers.

inorganic fertilizer when water availability is a problem, as in the drier region of Zimbabwe, there is a clear predominance of new cultivars and much less fertilization.

Substantial income gains are realized with the adoption of new cotton and maize technologies. In one Sudano-Guinean region of Burkina Faso, according to linear programming model results (presented in more detail in chapter 9), farm income increased 58 percent in hand traction households and 59 percent in animal traction households with the introduction of the intensive maize and cotton technologies (table 3-4). Wages per hour of work by the active household members increased 62 percent in hand traction households and 24 percent in animal traction households. When the new technologies were successfully introduced at a rapid rate in this region, the productivity of labor substantially increased, as indicated by the implicit wage rates calculated. Higher labor productivity leads to higher wages, according to economic theory. Is this relevant to within-family income distribution in African agriculture? How are these gains in household income divided within the family? Do women and children benefit from the rapid technological change, or is the household head the sole beneficiary of these changes? In chapter 9, we respond to the various attacks on the technology solution to improving the welfare of women.

## Rapid Introduction of Organic Fertilizers in Southern Mali

The farmers in the Sudano-Guinean zone who benefited from the increased incomes from cotton and maize have been investing their higher incomes in cattle.[10] In the absence of sufficiently high and secure returns in financial institutions, African farmers use large and small animals as their main investment and liquidity sources. With the rapid expansion of crops and trees (citrus and mango), the forests were being cut in the Sudano-Guinean zone, pushing back the tsetse fly. Trypanosomiasis had been a major barrier to increased livestock production in the subhumid zone and had given a comparative advantage in livestock production to the semiarid zone for most of the transhumance cycle.[11] In transhumance, herders from the Sahelian and Sahelo-Sudanian regions move south into the subhumid zone after the crop season. The animals graze the crop residues and in the process fertilize the farmers' fields. When the rains come, the herders move north again. When the cattle are owned by the farmers, the calf harvest is divided.

The rapid increases in cottonseed meal facilitated more intensive livestock operations in the Sudano-Guinean region. Farmers supplemented grazing with a feed, especially during the dry season. Supplementary feeding is especially important for plowing, because at this time the draft animals are in their weakest condition after the long dry season. In the last decade, cottonseed meal has become increasingly valuable and has been transported to other regions for intensive livestock operations.[12]

In the seventies and eighties, as farmers in the Sudano-Guinean zone were increasing their investments in cattle, the systems of the traditional transhumance herders from the north were breaking down. Herds were decimated by the 1968–73 drought, with losses estimated from 40 to 60 percent. Human casualties were relatively higher among the herders than among the farmers and were concentrated among both herders and farmers from the Sahelian agroecological region (Sen, 1981, pp. 115, 119, 121). Many of the Peuhl and Tauregs went to the urban areas and never returned. International donors and national governments supported programs to rebuild the herds and to improve their productivity. Unfortunately, after this major drought, rainfall remained approximately one standard deviation lower than the long-term norm through the 1980s (Glantz, 1987). Population concentrations and land degradation in the savannas make it more difficult for the herders to use their old routes and water holes.

Transhumance has been shifting southward due to combined factors of lower rainfall, rangelands degraded from overgrazing and the extension of cropland into former communal grazing areas, and the removal of some of the disease pressure in the southern zone. In the 1980s, many Fulani (Peuhl) moved their herds in a rotation between the Sudano-Guinean zone and the wet savanna of the northern coastal countries (northern Côte d'Ivoire, Togo, and Benin). Investment in these coastal countries in improved slaughtering facilities and expansion of trucking increased the profitability of livestock operations. Livestock and livestock products became easier to move to the major urban markets of the coastal cities of Abidjan and Cotonou.[13] The increasing migration of herders into the coastal countries in the late eighties led to violence as farmers in Côte d'Ivoire, Benin, and other countries reacted to the competition for resources with the itinerant herders. The Fulani (Peuhl) fled back to the Sahelian countries. In the Sudano-Guinean region, many herders are now becoming more sedentary, and the farmers are building up their herd sizes, so there is increasing concentration of cattle in the Sudano-Guinean region. The same phenomena of higher population density in agriculture pushing back the tsetse and enabling increasing animal concentrations further south, including the local Zebu, has also been documented in Nigeria (Bourn and Wint, 1994, pp. 13, 14). As in southern Mali, the increases in animal density are principally associated with increasing intensity of crop production in the Sudano-Guinean and Sudanian zones (Bourn and Wint, 1994, pp. 14, 16)

The shifts in cotton and livestock production to the principal Sudano-Guinean agricultural region of Mali-Sud in Mali are dramatic.[14] In this region from the 1950s to the mid-1980s, average cotton area increased more than 300 percent, from 32,000 to 130,000 hectares. From 1977 to 1986, the cattle herd of Mali-Sud had increased approximately one-half million head to 4.6 million cattle, an increase from 23 to 39 percent of the national cattle herd (Berthé et al., 1991, pp. 34, 43). The income gains from the new technology introduction for both cotton and maize made possible this substantial increase in the cattle stock.

In the eighties, agronomists in the cotton zones of Burkina Faso and Mali became concerned with the declines in organic matter and potential soil acidification associated with the use of inorganic fertilizers on cotton. In the late eighties, the structural reform programs of the World Bank included the elimination of subsidies on inorganic fertilizer and other farm inputs, for example, insecticides, petroleum, and credit. At this time in Mali, inorganic fertilizer prices increased 30 percent, while the cotton price stayed the same from 1985 to 1990. Cotton profits decreased, and use of inorganic fertilizer declined. The recommended application was 200 kilograms per hectare of the combination of compound fertilizer and urea. In Mali-Sud (Koutiala), farmers were using 190 kilograms per hectare on their cotton in 1980. Fertilizer use in the late eighties fell to 150 kilograms per hectare in one site and 120 kilograms per hectare in another (Raymond, Faure, and Persons, 1990, pp. 9–12). Finally, foreign exchange rationing required by overvalued currencies and low priority on fertilizer imports were factors discouraging imports of inorganic fertilizers.

In most of Burkina and Mali, the critical nutrient deficiency is phosphorus. Available nitrogen is also low and often inadequate. Initial potassium levels in the soil are sufficient, but continuous cropping, especially during the second and third years of sorghum in the cotton rotation, creates a potassium deficiency (Dureau, Traore, and Ballo, 1994, pp. 9, 10; Heathcote, 1974, pp. 469, 470).[15] Organic fertilizer can provide reasonable levels of nitrogen and potassium but the levels of phosphorus are generally insufficient. Phosphorus is the principal nutrient requirement or the first element that becomes constraining to yield increases of most crops in this region and especially cotton. It takes 5 metric tons per hectare of manure to provide the same level of phosphorus provided by 100 kilograms per hectare of the compound fertilizer generally used in Mali (table 3-5).[16] The high requirement of manure to supply the necessary phosphorus is limited by the number of animals that can be fed on most farms in the region and the high transportation costs of manure. Demands for labor are very high, to cut and transport the straw and dig and roof the compost heap, and for transportation to the compost heap and then to the field.

What do farmers in the Sudano-Guinean zone do about soil fertility? Interview data were taken by the Institut d'Economie Rurale over three crop seasons for farmers in the Koutiala region, one of the main cotton zones of

Table 3-5. Substitution Potential between Manure and
Inorganic Fertilizers for Major Nutrients

| Fertilizer Type | 14 N | 23 $P_2O_5$ | 12 $K_2O$ |
|---|---|---|---|
| Complex fertilizer (kg/ha) | 100 | 100 | 100 |
| Manure (t/ha) | 1.5 | 5 | 1 |
| Urea (kg/ha) | 30 | — | — |
| Potassium chloride (kg/ha) | — | — | 25 |

Source: Based on Dureau, Traore, and Ballo (1994, p. 32).
Note: One of the principal objectives of the applied experimentation with
manure is to improve the levels of the basic nutrients. The above are mean
values for four different types of manure preparation (Dureau, Traore, and
Ballo, 1994, p. 26).

the Sudano-Guinean zone of Mali. Sorghum and millet are the predominant
activities on these farms, with 2.4 hectares in monoculture sorghum, 1.3 hectares of millet, and 2.7 hectares of intercropped sorghum, millet, and other
crops. So, despite recent yield gains for cotton and maize, these farms are
still principally sorghum and millet producers. In the late eighties, sorghum
and millet yields in this region increased (Girdis, 1993, p. 19). As farmers
became wealthier, they could afford to use more inorganic inputs on their
staples. Also with increasing wealth, they were increasing their herd sizes. In
this sample in 1991, farmers' average herd sizes were 4.2 oxen for animal
traction, 13.8 cattle, 8.3 sheep, 3.4 goats, 0.9 asses, and various small animals. Manure and household wastes were used principally on cotton (1.4
metric tons per hectare) spread over the entire 3.45 hectares of cotton. On the
0.35 hectare of maize, levels of manure and household waste totaled 2.2
metric tons per hectare. Inorganic fertilizer use was concentrated on cotton
and maize at levels of 200 and 136 kilograms per hectare, respectively, of
compound fertilizers for the two crops and 41 and 55 kilograms per hectare,
respectively, of urea. Small quantities of urea and superphosphate and rock
phosphate were applied to peanuts and some rock phosphate to cotton (Coulibaly, 1995).

Farmers have been using organic fertilizers (manure and household wastes)
on their compound land for maize and vegetables in most agroecological
zones. They were reported to be using 175 to 681 kilograms per hectare of
manure in three sites in Burkina in the early eighties. Raymond, Faure, and
Persons, (1990, pp. 9–12) report farmers using 300 kilograms per hectare of

manure in Koutiala and Sikasso (southern Mali) in a remedial fashion on their cotton and maize fields. The sorghum and millet take advantage of the residual effect of fertilizer in the rotations. In the late seventies in northern Nigeria, where there are more cattle on farms than in much of the Sahel, 0.2 to 3.4 metric tons per hectare of manure were used by farmers without cattle and 1.4 to 4 metric tons per hectare by farmers with cattle (McIntire, Bourzat, and Pingali, 1992, pp. 90, 91). Without inorganic fertilizer, these are very inadequate levels of manure, since 5 to 12 metric tons per hectare are needed to supply the principal nutrients (ibid., p. 94). A survey in southern Mali found that farmers use both the compound fertilizer and 4 metric tons per hectare of manure on cotton but do not fertilize sorghum (table 3-6). Then there are residual effects of that fertilization for the following two years in which they grow sorghum on this land.

The rapid introduction on farmers' fields of more and higher-quality manure has been a recent innovation, occurring over the last five years. With the elimination of inorganic fertilizer subsidies, the increased size of cattle herds of farmers, and the more settled lifestyle of the herders, the relative price of inorganic to organic fertilizers has risen, encouraging applied research and farmer innovations to improve organic fertilizers. National and French scientists responded to the relative price signals. Practices to improve the quantity and quality of organic fertilizers were then developed or refined in applied experimentation, tested in on-farm experiments, and rapidly extended in the late eighties and early nineties (Coulibaly, 1995). One practice was to lay a bed of straw from the stalks of millet and sorghum for the animals in small confined areas of corrals. After several days, this mixture can be put into a covered compost pit. Alternatively, more layers of straw can be added to the corrals and then applied directly to the fields. The main innovation was to

Table 3-6. Crop Rotation, Fertilizer Use, and Yields over Three Years in the Cotton Zone of Mali-Sud (kilograms per hectare)

| Year | Crop Rotation | Compound Fertilizer | Urea | Manure | Yields |
|------|---------------|---------------------|------|--------|--------|
| | | | (kg/ha) | | |
| 1 | Cotton | 120 | 50 | 4,000 | 1,360 |
| 2 | Sorghum | 0 | 0 | 0 | 1,140 |
| 3 | Sorghum | 0 | 0 | 0 | 705 |

*Source:* Based on Dureau, Traore, and Ballo (1994, p. 9).

cover and water the compost heap and thereby maintain the quality of the manure.

The adoption by farmers of these organic fertilizers is also an excellent example of farmer responses to changes in the relative prices of land and labor. Land degradation, increasing population pressure, and the lack of sufficient demand for off-farm labor resulted in a falling price of labor relative to the implicit value of land. As the pressure on the land in the prime cotton zones increased with population concentration and qualitative deterioration of the land, farmers substituted for land with highly labor-intensive innovations. The collection of straw, compost-heap construction, and spreading of organic fertilizers are all extremely labor-intensive, even when farmers reduce labor requirements by only partially adopting these improved manure production practices (Coulibaly, 1995).

Cotton producers are accustomed to following technical recommendations and to obtaining a response to inorganic fertilizer. It is also traditional among farmers in the Sahelian countries to use manure and household wastes to fertilize the compound area immediately adjacent to the village. This practice has been substantially extended to larger land areas by increasing the quantity and quality of available manure.[17] With the shifts in land quality as land farther from the compound fields is fertilized with organic and inorganic fertilizer, settlement patterns in southern Mali are also shifting. To increase their land area, farmers had been going farther from the village. With the decentralization of the farming operation and the availability of more cattle and manure, farmers used the manure on these fields farther away. At first, farmers would sleep over in temporary facilities; then they build permanent housing on these more distant fields. Gradually, the settlement pattern in the cotton zone is decentralizing into isolated farmhouses replacing the villages.

## Soil Fertility: Alternatives and Myths

In the late eighties and early nineties, there was a dramatic, rapid introduction of organic fertilizers in both the Sudano-Guinean and the Sudanian regions of Mali.[18] However, supply increases of organic fertilizer are constrained by the number of animals and the production technologies to transform it. The devaluation in 1994 will have a short-run effect in reducing the demand for imports of inorganic fertilizer, but a long-run effect will be to increase prices of domestically produced food as imported agricultural products become more expensive.[19] With higher prices and an inelastic supply of organic fertilizer, the real price of inorganic fertilizer (price of inorganic fertilizer divided by cereal price) will decline, increasing the demand for this input. Hence, it is appropriate to review the problems and alternatives associated with the introduction of inorganic fertilizer.

Although the use of inorganic fertilizer in Sub-Saharan African agriculture increased 6.3 percent annually in the seventies and 5.5 percent in the eighties, it is still the lowest in the world. In the second half of the eighties, there were decreases in fertilizer use in Sub-Saharan Africa because of shortages of foreign exchange and the pressures of structural adjustment programs to eliminate fertilizer subsidies. In 1988, the fertilizer nutrients per hectare of arable cropland were 8 kilograms per hectare in Sub-Saharan Africa, compared to 85 kilograms per hectare in North America and 116 kilograms per hectare in East Asia. Twenty of forty countries surveyed in the region were entirely dependent on foreign aid for fertilizer imports. There were only three significant fertilizer producers in Sub-Saharan Africa (Bumb, 1991, pp. 41, 44, 46.)

In Sub-Saharan Africa, there is substantial interest in research on alternatives to inorganic fertilizer, including applied work on animal manure, crop residues, and rotations. The following list provides a summary of soil fertility alternatives for the Sub-Saharan countries:

- inorganic fertilizer
    imported
    locally available (rock phosphate)
- organic fertilizers
    manure
    incorporated plant residues
    alley cropping
- improving traditional alternatives to fertilization
    crop rotation
    intercropping
    use of fallow periods
- crop breeding
    low phosphorus tolerance
    aluminum tolerance
- sophisticated new technologies
    inoculation of legumes to improve nitrogen fixation
    mycorrhizae[20]

The interest in soil fertility alternatives is due to the foreign exchange requirements for fertilizer imports, the required cash expenditures for inorganic fertilizers, the risk, and the requirement that inorganic fertilizers be available to farmers at specific times. The main problem of organic fertilizer is that the supply is not large enough to provide the necessary basic nutrients. Although there are techniques that can be applied to improve the productivity of the manure and mulch in shaded compost heaps, the supply expansion potential of both manure and mulch is limited. Since the primary soil nutrient deficiencies presently are phosphorus and nitrogen, inorganic fertilizers are presently the most concentrated and lowest-cost sources of these principal nutrients in the Sudano-Guinean zone. Organic fertilization can supplement the inorganic fertilizers and improve water retention and the availability of other nutrients besides the major ones (nitrogen and phosphorus). So organic and inorganic fertilizers contribute different components to soil fertility and are complementary at low levels of both.

Breeders have been searching for methods to reduce the expenditures on inorganic inputs. Some recent crop-breeding programs have concentrated on cultivar selection for tolerance to low nitrogen or phosphorus or other soil stresses, such as aluminum or salt toxicities. Some gains have been made; however, the problems of low soil fertility will not be resolved by greater efficiency in nutrient utilization or even compatibility with agents in the soil, such as rhizobium or mycorrhizae, to increase nutrient levels. The problem is that there are presently very low levels of the two basic crop nutrients, nitrogen and phosphorus, in the soil in much of Sub-Saharan Africa; hence, increasing crop yields will mine these nutrients, even if they are more efficiently utilized. Even more efficient use of the nutrients does not ultimately resolve the long-term principle of agronomy: If you take nutrients out of the soil, you must put nutrients back into the soil to produce a crop. Where breeding for tolerances to soil stresses has been successful, as in Brazil, the introduction of new tolerant cultivars is associated with rapid increases in the use of inorganic fertilizer (Sanders and Garcia, 1994, pp. 40–44).

New agricultural technologies in Sub-Saharan African countries need to focus on improving the agronomic environment to enable sustainable increases in cereal yields. Producers adopting new soil fertility technologies face a learning curve. Hence, farmers are expected to obtain the full benefits of the new cost-reducing technologies only gradually. For inorganic fertilizer, scarce foreign exchange will need to be used and marketing structures improved for the more timely availability of inorganic fertilizer and to handle increased cereal supplies. In regions where farmers do not already use inorganic fertilizers, subsidies for the first few years probably can be justified to overcome the higher initial costs of learning to use them efficiently.

Unfortunately, the development of agricultural and economic policies to accelerate the introduction of inorganic fertilizer into the subhumid zone is delayed by the persistence of two myths about inorganic fertilizer: (1) inorganic fertilizer damages the soil, and (2) small farmers will not use scarce cash to purchase inorganic fertilizer, since it is too risky. The first myth supposedly is supported by long-term fertilization experiments in the Sudanian region of Burkina Faso (Sedogo, 1993; also see Bationo et al., 1993; Matlon, 1990, p. 23). These experiments showed that after eight to twelve years of inorganic fertilization, sorghum yields began to decline. There are two major problems with the conclusions of this research that inorganic fertilizer used without organic fertilizer damages the soil. First, agronomic research has consistently shown that continuous sorghum production can induce potassium deficiencies even with the use of a compound fertilizer with potassium and with adequate initial potassium levels in the soil (see Dureau, Traore, and Ballo, 1994, and the references cited there). There was no indication that the soil researchers tested for potassium deficiency when yields from inorganic fertilizer alone began to fall. Secondly, the experiment was conducted with present farmer practices of removing all the crop residuals. At higher yield levels, there would be less pressure on farmers to use all the crop residuals for animal feed and fuel; hence, farmers could incorporate these residuals. In the experiment, despite increasing sorghum yields for almost a decade, all the crop residues were removed from the field.[21]

A gradual decline of soil organic matter has also been observed in the Sudano-Guinean cotton zone, when only inorganic fertilizer has been applied (Savadogo, 1990, pp. 24, 25). Clearly, increases in organic fertilizer ultimately need to complement inorganic fertilizer. We have already discussed how manures are being used more efficiently in the Sudano-Guinean (and Sudanian) zones of Mali. However, continuous crop cultivation in the absence of fertilization clearly leads to soil degradation (Mokwunye and Hammond, 1992, p. 126, and references cited there.) The decline in soil organic matter is a second-generation problem of new technology introduction in the Sudano-Guinean region. The first-generation problem is how to increase crop yields in a situation of low levels of the basic nutrients of nitrogen and phosphorus. The use of inorganic fertilizers has been highly successful at resolving this problem in the Sudano-Guinean zone.

Contrary to the second myth, small farmers have purchased inorganic fertilizers in this Sudano-Guinean region and in other regions where there has been rapid introduction of yield-increasing varieties. In Latin America and Asia over the last two decades, 50 to 75 percent of the yield increases of food crops by small farmers have resulted from increases in use of inorganic fertilizer (Byerlee and Heisey, 1993, p. 28). Inorganic fertilizer was an important component of increased yields of cotton and maize in the Sudano-Guinean zone. Since usage levels are only moderate by international standards, farmers will continue to benefit from higher levels of inorganic fertilizer there. Public policy and private investments can facilitate the pace of greater input use.

## Conclusion

Cotton and maize have been impressive success stories of new technology development and diffusion in the Sudano-Guinean zone. These accomplishments are not generally known outside the region, except in the francophone literature, as the myth of general failure of agriculture and agricultural research in the semiarid tropics of Sub-Saharan Africa predominates in most popular and technical literature.

Cultivar introduction in Sub-Saharan Africa has been associated with substantial increases in agricultural chemicals, especially inorganic fertilizers and cotton pesticides. These increases in the use of inorganic fertilizer have spread from cotton to maize and, to a limited extent, to the rotation with sorghum. Hence, the improved input use in the cash crop has also increased yields of two basic cereals, maize and sorghum. Without these large increases in inorganic fertilizers, it is unlikely that cotton yields would have increased as much or that the new maize and cotton cultivars would have diffused as rapidly. A key component of the new technology introduction, then, is the combination of the new cultivars with increased inorganic fertilization.[22]

Since the principal soil constraints in the Sudano-Guinean zone have been lack of nitrogen and phosphorus, inorganic fertilizer has been the cheapest and most efficient source of nutrients. Over time, second-generation soil problems, such as declining organic matter and micronutrient and potassium deficiencies, have become important in the Sudano-Guinean zone. When the price of inorganic fertilizer increased in the late eighties with the removal of the subsidies, the supply of organic fertilizer increased, principally with qualitative improvements in manure. This increased organic fertilization was an impressive response by applied researchers and farmers to changing relative prices of two fertilizer sources, organic and inorganic, and to the falling price of labor relative to land.

A secondary effect from the devaluation of the CFA of 1994 after the increased costs of imported inorganic fertilizers will be the increasing price of domestically produced cereals as the price of imported cereals increases. The higher profitability of agriculture will encourage increased cash input use, while the supply of manure is constrained by the number of animals, the availability of land, and the available manure production technologies. Hence, the use of inorganic fertilizer will need to increase again in this region over the next decade.

Environmentalists have frequently raised objections to inorganic inputs in developed countries. The issues of increasing production or reducing inorganic input use are very different for developing countries, especially those with malnutrition and continuing pressures on their food supply systems. In developing countries, the use of chemical inputs in the better crop regions is expected to positively impact national environmental conditions by enabling some withdrawal of crop production from marginal areas (Byerlee, 1993, p. 9).

# 4

# Combining Water and Soil Improvements: The Sudanian Region of Burkina Faso

**N**EW CULTIVARS and better agronomic practices for both cotton and maize contributed to the successes of new technology introduction in the high-rainfall Sudano-Guinean region. In the Sudanian zone, rainfall is more limited and erratic, and there are considerable soil problems (especially crusting) that make infiltration difficult. This chapter reports on substantial fieldwork observing farmers' practices and evaluating technologies for the Sudanian zone of Burkina Faso. Modeling of these farms gives some insight into the process of technological change, especially the shift from extensive to intensive technologies and the evaluation of constraints to new technology introduction.

## A Sudanian Zone of Burkina Faso (the Central Plateau)

The Central or Mossi Plateau of Burkina Faso is composed of both the Sudanian and Sahelo-Sudanian agroecological regions and is principally settled by small farms of two to six hectares with approximately one hectare cultivated per active household member.[1] Farm size varies with the number of active workers in the household and the type of power source. Most labor is performed with simple hand tools. Donkeys are the principal source of animal traction and are becoming more common in the Central Plateau; oxen and horses are more prevalent in the southwest (Sudano-Guinean region) and in the eastern savanna (the more sparsely populated Sudanian region) (see fig. 4-1).[2]

The principal cereal crops in Burkina Faso are pearl millet *(Pennisetum americanum L.)* and sorghum *(Sorghum bicolor Moench)*, occupying an estimated 80 percent of the crop area. The land quality differences determine the

Figure 4-1. Climatic Zones, Research Sites, and Principal Cities of Burkina Faso

Source: Adapted from Nagy, Sanders, and Ohm (1988, p. 4).
Note: NLC is the northern limit of cultivation. Numbers given refer to isohyets in millimeters of rainfall at 90 percent probability levels.

allocation of cereal land. A small amount of maize is grown on the compound areas around the household. Here the animals are tethered or gathered at night, and household garbage further supplements soil fertility. The maize used is a short-season variety, to be harvested during the soudure shortly before the harvest of the pearl millet and sorghum.

Farther down on the toposequence, there are depressions and valleys where the runoff has resulted in more silt deposits and slightly heavier soils (Stoop, 1989; Vierich and Stoop, 1990). Sorghum is generally planted on the moderately better soils but still on the slopes. The principal crop, pearl millet, is planted on the sandier, less fertile upper portion of the toposequence.[3] Where there are less clear divisions of land quality, the sorghum and pearl millet are often intercropped. On the lowland heavier soils with poor drainage (*basfonds*), small areas of rice production are found. The crop allocation is adjusted to these topographical differences in soil fertility and water retention capacity. Of the cereals grown in this area, pearl millet is the most tolerant to low soil fertility and drought stress, and maize is the least tolerant.

Pearl millet and sorghum are often intercropped with cowpeas. As the production of cowpeas is limited by field and storage insects and by soil fertility problems, the yields, planting density, and total production are very low. A small area of peanuts is often planted to meet basic cash requirements. Various types of livestock, including chickens, guinea hens, goats, sheep, and donkeys, supplement the crop activities. On the Central Plateau and in the eastern savanna, cattle are often entrusted to the Fulani, who return them after the harvest to graze the stubble. In this way, cattle still can be used for the acquisition of wealth, even though the opportunity cost of their grazing land has become too high to keep them on the farm in many densely populated regions, as in much of the Central Plateau.

Cereal yields are low because inorganic fertilizers are not commonly used, and in much of the Central Plateau higher population pressures have broken down the traditional bush-fallow rotation system. Maize yields range from 1.0 to 1.7 metric tons per hectare, sorghum from 0.4 to 1.2 metric tons per hectare, and pearl millet from 0.2 to 0.7 metric ton per hectare. The areas planted in maize and sorghum are apparently determined by the quantities of higher-quality land available. In contrast, the area of pearl millet is extended as far as available labor will permit critical, seasonal operations.[4]

Land is communally owned, and village or land chiefs set long-term allocation rights for household heads. On the household land, the principal objective of production is to assure an adequate grain supply for the family during the year. Family members must provide labor on this land, as dictated by the household head. The household head also allocates private plots to family members, who provide the inputs and keep the output.

Because there are active seasonal and long-term migration flows to urban areas and to other countries, there is little agricultural use of hired labor. There is still access to land, even though land quality has been decreasing. Hence, farmers apparently prefer to work their own land rather than being hired labor. Labor exchange does exist, but most labor comes from the extended family system. The predominant characteristics of these production systems in the Sudanian zone are

- high population densities
- minimal use of purchased inputs
- decreased soil fertility resulting from disappearance or reduction of fallow time

• decline and reduced quality of grazing in the communal lands
• decreased cattle stocks

This chapter considers three water retention techniques: earth or stone dikes, the zaï and tied ridges. The simpler technique is the use of earth or stone dikes. These dikes are barriers ten to thirty centimeters high and ten to thirty meters apart, depending on the slope and the degree of the farmer's enthusiasm. These barriers reduce runoff, especially if they are constructed on the contour. In a small area (one to two meters behind a barrier), increased soil moisture raises yields, especially when organic fertilizer is used.[5] In Yatenga, the poorest and most degraded area of the Central Plateau, both earth and stone dikes were rapidly introduced during the late seventies and eighties (table 4-1).[6] In the less degraded regions of the Central Plateau, introduction of the dikes has been less rapid, even though the estimated rates of return for this activity in the undegraded region are higher than in the degraded region.[7] The dikes require an enormous labor input (up to 200 man-hours per hectare for dikes made of stone). Unless farmers are pressured by the soil deterioration and the falling labor-to-land price ratios, the implicit returns on these large labor inputs are apparently too low to interest them. The present diffusion of these dikes and their more rapid introduction into the more degraded regions appear to be consistent with the hypothesis, stated in chapter 2, that there is a shift to more labor-intensive technologies with increased population pressure and land degradation.

The Burkina Faso government estimates that in the seventies, 60,000 hectares were put into these earthen dikes in Yatenga. Heavy rainfall can destroy these dikes, and this often occurs at critical periods during the crop season. In the eighties, there was a switch in emphasis to stone dikes, which are more porous. By the summer of 1986, there were an estimated 6,500 hectares of the stone dikes in the Yatenga region (table 4-1). Diking of both types is encountered in other regions of the Central Plateau, but introduction has been most rapid in Yatenga, where the most serious land degradation has occurred. Since the stone dikes only slow down the water and increase infiltration, farmers in these degraded zones frequently combine dikes with the zaï technique. The zaï are also used in Yatenga without the stone dikes. This pitting technique consists of digging multiple holes all over the field. The holes are dug to a depth of 5 to 15 centimeters and a diameter of 10 to 30 centimeters, with about 50 to 100 centimeters between them. Some manure and organic matter are mixed with dirt and put into the zaï so there is a combination of water retention and soil fertility improvement. In the immediate vicinity, substantial

Table 4-1. Stages of Development of Water Retention and Soil Fertility
Technology on the Central Plateau of Burkina Faso

|  | Stage 1 | Stage 2 | Stage 3 |
|---|---|---|---|
| Environment and period for labor and technology input | Degraded soils; low implicit labor and land prices; water retention input in dry season | Undegraded soils; higher implicit labor and land prices; water retention input in dry season | Undegraded soils; water retention input in crop season; animal traction |
| Technologies | Earth or stone dikes; zaï | Earth or stone dikes; zaï | Improved land preparation; tied ridges |
| Stages of present diffusion | Earth dikes at wide spacing have been promoted by the Burkina government since the mid-1970s. The Burkina agency responsible for supporting these with funding from the World Bank estimated (1986) that it has participated in constructing almost 60,000 hectares of earth dikes. Stone dikes were actively promoted in the 1980s. They were most popular where there was more slope and stones were readily available. Often there is closer spacing of these stone dikes than of earth dikes at 10- to 20-meter intervals. In Yatenga since 1980, an estimated 6,500 hectares have been put into stone dikes. Both types of dikes were introduced where soils were already moderately to extremely degraded. The zaï is usually a complementary technique to the stone dikes; small holes are dug all over the fields to trap water. Some organic fertilizer is placed in the holes. | Some introduction of both types of dikes, but less farmer interest demonstrated here | Minimal introduction; substantial farm-level and experiment station testing |

*Source:* Based on Sanders, Nagy, and Ramaswamy (1990, p. 7).

yield gains are claimed, but the zaï again requires very large labor investments that need to be repeated annually (Reij, Mulder, and Begeman, 1988, pp. 44–47). This labor, as with the dikes, is done outside the crop season, and the final effect of storing water all over the field and planting adjacent to the water storage is an indigenous form of the tied ridges, only with wider spacing between the water storage areas than with the tied ridges. Both the dikes and the zaï technologies require very large labor inputs, but this can be done in out-of-crop-season periods, when the opportunity costs of agricultural labor have traditionally been very low.

We can now expand the theory of soil degradation and technological change to a three-stage development process (see table 4-1). On the most degraded lands, farmers adopt strategies for improving soil fertility and water retention with large labor inputs outside the crop season (stage 1). The returns are still low for this activity, but the farmers are pressured by the falling land quality and the need for some members of the family to remain in agriculture. If farmers were to adopt these technologies before the soils become degraded, the economic returns to increased moisture availability and moderate fertilization would be even higher (stage 2; see note 7 for the evidence). However, introduction of this technology is slower on these higher-quality soils, apparently because the returns in agriculture are still higher than in the degraded region and farmers can thus avoid these extremely labor-intensive techniques. On the undegraded soils, experiment station and farm-level testing have shown much higher returns when technologies to improve water retention and soil fertility are implemented during the crop season (stage 3) than for either stage 1 or stage 2 technologies above. This third stage of technology development will require more input expenditures and, in many cases, animal traction, because peak seasonal labor demand periods will often become a constraint.

## Extensive or Intensive Technology Introduction for the Sahelian Region?

Tied ridging is a water retention technique that consists of perpendicular ridges with a depression in the center, where water collects rather than running off.[8] The ridging can be done at planting, at the first weeding, or at the second weeding, but the best results for yield increases in the farm trials were at first weeding (Cantrell et al., 1983). The height and spacing vary with construction method (hand or animal tillage), farmer preference, soil type, and rainfall characteristics. The cereals are then grown on the ridges.

Since the compound land receives the household wastes and manure from tethered animals, inorganic fertilization in farm trials did not cause a significant maize yield increase. There was, however, a substantial yield increase due to the tied ridges. Over the 1982–84 period, sorghum yields in farm trials increased 1.9 to 4.4 times due to the combined use of tied ridges and a moderate level of inorganic fertilizer.[9] Yields increased approximately 50 percent with either tied ridges or fertilization (Table 4-2).[10]

We constructed a representative farm model for the Central Plateau to analyze potential adoption of and returns to these various technology combinations. This model considers the profitability of various new technologies, taking into account land quality, seasonal labor periods, two types of power

Table 4-2. Yields and Percentages of Farmers Who Took Cash Losses from Fertilization and Tied Ridges in Sorghum Production in Farm Trial Villages, 1983 and 1984

| | | | Yields (kg/ha) | | | | % of Farmers Losing Cash | |
| --- | --- | --- | --- | --- | --- | --- | --- | --- |
| Year/Village | No. of Farmers | Traction Source | Control | Tied Ridges | Fertili- zation | Tied Ridges and Fertilization | Fertili- zation | Tied Ridges and Fertilization |
| 1983 | | | | | | | | |
| Nedogo | 3 | Manual | 430 | 484 | 547 | 851 | 56 | 0 |
| Nedogo | 11 | Donkey | 444 | 644 | 604 | 962 | 58 | 42 |
| Bangasse | 12 | Manual | 406 | 493 | 705 | 690 | 21 | 17 |
| Diapangou | 24 | Manual | 363 | 441 | 719 | 753 | 8 | 8 |
| Diapangou | 25 | Donkey | 481 | 552 | 837 | 871 | 12 | 16 |
| Diapangou | 25 | Ox | 526 | 578 | 857 | 991 | 20 | 12 |
| 1984 | | | | | | | | |
| Nedogo | 11 | Manual | 157 | 416 | 431 | 652 | 27 | 9 |
| Nedogo | 18 | Donkey | 173 | 425 | 355 | 773 | 50 | 0 |
| Bangasse | 12 | Manual | 293 | 456 | 616 | 944 | 8 | 17 |
| Dissankuy | 25 | Ox | 447 | 588 | 681 | 855 | 28 | 0 |
| Diapangou | 19 | Manual | 335 | 571 | 729 | 1,006 | 26 | 0 |
| Diapangou | 19 | Donkey | 498 | 688 | 849 | 1,133 | 21 | 0 |
| Diapangou | 19 | Ox | 466 | 704 | 839 | 1,177 | 5 | 0 |

*Source:* Sanders, Nagy, and Ramaswamy (1990, p. 10).
*Note:* Cash expenditures were only for inorganic fertilizer. Tied ridges alone never increased cash expenditures. The only additional input for tied ridges was a substantial increase in the use of family labor.

sources, present and potential activities, and on-farm and off-farm resources (for further discussion of the model, see appendix to this chapter). If family consumption goals were not attained with farm production, higher or penalty cereal prices would be paid to reach the minimum required consumption, to reflect the additional costs of obtaining staples on the market during times of scarcity, when their prices increase. We used linear programming, even though there were substantial variations in crop yields and output prices in this region of Burkina Faso. The values for yields and prices were the expected values, based on almost a decade of field experience in this region. Although risk programming could provide further refinements, this was not considered to be essential to the technology and policy issues considered here.[11] (For further discussion of the risk issue, see chapter 7.) In the modeling, sorghum yields increased 50 percent with tied ridges or with fertilization alone and 100 percent with both tied ridging and fertilization (see table 4-2 for field results). The returns to both the tied ridging and fertilization were lower on the poorer bush land for millet; thus, we used a 50 percent increase in yields for the combined tied ridging and moderate fertilization on this type of land.

Because human labor is the only power source on 90 percent of the farms in Burkina Faso, our initial concern is those technologies that depend exclusively on human labor. In the first scenario, farmers are unable to obtain inorganic fertilizer. They have the option of using tied ridges on the compound land and on their higher-quality land, which is usually planted to sorghum. The adoption of tied ridges increases farm income by 13 percent as farmers plant all the maize-compound land (0.15) and half their sorghum land (0.78) using this new technique (table 4-3).

One alternative is to use inorganic fertilizer on the sorghum land, reserving tied ridges for the compound land planted with maize.[12] When this is done, the results are similar to those for tied ridges alone (household income of US $587 per household). However, the use of inorganic fertilization by itself is risky. Insufficient water at the critical times of plant development results in the lack of response to fertilizer, even in the Sudanian types of soils with very low fertility. In the 1983 and 1984 crop years, 5 to 56 percent of the farms in the farm trials would have lost their cash investments had they used inorganic fertilizer alone. However, the use of both tied ridges and fertilization resulted in no loss of money for farmers in five of the village sites in 1984. Moreover, the combined technologies resulted in a substantial decrease in the number of farmers losing money in both years across almost all of the sites, as compared with sites using fertilizer alone (Table 4-2).

Table 4-3. Cropping Patterns and Farm Income with Hand Traction, Donkey Traction, Fertilization, and Tied Ridge Technologies in the Central Plateau of Burkina Faso

| | Traditional Management | Intensive Yield-Increasing Technologies: Hand Traction | | Extensive Strategy: Donkey Traction | |
| --- | --- | --- | --- | --- | --- |
| | | Maize and Sorghum: Tied Ridges. No Inorganic Fertilizer Available | Maize and Sorghum: Tied Ridges. Inorganic Fertilizer Available | Maize and Sorghum: Tied Ridges. Inorganic Fertilizer Available. Rental Market for Donkey Traction[a] | Maize and Sorghum: Tied Ridges. Inorganic Fertilizer Available. No Rental Market for Donkey Traction |
| Total area (ha) | 5.84 | 6.02 | 6.02 | 6.48 | 7.35 |
| Maize (ha) | 0.15 CL | 0.15 CL,TR | 0.15 CL,TR | 0.16[b] CL,TR,DT | 0.20[b] CL,DT,TR |
| Sorghum (ha) | — | 0.73 TR | 0.73 TR,F | 0.60 TR,F,DT | No sorghum. New activities on high-quality land: Maize: 0.28 DT 0.32 DT,F |
| Sorghum-cowpeas (ha) | 1.42 | 0.78 | 0.78 | 0.90 HT | 0.90 HT |
| Millet-cowpeas (ha) | 4.00 BF | 4.06 BF | 4.06 BF | 1.20 BF,DT | 5.25 BF,DT |

| | | | | 3.20 BF,HT<br>0.25 BF,DT<br>0.17 BF,DT | |
|---|---|---|---|---|---|
| Peanuts (ha) | 0.27 BF | 0.30 BF | 0.30 BF | | 0.40 BF,DT |
| Urea (kg/farm) | — | — | 37.00 | 30.00 | 16.00 |
| Cotton fertilizer[c] (kg/farm) | — | — | 73.00 | 60.00 | 32.00 |
| Net farm income (CFA), including value of home consumption | 152,345.00 | 170,295.00 | 172,552.00 | 184,337.00[d] | 178,524.00[d] |
| Implicit wage (CFA/adult hr.) | 43.00 | 48.00 | 49.00 | 52.00 | 51.00 |

*Source:* Sanders, Nagy, and Ramaswamy (1990, pp. 12, 13).

*Note:* BF—bush-fallow land; CL—compound land; DT—donkey traction; F—inorganic fertilizer; HT—hand traction; TR—tied ridges. There are variations in the quality of the slightly better land where sorghum is grown. These differences and the distinction between red and white sorghum were included in the model and are summarized here. Opportunity cost of agricultural labor was CFA50 per hour (Jaeger, 1987). Currency of Burkina Faso is the CFA franc; exchange rate is CFA301 per U.S. dollar (average for 1987).

[a] Use of 23 donkey unit.

[b] Animal manure of work animal can be retained to improve soil quality and increase the area of compound land.

[c] Predominant fertilizer sold in Burkina Faso with NPK nutrient levels of 14:23:15.

[d] There were three different annualized cost estimates for donkey traction; the total field estimate of CFA17,000 used here was adjusted with a 10 percent cost inflation. Estimate was CFA24,000 in Roth et al. (1986). Estimate was CFA34,000 in Jaeger (1987).

In this second scenario, when inorganic fertilizer is available, sorghum with inorganic fertilizer and tied ridges replaces sorghum with only tied ridges. The increase in income from adding inorganic fertilizer to tied ridges is very small compared with the effect of tied ridges alone (table 4-3). However, this is a more stable, long-term solution, because the soil will not be mined. Soil fertility quickly becomes a limiting constraint on these soils when water availability is assured. Therefore, this solution of tied ridges combined with inorganic fertilization is considered to be a sustainable solution, while the tied ridges alone are not.

In absolute terms, incomes per household are still very low, ranging from $558 per household with traditional technologies to $632 per household with the combined technologies (exchange rate of CFA273/US$ in 1990). Note that cash income was substantially less than this, since the household income estimate included the market value of home consumption of crops. Depending on the region, only 10 to 20 percent of the cereals are sold. These farm incomes result in a $0.16 to $0.18 per hour adult-equivalent wage rate. These hourly incomes of CFA43 to CFA49 per hour are approximately the same as the average wage of agricultural labor (CFA50 per hour) in the region.[13] Moreover, the search for temporary labor would be costly for the farmers. Hence, it is not surprising that even with some new technologies on small areas of his land, the average farmer earns less than the agricultural wage rate for all his family's labor.

If the Burkina Faso government were to facilitate the development of a feeding industry for goat or sheep fattening or to encourage some substitution of sorghum and millet in breadmaking and successfully reduce cereal price collapses when weather conditions are good, farmers would earn more money for new cereal technologies. For example, at CFA55 ($0.20) per kilogram for sorghum and millet, improved agronomy (a combination of water retention and moderate inorganic fertilizer) would produce a household income of $733, compared to $558 with traditional technologies at CFA45 per kilogram of sorghum (a 31 percent increase).[14] With this slightly higher sorghum-millet price, the area in sorghum with tied ridges and fertilization increases to 0.93 hectare, according to this model.

In the tied-ridging period (first weeding), the shadow price of labor (marginal value product) was almost eight times the average hourly wage in the region. With this high value for labor, only 1.4 hectares of sorghum with tied ridges and fertilization would be produced on the farm, according to the model. Millet was also available with tied ridges and moderate fertilization on the poor soils, but farmers did not adopt this activity, according to model results.

Animal traction would reduce the labor requirements for tied ridges by 40 percent, from 100 man-hours by complete hand construction to 60 hours if the ridging were done by donkeys and the tying done by hand.[15] However, the introduction of donkey traction, even with the availability of tied ridges and fertilization on all three cereals, leads farmers to adopt more extensive strategies. Donkey traction is used principally to expand the cultivation of millet-cowpeas and peanuts on the bush-fallow.

If an efficient rental market for donkey services were to exist, farmers would use 0.23 donkey unit. In this model, farmers maintain the 0.15 hectare of maize with tied ridges in the compound area and slightly reduce the area of sorghum with tied ridges and fertilization in the higher-quality soils outside the compound. If farmers cannot easily rent donkey services or rent out their own donkey, they are forced to own a donkey and to use all their donkey services on the farm. In this case, bush-fallow cultivation of both millet-cowpeas and peanuts is further expanded with donkey traction (table 4-3). The peak season labor demand is then shifted to the first period for the planting of cereals, cereal combinations, and peanuts. According to the model, farmers shift from sorghum to maize in the high-quality land, since maize can be planted later outside this main planting period. Because of the large amount of seasonal labor required with tied ridges and fertilization, further expansion of these technologies was constrained both on the sorghum land and with millet on the bush-fallow land. However, even when this constraint was released by the use of animal traction, farmers in the model solutions still did not increase the tied ridges.[16] Rather, they extended the crop area farther into the bush-fallow land. This model result is consistent with field observations in the Central Plateau.

Why do farmers still choose the extensive technology when they adopt animal traction, and what factors will encourage them to shift to intensive technologies? These are the central concerns of the next section of this chapter. But first we need a reality check. Has there been some adoption of these intensive technologies of tied ridges and fertilization as predicted by our model? The models with hand traction predict that both tied ridges and fertilization would be adopted on small areas, but further adoption would be constrained by seasonal labor availability. In 1984, after several years of farm trials, Purdue researchers observed the fields of farmer collaborators to see whether these two technologies had been adopted. They then interviewed the farmers.

The diffusion results need to be separated by climatic zone. Bangasse is in the far north, reaching almost into the Sahelian zone. Since soils there are very sandy, their water retention capacity is low and their potential for using tied ridges is limited (see chapter 5 for more discussion of water retention techniques on sandy dune soils). Not surprisingly, the introduction of either tied ridges or inorganic fertilizer was minimal (table 4-4). In the two Sudanian sites of Nedogo and Diapangou, the diffusion results were consistent with model predictions of simultaneous introduction of fertilizer and tied ridges on small areas. On the average, the areas of the farmers' fields utilizing the new technologies were still approximately one-third of model estimates. This could be due to adjustment costs, as farmers were moving toward the model predictions. In the interviews conducted in the Sudanian villages, farmers identified labor constraints as the principal reason for not further extending the tied ridges. As both Poedogo and Dissankuy are near the isohyet division for the higher-rainfall Guinean zone, soil fertility was the principal constraint in most years. A high percentage of these farmers used inorganic fertilizer on a substantial area of these small farms (3 hectares). There was minimal adoption of tied ridges in these two villages, as there is less need for tied ridges in the higher-rainfall areas (see chapter 3).

In summary, the income increases from improved agronomy of the stage 3 type (table 4-1) are as yet still small, but there was farmer adoption despite an unfavorable economic environment of low output prices and high labor requirements to make the tied ridges. Both higher cereal prices and the avail-

Table 4-4. Adoption of Tied Ridges and Fertilizer in Farm Trial Villages of Burkina Faso

| Village | Farm Trial Involvement (years) | Number of Farmers | Farmers Adopting (%) | | Average Area of Technology Adoption (ha)[a] | |
|---|---|---|---|---|---|---|
| | | | Tied Ridges | Fertilizer | Tied Ridges | Fertilizer |
| Bangasse | 3 | 53 | 23 | 0 | .03 | .01 |
| Nedogo | 5 | 69 | 25 | 10 | .32 | .46 |
| Diapangou | 3 | 61 | 25 | 8 | .18 | .34 |
| Poedogo | 2 | 27 | 4 | 33 | .11 | 3.00 |
| Dissankuy | 2 | 60 | 3 | 97[b] | .03 | 3.00 |

Source: Sanders, Nagy, and Ramaswamy (1990, p. 15).
[a] Average of the adopters only.
[b] Figures relate only to land sown to cotton. Small amounts of fertilizer were used on cereals.

ability of an animal traction ridger are expected to hasten the introduction of the tied ridges.

## The Shift from Extensive to Intensive Technologies

The introduction of animal traction into the model released the seasonal labor constraints and enabled an income increase through area expansion. However, the more intensive water retention and fertilization activity in sorghum fields was actually reduced from 0.73 to 0.6 hectare with the availability of animal traction (table 4-3). Yet farmers, especially in the more degraded regions, were observed shifting to the labor-intensive, yield-increasing technologies of stone dikes and organic manure. The model does not yet explain these shifts.

Looking more closely at settlement patterns over time, we must further refine the land variable. In the model, there was a distinction between three types of land:

- high-productivity compound land around the village, which could be expanded if the farmer were to use the manure of more animals
- higher-quality land on the toposequence, usually planted in sorghum
- low-quality or bush-fallow land

We observed, and it has been empirically documented, that farmers often walk long distances to their plots (Chisholm, 1967; Stryker, 1976). These journeys have a cost in travel time. Moreover, in regions of higher population pressure, the total supply of bush-fallow land becomes fixed as the walking distance becomes too long.

When these higher costs resulting from the increasing scarcity of land are reflected in the model, there is a gradual shift to the intensive technologies. At a conservative cost estimate of one hour a day of walking to extend the bush-fallow area cultivated, the area in intensive technologies increases from 0.6 to 0.7 hectare (table 4-5). When the farmer has access to only 3.5 hectares of bush-fallow land, he shifts to using 1.4 hectares in the intensive technology). As the bush-fallow land supply becomes less available, farm incomes from traditional and new technologies are reduced. Nevertheless, in the three cases of land availability modeled, the shift to the more intensive technologies enables increases in income in all cases (table 4-5). Note that animal traction was also needed to put the full 1.4 hectares into intensive technologies.[17]

The farm incomes as a result of adopting either the traditional technologies

Table 4-5. Cropping Patterns, Input Use, and Income with Traditional and Improved Technologies As the Supply of Bush-Fallow Land Becomes Limited

| | Supply of Bush-Fallow Land Perfectly Elastic | | Supply of Busy-Fallow Land Moderately Elastic | | Supply of Bush-Fallow Land Highly Inelastic | |
|---|---|---|---|---|---|---|
| | Traditional Technology[a] | Improved Technology: Extensive Option[b] | Traditional Technology[a] | Improved Technology: Intensive Option[c] | Traditional Technology[a] | Improved Technology: Intensive Option[c] |
| Maize (ha) | 0.15 CL | 0.15 CL,TR,DT | 0.15 CL | 0.15 CL,DT,TR | 0.15 CL | 0.15 CL,TR,DT |
| Sorghum (ha) | — | 0.60 HQ,DT,TR,F | — | 0.70 HQ,DT,TR,F | — | 1.40 HQ,TR,DT,F |
| Sorghum-cowpeas (ha) | 1.40 HQ | 0.80 HQ,HT<br>0.10 BF,HT | 1.40 HQ | 0.70 HQ,HT<br>0.50 BF,HT | 1.40 HQ | — |
| Millet-cowpeas (ha) | 4.00 BF | 3.20 BF,HT<br>1.20 BF,DT | 3.60 BF | 3.20 BF,HT | 3.00 BF | 3.00 BF,HT |
| Peanuts (ha) | 0.27 BF | 0.25 BF,HT<br>0.17 BF,DT | 0.20 BF | 0.42 BF,HT,DT | 0.40 BF | 0.40 BF,HT |
| Total Area (ha) | 5.82 | 6.47 | 5.35 | 5.67 | 4.95 | 4.95 |

| | | | | | | |
|---|---|---|---|---|---|---|
| Urea (kg/farm) | — | 30.00 | — | 38.00 | — | 70.00 |
| Compound fertilizer (kg/farm) | — | 60.00 | — | 73.00 | — | 141.00 |
| Net farm income [d] $/year | 558.00 | 674.00 | 495.00 | 679.00 | 476.00 | 590.00 |
| Implicit wage [e] $/adult hour | 0.15 | 0.17 | 0.13 | 0.18 | 0.13 | 0.16 |
| (CFA/adult hour) | 41.00 | 46.00 | 35.00 | 50.00 | 35.00 | 44.00 |

*Source:* Ramaswamy and Sanders (1992, pp. 367, 370).

*Note:* BF—bush-fallow land; CL—compound land; DT—donkey traction; HQ—high-quality land; HT—hand traction; F—fertilizer activity. The moderately inelastic supply of bush-fallow land was modeled with a "time cost" of travel to outlying fields of one hour per day. In the highly inelastic case, the farmer had access to only 3.5 ha of bush-fallow. Exchange rate is CFA273/US$ (IMF, *International Financial Statistics*, 1990).

[a] Hand traction; no inorganic fertilizer or tied ridges.

[b] Use of animal traction.

[c] Tied-ridging on sorghum and maize, fertilization on sorghum, utilization of animal traction. This inorganic fertilizer is known as cotton fertilizer in Burkina Faso and has the composition of 14.:23:15 of NPK. The standard level utilized with the tied ridges on the sorghum land was 100 kilograms per hectare of this cotton fertilizer and 50 kilograms per hectare of urea.

[d] Includes market value of home consumption of cereals.

[e] To estimate the hourly wage for males, the net farm income is divided by the number of adult male equivalents in the household, the number of working days in the season, and the average daily hours worked on the farm. Females are 0.75 equivalents, and children ten to fourteen are 0.5 male equivalents. The average wage rate for this region is CFA50 per hour (Jaeger, 1987). For a more detailed description of the model, refer to Roth et al. (1986).

Figure 4-2. Farm Income with Traditional and New Technologies by Availability of Bush-Fallow Land (U.S. dollars, 1990 base)

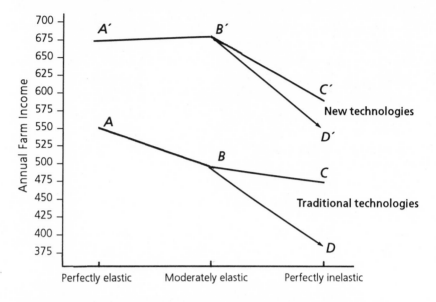

*Source:* Adapted from Ramaswamy and Sanders (1992, p. 368).
*Note:* D′ and D indicate conditions of severe land degradation and population pressure. Farm income includes the value of home consumption. The moderately inelastic land supply was modeled by introducing a time cost of travel. The perfectly inelastic land supply was modeled by fixing the supply of bush-fallow land at 3.5 hectares per farm. The exchange rate in 1990 was CFA273/US$ (IMF, *International Financial Statistics,* 1990).

or the intensive combination under different land availability scenarios are shown in figure 4-2. As land availability declines, the household increasingly adopts new technologies (compare points A and A′, B and B′, and C and C′; see also table 4-5). On the Central Plateau and in other heavily populated regions of the Sahel, such as the peanut zone of Senegal, the land is already severely degraded. This is represented for the case with the least available land with further yield declines ranging from a third to a half over the nondegraded case (point D in Fig. 4-2). Nevertheless, the more intensive technologies are still able to increase farm income by 36 percent to $530 a year (shift from point D to point D′). But even with these new technologies, farm incomes are absolutely higher when technology is introduced before land degradation begins.

To evaluate the impact of an improved economic environment on intensification, a range of output prices was considered. With improved transportation and communication, farmers would receive increased output prices through reduced marketing margins and reduced input costs. This better linkage to the market is expected to encourage intensification of agricultural production. For farmers in the intermediate land supply case with only 0.7 hectare of higher-quality land being intensively cultivated with sorghum, cereal prices were increased 22 percent and 44 percent (corresponding, respectively, to increases in the price of sorghum-millet from $0.16 to $0.20 and then to $0.24 per kilogram). With increasing profitability, farmers shift to more intensive technologies, extending the area in tied ridges and increasing fertilization, according to the model results (fig. 4-3). The creation of a profitable economic environment for farmers is one area in which governmental policy intervention would have a direct impact. For example, if the government were to encourage the development of a feed industry for goat and sheep fattening during years of good rainfall and consequent cereal price collapses, farmers' prices for these years would increase. Thus, farmers' expected incomes would increase.

According to the model, both the decreased availability of the lower-quality land and the improved economic environment result in the introduction of yield-increasing technologies. The income gains are small in absolute terms. On an adult-male equivalent basis, the hourly wage rate increases from $0.12 to $0.17 (see note e, in table 4-5, for details on calculation of these hourly wage rates). With the new technologies, these hourly incomes are approximately equal to the average wage of agricultural labor in this region of $0.17/hour. It is not surprising that farmers would be earning the average wage or below, because hired labor would not be employed full time and use of hired labor would incur search costs to find employment. Nevertheless, it is still possible to raise incomes moderately by introducing intensive technologies.

Since the new, intensive technologies (tied ridging, fertilization, and animal traction) in the model are found to be used only on the two small areas of higher-quality land (the compound land and the higher-quality land farther up on the toposequence), the effect on income of their introduction is still small. However, once farmers begin using these more complex management systems, they will be more open to further improvements, especially if the overall economic environment for increased crop production is improved. The addition of a new cultivar into this moderately improved environment is expected to further increase the profitability of these practices, as well as to accelerate the breeding and diffusion processes by making the breeding re-

Figure 4-3. Effects of Improved Economic Environment on Use of Intensive Technologies (model results)

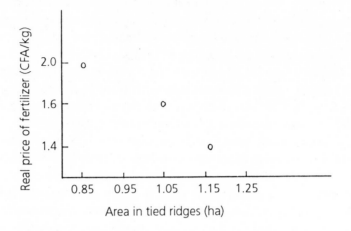

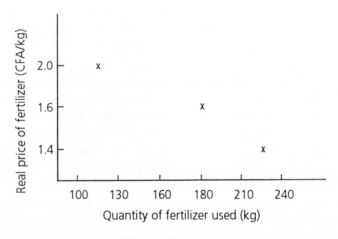

*Source:* Ramaswamy and Sanders (1992, p. 371).
*Note:* The relevant real fertilizer price is deflated with the cereals price. The weighted price of fertilizer is constant, with urea at $0.26/kg and compound fertilizer at $0.36/kg (1988 prices). The average price of sorghum-millet (price *S-M*) was $0.16/kg and increased to $0.20/kg and $0.24/kg, respectively. The prices of other crops were increased proportionally. Tied ridges and fertilizers were used as complementary inputs on the higher-quality sorghum land. On the compound area (or maize land) only tied ridges were used. Animal traction was used to make the ridges. The exchange rate in 1990 was CFA273/US$ (IMF, *International Financial Statistics,* 1990).

quirements less difficult. The breeders now need to orient some of their activities to producing new cultivars for a moderately improved agronomic environment.[18] Moreover, there is a dynamic aspect to increasing incomes as farmers then begin to demand more support from research agencies and input suppliers and both institutions get more confidence in their abilities to facilitate technological change.

The next logical question is: Why has there not been more adoption of these combined agronomic technologies on farmers' fields? First, in regions where farmers have observed these technologies for water retention and augmentation of soil fertility on other farmers' fields, there has been some adoption of the combined technologies (see Sanders, Nagy, and Ramaswamy, 1990, p. 15). Secondly, farmers and researchers have trouble evaluating technologies involving several new inputs (Byerlee and Hesse de Polanco, 1986). The desired optimal combination included tied ridges, inorganic fertilizer, animal traction, and a new animal traction implement. All, except the new implement, have been available in Burkina Faso for more than two decades, but extension agents and applied researchers have placed little emphasis on their complementarity.[19]

To what extent are farmers in the Sudanian zone already adopting labor-intensive, yield-increasing technologies? Earlier in this chapter, we discussed the rapid introduction of the stone (and dirt) dikes combined with organic fertilizer and the zaï in the more degraded regions of the Sudanian (and Sahelo-Sudanian) zones. Moreover, the ICRISAT village studies of the 1980s in Burkina Faso have been recording shifts over time to more-intensive techniques (Vierich and Stoop, 1990). The increased use of inorganic fertilizer and the growth of a cash market for the Fulani herd manure have both been observed in different Central Plateau villages. Increased out-of-crop-season production of fruits and vegetables for sale on the lowlands with labor-intensive watering methods is yet another shift to more-intensive production occurring in this region (Vierich and Stoop, 1990).

Both model results and the field observations indicate this shift to more-intensive (yield-increasing) technologies. The process has already begun in the Sudanian zone and in the southern Sahelo-Sudanian zone, despite low and irregular rainfall and soil fertility problems. Over time the pressure to introduce more-intensive or yield-increasing technologies will increase unless rapid nonfarm employment substantially raises the opportunity costs of labor. Continued strengthening and focusing of the agricultural research establishment will facilitate this production of intensive technology adaptation and introduction.

## Conclusion

As soil resources decline from soil depletion and erosion, farmers with low opportunity costs select more labor-intensive technologies to increase yields. It is not surprising that during the 1980s, dikes, the zaï, and organic fertilization were rapidly introduced on the degraded soils of Yatenga. These technologies also represent a capital investment of the state; the public sector has frequently helped with the transportation of stones for the dikes, as well as with construction of the earth dikes. The next stage in technology introduction (stage 2) could be the diffusion of this diking and zaï technology to the better soils, where the potential returns are higher (see note 7). Since farmers have higher opportunity costs in agriculture on these soils than on those in Yatenga, adoption has been slower. Constructing the zaï with an animal traction implement would be the next logical step for this region. The zaï are almost identical to tied ridges, except that they are dug manually outside the crop season, and the yield effects are much smaller. Moving to tied ridges and fertilization is the next logical step, but it will probably also require the use of the animal traction implement, the ridger. There has been substantial experimentation with two animal traction implements for tied ridges in Burkina and Mali. Further applied work in this area appears to offer a high return to the public and private sectors, especially for these less degraded regions.

Increasingly, population pressure and land degradation are reducing land availability, even of the lower-quality bush-fallow land. In the field observations and with the model runs, there are shifts to intensive technologies as land supply becomes more inelastic. Yield increases on these heavier clay soils, with their propensity for crusting and therefore very high runoff levels, depend on simultaneously resolving the constraints imposed by water availability and soil fertility. From technologies tested in Burkina Faso and those practiced in other countries, there are many alternatives to simultaneously address these two constraints. We consider several in this chapter. As farm testing and farmer observation have consistently shown the high profitability of these combined technologies to resolve problems of soil fertility and water availability, we are optimistic about their potential.

Income gains can be substantially increased with measures to avoid price collapses in years of favorable climate. With some demand expansion for sorghum, the returns to the technology combination of tied ridges with fertilization on maize and sorghum are sufficiently high to interest farmers in more rapidly adopting the new technology, according to model results. The fattening of sheep for sale at Tabaski (an Islamic holiday) is an example of activities that could put floor prices under grains; this fattening is an ongoing activity in southern Mali. The increase in potential profitability from a small increase in the sorghum price indicates the importance of simultaneously promoting technology introduction and agricultural policy measures.

To hasten the diffusion of intensive technologies, agriculture needs to be profitable. The public sector can facilitate this process with infrastructure investment, public policy to moderate price collapses in good rainfall years, the provision of adequate foreign exchange for inorganic fertilizer imports, and sufficient applied and maintenance agricultural research. Public sector support for water retention investments also would reduce the risks of inorganic fertilization.

One developmental dilemma has been the failure of Sahelian farmers to use yield-increasing technologies despite declining crop yields over time. The requirement of the simultaneous introduction of three or four new components of the intensive technology makes the new system difficult to diffuse, because farmers generally introduce one input at a time (Byerlee and Hesse de Polanco, 1986). Although all three of the technology components have been known and available in the semiarid Sahelian region for at least two decades, these intensive technologies have failed to be introduced on a wide scale. This could be due to the difficulty of introducing these technologies simultaneously and to the lack of an economic environment profitable enough to induce farmers to adopt new technologies (Repetto, 1989; Lal, 1991). The model indicates the natural evolution of these farming systems toward more intensive technologies on the higher-quality soils. According to model results, as expansion into low-quality lands becomes more difficult and expensive, farmers shift to more-intensive technologies on the better-quality soils.

Type of soil, labor availability, and economic environment are factors that will influence the choice of technologies for water retention and the improvement of soil fertility. We expect that these same types of intensive technology will be the critical factors for increasing farmers' incomes over a wide range of semiarid agricultural zones. As the intensive technologies that we evaluated substantially increase the demand for seasonal labor, the use of animal traction will be critical in overcoming constraints of seasonal labor.

The programming results for potential new technologies support the hypothesis that water availability and soil fertility are two principal constraints that need to be addressed simultaneously in the Sudanian zone of semiarid Sub-Saharan Africa. If plant breeders can develop new materials for a moderately improved agronomic environment, they are expected to be more successful. This is a sufficient agenda for breeders without also asking them to develop stress resistances for drought and various types of low soil fertility. If plant breeders attempt to develop all types of stress resistances for many microenvironments, continuing pressure will be put on more basic agricultural scientists, such as physiologists, for a better understanding of stress. However, only small farm-level yield increases will be attained even if new cultivars with some stress tolerances are introduced.[20] If adequate soil nutrients and water are not available, new cultivars can be developed to more efficiently mine the resources available. However, unless the nutrients are replaced, this still will not be a sustainable strategy.

The fact that technological change can be used to respond to decreasing land supply does not justify the continuing failure of governments and donors to act effectively on the staggering population growth rates in the Sahelian countries. The potential of agricultural technology is substantially reduced by the direct and indirect effects of population growth. Much of the literature about the agricultural prospects of the Sahel is not optimistic about the potential of agricultural technologies to raise farmers' incomes and increase the sustainability of the farming systems in semiarid regions. Our model and the field results, however, show grounds for cautious optimism. Nevertheless, the potential success from increased pressure on the available resources should not be a rationale to avoid introducing population control measures. Without sharply reducing birth rates, any improvements in living standards with technological change will be difficult and temporary.

## Appendix: The Linear Programming Model

A representative farm model was constructed for the Central Plateau. The decision-making unit maximizes a linear profit equation subject to a consumption constraint for maize and constraints on land, labor, donkeys, and capital. (For further details, see Roth et al., 1986, and Sanders, Nagy, and Ramaswamy, 1990.) The farm produces five commodities: sorghum, maize, millet, cowpeas, and peanuts.[21] The farm household maximizes the gross value of production (sales plus value of home consumption) less expenditures for inputs. There are two power technologies, hand traction and animal traction.

For hand tillage technologies, land and labor are the only inputs. Their costs are derived implicitly from land and labor constraints incorporated in the model. When animal power or fertilizers are introduced, purchased input costs are incurred. For each type of traction system, twenty-seven different activities are possible on the farm. The derived demand and supply of land resources is defined by

$$\Sigma X_{ij}^M + \Sigma X_{ij}^A \leq T_i,$$

where

$$j = 1 \ldots 27.$$

Demand for land type "1" is derived from cultivation enterprises $X_{ij}^M$ and $X_{ij}^A$. Supply of land, $T_i$, represents endowments of the particular land type owned or controlled by the household. Three land types are included: (1) high-quality land next to the farm household (also called compound land), on which maize is customarily planted (0.15 hectare); (2) intrinsically more fertile land lying farther down the toposequence, on which sorghum or sorghum-cowpeas are traditionally planted (1.4 hectares); and (3) sandy, infertile, poor-quality bush fields, on which primarily millet and peanuts are planted (Vierich and Stoop, 1990; Stoop, 1989). Initially, the farm household has fixed levels of the first two land types, but bushland availability is unlimited. This assumption about bush-fallow land is then modified to reflect increased population pressure.

The representative farm household here has eleven residents, including six active workers and five children. Among the active workers are two adult males and four adult females (Roth et al., 1986). The model does not allow for hiring labor. In normal and good rainfall years, farmers on the Central Plateau have difficulty finding seasonal labor, because most farmers want to cultivate their own plots (Binswanger and McIntire, 1987; Sanders, Nagy, and Ramaswamy, 1990).

There are ten rows denoting the sequential nature of agricultural operations from land preparation to harvesting. The technical coefficients, $A_{ij}$, represent the number of hours required per hectare in period $i$ for crop enterprise $X_j$. For each period $i$, the derived demand and supply of labor can be represented by the equation

$$\Sigma A_{ij}^M X_j^M + \Sigma A_{ij}^{MA} X_j^A \leq MHR_i * MA + FHR_i * FA.$$

Each term on the left-hand side of the inequality represents the demand for human labor in conjunction with the different technology regimes. The supply of labor is derived from the number of male adults *(MA)* and female adults *(FA)* "active" in the household. Male adults work $MHR_i$ in period $i$ and female adults $FHR_i$. The dual prices associated with the right-hand side labor resources, $MHR_i * MA + MA = FHR_i * FA$, are the marginal values of an additional hour of labor in period $i$. The demand and supply of animal traction are treated in a similar manner.

# 5

## The Same Principle, a More Difficult Environment: The Sahelo-Sudanian Region of Niger

**M**OVING NORTH from the Sudanian zone toward the Sahara Desert into the Sahelo-Sudanian zone, the level of rainfall decreases and its variability increases, while the soils have a higher proportion of sand and are even lower in fertility. Thus, developing new technologies for this region is even more difficult than in the agroecological zones discussed in the two previous chapters. Nevertheless, the principle of identifying technologies to simultaneously resolve the constraints of inadequate water availability and low soil fertility, applied to the Sudanian zone in chapter 4, is expected to be relevant here.

The farm population of Niger is concentrated in the Sahelo-Sudanian zone. Farther north in the Sahelian zone, rainfall is too infrequent and erratic above the 350 millimeter probability isohyet for crops, and most of the area of Niger (76 percent) is above this line (fig. 5-1) (Painter, 1987, p. 145). Niger has a very small Sudanian zone and no Sudanian-Guinean zone; hence, Niger is dependent for crop production on the Sahelo-Sudanian zone. Since the agricultural potential of the Sahelo-Sudanian zone is limited by both fragile soils and inadequate rainfall conditions, increasing output and attaining self-sufficiency will be more difficult in Niger than in the countries with larger areas having rainfall above 600 millimeters. Nevertheless, there have been some successes, and there is potential for further agricultural development in the Sahelo-Sudanian zone.

### Resource Endowments in the Sahelo-Sudanian Zone

The principal pattern of Nigerien agricultural development has been area expansion. From 1961 to 1982 the area in the principal cereal, millet, increased from 1.6 million to 3 million hectares, while yields fell from 550 kilograms per hectare to the 350–425 range as cultivation was pushed onto more marginal soils and soils deteriorated. Soils deteriorate from water and wind erosion and from the decline of organic matter when soils are opened up and exposed to the high temperatures (Painter, 1987, pp. 146–48). In many areas, the pressure of population densities and increasing profitability of agriculture are pushing for a shift from extensive to intensive production practices.

The two research sites in the Niamey region, Libore and Kouka (fig. 5-1), are characteristic of land shortage and land surplus systems. Millet-cowpea intercrop predominates on rain-fed fields in both systems. Libore lies farther south in the region and has the higher average rainfall of 570 millimeters. In addition to the predominant rain-fed activities, the Libore production system

Figure 5-1. Climatic Zones of Niger

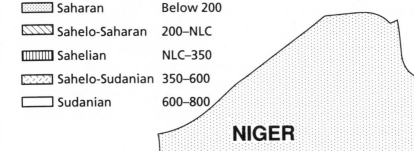

*Source:* Adapted from Gorse and Steeds (1987).
*Note:* NLC is the northern limit of cultivation. Numbers given refer to isohyets in millimeters of rainfall at 90 percent probability levels.

includes some irrigated acreage. Farmers in this dual system intercrop millet and cowpeas during the rainy season and raise irrigated rice during both the rainy and dry seasons. Land appropriate for irrigated agriculture exists only on the flood plain and terraces of the Niger River.[1] Population pressure is high because there is significant demand for the heavier, more productive soils suitable for irrigation. With government control, small-size parcels have been rationed to a large number of farm households. Most households along the Niger River farm irrigated parcels of 0.4 hectare. Intensification of irrigated activities has taken place, but not of rain-fed activities. Since farm households in this area have only a small area under supplemental irrigation, increasing rain-fed cereal production is an important goal for these farmers. Farmers claim that no land is available to extend either the irrigated or the dryland crop area.

Average family size at Libore is 6.8 equivalent male adults.[2] Average rain-fed farm size is only 3.9 hectares. The land-to-labor ratio is thus low relative to other regions of Niger and indicates the relatively high population pressure found along the Niger River.[3] Current production practices on rain-fed fields along the river are predominantly manual, and labor is mainly provided by household members.[4] Hired labor usage is substantial, however, in irrigated activities. Under current low-cash-input rain-fed practices, with increasing population density and poor rainfall in recent years, the quality of rain-fed land has been declining, as existing holdings have been fallowed less and more marginal land brought into production (Painter, 1986 and 1987; Raynaut, 1976). As yields decline and the land supply becomes more limited, the potential returns to more-intensive production practices increases.

At the site away from the Niger River at Kouka, where cereal crop production is exclusively rain-fed, average rainfall is only 430 millimeters. Cultivated area varies from 9 to 14 hectares, depending on the amount of seasonal rainfall.[5] There is a greater distance to the urban market of Niamey and less access to main highways; hence, crop product prices are lower than at Libore. Farm households have a limited amount of more fertile cropland near the village, only 3.5 hectares on average; however, substantial bushland is also available. Household sizes are also larger, with 8.6 members (adult male equivalents) on average compared with 6.8 members at Libore.

There is little hired labor available at Kouka; at times of peak demand for seasonal labor, farmers are busy on their own fields. Farmers plant the bush fields only after the fields closer to the village have been planted. Because bush fields are often far from the village, requiring farmers to stay up to several days at a time to carry out crop operations, it is difficult to give these fields proper attention. Due to the greater availability of land in Kouka, livestock production is more widespread than at Libore, and numbers kept by each household are larger. The average household owns eight goats and three sheep. For the marketing of livestock, Kouka is within the market sphere of the Niamey area, and the only differences in prices between Kouka and Libore are due to transport costs.

## Evolution of Irrigated Rice Production

The changes over time in irrigated farming activities along the Niger River have been dramatic. Where water and land resources have permitted, complete control irrigation has been developed.[6] This development has had an important impact on the incomes of those farmers who have been able to benefit from the intensification of rice production.

Although the irrigated parcels along the Niger River are very small (0.4 hectare on average), the model results suggest that this activity makes up over one-fourth (27 percent) of the rainy season income of these farmers (US$220). The income variability associated with irrigated rice production is very low (CV = 8 percent) and greatly decreases overall farm income variability. Rice production in government-controlled irrigation perimeters is thus an income-insurance policy provided by the government. Since irrigated rice is produced a second time during the dry season, it also helps ensure income for subsistence consumption during the hungry season, or soudure. Irrigated rice production along the Niger River includes high chemical input levels and the double-cropping of high-yielding varieties of rice. Farmers almost always choose to grow rice and use recommended exotic varieties such as IR 15, IR 21 and STB 26.[7] Land preparation is done with animal traction, and substantial amounts of inorganic fertilizer are utilized (Shapiro, 1990). Thus, irrigated rice production is a good example of combining water and high levels of other inputs, including fertilizers and new cultivars.

## Recent Rainfall Levels and Early Cultivars

In the Sahelo-Sudanian zone rainfall is low, the season is short, and the distribution of rainfall during the season is irregular.[8] For example, at Libore the average rain-fed-crop season is ninety-seven days. Convective storms occur often, and over 100 millimeters of rain can fall within a few hours. Intraseasonal drought is common. Furthermore, average rainfall for the last twenty years has been 66 millimeters lower than the long-run average for the last forty-four years. Throughout the West African semiarid tropics (WASAT), rainfall during the seventies and eighties has been one standard deviation below the long-term average (Gorse and Steeds, 1987). Whether this is a permanent or cyclical phenomenon is being debated (Glantz, 1987, p. 46 and references).

Farmers in both the Sudanian and the Sahelo-Sudanian regions of the WASAT have been adapting to the lower rainfall by selecting a higher percentage of shorter-cycle cultivars in the mix that they plant (Matlon, 1987; Vierich and Stoop, 1990). Farmers in Niger and elsewhere have been asking for shorter-cycle varieties of millet and cowpeas, and breeders have responded to this demand by selecting earlier-maturing material (Matlon, 1987; Reddy and Samba, 1989; Shapiro, 1990). Three experiment station millet varieties, CIVT, HKP, and P3 Kolo, are being adopted in areas near the origins of the parent materials.[9] The improved varieties are earlier than local material but resemble them in terms of other characteristics (taste, color, good seedling establishment, and resistance to pests and diseases) (Shapiro, 1990; Lowenberg-DeBoer, Zarafi, and Abdoulaye, 1992).

Adoption of early varieties with higher cowpea-planting densities increases expected rainfed-crop income 30 percent, to US$578 from US$446 under traditional agronomic practices, according to model results (table 5-1; see the

Table 5-1. Effect of Various Policy Instruments and Technology Strategies on Adoption of Fertilizer in Libore, Niamey Region, Niger

| Policy or Program | Fertilizer Use (ha) | Millet-Cowpea Income (US$) | Total Seasonal Income (US$) | Change in Crop Income (%) | Change in Total Income (%) | CV of Total Income (%) |
|---|---|---|---|---|---|---|
| Current practices | — | 446 | 812 | — | — | 40 |
| Improved short-season cultivars | | 578 | 921 | +30 | +13 | 39 |
| Input subsidy (10%) | 1.2 | 602 | 922 | +35 | +14 | 41 |
| Credit program (CFA10,000 at 0% interest) | 0.0 | 576 | 942 | +29 | +16 | 39 |
| Phosphorus only | 2.1 | 628 | 948 | +41 | +17 | 44 |
| Long-cycle millet variety | 1.5 | 624 | 944 | +40 | +16 | 42 |

*Source:* Shapiro et al. (1993, pp. 162, 166); Shapiro (1990, p. 98).
*Note:* Exchange rate is CFA298/US$.

appendix to this chapter for details on the model). Also, the shorter-cycle cultivars provide some drought escape through earliness, making rain-fed crop production more stable in lower rainfall years. Hence, the introduction of the improved cultivars lowers the variability of cash income from rain-fed crop production by 1 percent.[10] Farmers can adjust their cultivar strategies, depending on the early rains. In higher-rainfall years, the improved early cultivars at higher densities are not completely adopted, with local varieties still used on one-third of the area, according to the model results. Field evidence confirms that the improved shorter-cycle cultivars are indeed used more in lower-rainfall years (Shapiro, 1990; Lowenberg-DeBoer, Zarafi, and Abdoulaye, 1992).[11]

Diffusion of the improved cultivars in the Niamey region has been without fertilizer in the model results and generally on farmers' fields. The use of fertilizer for rain-fed crop production has been negligible at Libore, even though fertilizer is readily available from the cooperatives that service the irrigation perimeters, as well as from private merchants. New technologies that include the use of both nitrogen and phosphorus fertilizer have been shown to be promising when economically evaluated with partial budgeting and whole farm modeling (Adesina, 1988; Adesina and Sanders, 1991; Krause, Deuson, et al., 1990). Yet adoption of fertilizer has not taken place in the Niamey region.[12]

The use of improved shorter-cycle cultivars without fertilizer increases profits and reduces downside risks, stabilizing yields. However, without a means of maintaining the fertility of the soil, the use of improved cultivars alone will lead to further mining of the soil nutrients. Thus, the improved cropping system will not be sustainable unless the improved cultivars are accompanied by adoption of fertilizer.

## Soil and Water Constraints

There are two main soil types in the Niamey region: (1) sandy clay loam soils on the flood-plain of the Niger River, where rice is grown when there is irrigation,[13] and (2) sandy dune soils farther up on the toposequence, where most rain-fed agriculture is undertaken.[14] Unlike much of the Sudanian region where the clay content of the soils is higher, on the sandy dune soils of the Sahelo-Sudanian zone crusting is less of a problem; therefore, water infiltration is generally not a constraint. However, due to the lower and more variable rainfall and the sandy, porous soils, maintaining water in the soil for plants is still a major problem. These soils are also highly weathered and low in organic matter and natural fertility. Thus, nutrients and water reserves available to plants in these soils are low.

Accelerating soil degradation may be the greatest threat to sustained rain-fed crop production in the sandy dune soils commonly found in the Sahelo-Sudanian zone of Niger (Scott-Wendt, Chase, and Hossner, 1989). There is a high propensity for topsoil to be washed away by the frequent convective storms (Lal, 1984; IITA, 1987). Wind erosion can also deplete organic matter and plant nutrients. Sandblasting from the high winds that precede the early-season rains can damage seedlings and young plants. The above factors and the absence of fertilization lead to low yields on these sandy soils (Lal, 1984; Scott-Wendt, Chase, and Hossner, 1989).

How to alleviate the soil fertility constraint in this region has been much debated by agricultural scientists. The debate consists of several aspects:

- whether organic or inorganic fertilizers should be given priority
- whether imported or domestic rock phosphate is the appropriate source of phosphorus fertilizer
- what strategy will encourage the introduction of both nitrogen and phosphorus fertilizers

Some scientists and policymakers maintain that organic fertilizers, such as manure and crop residues, and cereal-legume rotations are the keys to improving soil fertility in this region. Imported inorganic fertilizer can be risky for the farm household, because the necessity for cash outlays can jeopardize the ability of the household to buy cereal to feed itself if the rains are not adequate and crops fail. Also, input distribution systems often do not function efficiently, and inorganic fertilizer can be available at the wrong times, lessening effectiveness. Meanwhile, sources of organic fertilizer, such as manure, are severely limited in most of semiarid West Africa. For most farmers, sufficient manure is available only for small areas surrounding family compounds (Sanders, 1989; see Williams, Powell, and Fernandez-Rivera, 1993, chap. 12, for a full discussion of this issue). Moreover, at the present time, most of the crop residue is removed for uses with higher economic value, such as feed, fuel, and building materials. Cereal-legume crop rotations or intercropping are already practiced, but raising yields still requires phosphorus and probably micronutrients (Bationo et al., 1993).

At the present time, inorganic fertilizers are the only technically efficient and economically profitable way to overcome the soil fertility constraint in the Sudanian and Sahelo-Sudanian zones for most regions and farmers. Until substantial on-farm and on-station experimentation with alternatives is more successful, the other measures of improving soil fertility with organic fertilizers and other techniques in these two agroecological zones must be considered as future complements to, rather than as actual substitutes for, inorganic fertilizers (Sanders, 1989; Nagy et al., 1988).

Potential problems with the use of inorganic fertilizer include soil acidification and aluminum toxicity due to low levels of organic matter with some types of fertilizers (Bationo et al., 1993). However, ICRISAT (International Crops Research Institute for the Semi-Arid Tropics) results consistently show that combining moderate levels of NPK fertilizer (forty-five, twenty, and twenty-five kilograms per hectare, respectively, of pure nutrients) leads to higher millet yields. With higher production, more crop residue can be left on the soil, raising the organic matter content (ICRISAT, 1985, 1986, 1987). The potential problems of acidification and aluminum toxicity associated with some inorganic fertilizers when combined with insufficient organic matter can thus be avoided.

With farm-level budgetary and government-level foreign exchange constraints discouraging the utilization of imported fertilizer, some Sahelian countries have been developing their own sources of phosphate. Recent research in Niger indicates, however, that high-quality rock phosphate from Tahoua, even when partially acidulated, can be competitive with imported super-simple phosphate only if supplied to farmers at approximately 25 percent of the price of imported super-simple phosphate. This implies that at present efficiency levels, rock phosphate is unlikely to become competitive with the imported inorganic sources, even after the devaluation of local currency by 50 percent in 1994 (Jomini, 1990; also see Mokwunye and Hammond, 1992, pp. 124, 125).

Improving soil fertility with inorganic fertilizer is critical to increasing agricultural output on Niger's sandy dune soils (ICRISAT, 1986; Bationo, 1988; Reddy, 1987). On these soils, inorganic fertilizer has both nutrient and water efficiency effects (Fussell and Serifini, 1985; ICRISAT, 1985, p. 42; ICRISAT, 1986, p. 41; ICRISAT, 1987, p. 72; Reddy, 1987). Fertilizer results in increased leaf area and root development and enables higher plant densities. With increased roots, higher plant density, and more organic material on the soil, plants can use more of the available soil moisture.[15] Moderate fertilizer use thus can simultaneously address the water and soil constraints in this low-rainfall region. The use of fertilizer would be combined with the higher plant densities and improved shorter-cycle varieties.

There is some disagreement about the best strategy for introducing inorganic phosphorus and nitrogen fertilizers. Although these soils are deficient in both phosphorus and nitrogen, some scientists recommend phosphorus use without nitrogen as an intermediate strategy (Reddy and Samba, 1989; Jomini, 1990).[16] In these sandy dune soils, nitrogen is so soluble that it can be rapidly leached out in the first rains and then not available in later stages of plant development. Increased levels of organic fertilizer or less soluble sources of nitrogen would be required for better nitrogen retention. Because phosphorus is so deficient in these sandy soils or unavailable due to insolubility, a large yield response is often obtained from the application of phosphorus fertilizer alone.[17] ICRISAT/IFDC (International Fertilizer Development Center) trials have shown that, although there may not be a response in poor rainfall years, there can be a significant economic carryover effect from the use of phosphorus fertilizer. Even without additional phosphorus application the following year, there can be a profitable response with moderate rainfall, because high grain prices usually occur following years of poor rainfall (ICRISAT, 1986, p. 67).

Advocates of using phosphorus fertilizer alone also point out that this strategy eliminates the cost and production risks associated with nitrogen fertilizer use. Nitrogen fertilizer will burn plants if there is insufficient soil moisture and can compound losses in poor rainfall years. Nitrogen deficiencies, however, soon limit plant growth when the plant increases its phosphorus use. Moreover, farmers can reduce the production risk associated with nitrogen fertilizer use by making adaptive decisions. If nitrogen is applied later in the season, such as after the first weeding, then the application decision can be made contingent on the amount of early-season rainfall.

The specific crop technology option recommended for the Niamey region has included both moderate phosphorus and nitrogen fertilizer use, improved shorter-cycle cultivars of millet and cowpeas, and higher cowpea planting density and better geometry. This last option simultaneously addresses the soil fertility and water constraints.[18]

## Interventions to Encourage Fertilizer Use at Libore

In the model results and on farmers' fields, the new cultivar and combined nitrogen and phosphorus fertilizer activity are not adopted, even in the high-rainfall years, when the response to fertilizer would be the highest. Rather, farmers use available cash to increase their small-animal stocks.[19] Moreover, making more credit available results in more livestock being purchased. Capital availability was not the critical constraint limiting the adoption of fertilizer (table 5-1).

After the successful introduction of shorter-season cultivars, the next step could be phosphorus fertilizer only, without nitrogen, in combination with the shorter-cycle cultivars and improved agronomy (Jomini, 1990).[20] Model results show that phosphorus fertilizer would be applied to 2.1 hectares before planting and that phosphorus alone raises total rain-fed crop income during the season 41 percent over current practices and 9 percent over the adoption of improved cultivars alone (table 5-1).[21] Thus, by first adopting moderate levels of phosphorus fertilizer, the incomes of these farmers would be increased over those achievable through the use of improved shorter-cycle millet and cowpea cultivars alone, and the increased nutrient requirements for more-intensified production would at least be partially met.

Although the adoption of inorganic phosphorus fertilizer alone on rain-fed fields has not taken place at the study sites, it has been ongoing among farmers in the Dosso region since the mid-1980s. Furthermore, although the Dosso farmers located in the same agroecological zone (Sahelo-Sudanian) began by adopting phosphorus only, some have since begun to use nitrogen fertilizer. For example, phosphorus fertilizer was first field-tested by IFDC in one village, Gobery, but the villagers have since adopted nitrogen (urea) and NPK as well (Mokwunye and Hammond, 1992). In interviews in 1987, ICRISAT found that over 98 percent of the farms were utilizing both nitrogen and phosphorus fertilizer. Adoption of new shorter-cycle millet varieties is also taking place.[22]

Adoption of phosphorus alone thus appears to be a viable alternative to the combined use of phosphorus and nitrogen. It could be part of a stepwise strategy while awaiting technological advances that would increase the profitability of simultaneous phosphorus and nitrogen fertilizer use. Meanwhile, the adoption of both phosphorus and nitrogen fertilizers at sites in the Dosso and Maradi regions suggests the possibility that policy interventions involving more extension efforts or lower initial fertilizer prices could increase adoption of the combined fertilizer in Niger.[23]

One relevant policy intervention that could encourage fertilizer use on rain-fed fields is an input subsidy on fertilizer. Since the border with Nigeria reopened in 1988, fertilizer has been brought into Niger and is in use in areas contiguous to the border, such as some of the adoption sites in the Maradi region. The market price of the fertilizer available in these border areas is lower than at the research sites in the Niamey region.[24] Would a moderate fertilizer subsidy result in increased farm-level adoption? This possibility was tested by placing a 10 percent subsidy on the existing price for simple superphosphate (SSP) fertilizer in the farm models for the two study sites.[25] This subsidy results in fertilizer adoption on 1.2 hectares of rain-fed fields at Libore and further rain-fed crop income increases of 5 percent from income levels of the introduction of the improved varieties alone (see table 5-1).[26]

Shortcomings of a fertilizer subsidy should be noted. First, in the late eighties and early nineties, the World Bank has been encouraging Sahelian governments to remove subsidies on fertilizer to avoid biased technological change and to decrease the burden on national treasuries. Another disadvantage is that farmers would use at least some of the subsidized fertilizer on their irrigated rice, which is more profitable and lower in risk. Nevertheless, these results show the potential for fertilizer adoption at Libore. Subsidizing nitrogen and phosphorus fertilizer use would be one way to get its use started while awaiting technological advances that would increase its profitability.

Since cereals require nitrogen and there is little nitrogen or organic matter in these sandy dune soils, farmers need to understand that this is an intermediate technology. Without nitrogen fertilizer, yields will decline after a few years. In higher-rainfall years, use of complete fertilizer, including nitrogen, is most effective. When additional phosphorus is provided to the cereal, requirements for other nutrients, including nitrogen, will be increased. This can best be met with inorganic nitrogen fertilizer.[27]

## Further Investment in Breeding Long-Cycle Cultivars

The principal advantage of short-season cultivars is their mechanism for drought escape, early maturity. The model results showed that there are fewer effects, or even negative effects, on yield increases over traditional cultivars in higher-rainfall seasons. In longer seasons, the early-maturing varieties are susceptible to yield-reducing pest infestation, because they mature first and attract all the insects and birds. If the cultivars mature when it is still raining, they are susceptible to grain quality problems. Furthermore, the early cultivars are not likely to be adopted with fertilizer in any type of season. We tested the potential effect on fertilizer use and income of having a mix of cultivars by adding such a combination of fertilizer and long-season cultivars to the activity choices in the farm model. Long-cycle varieties have the potential to yield more, since they remain longer in the field; hence, there is more potential for a response to fertilizer. We made the conservative assumption that the yields of improved longer-cycle and fertilized varieties would be 20 percent higher than those of shorter-cycle, fertilized cultivars in normal and better states of nature.[28]

The fertilizer–long-season-cultivar option is then adopted on 1.5 hectares before planting and results in 40 percent more income from rain-fed crops than that achieved with present practices. Income from rain-fed crops is 8 percent higher than income from adoption of shorter-cycle varieties alone. These estimated potential benefits from modeling must be compared at the experiment station with the expected costs and the probability of successful development of this cultivar type by breeders. Based on previous successes with farmer and breeder selections of short-season cultivars, this type of cultivar development would seem to be both feasible and socially profitable.

## Adoption of Potential New Millet Technologies at Kouka and Interventions to Encourage Fertilizer Use

It is more difficult to increase crop incomes in Kouka than in Libore, because rainfall and crop yields are lower. The overall income effects from the introduction of the improved agronomy and early varieties into this Kouka dryland system are an income increase of 20 percent and a lowering of income variability from a CV of 63 percent to a CV of 50 percent (table 5-2). Farmers in Kouka have been asking for improved early cultivars. Since the adoption

Table 5-2. Effect of Various Policy Instruments on Adoption of Fertilizer in Kouka, Niamey Region, Niger

| Policy or Program | Fertilizer Use (ha) | Millet-Cowpea Income (US$) | Livestock Income (US$) | Total Income (US$) | Change in Crop Income (%) | Change in Total Income (%) | CV of Total Income (%) |
|---|---|---|---|---|---|---|---|
| Current practices | — | 301 | 186 | 503 | — | — | 63 |
| Improved cultivars | 0 | 409 | 177 | 601 | +36 | +20 | 50 |
| Price support (CFA50) | 0 | 430 | 177 | 622 | +43 | +24 | 57 |
| Credit program (CFA10,000 at 0% interest) | 0 | 409 | 197 | 621 | +36 | +23 | 50 |
| Input subsidy (50%) | 0 | 409 | 230 | 653 | +36 | +30 | 54 |
| Adaptive livestock choices | 0 | 409 | 230 | 653 | +36 | +30 | 54 |

*Source:* Shapiro (1990, p. 127).
*Note:* Exchange rate is CFA298/US$.

of the new cultivars alone is not a more sustainable system than that which presently exists, the government may choose to intervene to encourage fertilizer use. As in the case of Libore, this could be done either by subsidizing credit or fertilizer or by supporting output prices. However, the results do not show potential for inorganic fertilizer to be adopted with any feasible policy shifts or even the introduction of higher-yielding, longer-season millet cultivars.

## Improvement of Livestock Activities in Land Surplus Areas

Improving livestock production and marketing in low-rainfall, land-extensive areas such as Kouka may be a more effective way to increase farmers' incomes. Developing more marketing opportunities and better availability of price information would increase the flexibility in the timing of livestock sales, making more sales possible after the rains start. Thus, the farmers could make better adaptive responses to rainfall conditions at the beginning of the season. This would result in increased profits from livestock activities.[29]

Adding to the model activities that represent the ability to sell livestock and buy livestock or fertilizer both before and after the rains begin results in more investment in livestock. Livestock income (US$230) is 24 percent higher than under current production practices (US$186) with the addition of this activity (table 5-2). This adaptive livestock strategy does not displace the use of improved varieties (see chapter 11 for a fuller discussion of the implications of these results for development of areas such as Kouka).

## Comparison of Rain-fed Crop Income at the Two Sites

Net returns per hectare under current practices are twice as high at Libore as at Kouka (US$115, as opposed to US$57, respectively; see table 5-3). Returns per hectare under present practices can be separated into those explained by yield differences and those explained by price differences. Under current low-input practices, higher yields at Libore can be attributed principally to higher rainfall, because the soil fertility is even lower there than at Kouka.[30] Higher prices at Libore are related to closer proximity to the major urban market of Niamey. Decomposing the revenue difference per hectare into yield and price effects shows that 60 percent of the difference is due to higher yields and 31 percent is due to higher prices at Libore.[31]

With introduction of fertilizer technology, the gap in net returns per hectare widens to over two times higher at Libore than at Kouka. Of the difference

Table 5-3. Expected Net Returns with Different Dryland Technologies at Libore and Kouka, Niamey Region, Niger

| Technology | Libore (US$/ha) | Kouka (US$/ha) | Ratio of Net Returns (per ha) |
|---|---|---|---|
| Current practices: millet-cowpea | 115 | 57 | 2.02 |
| Improved cultivars (low density) | 129 | 68 | 1.97 |
| Improved cultivars (high density) | 147 | 69 | 2.14 |
| Improved millet-cowpea with fertilizer | 175 | 76 | 6.30 |

*Source:* Shapiro (1990, p. 127).
*Note:* These are the standard net margins of linear programming.

in gross revenue per hectare, 57 percent results from yield differences and 38 percent from price differences. The introduction of the improved shorter-cycle varieties reduces the yield differences slightly between the two sites, but the effect of prices increases. There is much less potential for improving farmer incomes in areas such as Kouka through an intensification of crop production. More land is still available in Kouka, 8.8 to 13.5 hectares per farm, as compared with 3.9 hectares in Libore.

## Conclusion

Irrigated rice production provides a good example of our intensification strategy, since it involves high levels of cash inputs. Irrigation, where feasible, was shown to play an important role in income generation and stabilization for small farmers in this harsh environment. There is also considerable potential for the introduction of improved shorter-cycle varieties of millet and cowpeas. The introduction of fertilizer is also potentially viable and would be the logical next step in the intensification of dryland agriculture at Libore. This introduction is already taking place in the Gobery and Maradi regions, giving substantial field support to our model results.

The potential for adoption of phosphorus alone, according to model results as well as its use at other sites in the same agroecological zone, suggests that the fertilizer recommendation extended to farmers at sites such as Libore needs to be modified. Since farmers are known to adopt the components of a technology package in a stepwise fashion (this is what was observed at Gobery), phosphorus fertilizer alone needs to be recommended first at Libore to help begin the fertilizer adoption process. Furthermore, the successful experience at Gobery suggests that more farm trials for demonstration purposes will be required at Libore and elsewhere.

When the use of phosphorus is well established, a temporary subsidy on nitrogen (urea) and multiple nutrient fertilizers such as NPK may be appropriate while cultivars with more potential to respond to fertilizer are developed. The use of phosphorus will increase the demand by crops for nitrogen and other soil nutrients. Although, as part of the structural adjustment programs, the World Bank is advocating that governments in Sub-Saharan Africa eliminate subsidies on agricultural inputs, a temporary subsidy policy may be realistically required to encourage fertilizer adoption in Africa. This policy was successfully used in Asia as part of the Green Revolution (Lele, 1991).

The lack of a sufficiently profitable fertilizer technology that includes both nitrogen and phosphorus, relative to the alternative investments in small ruminants, helps to explain the present lack of intensification on rain-fed fields in areas such as Libore. At this time, only early or short-season improved cultivars are available for combined use with fertilizer. These cultivars are unable to take advantage of those years with a longer rainy season to produce higher yields through greater fertilizer response. If the crop mix contained normal or late-season improved cultivars, the model solutions included them with fertilization when the rains are early.

The recent emphasis in millet breeding in INRAN (Institut Nacional de Recherches Agronomiques du Niger) and other research organizations working in the West African semiarid tropics has been on earliness in response to lower rainfall and drought over the last twenty-five years. The strategy of breeding for earliness was introduced to reduce the risk from short seasons and irregular rainfalls, but it also limits the yield potential of these cultivars. Since farmers choose a portfolio of cultivars and crops, research institutions need to make available varieties with different maturity lengths. The availability of these longer-season cultivars is then associated with higher levels of fertilizer use.

For land abundant, lower-rainfall areas such as Kouka, efforts to intensify the cropping system to make it more sustainable are unlikely to be successful. Since the adoption of fertilizer use is not expected even with feasible policy changes or reasonable yield increases with new technologies, alternative strategies to improve incomes in this harsher environment must be found or out-migration facilitated. Encouraging improved livestock systems, including pasture and agroforestry systems, seems to be appropriate for this region (see chapter 11). Seasonal migration of most men is already occurring.

Technology development is an excellent tool for raising farm income. Even in the harsh rain-fed conditions at Libore, both new cultivars and different inorganic fertilizer strategies showed potential for raising incomes. Technology development does not appear, however, to be an efficient instrument for all regions, such as those with very low rainfall and low soil fertility, as in the Kouka case. In the lower rainfall regions of the Sahelo-Sudanian zone, a shift from crop research to concentration on research on agroforestry and improved livestock systems seems appropriate (see chapter 11 for further discussion of livestock and crop-livestock systems).

## Appendix: The Model

A one-year discrete stochastic programming model (DSP) was developed to capture farmers' adaptive decision making. Other DSP models estimated in Niger and northern Nigeria were Adesina and Sanders (1991); Krause, Deuson, et al. (1990); and Balcet and Candler (1982). The risk these farmers face is represented by minimum consumption constraints and stochastic input, output, and resource levels for each of the states of nature modeled. The modeling of several states of nature and the timing of decisions by farmers in this region are critical because of the uncertainty involved in rain-fed crop and livestock production. DSP captures the time factor by allowing adaptive decisions at specific critical points in response to stochastic rainfall events during the season. This is consistent with the strategies that these farmers were observed to follow (Balcet and Candler, 1982; Matlon and Kristjanson, 1988; Shapiro, 1990; Adesina and Sanders, 1991).

Risk reduction is a primary objective of these small farmers. First, farmers seek to assure minimum subsistence levels of cereals (Sutter, 1984, pp. 153, 157, 193–34; Shapiro, 1990; Adesina and Sanders, 1991). Thus, a minimum subsistence cereal production constraint for each state of nature was included in the model.[32] Second, farmers adapt their decisions during the season in response to the rainfall conditions. This adaptive farmer decision making was observed in the field and discussed with farmers (Shapiro, 1990; Adesina and Sanders, 1991). The responses to decisions about planting late or early cultivars and several fertilization decisions will depend upon rainfall.

Risk aversion was also evaluated in the modeling; however, variations in this farmer characteristic over a wide range had minimal effects on production decisions or incomes[33] (Shapiro, 1990). Therefore, these results were not reported, and the objective function maximized here was expected income with a subsistence constraint, implying a lexicographic utility function. The model is given below:

maximize

$$\sum_i \sum_j \rho_{ij} Y_{ij} \qquad (5.1)$$

subject to

$$A_0 X_0 + t_0 T \leq B_0 \qquad (5.2)$$
$$A_{0i} X_0 + A_i X_i - t_0 T \leq B_i, \text{ for each } i, \qquad (5.3)$$
$$- C_0 X_0 - C_i X_i + Y_{ij} = 0, \text{ for each } i, j, \qquad (5.4)$$

where

$Y_{ij}$     is the net revenue accounting activities for state of nature $j$ following state of nature $i$;

$\rho_{ij}$     is the vector of unconditional probabilities for state-of-nature $j$ following state-of-nature $i$;

$X_0$     is the vector of first-period activities;

$A_0$     is the matrix of first-period technical coefficients;

$B_0$     is the first-period vector of resource availabilities;

$X_i$     is the vector of activities for decision periods two and three for state of nature $i$;

$A_i$     is the matrix of technical coefficients for decision periods two and three for state of nature $i$;

$A_{0i}$     is the matrix of technical coefficients for first-period activities using or supplying resources in periods two and three for state of nature $i$;

$t_0$     is a vector of resource-transfer coefficients, which are zeroes or ones, depending on whether the resource can be transferred between periods;

$T$     is the vector of resource-transfer activities for period one to periods two and three;

$B_i$     is the vector of resource availabilities associated with state-of-nature $i$;

$C_0 \text{ and } C_i$     are the vectors of per unit net activity returns for decision period one ($C_0$) and periods two and three ($C_i$) for state of nature $i$.

The objective function (1) is to maximize expected income. Equation (2) is the resource constraint set for preplanting decisions, and equation (3) is the resource constraint set for decision periods two and three combined. There is a set of activities in periods two and three for each preceding state of nature. Similarly, technical coefficients and resource availabilities can vary with the preceding state of nature. The other terms *(T)* allow transfers of resources between periods when it is appropriate. For example, cash resources not used in the first period are passed to the second period. The coefficient $A_{0i}$ in equation (3) incorporates consequences of decisions in period one on resources in the next decision period. For example, fertilizing with phosphorus in period one supplies fertilized land in period two for each state of nature. Equation (4) sums the net contributions to profits of the activities for each final state of nature. Besides crop activities, there are livestock activities and the option of off-farm work in the model.

The agronomic and price data used in this study come from the INRAN on-farm research site at Libore in the Niamey Region for the period 1984–88 and from on-farm trial results of other research organizations, including ICRISAT, IFDC, FAO, and IITA, for the same period. The meteorological data are from the rainfall station at Niamey Airport, which is the closest to the INRAN site. Supplemental socioeconomic data from anthropologists who have done farm-level field work in Niger are also used. These anthropologists include Sutter (1984), Collion (1982), Raynaut (1976), and Painter (1987).

# 6

# A New Sorghum Hybrid in Low-Input and High-Input Environments: The Mechanized Rain-fed Zone and the Gezira of Sudan

SORGHUM accounts for 75 percent of cereal production in the Sudan and is eaten as an unleavened bread *(kisra)*, a porridge *(asida)*, a beverage *(abreih)*, and a local beer *(marisa)* (Ejeta, 1988, p. 29). When a new hybrid sorghum was released in the Sudan in the early 1980s, the main target zone was the mechanized rain-fed zone. This is the principal sorghum area of the Sudan, the site of 58 percent of sorghum production from 1980 to 1992 (table 6-1; also see Adam, Mohammed, and Hassan, 1981; Magar, 1986; Simpson and Simpson, 1984).

After the drought of 1984–85 and the consequent high sorghum prices, there was excitement about the large-scale release of the hybrid, Hageen Dura-1 (HD-1), and seed production was undertaken rapidly in both Sudan and the United States. The diffusion process came to an abrupt halt with the sorghum price collapse of 1985–86. As sorghum prices recovered and farmers noted the yield advantage of HD-1, diffusion then gradually resumed, and HD-1 became successful in the principal irrigated zone of the Sudan (see fig. 6-1 for the zones of mechanized rain-fed production and the Gezira irrigation project). Since its initial introduction in 1985–86, there has been minimal repurchase or diffusion of HD-1 in the drylands.

## The Three Sorghum Production Sectors

There are three production zones for sorghum in the Sudan: mechanized rain-fed, irrigated, and traditional dryland. The mechanized rain-fed sector produced an annual average 1.4 million metric tons of sorghum over the period 1980–92 (table 6-1; fig. 6-2). The mechanized rain-fed is the most im-

Table 6-1. Sorghum Area and Production in Sudan, by Sector, 1964–1993

| Crop Year[a] | Mechanized Sector | | Irrigated Sector | | Traditional Sector | | Total Sudan | |
|---|---|---|---|---|---|---|---|---|
| | Area | Production | Area | Production | Area | Production | Area | Production |
| 1964 | 854 | 863 | 206 | 334 | 317 | 152 | 1,377 | 1,349 |
| 1965 | 779 | 725 | 195 | 247 | 353 | 165 | 1,327 | 1,137 |
| 1966 | 867 | 780 | 174 | 220 | 303 | 95 | 1,344 | 1,095 |
| 1967 | 900 | 621 | 189 | 224 | 248 | 6 | 1,337 | 851 |
| 1968 | 1,562 | 1,672 | 206 | 278 | 207 | 30 | 1,975 | 1,980 |
| 1969 | 764 | 630 | 194 | 129 | 228 | 111 | 1,186 | 870 |
| 1970 | 1,124 | 862 | 249 | 246 | 405 | 244 | 1,778 | 1,352 |
| 1971 | 1,385 | 1,027 | 264 | 273 | 407 | 235 | 2,056 | 1,535 |
| 1972 | 1,278 | 1,072 | 215 | 215 | 421 | 304 | 1,914 | 1,591 |
| 1973 | 1,081 | 927 | 213 | 363 | 427 | 11 | 1,721 | 1,301 |
| 1974 | 1,041 | 822 | 229 (126) | 292 (226) | 1,045 | 577 | 2,315 | 1,691 |
| 1975 | 1,240 | 751 | 169 (65) | 171 (77) | 934 | 759 | 2,343 | 1,681 |
| 1976 | 1,282 | 1,183 | 258 (143) | 289 (204) | 1,195 | 688 | 2,735 | 2,160 |
| 1977 | 1,276 | 962 | 224 (136) | 221 (174) | 1,316 | 607 | 2,816 | 1,790 |
| 1978 | 1,236 | 837 | 219 (148) | 261 (190) | 1,435 | 964 | 2,890 | 2,062 |
| 1979 | 1,274 | 866 | 248 (145) | 245 (147) | 1,379 | 1,082 | 2,901 | 2,193 |
| 1980 | 1,039 | 592 | 184 (137) | 169 (163) | 1,134 | 701 | 2,357 | 1,462 |
| 1981 | 1,224 | 936 | 210 (126) | 154 (69) | 808 | 440 | 2,242 | 1,530 |
| 1982 | 2,342 | 1,239 | 243 (144) | 271 (89) | 1,522 | 558 | 4,107 | 2,068 |
| 1983 | 2,443 | 1,267 | 319 (135) | 233 (125) | 1,515 | 601 | 4,277 | 2,101 |
| 1984 | 2,198 | 1,084 | 279 (173) | 359 (216) | 977 | 363 | 3,454 | 1,806 |
| 1985 | 1,905 | 389 | 322 (176) | 436 (147) | 1,129 | 272 | 3,356 | 1,097 |
| 1986 | 3,587 | 2,328 | 472 (243) | 658 (318) | 1,468 | 609 | 5,527 | 3,595 |
| 1987 | 3,440 | 2,395 | 347 (188) | 459 (179) | 1,173 | 428 | 4,960 | 3,282 |
| 1988 | 2,232 | 853 | 299 (164) | 352 (141) | 858 | 158 | 3,389 | 1,363 |
| 1989 | 4,094 | 3,312 | 355 (179) | 468 (215) | 1,128 | 638 | 5,577 | 4,418 |
| 1990 | 2,449 | 850 | 317 (185) | 392 (238) | 1,035 | 290 | 3,801 | 1,532 |
| 1991 | 1,714 | 538 | 391 (213) | 516 (254) | 655 | 123 | 2,760 | 1,177 |
| 1992 | 3,899 | 2,386 | 579 (298) | 884 (482) | 672 | 265 | 5,150 | 3,535 |
| 1993 | 5,065 | — | 605 (261) | — (430) | 1,890 | — | 7,560 | — |

Source: 1964–88 data from Habash (1990); 1989–92 data from Merghani (1993); 1993 data from Sudan (1993).
Note: Annual data refer to the last year of the crop season, e.g., 1964 denotes 1963–64 crop. All area figures are in thousands of hectares. All production figures are in thousands of metric tons. Figures in parentheses reflect Gezira scheme portion of irrigated sector. Gezira is approximately half of the total irrigated area.

Figure 6-1. Mechanized Sectors in Sudan and Greater Gezira Scheme.

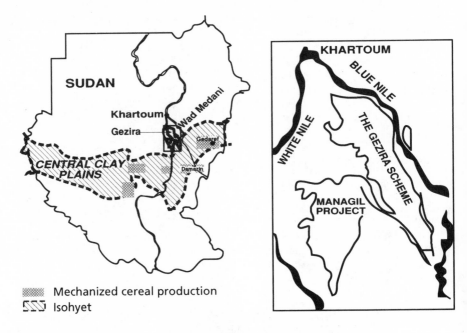

Source: Adapted from M. Ahmed and Sanders (1992, p. 74) and Salih (1993, p. 14).
Note: Shaded area represents isohyets of 400 to 800 millimeters of rainfall.

Figure 6-2. Production in the Three Sorghum Sectors of Sudan, 1964–1992

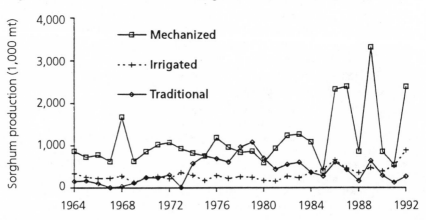

Source: Calculated from table 6-1.

portant sector, producing sorghum at approximately three times the levels of each of the other two sectors. Except for adverse weather years, the sorghum share produced in the mechanized drylands in the eighties was 55 to 75 percent of total output (fig. 6-3). The traditional dryland producers experienced a decline in annual production during the 1980–92 period, with output levels averaging only 419,000 metric tons annually. The irrigated sector increased sorghum yields in the last decade (fig. 6-4), and in the nineties the government loosened the area controls and sorghum became the predominant crop by area in the main irrigated scheme, the Gezira. The irrigated sector increased sorghum output over this period, producing 412,000 metric tons annually. Weather in the eighties varied considerably, with abrupt declines of sorghum production during the infamous 1984–85 drought but also in the 1987–88, 1989–90, and 1990–91 crop years (table 6-1; fig. 6-2). Following adverse weather in the drylands, the sorghum price usually rose sharply, and producers in all three sectors responded in the next year with increased output.

Development of the mechanized rain-fed zone was begun by the British during World War II. These heavy vertisols are difficult to work and have low organic matter. Their cracking characteristic gives them some water retention capacity when very dry, but they then seal when wet (Bein, 1980, p. 122; Dudal and Eswaran, 1988, pp. 9, 10, 13, 21). These soils are found all over

Figure 6-3. Sorghum Production Shares in the Three Production Sectors of Sudan, 1964–1992

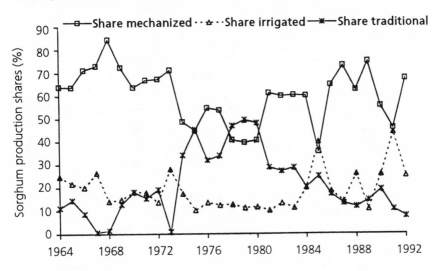

*Source:* Calculated from table 6-1.

Figure 6-4. Yields in the Irrigated and Mechanized Sectors of Sudan, 1976–1992

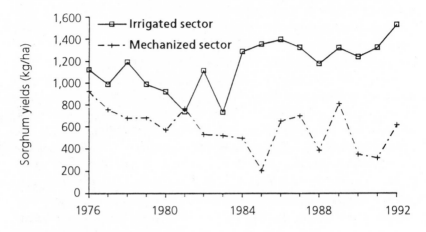

*Source:* Calculated from table 6-1.

the world, and in Sudan there are 40 to 50 million hectares of this soil type (Dudal and Eswaran, 1988, p. 8). Settlement on these plains was restricted by the lack of available water for people and the difficulty of land preparation with manual or even animal power.[1] The government began schemes to promote large-farmer, mechanized settlements in the 1940s. The area in mechanized dryland production increased from 5,000 hectares in 1944–45 to 1.6 million hectares in 1968 and to more than 5 million hectares in 1992–93. Besides the area directly available from the government through the Mechanized Farming Corporation (MFC), there was also an active rental market. In a land survey in 1989, 2.3 million hectares were leased from the MFC, and another 2.6 million hectares were farmed from the undemarcated land.[2]

In the mechanized rain-fed zone, there is some sesame, cotton, and millet production, but around 87 percent of the crop area was in sorghum over the 1980–92 period. The extensive production system of the mechanized vertisols includes land preparation and planting by tractor, one or two hand weedings, and hand harvesting with the use of combine harvesters, generally as stationary threshers. No fertilization or other chemicals are used. With subsidized land and machinery prices on a large frontier, it is not surprising that extensive settlement took place. Governmental promotion involved a nominal rent of $0.29 per hectare (1989 US$) on a twenty-five-year land lease, plus low interest rates and special foreign exchange rates on imported machinery (Habash, 1990, p. 15). Labor comes in by the truckload and includes temporary migrants from the west and from neighboring countries. Approximately 5,000 entrepreneurs operate these farms with 100,000 wage-earning employees and up to a million seasonal laborers for two months of weeding and harvesting (Holdcroft, 1989, p. 5).

There is a debate in the Sudan about whether the yields of the vertisols have been declining. Vertisols have a churning characteristic, pulling some soil from various layers. Vertisols also crack when dry, and this allows more water to penetrate into the soil. There have been some fallow rotation and shifts in and out of production in response to changing price expectations. However, the main contributor to the debate has been the irregular rainfall with the resulting substantial between-year yield variability. With the enormous variability of yields between years, it is difficult to observe a trend (see fig. 6-5). Hence, to estimate the effects of various traditional-farmer practices, a simulation model was constructed for a typical vertisol with its water, soil, and cropping system (Salih, 1993). When the cropping practice of continuous sorghum cultivation without fertilization is run, yields decline to approximately 60 percent of initial levels after sixteen years.[3] The observed and model yield declines to 500 to 600 kilograms per hectare indicate the soil

Figure 6-5. Historic and Simulated Yields in the Mechanized Sector of Sudan, 1964–1992

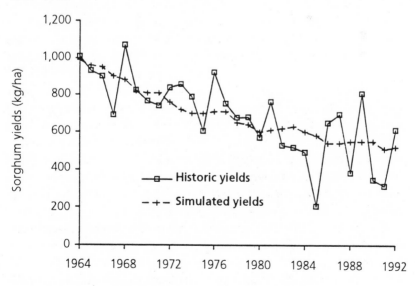

*Source:* Adapted from Salih (1993, p. 58).

mining of continuous sorghum without inorganic fertilizer or other fertilization sources.

In the 1970s, poor performance in the mechanized sector was offset by increased production in the traditional sector. However, in the eighties, the traditional sector was in decline, and the irrigated sector became an increasingly important source for Sudanese sorghum production. When yields in most of the mechanized dryland sector collapsed in the 1984–85 and 1990–91 crop years, the consistent 400,000 to 500,000 metric tons produced in the irrigated zone after 1984 was a key factor for domestic sorghum availability (table 6-1; fig. 6-3).

In the 1920s, the British began the Gezira scheme (Tothill, 1948). It is now one of the largest irrigation projects in the world. Approximately 875,000 hectares are cultivated in the Gezira, compared with 1.9 million total cultivated hectares in public scheme irrigation (D'Silva, 1986, p. 92). The Gezira scheme included approximately 12 percent of the Sudanese total crop area in the 1980s and 46 percent of irrigated area. Ranging in area from 6.3 to 16.8 hectares, 106,000 small farms in the Gezira provide full-time employment to 350,000 persons and four months of seasonal labor for another 450,000 (SGB, 1990; Holdcroft, 1989, p. 6; Youngblood, 1982, p. 6).

Historically, the main objective of the Gezira scheme management has been to increase foreign exchange by exporting cotton and reducing imports of wheat. In the 1980s, the Gezira produced 75 percent of Sudan's export crop, long staple cotton; 40 percent of the peanuts; and 85 percent of Sudan's wheat (SGB, 1990). For the principal crops, cotton and wheat, management provides extension, inputs, and marketing services. Input use and timing of operations for these crops are controlled by the project administration and verified by project staff. For these crops, the project is administered more like a mine than a farm.

In 1976, Gezira management began allowing farmers one-fourth of their farms to produce either sorghum or peanuts, or both (Ahmed, 1984; Fakki, 1982). On these crops, farmers make their own decisions. In the eighties, this percentage was higher than one-fourth and varied with sorghum availability, since droughts and a continuing civil war led to sorghum shortages in several years. In 1991, the restrictions on sorghum area were withdrawn, and farmers can now grow whatever crops they choose.

In 1984–85, the major drought year of the decade, the Gezira produced 13 percent, and all irrigated regions 40 percent, of Sudanese sorghum production. In that year, yields in the two dryland regions, mechanized and traditional, were 204 and 241 kilograms per hectare, respectively, as compared with 835 kilograms per hectare (calculated from table 6-1) in the Gezira.

Thus, the irrigated regions provide an important safety valve when sorghum production in the drylands collapses. In contrast, over the period 1980–92, the irrigated areas were only 8 percent of the total sorghum area and 18 percent of total production (table 6-1). Irrigated yields are approximately double those on the drylands and are more stable. Irrigated sorghum yields increased in the second half of the eighties after higher fertilizer levels, new cultivars, and other improved agronomic practices were introduced (fig. 6-4).

Following the high prices of these shortage years, such as 1984–85, 1987–88, and 1990–91, substantial sorghum area expansion, output increases, and then price collapses took place. So there were substantial variations in prices, with different incentives to producers (see Youngblood, 1982, p. 1). Sorghum area ranged from 26 to 48 percent of the crop area in the Gezira scheme from 1982 to 1993.[4] The sorghum area was 43 percent after the major drought year of 1984–85 and 48 percent in 1992–93. Over the 1981–82 to 1992–93 crop years, sorghum became the most important crop in the Gezira, with almost 36 percent of the crop area displacing cotton (30 percent) and wheat (21 percent). In the nineties, the governmental objective shifted to domestic food security as cotton fell to a 13 percent share of crop area for 1991–93, with wheat at 35 percent and sorghum at 45 percent (calculated from Sudan, 1993).

The third sector is neglected both by us (we have not done any research on the traditional rain-fed sector) and by the government (see UNDP, 1986; ILO, 1975). Almost all governmental attention and policy support were aimed at the mechanized rain-fed and irrigated sectors over the 1980–92 period, even though the traditional rain-fed sorghum producer is found all over the country. These are small farmers with manual power and a diversified crop mix. Few purchased inputs are used. Yields are even lower than in the mechanized rain-fed zone. Despite lack of governmental support for these small farmers, 28 percent of the sorghum area and 19 percent of the sorghum production came from this sector over the 1980–92 period (table 6-1).

## Success of HD-1 Diffusion in the Gezira Project

On regional trials with moderately high input levels, HD-1 outyielded farmers' cultivars 52 to 58 percent for irrigated and rain-fed conditions, respectively, over the 1979–82 crop seasons.[5] This new hybrid was then released in 1983. After the 1984–85 drought year, two public agencies and eleven private companies rushed into seed production in the Sudan (table 6-2). In 1985–86, with the high prices for sorghum following the drought, mechanized rain-fed farmers expanded their crop area from 1.9 million hectares in 1984–85 to almost 3.6 million hectares in 1985–86. Total sorghum

area in Sudan increased from 3.4 million to 5.5 million hectares, and Sudanese sorghum production recovered from 1.1 million tons in the drought year,
1984–85, to 3.6 million tons in 1985–86 (table 6-1).

Then in 1986, the real price of sorghum collapsed with the large area response to the high prices, the inelastic demand, and the export ban. The Agricultural Bank of Sudan, a principal buyer in the mechanized rain-fed zone,
stopped purchasing Hageen Dura-1 (Habash, 1990). A price differential of 40
to 50 percent was then observed between HD-1 and other local sorghums (fig.
6-6). Farmers and millers complained about the smaller, harder seed sizes of
HD-1 and about the blander kisra relative to the traditional sorghums. From
1986–87 through 1988–89, the Sudan Gezira Board was able to sell less than
20 percent of its seed stocks. The private seed companies stopped producing
HD-1 after 1986–87 (table 6-2).

After 1985–86, farmers in the mechanized drylands stopped purchasing
HD-1. The principal explanation for this withdrawal from HD-1 was the 35

Figure 6-6. Real Prices of Hageen Dura-1 and Traditional Varieties, 1985–
1990 (1989–1990 base)

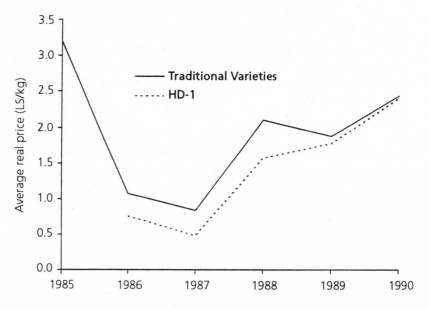

Source: M. Ahmed and Sanders (1992, p. 77).
Note: LS denotes Sudanese pound. The market or street exchange rate in summer 1990
was LS18/US$.

Table 6-2. Hageen Dura-1 Certified Seed Production and Sales by Public and Private Seed Producers in Sudan

| | Sudan Gezira Board | | | National Seed Administration | | | Private Companies | | |
|---|---|---|---|---|---|---|---|---|---|
| | | Sale | | | Sale | | | Sale | |
| Season | Production (mt) | (mt) | % Stock | Production (mt) | (mt) | % Stock | Production (mt) | (mt) | % of Stock[a] |
| 1983–84 | 18.00 | — | — | — | — | — | — | — | — |
| 1984–85 | 75.27 | 18.00 | 100 | 12.47 | — | — | — | — | — |
| 1985–86 | 412.83 | 75.27 | 100 | 81.81 | 11.20 | 90 | 162.09 | — | — |
| 1986–87 | 23.40 | 61.83 | 15 | 36.41 | 66.62 | 81 | 21.87 | 33.40 | 20 |
| 1987–88 | — | 72.00 | 18[b] | 22.85 | 51.60 | 100 | — | 18.00 | 12 |
| 1988–89 | 31.38 | 17.98 | 19 | 36.20 | 25.40 | 89 | — | — | — |
| 1989–90 | 89.78 | 103.18 | 100 | 8.60 | 36.00 | 21 | — | — | — |
| 1990–91 | 330.12[c] | 108.36 | 100 | 85.85 | 85.00 | 100 | 0.67[c] | — | — |
| 1991–92 | 220.00 | 215.60 | 98 | 30.60 | 30.60 | 100 | 88.00[d] | 88.00[d] | 100 |
| 1992–93 | 210.00 | — | — | — | — | — | 50.00[d] | — | — |

Source: Yousif (1989); SGB (1990); M. Ahmed and Sanders (1992, p. 76, table 2, updated for 1991–92). Data for 1991–92 and 1992–93 are from unpublished data provided by the Sudan Gezira Board, the National Seed Administration, and the Pioneer Seed Co., Sudan.
Note: Production is one-year lagged, e.g., the seed produced in a season will be available for sale the next season.
[a] Sales as percentage of accumulated stock.
[b] Including the Rahad scheme production of 1986.
[c] Estimated from planting date and past yield averages.
[d] Pioneer Seed Co.

percent expected price differential, according to farmers surveyed in 1989 in the Gedaref region of the mechanized rain-fed zone. Farmers were confident that HD-1 would outyield the local sorghums (Feteritas, Debar, and Gadam el Hamam), but they expected this large price discount to continue. The cross-over point at which farmers were expected to be indifferent between HD-1 and the local sorghums was with a price discount for HD-1 of 16 percent. At a 10 percent price differential, they would almost completely substitute HD-1 for traditional sorghums, according to model results (Habash, 1990, pp. 60, 61).

In the irrigated regions, a different phenomenon occurred with HD-1 in the second half of the 1980s. Farmers noticed the high yields of HD-1 when combined with chemical fertilizer. With continuing consumption of HD-1,

Gezira farmers and other consumers and their families apparently began to change their tastes. The price differential between HD-1 and other local sorghums narrowed and then disappeared (fig. 6-6). Of fifty-six farmers interviewed in the Gezira in 1990, 90 percent reported that HD-1 kisra was equal to or better than that of traditional sorghums. The introduction of HD-1 enabled producers to shift from purchasers to sellers of sorghum. Over the period 1984–90, farmers producing the local sorghums purchased 12 to 26 percent of their domestic requirements in three of these years. In contrast, farmers producing HD-1 sold 25 to 33 percent of their production during these years, staggering their sales during the off-season to avoid the postharvest price collapse (M. Ahmed and Sanders, 1992, p. 78).

At the beginning of the 1990s, the introduction of HD-1 accelerated (fig. 6-7), reaching 37,600 hectares or approximately 12 percent of the sorghum area in the Gezira in 1991–92. Even if the diffusion were to stay at only this absolute area and not continue increasing, there would be an internal rate of return to this research of 97 percent (M. Ahmed, Masters, and Sanders, 1995,

Figure 6-7. Adoption of Hageen Dura-1 in the Gezira, 1985–1992

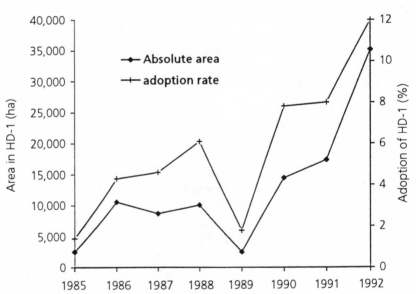

*Source:* Adapted from M. Ahmed and Sanders (1992, p. 77) and Nichola (1994).
*Note:* Adoption on the secondary axis is the percentage of the total area in sorghum in the Gezira scheme.

p. 29). The returns are large for developing countries to implement breeding programs by selecting from the wide range of cultivars available from the international research centers and from developed-country breeding programs (Texas A&M University, in this case). A good breeder in Sudan can and quickly did identify and then promote and distribute to governmental seed agencies a new hybrid with adaptation and high yields. The developing-country breeder has a wide range of germplasm from outside agencies to draw on if he knows how to access the world scientific networks.

In field interviews in 1990, Gezira farmers reported that there was no yield advantage to HD-1 without fertilizer. At a low level of nitrogen (47.5 kilograms urea per hectare), traditional sorghum cultivars yielded 1.45 metric tons per hectare, compared with 2.05 metric tons per hectare for HD-1. Increasing fertilization to moderately high levels (95 kilograms urea and 95 kilograms triple superphosphate per hectare) enabled a doubling of yields to 3.1 metric tons per hectare for HD-1 (table 6-3). Increasing levels of inorganic fertilizer and the diffusion of HD-1 were strongly associated. In the early nineties, many farmers in the farm survey of HD-1 diffusion in Gezira in 1990 complained about their inability to obtain HD-1 seeds and chemical

Table 6-3. Average Sorghum Yields for Hageen Dura-1 and Traditional Cultivars in the Gezira Scheme, 1985–1989

| Cultivar | Fertilizer Level (per ha) | Mean Yields (mt/ha) |
|---|---|---|
| Hageen Dura-1 | 190 kg urea and 95 kg simple superphosphate | 3.28 |
| Hageen Dura-1 | 95 kg urea and 95 kg simple superphosphate | 3.07 |
| Hageen Dura-1 | 190 kg urea | 2.84 |
| Hageen Dura-1 | 95 kg urea | 2.35 |
| Hageen Dura-1 | 47.5[a] kg urea | 2.05 |
| Hageen Dura-1 | no fertilizer | 1.17 |
| Traditional cultivar | 47.5[a] kg urea | 1.45 |
| Traditional cultivar | no fertilizer | 1.13 |

*Source:* These data were from interviews in 1990 of fifty-six farmers in four different regions of the Gezira project. Farmers were asked to recall data about cultivars, yields, area, prices, costs, and production practices over the last five crop seasons. Data were recorded only when farmers expressed certainty about the specific values. Since sorghum was the principal food crop and they were the decision makers growing it, most farmers did not have difficulties in recalling the principal information.

[a] Above zero and less than ninety-five kilograms per hectare. Mean value used.

fertilizer for sorghum. The apparent constraint to further diffusion of HD-1 was the functioning of the input industries. The standard recommendation is to open up the seed industry to the private sector. However, the private seed companies stopped HD-1 production in 1986–87 after the postdrought price collapse (fig. 6-6). The public-sector companies remained in sorghum seed production, and diffusion of HD-1 gradually resumed. By 1989–90, the two public seed companies had sold their remaining stocks of HD-1 and were having difficulty expanding seed production fast enough to meet the rapidly increasing demand (table 6-2). Pioneer Seed Company returned to hybrid sorghum seed production in Sudan during 1991 and 1992.

If the input industries for hybrid seed production and chemical fertilizer distribution can respond to the rapidly increasing demands for inputs, HD-1 is expected to expand into a substantial area of the entire public irrigated scheme.[6] In the past, fertilizer imports have often been dependent on foreign aid. A higher priority needs to be put on making foreign exchange available for the required fertilizer for sorghum and for other irrigated and nonirrigated crops. With small additional public investments, this diffusion onto other irrigated projects could be accelerated by facilitating the availability of seeds, fertilizer, and farm trials.

The diffusion of HD-1 is only in the initial stages in the largest irrigation project, the Gezira, and has not been successful in the drylands.[7] Nevertheless, there already are high returns to the research investment in HD-1. Successful technologies in the Gezira are expected to move quickly into the other irrigated projects. Irrigation technologies are self-contained units similar to chicken broiler technologies, so much less regional adaptation is required than for most agricultural technologies. In the Rahad irrigation project in 1990, farmers requested the project administrators for HD-1 seed.

The principal constraint to a more rapid introduction of the high-yielding cultivar, according to the farmers interviewed in 1992, is the ability of input suppliers to produce adequate quantities of high-quality seed and to provide sufficient fertilizer.[8] There were complaints about the quality of the seed. Moreover, there would have been 51 percent more adopters if all those who wanted to buy seed had been able to get it (Nichola, 1994). The reentry of the private seed producers is presently occurring and increases the responsiveness of the seed sector to rapidly increasing farm demands.

In diffusion models, entirely misleading results can be obtained if no adjustment is made for input supply shortages. If the frequent failure of the seed and fertilizer firms to provide seed and fertilizer to all who would buy it is not taken into account, we get the conventional results for diffusion studies (table

6-4). Statistically, the probability of purchase is greater for the more educated and wealthier farmers, and therefore extension and other diffusion programs should be aimed at them. However, if we adjust for seed and fertilizer short-ages by treating all who said they would buy as adopters, these farmer charac-teristic variables no longer influence the rate of diffusion. Rather, diffusion is only determined by the taste variable (whether the farmer likes the taste of Hageen Dura 1) and by the number of extension visits (table 6-4). Apparently, farmer characteristics such as greater size, wealth, and higher education deter-mine the ability of farmers to obtain a rationed, subsidized input. The policy implication is not to concentrate extension efforts on this wealthier group of farmers, as implied in many other diffusion studies that do not adjust for this inability of the input sector to respond. The appropriate policy is to improve the functioning of the input industries.

In the input industries there is also a difficult pricing issue for public firms. A subsidy on the price can be justified for equity or welfare reasons, but the consequence of a subsidized input is that there will be excess demand and then rationing of the input. When rationing occurs, the principal beneficiaries are usually the larger, more influential farmers. Hence, a measure ostensibly designed to improve income distribution can in practice make income distri-bution worse. Moreover, a subsidized price for the hybrid in the public sector will make it more difficult to develop a private seed sector.

Price collapse often results in years of good rainfall when the rain-fed output is high.[9] In lower-rainfall years, cereal shortages and high prices are observed. Thus, there is substantial price instability between years, which adversely affects sorghum production. On the policy side, price supports and storage are expensive policies, given the size of the sorghum sector. An alter-native solution to avoid price collapse in high-rainfall years is to introduce new uses for sorghum. Using sorghum as a feed for poultry and livestock is another way to expand demand in high-rainfall years. Unfortunately, a feed-ing operation cannot start up rapidly after a high-rainfall year, run one year, shut down, and then reopen. Changing the composition of bread flour has fewer continuity demands than developing a livestock feed industry, once the milling capacity for both grains is in place. The commercial production of composite flour from wheat and sorghum for bread making can use surplus supplies of sorghum and reduce wheat imports. The feasibility of this technol-ogy was demonstrated by the Food Research Center of the Agricultural Re-search Corporation (Wicker, 1989). Taste differences of bread with low levels of sorghum flour (10 to 20 percent) are negligible. In the long run, the best way to increase demand for sorghum may be to make public investments in infrastructure and international marketing information to enable Sudan to become a sorghum exporter.

In the Gezira, farmers have already obtained sorghum yields over three metric tons per hectare with inorganic fertilizer, improved land preparation, adequate irrigation water, and other agronomic improvements (table 6-3). However, in most countries, food staple cereals, except for rice and wheat, are of too low value to be produced under irrigation unless there are substantial price distortions or supply crises, such as the droughts and civil wars in Sudan. Hence, in the long run, sorghum is expected to be pushed out of the irrigated zones by high-value crops. Vegetable production in the Gezira in 1988–89 occupied 3 percent of crop area, but it is not expanding, since in-

Table 6-4. Determinants of Farm-Level Adoption of Hageen Dura-1 in the Gezira, with and without Adjustments for Input Supply Shortages (probit model)

| Determinant | No Adjustment for Input Supply Restrictions | Adjustment for Input Supply Restrictions |
|---|---|---|
| Experience | 0.011 | −0.001 |
| | (1.0) | (0.1) |
| Education | 0.089 | 0.03 |
| | (2.0)** | (0.7) |
| Family size | −0.002 | 0.02 |
| | (0.1) | (0.4) |
| Farm size | 0.035 | 0.19 |
| | (2.8)*** | (1.6) |
| Indebtedness | 0.0000096 | 0.000006 |
| | (1.6)* | (1.0) |
| Extension | 0.20 | 0.11 |
| | (4.5)*** | (2.8)*** |
| Taste | 0.84 | 0.62 |
| | (2.5)*** | (2.1)** |

*Source:* Based on Nichola (1994, pp. 70, 73).
*Note:* Numbers in parentheses are *t*-values.
*Asymptotic *t* value of 10%.
**Asymptotic *t* value of 5%.
***Asymptotic *t* value of 1%.

come growth has been stagnant. As technical and marketing problems of vegetable and fruit production are resolved and as urban incomes increase, irrigated vegetable and fruit production will become the dominant use of the irrigated crop area over which the farmer has control, but this development is expected to take five to ten years if the government supports research on these crops and marketing infrastructure improves. The foreign exchange crops of cotton and wheat are expected to remain in the product mix in the Gezira.

## Requirements for Intensive Technology Introduction in the Mechanized Rain-fed Zone

The center of Sudanese sorghum production in the long run needs to be the drylands, despite the higher yield potential in the irrigated region. With increasing incomes, the opportunity costs of keeping high-value irrigation land in low-value cereal crops will become too high, and sorghum will be replaced by fruits, vegetables, and other high-value crops. Presently, sorghum yields in the drylands average 0.5 to 0.7 metric ton per hectare, compared with mean irrigated yields of more than 1.2 metric tons per hectare (fig. 6-5). In the drylands, aggregate yields are declining as farmers continue extensive agriculture and land area expansion becomes more expensive.

The mechanized rain-fed area has become almost a monoculture sorghum area of large mechanized farms. Chemical inputs are not purchased. HD-1 was experimented with in the mid-eighties, and farmers then returned to traditional sorghums (see the qualifications to this in note 7). One explanation for farmers' present lack of interest in HD-1 in this region is its poor yield and grain quality without additional inputs (Habash, 1990). Even in irrigated regions, farmers report no yield advantage for HD-1 over traditional cultivars in the absence of inorganic fertilizer (table 6-3).

With a simulation model, the long-run potential effects on yields and sustainability of various new technologies on the mechanized rain-fed area were evaluated. Introducing only a new cultivar would increase yields approximately 13 percent over the sixteen-year period, with the yield advantage declining over time as soil fertility decreases (fig. 6-8). Combining the new cultivar with 47 kilograms urea per hectare increased yields 58 percent over the improved cultivar alone, approximately doubling yields of the traditional cultivars, according to model results. These yields are sustainable in contrast with traditional practices or with a new cultivar alone. This combination of moderate fertilization combined with an improved cultivar increased profits 95 percent (M. Ahmed, 1994).[10] Doubled yields is a surprising increase for

Figure 6-8. Simulated Sorghum Yields of Actual and Potential Technologies in the Mechanized Rain-Fed Zone, 1973–1989

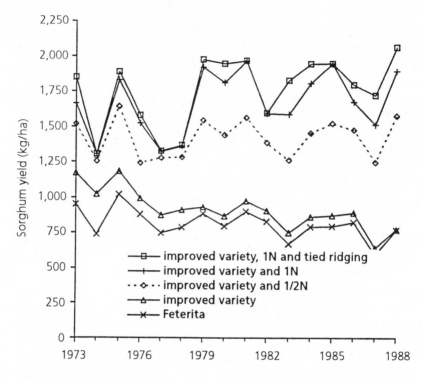

*Source:* M. Ahmed (1994).
*Note:* 1N denotes application of ninety-four kilograms urea per hectare and ½N is forty-seven kilograms urea per hectare.

low fertilization and a new cultivar. However, these heavy soils have adequate levels of other nutrients and rainfall, so increasing nitrogen has a large effect.

Doubling the fertilizer level increases the yield levels 30 percent above the lower fertilizer level, but the additional effect of the tied ridges is minimal, only 6.5 percent (fig. 6-8; M. Ahmed, 1994). This is unexpected, since a water retention technique is already used by many traditional producers. Small traditional producers use *teras*, a hand-constructed series of bunds built on three sides on the contour to prevent runoff.[11] This region (Sim Sim) is definitely semiarid, at a mean rainfall of 630 millimeters. However, the greater water-holding capacity of these heavy clay, cracking soils evidently makes the additional water-holding capacity of tied ridging insufficient to be profitable and therefore adopted by farmers. At higher absolute yield levels, as on the vertisols of the Texas high plains (Krishna et al., 1987) or at lower rainfall levels, the tied ridges may become a profitable activity. But for the moment on these vertisols the addition of nitrogen and new cultivars are the critical innovations and do not need to be combined with a water retention technique.

In summary, in the rain-fed vertisols, the introduction of a new variety alone increased yields 13 percent but was not a sustainable long-run strategy. When combined with moderate fertilization, the two practices doubled yields and maintained them at approximately 1.5 metric tons per hectare, according to the simulation model. Once soil fertility is improved, a new cultivar needs to be used, since new cultivars respond better to inorganic fertilizer than traditional land races, such as the Feterita sorghums.

## Conclusion

The introduction of Hageen Dura-1 is now accelerating in the Gezira. Problems of taste and milling differences have apparently been overcome. This narrowing of the price differential over time between the new and traditional cultivars may indicate that tastes are dynamic and respond to the higher yield potential (lower costs) of the new cultivar. Further research on the evolution of tastes in response to economic opportunities offered by a new cultivar is important to give plant breeders more flexibility in their development of new cultivars.

In the Gezira there was a tradition of using inorganic fertilizer on cotton and wheat. There were organized channels for obtaining fertilizer and seeds. It was not difficult for Gezira farmers to convince irrigation-scheme officials that they wanted hybrid seeds and inorganic fertilizer for their own crop, sorghum. When water availability is assured, as in these irrigation schemes, there is a larger response and less risk from fertilization than in the dryland regions. Farmers in the Gezira adopted HD-1 with low levels of inorganic fertilizer and then increased fertilization over time (M. Ahmed and Sanders, 1992). Without fertilizer, even with assured water in the Gezira, there was no advantage to HD-1, according to the farmer interviews. The Gezira had all these favorable conditions of a substantial, stable response to inorganic fertilizer and a history of access to this input. The economic returns to the investment in research on HD-1 have been high for the Gezira.

In contrast, in the mechanized rain-fed zone, fertilization is more difficult because access to this input is lacking. Farmers in the mechanized rain-fed zone do not presently use fertilizer. The simulation results indicate the need to introduce inorganic fertilizer along with a new sorghum cultivar in the mechanized vertisols. Inorganic fertilizer is presently a key component to make the sorghum systems in the mechanized rain-fed region more profitable and sustainable. Without inorganic fertilizer here, the introduction of a new cultivar is not sustainable, because yields decline with continuing cultivation as farmers mine the soil.

So in the Gezira region, where farmers were willing and able to use inorganic fertilizer, there was adoption of HD-1. Where farmers did not use inorganic fertilizers, the mechanized rain-fed zone, adoption of HD-1 quickly ceased after the price collapse of 1985–86. To obtain a profitable and sustainable yield advantage from this new cultivar, fertilization was required in both zones. Sudan needs to put a high priority on making more inorganic fertilizer and improved cultivars available to farmers on both the rain-fed and irrigated regions. For both, the functioning of the fertilizer and seed input markets appears to be a critical factor in accelerating technology introduction.

Tied ridges were not sufficiently profitable for farmers to introduce them on these heavy vertisols in the semiarid zone of the Sudan. There is a yield effect from the tied ridges. However, in contrast to the vertisols on the Texas high plains, the yields in Sudan are still too low to pay for the additional costs of the ridging, including knocking them down in heavy rainfall years to avoid problems of excess water (Gerard, 1985; Krishna et al., 1987). As yields on the vertisols are further increased with higher fertilization levels and continued introduction of new cultivars, the tied ridges are expected to become profitable and to be adopted as they are in Texas. Meanwhile, these soils of heavy clay with cracking characteristics have water retention advantages over the crusting ferruginous soils and the sandy dune soils predominant in West Africa (see fig. I-3).

Comparison of chapters 4 to 6 indicates the need to make rainfall-regime and soil-specific adjustments to the strategy of identifying technologies to respond to the water availability and soil fertility constraints in the dry savanna. Other region-specific adjustments, including the expected profitability and riskiness of agriculture in different sites, are also expected to be important in defining the appropriate technologies to introduce.

# III

# Critical Research and Planning Issues for Technology Development

# 7

# Risk and Intensive
Technology Introduction

I N PREVIOUS CHAPTERS, farmers have been shown to adopt new intensive, yield-increasing technologies when there was adequate rainfall (chapter 3), when they used water retention devices (chapter 4), when moderate
fertilization and higher densities increased water use efficiency (chapter 5),
and when irrigation was available (chapter 6). Once water availability was
assured, many farmers used soil fertility improvements generally involving
higher input purchases.[1] Is risk a critical constraint to higher input purchases?
We focus on that question in this chapter.

In semiarid regions, farmers are, on the average, strongly averse to risk
(Dillon and Scandizzo, 1978; Binswanger, 1980; Hamal and Anderson, 1982;
Anderson and Dillon, 1992; Anderson, Dillon, and Hardaker, 1977, 1986).
They often have few farm resources or ready access to credit. Their environment is also unpredictable. Yields vary substantially with the low and highly
variable rainfall. Insect and disease pests also can substantially affect yields.
Prices fluctuate with the large weather-related changes in supply and the inelastic demand. Fortunately, prices often move in the opposite direction to
yields, thereby reducing income variability.

## Farm Household Mechanisms for Reducing Risk
## in Semiarid Regions

Farmers use several insurance mechanisms to reduce their exposure to risk,
including diversification, networking, and migration. Crops have different
capabilities to respond to drought, soil-fertility stress, and position on the
toposequence (Vierich and Stoop, 1990). A crop mix will spread labor operations over the crop season. Diversification responds to both variations in soil
quality and seasonal labor constraints. Diversification is also a standard portfolio strategy to reduce risk exposure by farmers holding different assets.

Besides intercropping, farmers in semiarid regions plant several varieties with different maturity periods. These mixtures of cultivars and crops reduce the impact of stresses from insects, diseases, and climatic variation (Lynam and Blackie, 1994, p. 112). There is a trade-off or cost of greater risk reduction, leading to less yield potential, under favorable conditions. For example, a shorter-season cultivar can provide drought escape, whereas with "normal," better weather a longer-season cultivar has the potential to respond to additional time in the field.

Farmers in West Africa develop complicated networks of friends and relatives. They exchange labor, gifts, and favors. Much household effort is put into maintaining these networks. In emergencies they can then call on these contacts. But they also have reciprocal responsibilities when harvests are good. These obligations to share increases in income with relatives and others can reduce the incentives to use new technologies. Unfortunately, these contacts will not be sufficient if there is a widespread drought or a price collapse over the region (Binswanger and McIntire, 1987; Bromley and Chavas, 1989). During droughts, governments and donors often intervene with food aid. With good production conditions and the resulting price collapses of the staple foods, in most countries in Sub-Saharan Africa there has been insufficient public will or revenue to support the prices.[2] Yet, these price collapses, by reducing expected incomes and increasing income variability, can be a principal disincentive to adopting new technologies (chapter 4).

In large families, one way of reducing agricultural risk is for family members to migrate to nonfarm work. An estimated 25 percent of the potential labor force in Burkina Faso in the late seventies worked outside the country (Zachariah and Conde, 1981). Such nonfarm work serves as a hedge against agricultural risk, including a generalized drought or agricultural price collapse. Nonfarm earnings have been shown to be a significant component of income in both Burkina and Niger (Reardon, Delgado, and Matlon, 1992; Painter, 1986, 1987). Even in the more prosperous agricultural regions, as in southwest Burkina Faso, off-farm labor was an important income source. In this region half the income and three-fourths of the cash for average households come from nonfarm sources (Savadogo, Reardon, and Pietola, 1994, p. 2). This income then enables farm investment and provides additional income security.

There are many techniques for hedging risk; the apparently more effective techniques, the networks and off-farm family labor, do not involve adjustments in crop decisions. Rather, the primary techniques are adjustments in family decisions to maintain kinship networks for family members to obtain off-farm work.

## Farm-Level Risk and Modeling

Risk aversion is one hypothesis sometimes advanced to explain why farmers may be hesitant to adopt technologies requiring input expenditures. To evaluate this hypothesis, we have to take into account the various sources of risk and how farmers respond.

Most real decision making involves distributions of critical variables and outcomes. The cases of production relationships, prices, and costs having one value, known with certainty—as in the basic production economics theory—do not occur in real-world decisions. Engineering processes may have almost certain outcomes, but agricultural processes do not. Nor do most economic phenomena occur with certainty, even with governmental intervention. In more risky agricultural environments, as in much of Sub-Saharan Africa with low and erratic rainfall, low fertility, and fragile soils, variation in yields can be very large. On the product-price side, governmental efforts to stabilize variations are often unsuccessful for principal crops in poorer developing countries.

Farmers not explicitly incorporating probability distributions in their expectations often make partial efforts to incorporate them. In research, budgeting analysis is extended to sensitivity analysis of key parameters. Linear programming is adjusted to expected values rather than using the single-period observations collected. In both cases, some knowledge of the distribution is incorporated, either in the range of the sensitivity analysis or in the adjustment of the observed to expected values. With simulation, more complete yield distributions can be generated for the analysis.

Much intellectual energy in the risk literature has gone into measuring risk aversion and into adjusting for farmers' risk aversion.[3] The degree of risk aversion is frequently hypothesized to be an important negative factor discouraging technology adoption. Farmers may not be very risk averse but may be pessimistic about the distribution of profits from a new activity. Thus, their perceptions of the riskiness of a new activity may be a more important factor than their aversion to risk in the adoption decision (Goodwin, Sanders, and de Hollanda, 1980).

Farmers in developing countries frequently respond to climatic events by modifying their production practices. Some farmers in Niger use nitrogen fertilizer as side-dressing after the planting period. When rainfall is low or nonexistent, they desist from fertilization. This response to the observed weather allows for adaptation of practices to climatic factors. Other examples of sequential response to risk have been observed in high-risk environments.

In summary, five components of risk analysis are considered here:

- variability of yields, prices, and costs
- farmers' aversion to risk
- farmers' perception of risk
- farmers' use of insurance techniques, such as producing and storing sufficient cereals for their subsistence needs during the year or sending relatives off to work elsewhere
- farmers' responses to weather and price information during the crop season or production cycle

Our principal interest here is the impact of risk aversion on farmers' production decisions. The first requirement in risk modeling is to generate the distributions of the risky variables. The most reliable type of information is multiyear farm data and experiments, where there is sufficient climatic information to generate probability estimates for different types of year.[4] In applied work with agricultural scientists, there is a fear of economists' black boxes. Using scanty data in a rigorous, clear fashion may be more convincing to agricultural scientists than the more sophisticated techniques for distribution generation with scanty data. In the modeling, the principal emphasis was on collecting data on the basic production and economic variables over time. The yields, prices, and costs for present and new technologies were estimated based on the available field data, farmer interviews, and secondary data. These were supplemented with experimental data and expert estimates for new technologies.

Risk-aversion coefficients were not elicited from farmers, but risk aversion was included in the sensitivity analysis. Finally, discrete stochastic programming (DSP) was utilized in most of the studies to enable the decision maker to react during the production period by altering his choices in response to some stochastic events (Cocks, 1968; Rae, 1971a, 1971b). This sequential decision making enables choices to be made in response to the risky events as they unfold during the period studied. In the two Sudan cases below there was no observed farmer adaptive response to climatic events, so DSP was not used.

## The Impacts of Risk Aversion on Technology Choices and Farmers' Incomes: Some Field Results and Implications

For small-scale farmers in two regions of Niger and large-scale farmers in two regions of the Sudan, the crop technology decision was modeled with variations in the risk-aversion coefficient. Despite these large modifications in risk aversion, there was little impact on farmer choices in three of the four cases (table 7-1). Similar results of only small effects on technology choices from substantial variations in risk aversion were also found for modeling of farmer decisions in Portugal (Serrão, 1988) and Honduras (Lopez-Pereira, 1990).

These were surprising results, since in much of the literature there is an expectation that risk aversion will play an important role in technology choice for farmers in semiarid regions (Anderson and Dillon, 1992, and the references cited there).[5] We have three hypotheses to explain these results:

- Incorporation of a subsistence goal and an adaptive ability to modify decisions in response to the climatic variables in the models enables the farmer to adequately respond to risk.
- Combined technologies reduce the riskiness of farm activities or increase risk very little with a substantial gain in profitability.
- Farmers may be less influenced by risk aversion than by their inability to predict the outcomes of new activities.

Risk aversion and subsistence goals may be impossible to separate. Small-scale farmers would be expected to be primarily motivated by the need to assure adequate family food consumption and therefore to have target minimum income and consumption goals. Small farmers in the Sahelian countries clearly state that cereal subsistence goals are their primary concern in agricultural decisions. These goals are included first in the modeling for small farmers. When sequential decision making was observed in the field, this was also incorporated into the modeling. Some of the risk-aversion and risk-response strategies were thus already incorporated.

Closer examination of these technologies shows that in several cases risk is reduced by various new technology components. New short-season cultivars of millet and cowpeas are better able to respond in dry years to the cessation of rainfall in September. This early cutoff of the rainfall has been a chronic problem from the 1968–73 drought to the present. When combined with moderate levels of inorganic fertilizer, the new cultivar technology sub-

Table 7-1. Farm Characteristics, Programming Models, and Impacts of Risk Aversion in the Farm Models Evaluating New Technology Introduction

| Region | Farm Characteristics | Subsistence Cereal Production | Programming Type | Impacts of Risk Aversion on Technology Introduction and Income Increase |
|---|---|---|---|---|
| 1. South Central Niger (Maradi region) | Small: 2 to 4 ha | 800 kg cereals annually for household equivalent of 3 adults | DSP | Modest[a] |
| 2. Western Niger (Niamey region) | Small: 2 sites: partial irrigated system with 0.4 ha irrigated and 3.9 ha dryland; dryland only, 8.8 to 13.5 ha cultivated | 730 kg cereals per household of 8.6 adult (male equivalent) in the dryland | DSP | Modest[a] |
| 3. East central Sudan (Gedaref vertisols) | Large: 630 ha state grant; 151 ha rented from other farmers | None[b] | Target: semivariance | Small. As the relative risk aversion coefficient was increased, farm income declined only 1.3%. Similarly, changes in target income goals had only minor effects on farm income. |
| 4. East central Sudan (Sim Sim vertisols) | Large: 420 ha state grant; 295 ha rented from other farmers | None | MOTAD[c] | Moderate. At higher risk aversion levels, the land area rented decreased substantially. Farm income fell 30%. |

*Source:* (1) Adesina and Sanders (1991); Adesina (1988); (2) Shapiro (1990); (3) Habash (1990); (4) M. Ahmed (1990).
[a] Includes risk aversion in the initial modeling. Substantial variations in risk aversion had little effect.
[b] The hired workers were paid in sorghum. Moreover, there were different targeted income goals to repay the credit.
[c] MOTAD is defined as the minimization of total absolute deviation. The standard deviation was estimated from the absolute deviation with the standard formula.

stantially increased cash and total income and reduced the coefficients of variation (CVs) in Maradi, Niger (Adesina, 1988; table 7-2).

In Niamey, Niger, in one site, inorganic phosphorus fertilizer combined with a new cultivar and at a higher density increased the CV only slightly, while substantially increasing farm income. In the other site, with lower rainfall, farmers adopted only the new cultivars and no inorganic fertilizer. This change reduced the CV. Researchers were successful in producing technologies that either increased risks only moderately for large income gains or reduced risk (table 7-3).

In the Sudan, the new rotations with or without the water conservation device had minimal effects on income but also reduced the CVs. In contrast, fertilization alone of sorghum and sesame increased incomes 25 percent and 19 percent respectively and increased CVs slightly in the two studies (table 7-1; Habash, 1990, p. 69; M. Ahmed, 1990, p. 77). In Sudan the new technologies also generally reduced risks or increased risks only slightly. Part of the selection criteria by researchers for new technologies in semiarid environments is for yield stability. Improving the yield response for adverse rainfall regimes raises mean yields.[6]

In summary, one principal factor to explain the lack of impact of risk aversion on technology adoption and incomes was that the new technologies increased risks only slightly or actually reduced risks. Hence, they were an easy choice for all decision makers, from those indifferent to risk to those

Table 7-2. Expected Income and Risk of Traditional and New Technologies at Maradi, Niger

| Income | Traditional Technologies | Improved Cultivars and Agronomy |
|---|---|---|
| Expected cash income ($/farm) | 92.00 | 116.00 |
| CV of cash income (%) | 72 | 69 |
| Expected total income ($/farm) | 156.00 | 195.00 |
| CV of total income (%) | 52 | 42 |

*Source:* Adesina (1988, pp. 71, 86).
*Note:* The new technology included moderate fertilization (fifty kilograms per hectare of urea and fifty kilograms per hectare of simple superphosphate), a new millet cultivar, and higher density. The total income estimate included the value of home consumption of agricultural production (Adesina, 1988, pp. 34, 37). Exchange rate is CFA298/US$.

Table 7-3. Expected Income and Risk of Traditional and New Technologies at Libore and Kouka, Niamey Region, Niger

| Region | Income | Traditional Dryland Crop Technologies | Improved Dryland Crop Technologies | Technologies Introduced |
|---|---|---|---|---|
| Libore | Expected crop income ($/farm) | 446 | 628 | Improved shorter-cycle cultivars of millet and cowpeas[a] with phosphorus fertilizer |
| | CV of cash income (%) | 52 | 56 | |
| Kouka | Expected crop income ($/farm) | 301 | 409 | Improved shorter-cycle cultivars of millet and cowpeas[a] without fertilizer |
| | CV of crop income (%) | 49 | 39 | |

*Source:* Calculated from Shapiro (1990, pp. 92, 98, 125).
*Note:* Exchange rate is CFA298/US$.
[a] The improved cowpeas were planted at four times the density of traditional varieties.

more strongly averse. One initial selection emphasis of technology development in semiarid agriculture at low incomes is for income-stabilizing technologies.

In semiarid systems in which the fallow rotation is breaking down, the main constraint to increasing yields is to find alternatives to increase soil fertility. These alternatives generally involve increased input expenditures and can increase risk moderately due to the variability of their response under different climatic conditions. By providing some additional measures to reduce the downside risk, such as by assuring more water under adverse conditions or introducing shorter-season cultivars, the total risk of the combined technologies was reduced. Thus, the first round of intensive technology improvements are already responding to the farmers' requirements to raise incomes without large increases in risk.

## Conclusion

Risk aversion had a minimal impact on intensive technology introduction in the modeling cases analyzed. We believe that the principal explanation is the low risk levels of the technologies introduced in these regions. However, we were not able to test for differences in the three hypotheses raised, and all three factors were undoubtedly important. One of the components of the first stage of technology selection for low-income, high-risk agriculture was to improve yields in the adverse climatic states. The new technologies generally included moderate increases in inorganic fertilization, and they all had measures to increase yields in adverse seasons either through earlier cultivars or improved use of available water. These combined technologies do not imply much higher risk levels. Rather, they either reduced the coefficients of variation or increased them moderately while increasing incomes.

Introducing this first stage of new technologies into semiarid agricultural systems implies only small income gains but, nevertheless, welfare improvements for these farmers. The principal point is that for the first round of technology introduction, the observations of farmer adoption (chapters 4 and 6) and the review of model results in this chapter indicate that risk aversion will not be a barrier to new technology introduction.

Once the first round of risk-reducing technologies are adopted by farmers in these semiarid agricultural systems, the next round of new technologies would imply even higher levels of purchased inputs and higher risks as inorganic fertilization is increased. Hence, the risk-aversion characteristics of the farmers could become more important in the second stage of technology introduction. However, with the increased wealth generated from the first round of technology introduction, risk aversion levels are expected to decline, according to risk theory.

An important factor to explain slower adoption rates on farmers' fields than in the modeling is that farmers may poorly perceive the distribution of risky outcomes from new technology introduction. Farmers' tendencies to be pessimistic about possible yield gains until they have more information may be more important than risk aversion as an impediment to higher diffusion rates. This risk-perception factor needs to be included in future fieldwork and modeling. The expected importance of this poor-perception factor also apparently indicates the potential returns to public support of on-farm demonstrations of the new technologies and other extension activities.

# 8

# Sustainability, New Intensive Technologies, and Land Market Evolution in West Africa

**O**NE OF THE main attacks on new technology introduction in the eighties and nineties has been on the soil degradation and water pollution resulting from intensive agricultural production systems. In developed countries, an antichemical input orientation has frequently been an integral part of environmental movements. One principal problem of using high levels of chemicals is the effect of chemical by-products on water downstream or underground and on the ecosystem in general. Increasing scientific knowledge in developed countries has made us more aware of the adverse consequences of this pollution.

In contrast with the high levels of chemicals in developed countries, natural and man-made causes have increased degradation and destruction of the environmental systems and natural resource base in Sub-Saharan Africa. Soil fertility is low before cropping and is mined as the fallow system breaks down. The traditional long-term fertility maintenance system of fallow rotation is not being replaced with purchased inputs in most of semiarid Sub-Saharan Africa; purchased input use on most food crops is minimal with some significant exceptions. Nevertheless, even without chemical (or industrial) inputs, soils are being eroded, forests eliminated, and grasslands overgrazed, thereby threatening long-term sustainable agriculture.

In Africa, according to the latest Global Assessment of Soil Degradation funded by the United Nations Environmental Program, 14 percent of the cropland excluding unused wasteland has been at least moderately degraded (Oldeman, Hakkelin, and Sombroek, 1991, pp. 28–29). There is a substantial range in the degradation, but for water erosion, 45 percent was in their serious problem category. The damage is concentrated in the semiarid regions, and one principal causative factor is overgrazing (Oldeman, 1994, pp. 99, 108,

109, 113). The reduction of available land and the extension of farmers and herders into marginal land areas has accelerated the land degradation.

As the resource base deteriorates, the ability of Sub-Saharan countries to feed themselves is reduced. Meanwhile, there is already substantial malnutrition in Sub-Saharan Africa. The continuing rapid population growth and renewed economic growth will result in large increases in the domestic demand for food. Hence, important aspects of the sustainability debate in Sub-Saharan Africa are first expanding food supplies to keep up with population and income growth and then improving the quality of human life of the poor through adequate nutrition (von Braun and Webb, 1989; von Braun, 1991; Webb, Bisrat, and Coppock, 1991). Given the large number of households dependent on farming and thus on the natural resources of water and land, there is an urgent need for policymakers and researchers to focus on the adoption of sustainable agricultural technologies.

## Sustainable Agriculture and Societies

The sustainability movement has had a wide range of concerns, including soil erosion, effects of agrochemicals on the environment, tropical deforestation, loss of genetic diversity in crop species, and implications of global warming (Lynam and Herdt, 1989, p. 382; also see Cheru, 1992). We are directly concerned here with soil degradation and agrochemicals. Indirectly, the introduction of technological change in the semiarid and subhumid zones could reduce the pressures to develop the humid zone and the more marginal agricultural regions, thereby slowing deforestation in humid zones and reducing settlement in the more fragile agricultural regions.

The sustainability focus on natural resources becomes more difficult in low-income countries, where many of the country's inhabitants are not receiving minimum nutritional levels or other basic requirements. From a societal perspective, a country's residents must be adequately fed and provided with other basic social services to fulfill their potential as human beings (Drèze and Sen, 1989; Chopra and Rao, 1991). Sustainable societies provide these basic social services for their populations. The sustainability concept in Sub-Saharan Africa has to include a much more rapid rate of agricultural output growth than the historical growth while being concerned with the future productivity of land and water resources.

Sustainable agriculture is defined in this chapter as the successful management of resources for agriculture to satisfy changing human needs.[1] With this criteria, an acute failure of sustainable agriculture is indicated by famine and a chronic failure by malnutrition. Both famine and malnutrition are common in Sub-Saharan Africa; hence, these pressing problems require that rapidly increasing food output growth be a fundamental component of any strategy for sustainable agriculture.[2] If the present generation also puts a high value on maintaining the resource base for future generations, another requirement of sustainable agriculture is to maintain or enhance the quality of the available resources.[3] If sustainable agriculture stabilizes output along an increasing trend while maintaining a balance in environmental resources, economists can obtain help from agricultural and biological scientists about the appropriate constraints and estimate the trade-offs in costs and benefits of various levels of environmental constraints.

The conceptual difficulty comes with a more limiting form of sustainable development as a minimization of the use of natural resources. This view implies that exceeding some critical level of natural resource exploitation could lead to an irreversible catastrophe. Thus, resource utilization needs to be minimized until this danger is understood, causal relations are identified, and resource use can be adjusted so as to avoid the catastrophe. This concept of sustainable development emphasizes the limits of the assimilative capacity of the environment and the incapacity of technology both to enhance human welfare and to rectify environmental damage resulting from technological change (Mellor, 1988; Batie, 1989, pp. 1084, 1085; also Lynam and Herdt, 1989, pp. 385, 386). If the damages of the irreversibility are being overstated, the environmentalists could make agricultural development more difficult by imposing more restrictions than are necessary. Due to the lack of agreement on whether these disasters will occur or are irreversible, the debate between economists and ecologists often breaks down.

## Agricultural Technology Development: Beyond the Boserup Effect

A few decades ago, Ester Boserup challenged the classical Malthusian perspective of population increasing faster than food production and leading to disaster, arguing that as a result of increasing population pressure, a traditional agrarian community moves from slash-and-burn fallow to a bush-fallow, to annual cropping, and finally to multiple cropping.[4] Each sequence represents a growing intensification of the farming system. Technological change comes as a response to adversity, which in the Boserup scenario results from increasing population pressure (Boserup, 1965). Several attempts have been made to formalize and test the Boserup hypothesis (Stryker, 1976; Darity, 1980; Pryor and Maurer, 1982; Robinson and Schutjer, 1984; Bilsborrow, 1987; Binswanger and McIntire, 1987).

In the Sahel, Boserup's hypothesis is relevant in explaining the historical evolution of farming systems. Initially, settlement took place on the lighter soils, since these soils were easier to work and land was abundant relative to labor. Population pressure then began to push farmers on to the higher quality, heavier soils. Frequently, animal traction was necessary on the low-lying, heavy soils to facilitate preparation and to extend the cultivated area (Pingali, Bigot, and Binswanger, 1987; Jaeger and Matlon, 1990).

However, as population density has continued to increase, negative consequences have occurred, including overexploitation and degradation of the natural resource base of agriculture (Broekhuyse and Allen, 1988). The problem is exacerbated in low-productivity, high-risk environments such as the Sahel, for not only is nature's biomass diversity low, but recovery speed of once damaged land and vegetative resources is slow (Gorse and Steeds, 1987). By the early eighties in some regions of the Sahel, population densities had reached high levels (around forty-eight persons per square kilometer in the Central Plateau of Burkina Faso).[5] Here, substantial water erosion, crusting, and soil fertility mining have taken place on soils that have been characterized as low in fertility and fragile before the degradation process (Matlon, 1987). Crop yields have reached low-level equilibriums, declining by a third to a half of those levels of an earlier period with an adequate fallow system (Broekhuyse and Allen, 1988). Extensification by animal traction has pushed cultivation into even more marginal land, further decreasing yields (Vierich and Stoop, 1990, p. 123).

Without inorganic fertilizers, soil fertility will not be replenished once the fallow system breaks down. Even with the addition of more animals, the amount of manure and compost produced on the farm in the traditional or even extensive technology system with animal traction will not be sufficient to replace the major nutrients mined from the soil by crop production (Nagy, Sanders, and Ohm, 1988).[6] Thus, there will be a long-run yield decline and eventually land abandonment unless more-intensive technologies, including inorganic fertilizers, are introduced. Alternative techniques can supplement but not replace the inorganic fertilizer. "Although the amount of fertilizers required can be reduced by incorporating appropriate legumes in rotation or adding organic materials, chemical fertilizers cannot be completely dispensed with for commercial farming." (Lal, 1987, p. 1075)

Intensive or yield-increasing technological change is necessary to reverse the land degradation and to increase crop yields. We have discussed the process of the introduction of these intensive technologies in chapters 3 to 6. In regions with adequate rainfall or irrigation, the process of technological change has been rapid. We have pointed out the need for a combined series of new technology components to be simultaneously introduced in the semiarid regions along with governmental policy changes to support the introduction of these technologies. Historically, policymakers have been more concerned with keeping food prices low in urban areas than with increasing the profitability of agricultural production (Bates, 1981). Food imports have been increasing into most Sub-Saharan countries. In these circumstances, the Boserup scenario of population pressure automatically leading to more intensive agricultural systems has not been occurring in the semiarid regions, due to the low profitability of agriculture (see chapter 4 for empirical support).

## Sustainability Problems: Design and Implementation of Appropriate Technologies and Policies across Agroecological Zones

These intensive technologies of water retention and fertilizers maintain yields and soil quality. Hence at higher population densities, this system with higher inorganic inputs is more sustainable than the traditional systems. The long-run effects of high levels of agricultural chemicals are an increasing environmental hazard in developed countries. However, at extremely low levels of purchased inorganic inputs, as in the case of most of semiarid Sub-Saharan African agriculture, these inorganic inputs are expected to be necessary complements to the organic and other methods of increasing yields, such as manure, residual incorporation, or cereal-legume rotations. It is necessary to distinguish between inorganic fertilizers, which are principally made of elements already in the soil, and the more dangerous pesticides and herbicides. Until we know more about long-term effects, a much stronger case can be made for slowing the introduction of pesticides and herbicides than can be made for doing this with inorganic fertilizers. For many developing countries, the immediate problems of increasing food production often are so urgent that there will be pressures to use any chemical means to increase food production.

The pollution problem of agrochemical uses is often treated as a market failure. When polluters must pay for additional costs they impose upon society, the natural functioning of a market economy can be extended, by governmental action, to tax polluters (Lynam and Herdt, 1989, p. 388). As developed countries identify new institutions to create these markets and force polluters to pay these costs, developing countries would be expected to adopt these institutional innovations with a time lag. This time lag reflects the lower social priority expected to be given to pollution control in low-income societies.

In table 8-1 some of the predominant soil and pest problems in the Sahel

Table 8-1. Some Specific Sustainability Problems in the Major Agroclimatic Zones in Semiarid West Africa

| Zone | Rainfall[a] | Population Density | Crop Technology Development Potential | Soil Sustainability Problems | Some Principal Pest Problems |
|------|---------|------------|-----------------|-----------------|----------------|
| Sudano-Guinean | 800–1,100 | Moderate; high human and animal disease risks | High | Declining organic matter | High levels of pesticides on cotton, storage insects, Striga. |
| Sudanian | 600–800 | High | Moderate | Water and wind erosion, soil-crusting, low organic matter, low soil fertility | Headbugs and stemborer in sorghum and cowpeas (see below), Striga. |
| Sahelo-Sudanian | 350–600 | High in southern section, but declining farther north | Lower than Sudanian for sorghum system; low for millet-cowpea system | Water and wind erosion; low soil fertility and organic matter; poor water and nutrient retention in sandy, dune soil. | Headgirdler and stemborer on millet; thrips and maruca on cowpeas in field and bruchids in storage; Striga |

*Source:* Gorse and Steeds (1987, p. 2); Sanders (1989); Posner and Gilbert (1991). For pest problems in the Sudanian and Sahelo-Sudanian zones, Don Paschke, Professor of Entomology at Purdue, provided useful inputs from his fieldwork in the Sahel.
*Note:* The other agroclimatic zone in semiarid West Africa is the Sahel, with less than 350 mm of rainfall (90% probability). This region was not included, as rainfall is too low for crop production, except in oases or with irrigation.
[a] In millimeters, 90 percent probability.

region are identified. The scientific knowledge and management skills are presently available for handling soil fertility, crusting, and some of the erosion. The technology includes purchased inorganic fertilizers and improved water-retention techniques. However, increasing use of inorganic fertilizers will not resolve the problem of declining organic matter. In considering soil specific characteristics, we have focused on the first two of the following five characteristics noted by Crosson and Anderson (1994): nutrient content, water-holding capacity, organic-matter content, acidity, and topsoil depth. Clearly, it is appropriate to dedicate more research attention to organic-matter content as farmers become more successful at overcoming constraints from the deficiencies in nutrient content and water-holding capacity.

Management changes and biological controls are required for some of the pest problems. Adaptive research will be necessary for economically viable, integrated systems of soil fertility and pest management.[7] This research would be aimed at reducing but not eliminating the requirements for chemical input use (pesticides) through the development of improved crop systems and better farmer management. (For details, see Lal, 1991, and Edwards, Thurston, and Janke, 1991.)

## Sustainability Issues in Moderate-Input Regions

In the regions we consider in this book, the most rapid technological change in agriculture has occurred in the highest-rainfall region, the Sudano-Guinean zone. This also appears to be the region with the greatest future potential for continuing output increases (chapters 3 and 10). Crop yields are still low by international standards. Moreover, the population densities are lower here than in the other two regions, the Sudanian and the Sahelo-Sudanian zones. Areas of higher rainfall have greater potential for output increases, but these areas have been associated with higher human and animal disease risks (see chapter 10). Rapid human and animal migration into these regions is now occurring (Bourn and Wint, 1984, pp. 12–14; see also chapter 3).

In the Sudano-Guinean zone, inorganic fertilizer use is moderately high on cotton and maize, and there is an indirect impact from fertilization on sorghum through crop rotation. In this zone there is a complicated technical problem of reversing the decline of organic matter on farms where plant residues are grazed, harvested for building materials, or burned. Inorganic fertilizer does not help build up the level of organic matter and can aggravate its decline. In some regions, such as southern Mali, there is increasing use of organic fertilizers (chapter 3). Introduction of a legume into the rotation, incorporation of plant residues, and other measures to raise organic matter have been introduced into the research agenda for the Sudano-Guinean regions.

As the yield gaps between developed countries and the moderate-input systems in Sub-Saharan Africa are reduced, implementing systems of maintenance research to respond to emerging problems will become increasingly important (Plucknett, 1990). The closing of the yield gap between this region and developed countries is probably a decade away, but the national agricultural research systems in Sub-Saharan Africa presently need to be creating the scientific manpower and institutions to respond to new problems experienced over this decade and beyond. Agriculture takes place in a biotic system undergoing continuous change from natural and man-made factors.

## Sustainability in the Low-Input Regions

In the Sudanian and Sahelo-Sudanian zones, the principal economic and sustainability problem is to increase crop yields. Intensive technologies increase yields but require moderate levels of inorganic fertilizers (see chapter 4 and 5). In Sub-Saharan Africa, foreign exchange shortages can be a constraint to increasing fertilization levels. Policymakers can be deluded by the illusive prospect of a local solution not requiring imports or farmer expenditures. Manure, rotations, local rock phosphate, nitrogen fixation with a cereal-legume rotation, and other alternatives have been suggested. Field-testing and economic analysis have indicated that these alternatives are either not available in sufficient supply (such as manure and crop residues), do not have the expected technical impacts, or are not profitable (such as local rock phosphate) (Nagy, Sanders, and Ohm, 1988). Nevertheless, it continues to be important to do basic and adaptive research on these soils and on the multiple alternatives to reduce fertilizer costs and to modify the technical and economic constraints impeding the profitable use of various soil amendment techniques.

Low organic matter and low soil nutrients are common problems in the Sudanian and Sahelo-Sudanian zones. Once crop yields are stabilized and increased, there will be more crop residues available for incorporation into the soil. Increased cereal production will enable a withdrawal from more marginal lands, where grazing can then be increased, supporting larger herd size, which produces more manure. As in the high-input regions, better rotations, including a grain legume in the rotation and incorporating more crop residues, can help resolve the organic-matter problem.

The sandy, dune soils in much of the Sahelo-Sudanian region support subsistence levels of millet and cowpeas. In some countries, such as Niger, these are important cropping systems for a major sector of the farm population. However, with scanty rainfall and low soil fertility, these production systems do not become sustainable without fertilizers. In some of these regions, even with feasible technical improvements and new policies, it still would not be profitable to adopt fertilizer (see chapter 5). Hence, in some of these areas, crop production needs to be replaced with trees and grazing, and crop researchers need to concentrate in other regions where there is more potential.

## Sustainable Agriculture and Indigenous Land Tenure Systems in the Sahel

In many regions of Sub-Saharan Africa and especially in the Sahel, there is an ongoing deterioration of the environment resulting from cultural practices, policies, and institutional arrangements evolved to support low population pressures, and shifting agricultural systems. Technological change can resolve some of these sustainability problems by increasing yields, maintaining soil quality, and reducing runoff and erosion.

Does the land tenure system of communal holdings impede the introduction of these new technologies? The system of land rights is a low-population-density system in which migrants from inside or outside the region or the lineage can obtain access to land. Historically, land use rights have been granted to all upon request made to the appropriate land use authority in the region. Land rights can be grouped into those concerned with use (cultivation, planting of trees, construction) and alienation (the right to sell or rent) (Feder and Noronha, 1987). The system of land rights in the Sahelian villages vests use rights at the level of the individual household and alienation rights at the level of the community or group (Matlon, 1991). While an individual may have rights to cultivate a particular plot, the land itself remains communal property, irrespective of the period of cultivation. In particular, the individual does not have the right to alienate such land from the community through sale or lease. The communal nature of property rights is derived from quasi-religious beliefs that serve to guarantee use rights for future generations. This land-use system minimizes violence over land and provides a safety valve for population pressures in other regions. However, at higher population pressures, the system discourages fallow, since failure to crop the land can lead to a loss of usage rights if there are other claimants. Moreover, those obtaining temporary use rights as outsiders are discouraged from making long-term investments in the land, as these investments can be considered as hostile attempts to take over the land (Southgate, Sanders, and Ehui, 1990).

If there were evidence that the indigenous land tenure systems were in fact constraining the adoption of new agricultural technologies, then there would be a need for large-scale, expensive land-titling arrangements. Yet, with few exceptions, land rights are not found to be a significant factor in determining investments in land improvements, use of inputs, access to credit, or the productivity of land (Matlon, 1991; Place and Hazell, 1993). There are many other factors besides tenure reform that affect returns to investment in agriculture, including infrastructure, rural health and education, and price incentives (Boserup, 1981; Pingali, Bigot, and Binswanger, 1987). Indigenous tenure regimes have been shown to be dynamic in nature, evolving in response to changes in the economic environment (Uchendu, 1970; Cohen, 1980; Noronha, 1985; Matlon, 1991). As population pressure and agricultural commercialization have proceeded in Sub-Saharan Africa, there has been a greater individualization of property rights, and a similar evolution is expected over time in other regions (Matlon, 1991; Migot-Adholla et al., 1991; Binswanger and Ruttan, 1978, pp. 327–57; Pingali, 1990, p. 249). It is easy to overrate the importance of land rights as a precondition for successful increase in agricultural output or technology introduction, since the landholding system is so different from Western tenure systems. However, the empirical evidence does not support this belief.

Figure 8-1 outlines two types of connections between population pressure, communal land systems, and agricultural technological change. The adverse impacts of population pressure can result in land degradation and ultimately depopulation. In other regions with more agricultural potential, the decreasing availability of land and increasing profitability of agriculture can act as inducements for farmers to adopt intensive technologies. Technological change is expected to create pressures for land rights systems to move toward individual ownership. This in turn will enable land to be increasingly used as collateral against credit. The credit enables farmers to invest more in land-improving investment, thus making the farming system more sustainable. The synergistic interaction between agricultural technological change and the evolution of traditional institutions is hypothesized to be a key element for making the production systems more sustainable by creating a profitable, dynamic environment for further long-term investments in land productivity.

Figure 8-1. Links between Population Pressure, Technological Change, and Institutional Change

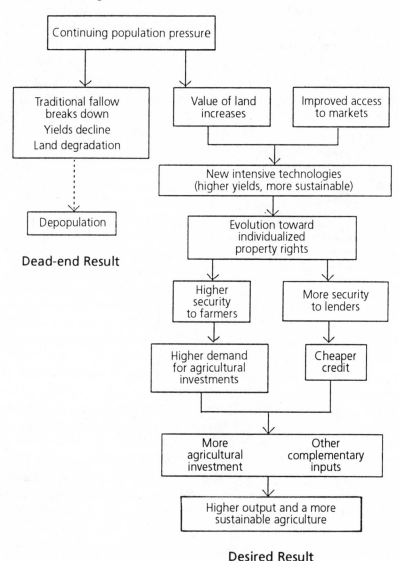

## Conclusion

In Sub-Saharan Africa, the most important goal of sustainability is the improvement of the quality of life of the population. This implies rapid growth in agricultural production. "Sustainable" then means reversing crop yield declines in some of the low-input systems and increasing yield gains in the moderate-input systems. Fortunately, the shift to more-intensive technologies also implies an improved management of natural resources (land and water) as compared with the extensive strategies often pursued in the low-input systems. The combination of technologies to improve soil fertility and to increase water retention has demonstrated the potential to produce higher outputs and to increase land productivity (chapters 3 to 6).

Some ecologists argue that high-input, industrial technologies, especially the use of inorganic fertilizers, will only temporarily create increased yields and will then lead to some combination of a long-run yield decline and increased farmer dependence on input purchases. We discuss the first claim in chapters 3 to 5. The field and experimental evidence are now increasingly convincing that long-run cereal yield declines from continuous cropping can result from failure to incorporate organic matter and from the lack of sufficient $K_2O$. Correction depends on further inorganic fertilization and finding more economically efficient ways of incorporating plant residues and manure. These potassium and organic-matter deficits are second-generation problems that can be corrected. The first-generation problem of low soil fertility is still most efficiently resolved by the rapid introduction of inorganic fertilizers (nitrogen and phosphorus) (again, see chapters 3 to 5). Moreover, higher input expenditures have consistently accompanied rapid agricultural output increases in developing and developed countries. With modeling, we have shown in chapters 4 to 6 that in these low-input systems, intensive agricultural technologies are profitable and enable the achievement of sustainable yield increases. With the disappearance of frontiers and especially with soil depletion, farmers need to use intensive technologies to increase the productivity of land.

Sustainable development priorities need to focus first on increasing purchases of inorganic fertilizers, rather than on some of the more complicated management concepts stressed in the ecology literature, such as nutrient cycles or integrated pest management (for a discussion of these two, see Lal, 1991; Edwards, Thurston, and Jauke, 1991). These labor-intensive, low-input systems attempt to substitute high management capabilities and large extension inputs for cash expenditures on inputs by farmers. Neither high management levels nor extension services can be assumed to be available or low cost in most of Sub-Saharan Africa. So the only meaning to the "low input" is reduced cash expenditures; it is necessary to put low implicit values on farmers' labor and management abilities, and on the extension services, to consider these alternative technologies as low-input systems (Lynam and Herdt, 1989, pp. 389, 390). New integrated management systems can ultimately build on moderate levels of industrial inputs, once the local adaptive research is done, extension capacity is increased, and farmers' abilities to manage sophisticated systems, such as pest monitoring, are improved.

In many countries the principal emphasis of technology development needs to be focused on the regions with better resource-bases (the Sudano-Guinean and Sudanian zones), since the returns to investment and research are expected to be higher in regions with more water availability and better soil fertility. For countries, such as Niger, with very little area in these two climatic zones, identification of research priorities for the highest potential regions in the Sahelo-Sudanian zone will be especially important, since research and other resources are limited. Technological change is not an efficient instrument for the attainment of all income distribution objectives within agriculture.

# 9

# Technological Change in Agriculture and the Welfare of Sahelian Women

I N THE SAHEL, the family farm area can be divided between family fields and privately cultivated fields. On the family fields, the household head has to mobilize labor and other resources to meet the household's subsistence needs. Once the family members have provided their labor on these family fields, they can work their own private fields. The private fields are allocated by the household head to the other adults in the household as partial payment for their labor on the commonly farmed fields. These are temporary-use rights, which the household head can revoke.[1] The family lands are generally the most fertile fields on the farm and the closest to the household. In contrast, the private fields are frequently located on poorer quality or marginal land and farther away. New technologies, such as fertilization of major cereals and cultivation of cash crops such as cotton, are adopted principally on the family fields.

Historically, women in the Sahel have played a significant role in food production. However, as new agricultural technologies are adopted, the men acquire them and the women work more on the family lands and less on their private land, where they had control of the output. The women are frequently unable to obtain the agricultural technologies embodied in new inputs and crops. Hence, researchers have hypothesized that the introduction of agricultural technology may have little or even negative impact on the economic status of women. To remedy this, development projects and other institutions are advised to provide women with access to inputs, credit, and female-specific extension services (see Boserup, 1970; Davison, 1988, pp. 1–32; Gladwin and McMillan, 1989; Kumar, 1987, pp. 135–47; Tinker, 1990; Due and Gladwin, 1991.)

## Tasks, Technology, and Gender Division of Labor

Citing data from the thirties, Ester Boserup reported that African women performed 60 to 80 percent of the agricultural labor.[2] Traditionally, women specialized in food crops, while in different periods and regions men hunted, went off to work in mines or on plantations, or specialized in export crops promoted by the government. Some recent studies show that there is an increasing male dominance of agricultural activities, including food production. A detailed field study in Gambia documented that males provided one-half to two-thirds of the agricultural labor supply (von Braun and Webb, 1989).

Due to the combination of agricultural labor and household chores, rural women work much longer hours than rural men or urban women (Buvinic and Mehra, 1990, pp. 290–308). For additional activities, women must reduce their private-plot participation, because their household chores make fairly inflexible demands on their time. The most basic household tasks of bringing water, gathering firewood, caring for children, and processing and preparing food are time-intensive. These routine activities have been estimated to employ one-half of a normal eight- to ten-hour day (Buvinic and Mehra, 1990, p. 294).[3]

There are many regional and ethnic differences, but there is usually some task division by gender. Men are primarily responsible for land clearing. Seeding and weeding activities are undertaken by the owner or operator of the land. Postharvest operations, especially processing and marketing, and livestock care are generally activities concentrated among women.[4] The predominance of women in the difficult, menial tasks of weeding, harvesting, and food processing give them a full schedule of agricultural activities.

As agricultural activities become more lucrative and less menial, men systematically replace women in agriculture. Animal traction operations to prepare the soil or to cultivate it are male activities. The introduction of cash crops in the colonial period was almost exclusively performed by men. Similarly, yield-increasing technologies have been principally associated with an increasing male dominance of agricultural activities (Gladwin and McMillan, 1989, pp. 350–56; Buvinic and Mehra, 1990, 290–91).

The predominance of women is noted on small farms with primarily manual inputs aimed at production for subsistence consumption. The lack of access or failure to use purchased inputs results in female activities being labor-intensive and paying low returns (Buvinic and Mehra, 1990, p. 292; von Braun and Webb, 1989, p. 525). Male predominance in production activities increases as production shifts to larger farms, as more animal traction is used and more cash crops are produced.

In farming systems with much higher labor demands, such as expanded crop areas with animal traction or irrigation, the demand for labor is substantially increased. For example, the use of animal traction is a male activity that reduces labor requirements per hectare, but it also enables crop area expansion by overcoming the seasonal labor cultivation constraint. Thus, there can be an increased total demand for labor, including female labor for other non-mechanized operations. The more intensive or yield-increasing technologies considered here of inorganic fertilizers, water retention techniques, and improved cultivars substantially increase labor demands per hectare.

The farm household responds to these profitable technologies by mobilizing more labor (and other factors of production) from within the household or from outside markets. The household head can hire labor from outside the farm. He can marry another woman or get more unmarried relatives working on the farm. If labor is mobilized from within the household, it implies that the various members would have to allocate labor away from their private holdings and other activities to satisfy the increased requirements on the communal lands. Are women within these farming households thus getting more marginalized as a result of these new agricultural technologies? This is a crucial question and deserves more empirical investigation.[5]

Clearly, there is discrimination against women in rural areas of many developing countries. Higher mortality rates among female children in India is in direct contrast with the lower rates in developed countries. Assuming equal care between sexes in developed countries, these differences indicate lower health or other investments in females in Indian households (Rosenzweig and Schultz, 1982). There is also some between-country evidence that shows lower human capital investments in areas other than health, such as in schooling for females (Lele, 1986a; von Braun and Webb, 1989). Finally, in Sub-Saharan African agriculture, less access to the critical inputs of information, credit, purchased inputs such as fertilizer, and land make adoption of new technologies more difficult for women and reduce the returns when new technology is introduced (Gladwin and McMillan, 1989, p. 356; Lele, 1986a, p. 212). Discrimination between sexes has an economic cost to these societies, and we expect a high return from its elimination.

What is the impact of new technology introduction on the income (welfare) of women? With the introduction of intensive technologies, women's participation on private plots has consistently declined. As women work more on the family land, they have less direct control of the food or cash resources from production.[6] The independent incomes of women give them some economic power. Some report that women prefer a reliable source of independent personal income, as from private plots, brewing beer, or processing and marketing food, to working for their husbands or fathers (von Braun and Webb, 1989, p. 20; Jones, 1983; Dupire, 1960, p. 14; Obbo, 1980).

In most cases, it is unknown whether the women are compensated for the increased labor on the family-operated fields with income, gifts, or increased food supply or are not compensated at all. Recent field studies have investigated this question. A detailed study of within-household income distribution in Cameroon found that the women were paid their opportunity costs for the additional labor, but the income they received was only one-fourth of the income generated by this additional work on the family area (Jones, 1983, 1986). In another detailed study in Gambia, no increased wage compensation was noted with the introduction of new technologies, but there were consumption benefits to the entire family.

The conventional wisdom on consumption is that men will use increased income first for their own consumption, accumulating animals and then more wives, and women will purchase improved family nutrition, clothing, education, and family health (Lele, 1986b, p. 204). In the Sahelian family, the primary responsibility for children is borne by the wife. The man's responsibility is principally for the wife (Guyer, 1986). Hence, verifying the income distribution consequences to the women also broadens the equity concerns to the children.

What can we say about within-family welfare improvements from technological change based on empirical studies? In the Gambian study referred to above, household food consumption increased as a consequence of the introduction of new rice technology on family fields. On the negative side, the women had even less time and less access to other resources for their private fields after new technologies were introduced. The labor productivity of women on their private fields was 65 percent that on the men's private fields and even further below labor productivity on the communally operated fields (von Braun and Webb, 1989, pp. 525–30). In summary, when new technologies were introduced on the family areas in field studies in both Cameroon and Gambia, female welfare increased, with either more wages for the females or higher family consumption, including hers.[7]

## Theories of Household Behavior and the Labor Market Applied to Sub-Saharan African Agriculture

In the Sahelian countries, the first obligation of the household head at low income levels is to provide for the subsistence consumption of the extended family, defined by anthropologists as those who eat from the same pot (Gladwin and McMillan, 1989, p. 356). To achieve these subsistence objectives, the household head may dictate to household members, his wives, other relatives, and adolescent children the labor they need to provide on the communally farmed area. This labor on the family fields for basic subsistence takes priority over other objectives (Adesina and Sanders, 1991). In compensation, the household members receive grain for themselves and their dependents during the year. Besides the common fields, the household head also allocates small areas of private fields to other household members. They can spend their remaining time here after finishing their obligatory time on the family fields—and, for the women, also the household chores. These individuals have a right to the production on these private plots.

The intensive technologies increase the demand for labor on the family fields during the crop season. As higher household incomes are earned, at what point will the adult family members, including the women, demand a share of the new income stream in cash, grain, or gifts? There are essentially three household theories in the literature that give insights into this question:

- the exploitation theory
- the altruistic household head or joint family decision theory
- the cooperation-conflict case

### Exploitation Theory

The household head substitutes for the capitalist in Marxist theory. Given the power structure of the society, the household head can control the labor supply of all the adult women in the household through social traditions, and he can exploit that power to his own personal advantage.[8] In the traditional society, women work for men and provide a certain part of the food that the husband eats (Saunders, 1980). Their labor obligations are acquired with the payment of the bride's price. Within-family conflict can be provoked if women rebel against this role. Moreover, there are strong community pressures to maintain traditional roles (Jones, 1986, pp. 112–13).

As the introduction of new technology requires reduced labor activities on the private plots, the women (and other adult males in the household) produce less of the food and cash crops that they directly control. Following the logic of exploitation theory, the household head could still demand the additional family labor on the family fields associated with the new technologies, without increased compensation. Even though total family income would increase, the income and nutrition of these family members and their dependents could decline. Whether households can function in this manner as new technologies are introduced and incomes increase above subsistence levels is an empirical issue.

### Altruistic Theory

The household head, either in combination with other household members or by himself, maximizes the welfare (utility) of the entire family in an altruistic way. This type of family decision making follows the neoclassical tradition so that, as in the exploitation case, there is one potentially dictatorial decision coming from the family head, who is usually the patriarch (Becker, 1973; 1981, p. 27). However, there may be consultation before making this decision. In pure theory, the household head would be maximizing the group's welfare. There is a high degree of interdependence of welfare among family members, and the household head benefits from improvements in the welfare of other family members. With technological change, all family members are better off from increases in household income or food consumption or from gifts.[9] The joint-welfare maximization approach based on altruism obscures any conflicts and separate interests that exist within the household. It does seem paradoxical to argue that economic agents are driven by self-interest in the marketplace but that the very same agents become altruistic once they cross the family threshold (Folbre, 1986). Perhaps this theory is more appropriate as an ideal form of decision making but difficult to attain in practice.

### Cooperation-Conflict Theory

Typical intrahousehold behavior observed in Sub-Saharan Africa does not reflect either altruism or exploitation. The observation that the household head had to pay women their opportunity costs to obtain the additional labor for new technology introduction in rice farming is not consistent with either of these two theories (Jones, 1983). Nor do the observations of husbands purchasing water from the wives, selling firewood to wives, or lending money at usurious interest costs within the family fit with these theories (Hafkin and Bay, 1976). The cooperation-conflict approach challenges the traditional view of the Beckerian household and provides a rationale for the observed intrafamily monetary transactions.[10]

The members of the farm household have to decide simultaneously about cooperation, adding to total availabilities, and conflict, dividing the total availabilities among the various members.[11] To meet the increased labor requirement associated with new technologies, the household head must mobilize more labor. Given the additional cost of searching for and supervising hired workers,[12] it is in the household head's interest to bid his own family workers away from their private plots to work on the family fields, even if it means compensating them either monetarily or with gifts. Within a sufficient range of compensation, women are expected to prefer to work on the farm, since they would thereby avoid the search and transportation costs of looking for work and would be nearer to their homes and children.

A nagging question is: Why should the household head compensate the women for their additional labor? Will not the traditional and patriarchal rights vested in the household head be enough to force the women to work the extra hours? The conventional wisdom in the literature on women in development certainly emphasizes the exploitative and dictatorial nature of the patriarch within the household. However, there is evidence from Cameroon that after a few seasons, female farmers refuse to work on the communal fields unless implicit wages are increased (Jones 1983, 1986).

The cooperation-conflict model seems to be a more realistic description of household decision making than the model of the household head being able to coerce the other adult workers into performing more labor. In a pure subsistence economy, more coercion may be possible. Once this family-subsistence objective is assured, the competing objectives of household members to obtain part of the gains of the new technologies would ensure some division of the increased product. With the introduction of technological change, both male and female adult workers are observed reducing their participation on the private plots (Savadogo, Sanders, and McMillan, 1989). This reduction of time on the private plots is an entirely rational response of independent economic agents, if compensation is paid in wages or other benefits for increased labor on the family-operated area.[13]

## Modeling a Representative Farm in a Region of Rapid Agricultural Technological Change

The Solenzo region lies in the southwest corner of Burkina Faso. The region has a Sudano-Guinean climate, with rainfall over 800 millimeters per annum (90 percent probability) spread over a period of five months. The region has adequate water resources, relatively fertile soils, good market access, and a moderate population density. Among all the regions in Burkina Faso, the southwest has demonstrated the most potential for development.[14] The southwest is a cereal exporter to the rest of the country in most years. Although Solenzo is actually geographically north of the rapid growth area of the southwest, it has experienced rapid growth in the last decade after the recent elimination of river blindness (onchocerciasis) (see chapter 10).

In the Solenzo region, most farm households have four to seven hectares of crop area if cultivation is based on human labor alone. Farms using animal power (donkeys and oxen) are five to twelve hectares in size. A small number of farms in this region also use microtractors; these mechanized farms are much larger in size, ranging from ten to twenty-five hectares. Historically, the French invested heavily in agricultural research, extension, and marketing of cotton. Inorganic fertilizers, other chemicals, improved cultivars, and better agronomy for cotton have had spillover effects, since farmers have begun to use fertilizers for maize production with favorable results. The farmers also use insecticides for the cultivation of cotton, cowpeas, and peanuts (Savadogo, Sanders, and McMillan, 1989).

In Solenzo, crop production (except for grain legumes) is almost entirely concentrated on the family fields. The major subsistence crops (maize, sorghum, and millet) and cash crops (cotton and peanuts) are cultivated there. Maize is also an important cash crop for the larger producers. Members of the family household use the private plots to produce a small quantity of cereals (mainly red sorghum), some grain legumes, and vegetables (okra) for dietary and financial diversification (table 9-1). The red sorghum enables women to produce beer, thereby obtaining a higher-value-added product. Because there are numerous field and storage insect problems, yields are low for these legumes and vegetables. The private plots give a low return to labor, as they are generally on poorer quality or marginal land and there customarily is little expenditure on inputs such as improved seeds, insecticides, and fertilizers (Savadogo, Sanders, and McMillan, 1989).

To analyze the impact of new technologies on household income, we constructed a representative farm programming model for the Solenzo region.[15] We then incorporated the farm model into the bargaining model. (For details on the bargaining model, see the appendix to this chapter.) With new technology, the household head has to increase his labor inputs on the communal land. His maximum cost of labor would be the daily wage *(w)* plus the search and supervision costs *(S)* of finding and overseeing temporary employees. If there is no option of off-farm work, the wife's initial offer price would be the marginal return from her labor on her private plot. If the wife can work off

Table 9-1. Agricultural Production on Communal Fields and Women's Production on Private Plots in the Solenzo Region of Burkina Faso

| Crop | Production on Farm (kg) | Production on Communal Fields (%) | Production by Women on Private Fields (kg/farm) |
|---|---|---|---|
| White sorghum | 1,721 | 95 | 39 |
| Red sorghum | 1,705 | 88 | 223 |
| Millet | 692 | 90 | 69 |
| Maize | 9,037 | 100 | 0 |
| Sesame | 60 | 100 | 0 |
| Cotton | 6,578 | 100 | 0 |
| Cowpeas | 124 | 94 | 18 |
| Groundnuts | 99 | 65 | 89 |

Source: Savadogo, Sanders, and McMillan (1989, p. 19).
Note: Figures are based on a sample survey of fourteen villages from the Solenzo region (1988–89). The average family size is twelve to fifteen members, of which six to eight are women. Minimal amounts of rice and soybeans are also produced.

the farm, her minimum acceptable wage to work on the farm would be the daily wage minus the search and transportation costs. With the availability of off-farm labor, the two would negotiate over a range from $(w - s)$ to $(w + S)$. Utilizing the Nash equilibrium solution to the bargaining model, the participants will split the difference between their threat points (Nash, 1953). The threat points are the upper and lower bounds of values at which negotiations would break down and one of the collaborators would refuse to deal with the other. This is analogous to strikes and lockouts in labor-management negotiation.

The farm household maximizes profits subject to constraints on available land, labor, donkeys, oxen, and capital. The farm produces six commodities on the communal fields: cotton, sorghum, millet, maize, cowpeas, and peanuts. The model explicitly takes into account different land types and also differentiates between various communal land activities and private land activities.[16] Maize is cultivated on the higher-quality soils and is very responsive to fertilizer inputs, yielding 1.5 to 1.9 metric tons per hectare. Sorghum yields range from 0.85 to 1.1 metric tons per hectare, and cotton yields range from 0.9 to 1.3 metric tons per hectare. Millet yields are comparatively low, ranging from 0.5 to 0.7 metric ton per hectare. Donkey and oxen traction extend the cultivated area on the communal fields.

The private lands (0.6 to 1.0 hectares) are the less fertile lands on the edge of the farm, on which primarily red sorghum and small amounts of millet, vegetables, and peanuts are planted. Red sorghum yields on the private plots are approximately 50 to 60 percent of the corresponding yields on the better-quality communal land. Sales from these private plots accrue only to the individual family members. The representative farm household has twelve to fifteen residents and six to seven adult equivalents.[17]

## Impact of New Agricultural Technologies on Households and Women in the Sahel

With the modeling of the traditional system, before the introduction of technological change, the female farmer cultivated 0.75 hectare of private land.[18] When the new technology was introduced on the communal fields, the area she cultivated on the private plot declined 56 percent. This is the phenomenon that many deplore. When the new intensive technologies were introduced on the communal lands, household income increased from US$922 to US$1,556. Because the household head must bid for the labor of the woman to persuade her to reduce her efforts on the private plot, her income was increased from US$36 to US$85, the difference reflecting the compensation paid to her by the household head. The incomes of both the household and the individual female were increased, even though she reduced her time on her private field. These model results are consistent with preliminary results from field surveys, which indicate that women's (and even men's) participation rates on private plots in Solenzo have declined in comparison with other regions. Furthermore, total farm income in Solenzo has been rising rapidly, and women's discretionary income is reportedly higher (Savadogo, Sanders, and McMillan, 1989, pp. 24–29).

As a next step, we used the model to evaluate the potential impacts of various policy suggestions from the literature. Forcing the new technology to be introduced only on the private fields decreased both the income of the woman and the overall farm income (table 9-2). Even with another 1 hectare available to her (for a total of 1.75 hectares of private land), the income of the woman farmer still declined. The explanation for this decline in household income is that both the use of inputs and the productivity on the private fields were lower than on the family fields. If the bargaining process within the household is functioning, the woman and the farm family would have higher incomes with the technology introduced only on the family fields.

If exploitation rather than cooperation-conflict were the norm, then women would not be able to obtain the increased compensation of $85. In such a

Table 9-2. Farm Income and Women's Income from New Technologies and Off-Farm Employment in the Solenzo Region of Burkina Faso (model results in U.S. dollars)

| | Traditional Technology and Animal Traction | New Intensive Technologies on Communal Fields[a] | New Intensive Technologies on Private Fields Only[b] | New Intensive Technologies on Communal and Private Fields | Improved Off-Farm Options; also Technologies on Both Types of Fields[c] |
|---|---|---|---|---|---|
| Farm income from communal fields[d] | 922 | 1,566 | 804 | 1,414 | 1,106 |
| Income of adult female worker | | | | | |
| private plot | 36 | 14 | 68 | 68 | — |
| communal field | — | 71 | — | 45 | 125 |
| off-farm | — | — | — | — | 71 |
| Total per female worker | 36 | 85 | 68 | 113 | 196 |

*Source:* Calculated from Ramaswamy (1991, p. 99).
[a]The household head must pay more to the female worker for the increased labor on the communal field. The private field available is only 0.75 hectare.
[b]The land available to the female worker is increased to 1.75 hectares and the technology is introduced first on the private fields, in spite of the lower productivity. This is done by forcing the model in the programming. It is equivalent to a preferential policy of directing the technology first toward the female farmer (and increasing her land area).
[c]The new agricultural technologies were available for use on both the communal areas and private plots. However, since nonfarm activities and work on the communal plots were more remunerative, the private plots were not cultivated.
[d]Family income including the value of home consumption of food. This includes only crop income from the communal land. The farm with animal traction includes seven adult equivalents.

case, concentrating technology policy on the women would improve their situation. The farm household, however, would suffer substantially, since the farm as a whole loses almost 50 percent of its income as compared with the previous case of intensive technology introduction (table 9-2). In this case, there would be substantial pressure on the household head to move from exploitation to a bargaining decision-making process, to gain access to the new technologies.

In the fourth scenario of table 9-2, we introduce new technologies on both the private and family fields, but we must introduce these technologies first on the expanded private fields of 1.75 hectares. The female's private-plot income remains the same as that in the previous case, but she is also able to receive earnings from the new technology introduced on the communal field. The female's income is increased here, but the household income is reduced compared to the case of the introduction of new technology only on the communal fields. The female farmer's income is increased from US$85 to US$113. Family income declines slightly (from US$1,556 to US$1,414), due to the fact that the productivity and input use is lower on the private land than on the communal land. The household head is also forced to contract outside labor at a higher wage.

There are two ways of increasing women's incomes without reducing allocative efficiency on the farm. First, future technological change could increase the productivity of her land. If land productivities are equal, then adopting technologies on the private land is an efficient policy. A more viable alternative presently may be to facilitate the growth of nonfarm employment, thereby raising the opportunity costs of women. This would also be expected to help women in the bargaining process, through increasing the value of their threat point.

When off-farm labor is available in the model, the female worker entirely eliminates work on the private plot (table 9-2). Since she earns more on the communal field and is more productive there, she continues to contribute labor there to facilitate introduction of new technology. In this scenario, she increases her income 73 percent as compared with the introduction of new technology on the private and communal fields (table 9-2). However, as the household head has to pay more for the female's on-farm labor and even more for some off-farm labor, total farm income is reduced. The off-farm labor market, combined with new technologies on the communal fields, gave the highest returns for women.

Using the same bargaining models but with some differences in the technical coefficients based on more recent data, another study compares the effects of new agricultural household technologies on the income of women with the three different decision-making techniques for both hand traction and animal traction households (table 9-3). No matter how household decision making is done, the combination of agricultural and household technologies increases the welfare of women. The household technologies are an improved stove and more efficient grain processing. Both household innovations are being introduced in the cotton-boom regions, such as Mali-Sud, and are promoted by some public and private efforts (Lawrence, 1993, p. 98). Household technologies release labor time from uncompensated activities.[19] The mud and metal stoves save 35 to 40 percent and 40 to 50 percent, respectively, of the wood requirements (S. Brunisma, CMDT, unpublished data). If the combined household technologies of more efficient stoves and a grain-processing innovation reduce labor requirements by 1.5 hours a day, women are able to in-

Table 9-3. Effects of Household Decision-Making Behaviors on Women's Income under Traditional and New Technologies in the Solenzo Region of Burkina Faso (U.S. dollars, 1992 base)

| Household Behavior | Traditional Agriculture | | New Agricultural Technology | | New Household and Agricultural Technology | |
|---|---|---|---|---|---|---|
| | Hand Traction | Animal Traction | Hand Traction | Animal Traction | Hand Traction | Animal Traction |
| Competition | 100 | 158 | 160 | 196 | 217 | 257 |
| Exploitation | 100 | 125 | 100 | 125 | 137 | 171 |
| Cooperation-Conflict | 100 | 135 | 137 | 175 | 185 | 228 |

*Source:* Based on Lawrence (1993, p. 98).
*Note:* As in table 9-2, this is the income of one woman from all sources.

crease their labor in agriculture. Incomes of women are increased 68 to 85 percent by the combined household and agricultural technologies in the system with household bargaining. In a competitive system, where women are paid their VMP, female incomes are increased even more. Over time, we would expect household decision making to evolve from exploitive to bargaining and, finally, to a self-sacrificing or altruistic decision-making process.[20]

## Conclusion

Of the three theories of household behavior, the cooperation-conflict pattern is the most consistent with the observed behavior of economic transactions within the African family and with human behavior in general. If the cooperation-conflict or altruistic decision making takes place within the household, then measures to direct technologies specifically to women or to the private plots would not be as efficient as the natural functioning of the marketplace. If the exploitation model is relevant, then the specific policy measures advocated for women would benefit them but would also reduce household income. Even in this case, increasing the off-farm options of women would raise their opportunity costs, thereby pressuring the household system to move from exploitation to the bargaining type of household decision making.

To develop policies that are more focused toward women, we need to compare the benefits and costs to productivity-increasing measures (more input purchases or female-specific extension services) on private land with the benefits and costs of increased off-farm employment or of household technologies. Meanwhile, with some reasonable assumptions about the bargaining process within the household, technological change improves the welfare of the entire household *and* women, even if technology is introduced only on the family lands. Women benefit more from the combination of the introduction of new technology on the family fields and increased off-farm employment than from specific measures to introduce new agricultural technologies directly to them. This is essentially due to the fact that the communal lands have higher productivity than the private lands.

Women should have more access not only to the new technologies but also to better land. However, attempting by policy to direct new technologies toward less productive land makes all worse off, as would policy measures to slow the introduction of new technologies. Technological change by itself may change the institutional relationship by increasing the value of household adult labor, thereby encouraging more bargaining and enabling women to get a larger share of the gains from technological change. This will not be an automatic process, and policy measures to improve the bargaining position of women are recommended.

Under reasonable assumptions about household decision making, women benefit from the introduction of new agricultural technology. But their potential income increases are reduced by some policies advocated to direct agricultural technologies to their fields unless the productivity of their fields and their access to other inputs are simultaneously increased. A reasonable two-stage operation that would benefit women is to first introduce agricultural technologies on family fields of the farm and then introduce household technologies for them. This is a natural sequence substantially benefiting both the household and the women.

In all of the above cases, the wage rates for women are still low. As these are low-income systems, these changes will make only small impacts on welfare. Nevertheless, the process of improving these systems will gather its own momentum as small changes are made. It is important that policy measures do not reduce the welfare of the women and the household by encouraging inefficient allocation of resources. The production and diffusion of new agricultural technologies is expected to be the principal continuing policy measure to increase household incomes. Slowing down this technology introduction will not benefit women. Combining agricultural technology introduction with various measures to save women's time and to increase their bargaining power will unequivocally raise their incomes, according to model results and the various empirical studies cited.

## Appendix A: Microeconomic Foundations of the Production Structures and Labor Markets in the Sahel

Initially, the farm household uses traditional means to work on communal lands and private fields and to do household chores (especially the women). These household chores require an almost fixed amount of time, and so we assumed that to be fixed; the remaining time is allocated between activities in the other two sectors—the communal fields and the private fields.

The labor allocation problem can be analyzed in a standard Ricardo-Viner specific-factor model popularized in the international trade literature. Land is the specific factor that is immobile between the two sectors; that is, private fields are not substitutable for communal lands, and the latter are inherently of a superior quality. The other inputs—capital and labor—are mobile between the two sectors. Output prices are assumed to be fixed and exogenously specified to the model.

Figure 9-1 describes the traditional farm household. *OL* is the total labor

Figure 9-1. Labor Allocation between Communal Lands and Private Fields in the Solenzo Region

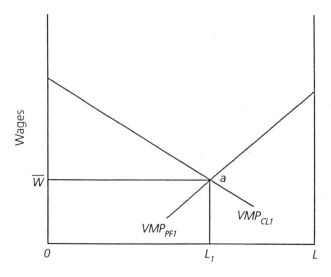

time available. $VMP_{CL1}$ is the value of the marginal product of labor on the communal lands, while $VMP_{PF1}$ is the value of the marginal product of labor on the private fields. $\hat{W}$ denotes the existing wage rate, implicit or explicit, and this can be assumed as the subsistence wage. $OL_1$ is the amount of time spent on the communal lands, while $L_1L$ is the remaining time spent on private fields.

With the introduction of new technologies, the farming system undergoes a transformation. Agricultural technologies have been introduced on both the communal lands and private fields; however, the adoption rates and returns have been higher on the better quality communal lands. This raises the *VMP* of labor on the communal lands by a larger magnitude compared with the corresponding shift of the *VMP* curve for the private fields (figure 9-2). As a result of the new technologies, members of the household work less on the private fields and more on the communal lands to alleviate the labor shortages associated with time intensive activities.

The framework (figure 9-3) can be used to show why the exploitative model of household decision making results in an inefficient allocation of resources. For simplicity, let the new technologies be introduced only in the

Figure 9-2. Impact of New Agricultural Technologies on Labor Allocation Patterns

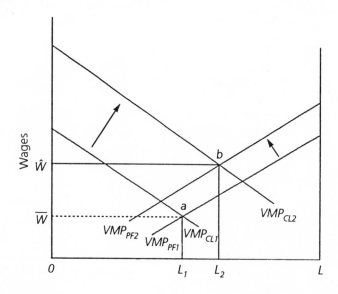

Figure 9-3. Inefficient Allocation of Resources under Exploitative Decision Making

communal lands. The new equilibrium would be at *b*, with $OL_2$ being allocated to communal lands and the remainder $L_2L$ going to private fields. If the household head persists in exploiting the women by paying only $\bar{W}$, then more time $(L_2L_2')$ is spent on the communal lands than is optimal, and this results in a deadweight loss (area 1) due to a misallocation of resources and a redistribution of income, with the household head appropriating all the gain from new technology.

In the next scenario (figure 9-4), the option of working off farm is introduced. It is assumed that the off-farm work is highly productive and that the market wage is exogenously determined at $W^*$. Employment in the private fields dropped to $L_PL$ and even on the communal lands to $OL_C$. The remaining time $L_CL_P$ is spent working off the farm for the higher wage rate $W^*$. $\bar{W}W^*$ denotes the range of bargaining between the household head and the women. The introduction of other income-earning opportunities raises the women's threat point and improves their bargaining position within the household.

Figure 9-4. Off-Farm Work and New Agricultural and Household Technologies

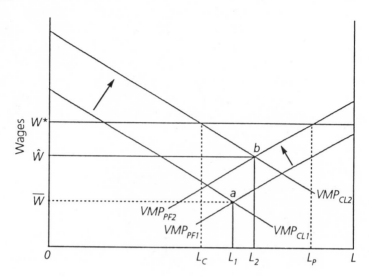

## Appendix B: The Bargaining Model

The consumption equation of the women can be formalized:

$$C = rl_1 + Wl_2 + qA(h, l_3),$$

where $l_1$ is the amount of labor supplied on the communal fields and $r$ is the compensation wage rate paid out by the household head to mobilize labor from within the family; $W$ is the net wage received for off-farm employment, and $(W = w - s)$, where $w$ is the market wage rate and $s$ is the search cost incurred by women in seeking off-farm employment; $l_2$ denotes the time spent on off-farm employment activities; $q$ is revenue from sale of produce on the private plots; $A$ is the production function relating the amount of land cultivated by the women on the private fields $(h)$, and $l_3$ denotes the time they spend on the private fields.

The optimization problem is to maximize income subject to the following constraints (all income is consumed):

$$l_1 \leq L_1; \; l_3 \leq L_3; \; l_2 \leq L - L_1 - L_3; \; leisure = 1 - L.$$

$L_1$ refers to the maximum time that can be spent on the collective fields. Intuitively, all agricultural activities require that only so much time be spent on the fields. The same holds for labor input on the private fields ($l_3$).

From the household head's perspective, he is willing to pay ($r' \leq w + S$), where $S$ is the additional supervisory costs. Supervisory costs are expected to be lower for family labor. Seasonality in agriculture is crucial—certain tasks (such as planting and first and second weedings) have to be accomplished at fixed times, with a yield penalty if they are not finished rapidly. It is the responsibility of the household head to contract sufficient numbers of casual labor at the right times to perform various time-intensive activities. The greater the reliance on family labor, the less risk there is from these seasonal operations.

The women's asking price is ($r \geq w - s$), where $s$ is the search and transportation costs incurred by the women to find off-farm employment (Bryson, 1981). Clearly, there is scope for bargaining within this range. The head would try to pay a wage rate close to $r$, while the women would try to bargain for an $r$ close to $r'$. Now the decision problems of the female farmer and household head need to be put into a bargaining framework to calculate the optimal wage rate.

The female farmer's profits from her various activities are

$$Y^1 = rl_1(r) + Wl_2 + Qa(h,l_3). \tag{9.1}$$

The household head's net profits from mobilizing labor on the communal fields are

$$Y^2 = PQ\{T, nl_1(r) + Z\} - rnl_1(r) - W'l, \tag{9.2}$$

where $P$ is the price vector of crops cultivated on the communal fields; $Q$ is the output vector and is a function of the land available *(T)* and the amount of family labor ($nl_1$) and outside labor *(Z)*; $W'$ is the wage paid to hire outside labor and is equal to ($w + S$), where $w$ is the market wage rate. If the two agents fail to agree on the wage rate paid for family labor, the respective incomes are

$$y^1 = wl_2' + qA(h,l_3') \tag{9.3}$$

and

$$y^2 = PQ'\{T,l_1\} - W'l', \tag{9.4}$$

Where $l_2'$ and $l_3'$ denote the adjustments made in labor time spent on the other two activities by the women. $Q'$ is the new output vector, which is now a function of all hired labor ($l'$).

The disagreement payoffs, $y^1$ and $y^2$, reflect the bargaining power of the women and the household head, respectively, and these threat points prevail when bargaining breaks down. To arrive at a solution to this bargaining game, the Nash method is used, where

$$N = \{Y^1 - y^1\}\{Y^2 - y^2\}. \tag{9.5}$$

The value of $r$, which maximizes $N$, is a solution assuming that the solution is unique. Nash's solution also stipulates that the parenthetic terms be greater than zero (i.e., both parties will not enter nonremunerative contracts).[21] Using equations (9.1) to (9.4), equation (9.5) can be written as

$$N = \{rl_1(r) + Wl_2 + Qa(h,l_3) - [wl_2' + qA(h,l_3')]\}$$
$$\times \{PQ[T,nl_1(r) + Z] - rnl_1(r) - W'l - [PQ'(T,l') - W'l']\} \tag{9.6}$$

$N$ is a function of $(l_1$ and $r)$, which makes it difficult to solve for the optimal value for $r$. However, at $r$, the women will supply all the labor associated with the new technologies on the communal fields equivalent to $L_1$. This implies that in the above equation, $l_1$ is set at $L_1$, and the first order condition with respect to $r$ will solve for the optimal level $(r^*)$:

$$\frac{\delta N}{\delta r} = L_1\{PQ(T,Nl_1 + Z) - rnl_1 - W'Z - [PQ'(T,l')$$
$$- W'l']\} + \{Rl_1 + Wl_2 + Qa(h,l_3) - wl_2' - qA(h,l_3')\}(-Nl_1) = 0 \tag{9.7}$$

and

$$r^* = \frac{-1}{2nL_1}\{nW(l_2 - l_2') + nq[A(h,l_3) - A(h,l_3')] + P[Q(T,Nl_1 + Z)$$
$$- Q'(T,l')] + W'(l - l')\}. \tag{9.8}$$

In the traditional system, the only profitable alternative to working on the private fields is working on the communal fields. In such a case, the household head would offer $r$ just greater than the marginal value product of labor on the private plots $[VMP(L_3)]$ to mobilize the family labor.

If

$$r^* > VMP(l_3),$$

then

$$l_1 = L_1; \; l_3 = L_3; \; leisure = L - L_1 - L_3.$$

The mobilization of female labor is conditional on her opportunity costs. Experience across households would vary with other factors, influencing the relative power positions. For example, in households with a number of senior wives and women whose husbands still owe bride's wealth to their wives' families, the men must complete the transfer of bride's wealth cattle. The men cannot afford to get into a dispute over a wife's compensation, since the additional labor she provides is critical on the communal lands. Also, when there are more senior wives, the husband may be less inclined to dispute her, since she would traditionally be accorded a senior status and will have helped him over the years to accumulate wealth, which enables him to marry other women (Bryson, 1981, pp. 29–46).

# IV

## Alternative Strategies?

# 10

# Disease Control, New Land Settlement, and Technological Change

*Della E. McMillan*

*Kimseyinga Savadogo*

**T**RADITIONALLY, agricultural output is increased through area expansion. Once the frontier is exhausted, however, farmers are pressed to find new alternatives. Intensive or yield-increasing technologies have been the response of developed countries. In much of Sub-Saharan Africa, land is increasingly being depleted and crop yields declining. There are, however, large areas with lower settlement rates due to the high incidence of human and animal diseases. Four debilitating diseases endemic to much of Sub-Saharan Africa are bovine trypanosomiasis, malaria, schistosomiasis, and onchocerciasis (river blindness). These diseases reduce settlement or seriously weaken the population in large areas of Sub-Saharan Africa and have enormous economic impact.

Donors are attracted to large-scale disease control programs for a dramatic impact. The United Nations supports a program to recover part of the 700 million hectares in Sub-Saharan Africa where the tsetse fly historically restrained the expansion of livestock production, except for one resistant species (Jahnke, 1982; FAO, 1986a).[1] Malaria and schistosomiasis control would increase agricultural labor productivity by improving health (Goering, 1978; Miller, 1992; Liese, Sachdeva, and Cochrane, 1992). Of particular concern to the semiarid region of West Africa is a World Health Organization program to control river blindness.[2] This disease has historically been so debilitating that whole villages have fled from infected areas. River blindness "constitutes for the [West African Sahel] area the most important single deterrent to human settlement and the subsequent economic development of many fertile valleys, which lie uninhabited and unproductive" (PAG, 1973, p. 1).

Now, after more than two decades, the Onchocerciasis Control Programme

(OCP) is considered to be one of the most successful health programs ever launched. The program estimates that 30 million people are now protected from further transmission of river blindness. Nine million people born since the OCP began face no risk of contracting the disease, and 1.5 million people once seriously infected have no further trace of the disease. The OCP further estimates that it has created new settlement opportunities on 25 million hectares of potentially highly productive land (World Bank, 1994).

Low-income settlers from poorer or degraded regions were expected. Thus, the disease erradication program would increase output and improve income distribution. Does a disease control program, such as the very successful river blindness program, serve as a substitute for or a complement to the private and public investments in intensive agricultural technologies recommended in this book?

## Onchocerciasis Control in West Africa

River blindness control was one of the principal development concepts that emerged from the 1968–73 drought. River blindness has been an important factor in the underpopulation of large areas of agriculturally valuable land. When the OCP began, there was no viable drug treatment for the disease.[3] Therefore, the early program focused on controlling the black-fly vector. Since 1974, the OCP has sprayed the infected river basins repeatedly with biodegradable insecticides, which destroy the fly's larvae. The program's original sphere of operations covered 764,000 square kilometers in seven countries—Benin, Burkina Faso, Côte d'Ivoire, Ghana, Mali, Niger, and Togo. In 1986, the control zone was expanded to cover 1.3 million square kilometers, including the additional areas of Benin, Ghana, Mali, and Togo and parts of Guinea, Guinea-Bissau, Sierra Leone, and Senegal (fig. 10-1).

Fifteen years after control started, the OCP was considered to be one of the most successful disease control programs ever launched (Younger and Zongo, 1989). River blindness is no longer a public health problem in the core control zone, and large areas of the river basins have been recolonized (World Bank, 1994; WHO, 1985; OCP, 1986).

The OCP has emphasized that the settlement and development of the relatively uninhabited fertile lands of the Volta River basin was the major objective of control; however, the program has not taken a direct role in either the planning or administration of these efforts. Although the program has sometimes helped national governments in finding external funding for specific projects, the main responsibility for settlement has been vested in the national

Figure 10-1. The Onchocerciasis Control Programme (OCP)

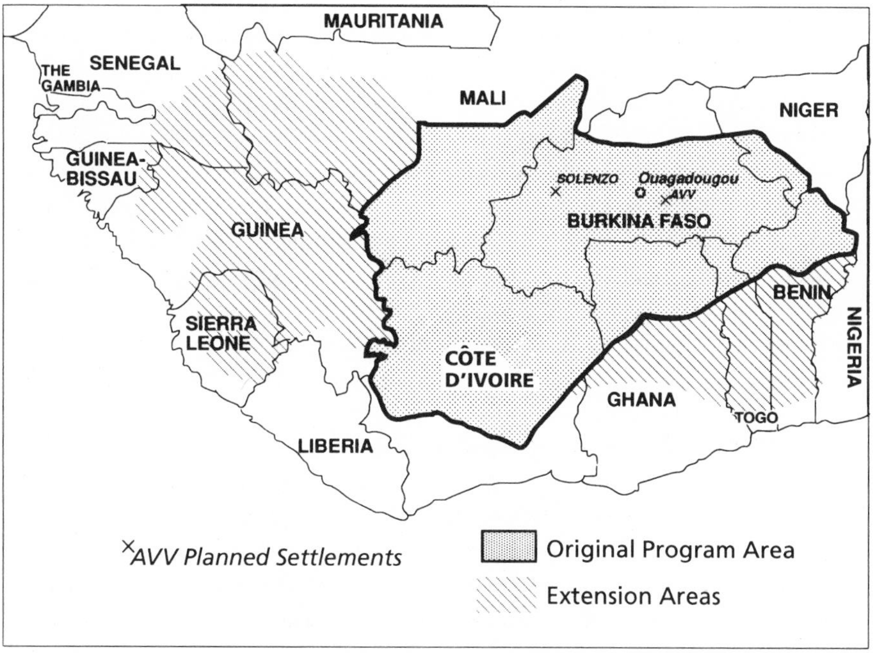

*Source:* Adapted from McMillan, Painter, and Scudder (1992).

governments. Burkina Faso, the country with the largest area affected by the OCP, was the only country to implement a highly centralized program of planned settlement and agricultural extension (McMillan, 1983; McMillan, Painter, and Scudder, 1992; WHO, 1985; OCP 1986).

## Introduction of Extensive Cultivation Practices

Most settlement taking place in the affected river basins can be classified as spontaneous, with little access to basic infrastructure or services. One major criticism of spontaneous settlement in the OCP area and worldwide is that settlers introduce extensive cultivation and forestry practices.[4] These extensive crop and livestock systems are expected farmer responses when land with good potential for rain-fed agriculture is still easily acquired and cleared and where there are few social and economic costs to abandoning worn-out land.

If population densities are low, extensive agricultural cultivation can be ecologically and socially sustainable. In addition, there is usually little social or economic infrastructure (other than access roads and markets) that makes one village setting more attractive than another for outside migrants. Under these conditions, the primary factor determining household production levels is the size of the family labor force. The rational strategy for settlers, therefore, is to clear and plant the largest area possible, constrained only by the seasonal labor supply, and to abandon older fields with declining fertility. For example, farmers in the Niangoloko region (on the Burkina–Côte d'Ivoire border) and in the Kompienga region (on the Burkina-Togo-Benin border)— two areas once highly endemic for river blindness—have traditionally farmed a field only five years before leaving it fallow for an average of twenty to twenty-five years (Nana, 1989; Agrotechnik, 1990; McMillan, Nana, and Savadogo, 1993). This long fallow/rotation system was made possible by the abundant supply of land.

With increasing population densities, fallow systems are shortened or entirely eliminated. If agriculture is not sufficiently profitable to use chemicals or other soil amendments to maintain soil fertility, then yields will decline, and cropland will be extended into more marginal grazing areas. If land is available and easily accessible, pastoralists and agriculturalists will often move at this point in the settlement cycle. When land is not available, increased pressure on agricultural land causes rising levels of social conflict. These conflicts can be precipitated by livestock damage to agriculturalists' fields, lack of access to potable water, pastoralist resentment at being denied their traditional grazing areas, and a diminished supply of firewood. Violence from these types of conflicts is increasingly observed in the Sahel countries and in surrounding countries (McMillan, Nana, and Savadogo, 1993).

## Introduction of Intensive Cultivation Systems

### The Volta Valley Authority

Large-scale spontaneous migration away from the Mossi plateau to Burkina's less populated southwest was well underway when the OCP began in 1974. The Volta Valley Authority (AVV, or Autorité des Aménagements des Vallées des Volta) planned-settlement program was a deliberate attempt to offset rapid, uncontrolled forest clearance and spontaneous settlement of new lands in the OCP river basins.

Between 1974 and 1985, the Burkina government created twelve groups of AVV-sponsored settlements (AVV, 1985). The highest concentration of planned settlements was along the Nakambe (formerly White Volta), to the east of Ouagadougou along the paved highway that links the capital Ouagadougou with eastern Burkina, Togo, and Niger (fig. 10-1). In this Sudanian zone, with an annual rainfall from 600 to 800 millimeters (90 percent probability), there is a high risk of inadequate water availability during the production season. These river basins do, however, have more alluvial soils and higher initial soil fertility than does the plateau region. Prior to the creation of the first AVV planned settlements in 1973, there had been little immigration to the region. Since control, however, the area around the sponsored settlements has attracted large numbers of spontaneous agricultural and pastoral migration (Nana and Kattenberg, 1979; AVV, 1985; McMillan, Nana, and Savadogo, 1990).

When the first pilot AVV planned settlements were created in the Nakambe River basin in 1973, farmers were required to cultivate a rotation of cotton, cereals, and legumes in combination with inorganic fertilizer. The program focused heavily on commercial cotton production, as these sales provided the means of reimbursing short-term credit for inputs and longer-term credit for ox-drawn plows and donkey-drawn carts. The average project farm consisted of a one-hectare home site and six 1.5-hectare bush fields.[5] Under the prescribed system of crop rotations, each of the six bush fields was supposed to lie fallow for two years as part of a six-year rotation that included sorghum, cotton, and legumes. The AVV also specified the type and level of fertilizer, seed, and insecticide for each crop.

When settlers joined the project, they signed an agreement to follow the recommended program. Their participation was then closely monitored. During the first five years, each planned settlement included one male extension agent for every twenty-five settler households and one female agent for every fifty households. Although the project administration only rarely exercised its right to expel farmers for not adhering to the proposed technology and land use program, the threat of expulsion (or of being refused access to short-term credit) carried weight.

The results of the 1979 AVV farm-monitoring survey showed that food aid, tractor plowing, animal traction, and the newly cleared soils were successful in helping the settlers achieve high levels of growth in agricultural income during the first years of the project (Murphy and Sprey, 1980; McMillan, 1983, 1986, 1987a, 1987b, 1993). Settlers who had been at the project for shorter periods of time tended to follow the extension package more closely than those who had been there longer. Cotton was the only crop on which the recommended package of intensive cultivation techniques was consistently applied. This package included monocropping, chemical protection, planting in rows, use of recommended quantities of fertilizer, thinning, and timely weeding with animal traction.

Since the AVV recommendations for fertilizer were not combined with water-retention technologies such as stone dikes *(diguettes)*, tied ridges, or improved land preparation, fertilization was a risky activity during crop seasons with inadequate water availability. Hence, the loss of interest in recommended technologies, especially fertilizer, is not surprising. Applied research on the basic technological recommendations for this marginal cotton area was lacking at the start of the project (for a discussion of these technologies see Nagy et al., 1988; Sanders et al., 1990; Deuson and Sanders, 1990; Sanders, 1989; Jayne et al., 1989). Mounting evidence of soil erosion in the older AVV-sponsored settlements led to a reorientation of extension advice and recommendations after 1986 (AVV, 1985). Most notably, the revised program promoted the use of manure pits and stone dikes to improve soil fertility, arrest erosion, and retain more of the runoff. Unfortunately, the stone dikes do not capture much water, except for the crop rows immediately adjacent to the dikes.

Without significantly increased water retention, it is not surprising that the 1989 restudy did not show any improvement in settlers' use of either manure or fertilizer on crops other than cotton (McMillan, Nana, and Savadogo, 1990; Savadogo, 1989a, 1989b). In the AVV case study in 1979, the Mogtedo V3 (Village 3) settlers used fertilizer on 87 percent of their cotton fields and on 33 percent of their sorghum fields. Ten years later, fertilizer use was confined exclusively to cotton, and at lower levels than recommended by the project.[6]

By 1988, many settlers had virtually abandoned the prescribed five-year rotation of sorghum, cotton, legumes with two years of fallow. Instead, there was a growing trend toward continuous cultivation of the more accessible fields, with the better fields being planted alternatively to cotton and sorghum. Despite the settlers' failure to practice the prescribed cultivation package, the project records showed no substantial change in yields.[7] However, these valley soils were more fertile than the plateau soils and had residual effects from fertilization of the cotton.

Production costs were increased with the elimination of the input subsidies after the mid-eighties. Cotton was increasingly replaced with sorghum and millet. Over the decade, real income per worker declined 39 to 47 percent (table 10-1).[8] Consequently, a decade after colonization began, many of the

Table 10-1. Real Agricultural Income Per Worker in the Older AVV-Planned Settlements, 1979 and 1988

| Village | Communal Fields | | Communal and Private Fields | |
|---|---|---|---|---|
| | 1979[a] | 1988 | 1979 | 1988 |
| Linoghin | 92,718–107,282 | 61,315 | | 76,766 |
| Bombore | 91,586–105,718[b] | 54,988 | | 64,329 |
| Mogtedo | 91,586–105,718[b] | 51,072 | | 65,742 |
| Mogtedo Village 3 | | 55,101 | 122,275 | 72,588 |

Source: Savadogo, Sanders, and McMillan (1989); Murphy and Sprey (1980, p. 69); McMillan (1983); IMF (International Financial Statistics, 1989, p. 256).
Note: Income per adult labor equivalent, in real CFA (1988 base); adjusted for inflation, using IMF consumer price index for Burkina Faso (1988 base). Both 1979 and 1988 were good rainfall years.
[a] The first figure refers to farmers in their third year, and the second to farmers in their fourth or higher year.
[b] Average incomes of the Bombore and Mogtedo settlements in 1979.

best farmers were migrating out of the region (McMillan, Nana, and Savadogo, 1993).

*Solenzo*

Solenzo is located on the northern fringe of an area that was highly endemic for river blindness before 1974. Solenzo has higher rainfall and better soil fertility, however, than the AVV-sponsored settlements in the upper Nakambe. In addition, the Solenzo region and the surrounding Mouhoun (formerly Black Volta) River basin were already experiencing an agricultural immigration in the late 1960s, before control started (Hervouet, Clanet, and Some, 1984; Conde, 1978; Ancey, 1974; Capron and Kohler, 1975; Terrible, 1979). The rate of spontaneous settlement to the area then accelerated after 1974.

The crop extension program applied by settlers to the Solenzo area was developed over several decades, first by the French colonial government and later by the Burkinabè cotton agency, SOFITEX. There was, therefore, a base of applied research and farmer experience before control started in 1974. Although the basic package focuses on increasing cotton yields, it includes crop rotations, fertilizer, and cultivation techniques to reduce the long-term

Table 10-2. Crop and Livestock Production Per Worker in Solenzo, 1988–1989

| Village and Power Source | Number in Extended Family | Number of ALEs | Communal Field Area (ha/farm)[a] | Communal Field Area Per Worker (ha/ALE) | Cotton Productivity Per Worker (kg/ALE) | Sorghum-Millet Productivity Per Worker (kg/ALE) | Maize Productivity Per Worker (kg/ALE) | Net Crop Income Per Worker (CFA/ALE)[b] | Annual Livestock Income Per Worker (CFA/ALE) |
|---|---|---|---|---|---|---|---|---|---|
| DAR-ES-SALAAM | | | | | | | | | |
| Manual | 8.0 | 2.8 | 4.4 | 1.4 | 148 | 422 | 42 | 24,416 | 1,000 |
| Animal traction | 13.5 | 5.3 | 7.0 | 1.6 | 548 | 694 | 135 | 79,821 | 11,200 |
| Tractor | 29.5 | 10.9 | 37.7 | 3.4 | 2,789 | 808 | 4,292 | 521,167 | 71,907 |
| DABOURA | | | | | | | | | |
| Manual | 8.1 | 2.6 | 2.7 | 1.5 | 133 | 411 | 132 | 39,134 | 3,737 |
| Animal traction | 7.5 | 2.5 | 5.8 | 1.9 | 513 | 1,252 | 94 | 104,988 | -4,911 |
| Tractor | 37.0 | 13.8 | 29.9 | 2.2 | 869 | 737 | 1,488 | 182,850 | 10,921 |
| ALL | | | | | | | | | |
| Manual | — | 2.7 | 3.5 | 1.4 | 138 | 410 | 88 | 31,978 | — |
| Animal traction | — | 4.1 | 6.5 | 1.7 | 537 | 838 | 124 | 86,398 | — |
| Tractor | — | 12.2 | 34.5 | 2.8 | 1,824 | 771 | 2,864 | 297,331 | — |

*Source:* Adapted from McMillan, Nana, and Savadogo (1993); and Savadogo, Sanders, and McMillan (1989).
*Note:* ALE = adult labor equivalent. See note 5, this chapter, for weights used to derive ALE. Sample sizes were very small. Households in the Dar-es-Salaam sample for manual, animal, and tractor power were six, eight, and five, respectively. In Daboura, the households were seven, six, and four, respectively.
[a] Measurements for the fields of the household head and one wife were estimated by calculations of length and width. A subsample of fields was subjected to more rigorous field measurements to verify the accuracy of estimates.
[b] This is for all fields. CFA315/US$ (1989).

deleterious impact of cotton production on area soils. There have been substantial effects from these combined technologies in the southwest on cotton and maize yields (see chapter 3).

In contrast to the AVV, the cotton package at Solenzo has allowed migrant farmers to enjoy a sustained rate of income growth from commercial farming since the late 1960s through an increase in yields and of the total area farmed. The average yields for cotton increased from 544 kilograms per hectare in 1972–73 to 870 kilograms per hectare in 1980–81 and to 1,140 kilograms per hectare in 1990–91 (CRPA, 1989; Nana, 1989; McMillan, Nana, and Savadogo, 1993; CFDT, 1992).

Fertilizer use in the Solenzo area is among the highest in the country. The most concentrated applications tend to be on cotton and, to a lesser extent, maize, which was grown as a cash crop by the tractor farmers beginning in the early 1980s. Chemical fertilizer use in 1987–88 was estimated to be 143 kilograms per hectare NPK for cotton and 80–90 kilograms per hectare NPK plus 50 kilograms per hectare urea for corn, with about 95 percent of the area planted in cotton and 80 percent of the area planted in corn using some fertilizer (CRPA, 1989, pp. 32–33). In the field study, 80 percent of the cotton fields received NPK fertilizer at 100 kilograms per hectare or more, and 57 percent of the maize fields received lower amounts of NPK fertilizer. Only 23 percent of the red sorghum and 21 percent of the white sorghum fields received any fertilizer. In general, the tractor farmers used the largest amount of fertilizer per hectare. Only the tractor farmers received a guaranteed price for their maize production from the cotton parastatal, which also financed their tractors. Hence, maize production was concentrated on their farms (table 10-2). These guaranteed maize prices lasted only three years and were then discontinued (Bruno Barbier, personal conversation).

The lower use of fertilizer on cereals can be attributed to several factors. Farmers fertilize a rotation, with the residual effects being passed on to the maize and sorghum crops the next year. Twenty-six percent of the sorghum and 55 percent of the maize fields included in the CRPA du Mouhoun's farm-monitoring program in 1987–88 were planted on fields preceded by cotton.

High levels of fertilizer use on cotton, in combination with the high-quality area soils, have allowed the Solenzo area farmers to sustain high yields. These favorable circumstances have encouraged the more successful farmers to invest in minitractors and additional plows. The acquisition of animal and mechanical traction is also associated with much larger extended-family sizes (table 10-2).[9]

Increasing population densities will constrain the more ambitious farmers' attempts to exploit a larger area. We observed substantial differences in labor productivity and individual crop output per worker for the tractor farmers between the two settlements (table 10-2). The older settlement, Daboura, which experienced high rates of immigration in the early 1960s, is located on the main highway linking Dedougou and Solenzo. This village does not have any idle land in the area immediately adjacent to the river. In contrast, the newer settlement, Dar-es-Salaam, did not begin to develop until after 1974. This newer village possesses a large uninhabited bush between the core village and the Mouhoun River. Because of this large supply of uncultivated land, the tractor farmers in the newer settlement can still expand toward the river, and they achieved much higher labor productivities (table 10-2).

Although the use of inorganic fertilizers is widespread, there is mounting concern in Solenzo and the greater cotton zone of southwest Burkina about the steady decline in soil organic matter. Hence, there is an increasing need for organic fertilizers, including manure and incorporation of crop residues. Migrants farm the largest area possible, rather than adopting these soil conservation practices (CRPA, 1988).[10]

This problem of declining soil organic material and the research-and-development agency responses of improved rotations and higher utilization of organic fertilizers are second-generation problems of successful intensive technology introduction. In the Solenzo region, yields have been increased, incomes continue to rise, and in-migration continues after a decade of already high levels of in-migration. Good soils and adequate rainfall are found here. Two important advantages to this region are that intensive technology introduction was facilitated by research and that input and product-marketing infrastructure for both cotton and maize were well developed.

## Conclusion

The 1979 AVV farm-monitoring survey (Murphy and Sprey, 1980) and the ten-year restudy in 1988 (McMillan, Nana, and Savadogo, 1993) showed that various elements of the AVV extension package—food aid, tractor plowing, animal traction, and new soils—helped farmers with limited resources to achieve high levels of agricultural income growth over the initial five years of the project. However, this technical package was insufficient to allow them to continue to raise their annual standards of living on the same fixed land base. The principal apparent reason was the lack of a strong research base for the Sudanian region. More recent research in the 1980s showed that, unless combined with a water retention measure, fertilizer is a risky activity in the Sudanian zone (Nagy, Sanders, and Ohm, 1988).

In contrast, the Solenzo site was characterized by the successful introduction of a high-yielding package for commercial cotton and maize production. The cotton package has allowed migrant farmers to enjoy a sustained rate of income growth from commercial farming since the late 1960s. This successful crop technology package did not develop overnight. In colonial and postcolonial times, the French invested substantially in technology development for cotton. The Burkinabè have continued these investments in research, extension, and policy support to cotton and maize producers.

The comparison of the Solenzo and the AVV-sponsored settlements supports the need to reinforce the intensive technology research programs described earlier in this book. Even without public investment in planned colonization, the Solenzo development had the research base and has been successful and sustainable. In contrast, the AVV-planned settlement program was excellently supported by the public sector but could not maintain income growth over time due to technological limitations. Although the new technologies for water-harvesting in this zone (see chapter 4) are potentially important, they are not well known.

Another important research area is the need to increase the diversification of local crop and livestock systems. At present in the Solenzo region, most intensive crop production packages focus almost exclusively on cotton, with lower levels of support for maize. Cotton demands almost twice the amount of labor per hectare as other crops, and both crops are hard on soils due to nutrient depletion and soil degradation. Research can contribute to the development of more diversified crop production systems by developing rain-fed grain legumes, increasing livestock productivity, and testing new activities for dry-season irrigated gardening.

Foreign donors will continue to finance large-scale control of human and animal diseases in Sub-Saharan Africa, since these programs offer a rare opportunity to have an immediate and direct impact on income and productivity. However, this donor investment in disease control cannot be considered a substitute for the development of better adapted, intensive crop and livestock technology. Rather, the availability of this "new" land in Africa's semiarid zones offers "a vitally needed breathing spell, time to address the fundamental problem: improvement and eventual transformation of farming practices, in the direction of permanent, intensive cultivation" (Berg et al., 1978, p. iv). To make these settlement schemes sustainable and profitable in the long run, research and a profitable environment for agriculture must enable the shift to more intensive agricultural systems. Area expansion through disease control requires a complementary investment in the development and introduction of intensive agricultural production systems in order to move to higher-income, sustainable agricultural systems.

# 11

# Livestock Development through Intensification or Improvement of Mixed Farming Systems?

**I**N THE SEMIARID ZONES, livestock is found predominantly on smallholder mixed crop-livestock farms. In these mixed systems, a critical issue is whether further improvements in crop-livestock interactions are viable alternatives to more intensive crop and livestock activities that depend on purchased inputs.[1] For the drier areas of the semiarid region where there is relatively little potential for crop production (such as the more northerly, drier parts of the Sahelo-Sudanian zone of West Africa; see chapter 5), the question is whether livestock development can substitute for the marginally profitable crop-livestock systems presently practiced.

## Livestock Specialization Involving Intensification

Some types of specialized livestock production rely on high levels of inputs, both those produced on-farm and those purchased off-farm, and thus provide good examples of the intensification strategy proposed by this book. These specialized activities occur near urban population centers and include peri-urban dairying[2] and finishing operations for meat production.[3] The income elasticities are higher for livestock products than for cereals, and access to urban markets results in relatively high livestock prices. Due to high prices, these specialized livestock activities can be intensified, even with the rising costs of land and other inputs resulting from increasing population pressure (McIntire, Bourzat, and Pingali, 1992). As development proceeds, cheap industrial by-products, such as fish by-products in Senegal, are increasingly used in intensive livestock operations.

Intensified smallholder peri-urban dairying is developing rapidly all over the continent to serve population centers (see appendix for further discussion of the characteristics of these intensified dairy operations). While traditional African export crops suffer from depressed world prices, dairying offers immediate income-generating opportunities for peri-urban farmers in many countries in Sub-Saharan Africa (Walshe et al., 1991). Policy changes on the part of the European Common Market, the United States, and other major dairy exporters have led to a decline in world milk supplies, pushing up world market prices and making domestic milk production more competitive with imports from Europe. Even if world market prices do not continue to rise as expected (Shapouri and Rosen, 1992; Shapiro, Jesse, and Foltz, 1992), domestic milk production in many Sub-Saharan countries will remain competitive due to recent devaluations of local currencies (Walshe et al., 1991).

Smallholder units are especially effective in peri-urban dairy production, since it is labor- and management-intensive. Although dairy development is easier where disease pressure and climate are not major constraints, such as in the semiarid region, high prices enable smallholder peri-urban producers to take advantage of intensified feed technologies and better management practices in higher-rainfall regions. Costly preventive health technologies such as spraying and pour-ons can be used to mitigate the effects of trypanosomiasis, and dipping can be used to prevent and control East Coast fever and other endemic cattle diseases, thus allowing grazing to remain cost-effective even in subhumid lowland areas. Stall-feeding, involving produced or purchased products, also facilitates control of diseases such as dermatophiliasis and other technical problems such as heat stress. These feeding and health measures enable dairy activities to expand even in wetter lowland and coastal areas.

International and domestic policy changes are having supply-side effects on meat markets in Africa as well, since they are making domestic products more competitive in urban markets compared to non-African imports. Price liberalization and currency devaluation in most African countries have improved the competitiveness of meat domestically produced. Furthermore, livestock production in the semiarid areas in West Africa, as well as in eastern and southern Africa, has a comparative advantage relative to livestock production in coastal, humid countries, improving the prospects for interregional trade.[4]

Finishing operations for meat production are also located in or around urban areas across the continent. Presently, these finishing operations function mainly as collection and marketing points. Unlike in developed countries, where animals are fattened to increase value added, in Sub-Saharan Africa animals are fed in finishing operations mainly to maintain weight while they are being held for sale until prices are higher during demand peaks (Metzel and Cook, 1993). Nonetheless, these finishing operations still use a zero-grazing feeding technology similar to stall-feeding dairy cattle, because land for grazing is not available where finishing takes place near consumer markets. Again, the choice is for a labor-intensive technological change. Besides purchased hay and straw, supplements such as industrial by-products are used. Although finishing operations are rarely smallholder operations, the hay and straw they purchase usually comes from smallholder mixed farms.

With rapid population growth and increased urbanization, demand for both dairy and meat products is expected to continue to grow in Sub-Saharan Africa. In the twenty-five years prior to 1987, milk production grew by 3.2 percent in Sub-Saharan Africa, but consumption increased even faster (von Massow, 1989). Despite weakening economies and foreign exchange constraints, imports were still 11 percent of consumption in 1989 (1.2 million metric tons). Even if the growth rate of milk production remains the same, at the present rate of population growth in Sub-Saharan Africa, imports of 11 million tons of milk would be required by the year 2015. At current population growth rates, meanwhile, the demand for meat in urban areas in Sub-Saharan Africa is expected to grow at a rate of at least 4 percent per annum through the year 2025, while meat production is presently growing annually at less than 3 percent (Winrock International, 1992).

Demand for livestock products in Sub-Saharan Africa will thus grow, even if incomes continue to stagnate as in the eighties (Walshe et al., 1991; Winrock International, 1992; Metzel and Cook, 1993). More optimistically, with the positive effects of structural adjustment and debt forgiveness by Western governments and international agencies, growth of African economies will take place. In this case, even more rapid acceleration of demand for livestock products will occur.

## The Evolution of Mixed Systems in Semiarid Areas

Mixed crop-livestock farming predominates in most of semiarid Sub-Saharan Africa. Until recently, arable land has been abundant relative to labor. Extensive bush-fallow crop production was practiced with little use of cash inputs and low levels of management. Rapid population growth, however, is taking place in semiarid areas. The immediate response to increasing population is an expansion of cultivated area to maintain per capita crop output (Boserup, 1965, 1981; Ruthenberg, 1980). Fallow periods for maintaining soil fertility on cropland are declining or disappearing in many semiarid areas, and pastureland is being put under crop cultivation (see chapters 4 and 5; also see Peyre de Fabreques, 1986).

Livestock and crop activities thus become competitive for land resources under increasing population pressure. The expansion of crop production onto land previously used for grazing results in increased crop residues that can be used for animal feed but do not provide more animal feed than the lost grazing land. Furthermore, animals have to be kept off the fields during the crop season. In some regions, such as the Sudanian zones, this competition has resulted in the system of leaving the large ruminants in the care of the transhumant Fulani. Manure from these herds, thus, cannot replace fallowing practices as a means of maintaining soil fertility.

Continuing population growth eventually reduces farm sizes. However, more importantly, land becomes limited in quality as well as quantity as the fallow system breaks down and cropping is extended onto the less fertile lands previously used for grazing (see chapter 2). The use of inorganic fertilizer is increasing where rainfall is high enough for the combination of fertilizer with higher-value crops to be profitable, as in the subhumid region and the Sudanian part of the semiarid region of West Africa (see chapters 3 to 5). Here the land constraint, in terms of both quality and quantity, and potential profitability of intensified crops cause fertilizer to replace or be combined with manure in farmer strategies to maintain soil fertility.[5] Livestock is usually of secondary importance to crops where rainfall can sustain cropping, and intensification of crop production usually takes precedence. In spite of this, market forces can cause some livestock production activities to be highly profitable, resulting in intensified livestock production in mixed systems or specialized activities such as those activities mentioned above. Possibilities for intensified livestock activities on mixed farms in such areas include milk production with crossbreeds or improved breeds and fattening of large and small ruminants, especially strategic fattening to meet demand peaks for meat at holidays (Metzel and Cook, 1993). Labor also becomes constraining due to intensified crop production, and animal traction is often required where the soils are heavier (see Matlon and Adesina, 1991; also chapter 5, this volume).

Spatially uneven population growth combined with drier climatic conditions results in a relative abundance of land in more remote and drier areas, favoring livestock production over crops. In the more northerly, semiarid areas of West Africa, animal agriculture would be expected in the long run to replace crop production, as livestock prices rise relative to crop prices, due to structural adjustment. Such specialized, but low-input, livestock activities could also be integrated with low-cash-input sown grasses or forage legume crops. However, these systems are unlikely to be viable activities for smallholders, as they need to be practiced on a large scale. Hence, commercial farmers, including urban businesspeople and civil servants, who presently have crop farms in such areas, can be expected to switch to or expand livestock production as livestock prices increase. There is a danger of overgrazing these marginally productive lands, leading to land degradation in the drier areas of the semiarid region. Public policy measures to respond to the common property dilemma may be needed to avoid such consequences of the expansion of livestock.

## The Economic Role of Livestock in Mixed Systems

Livestock plays an essential role in diversifying the portfolio of economic activities of farm households in the semiarid region. Livestock often is the primary investment opportunity for many smallholder mixed farmers and their major source of on-farm cash income.[6] The ability to sell livestock in drought years to purchase food increases food security for farm households (Swinton, 1988; Adesina and Sanders, 1991). Unfortunately, in serious droughts, as in semiarid West Africa in 1972–73 or 1984–85, as the available food supply disappears the livestock either die or their price collapses as no one else can feed them, and there is widespread panic selling. Small ruminants thus play a greater role as food security, since they have a greater ability to survive drought and they can be more easily liquidated for cash or exchanged for cereal.

Some researchers have maintained that livestock is primarily kept as a store of wealth in peasant societies to enhance social prestige (Doran, Low, and Kemp, 1979; Low, Doran, and Kemp, 1980). There is growing evidence, however, that the cultural attitudes of farmers are consistent with economic motives. For example, village-level data from Niger indicate that livestock, as well as off-farm activities and remittances from relatives, can provide cash to buy inputs needed to change crop production methods (Sutter, 1979, 1984; Collion, 1982; Painter, 1986). Moreover, the same data show that other farm and off-farm activities, including livestock production and trading, rather than new crop technologies for dryland crop production, have been attracting this investment capital (Raynaut, 1973; Painter, 1986).[7]

Due to the climatic variability in the semiarid region, it is sometimes argued that on-farm sources of organic fertilizers, such as crop residues and manure, are better alternatives for maintaining soil fertility than inorganic fertilizer. The availability of crop residues for soil fertility maintenance in this harsh region, nevertheless, is limited, since most crop residues are removed for animal feed, fuel, and building materials. These uses are recognized by farmers to have higher economic value (Shapiro, 1990). While the use of manure can make livestock complementary to crops, crop residues are also the main source of animal feed, so there is a trade-off in using animals to maintain soil fertility.[8]

Policies and technologies designed to integrate a larger number of animals into crop-livestock systems are not likely to enhance soil fertility and thus result in increased crop production, even in the early stages of the development process. The manure supply is sufficient only to maintain yields on small areas surrounding family compounds (Sanders, 1989). Organic fertilizer sources are generally not sufficient for maintaining moderate levels of soil nutrients when population pressure is low and animal stocks fairly large. Approximately ten hectares of grazing land is required for each hectare of cropland to provide sufficient manure to maintain soil fertility (Williams, Powell, and Fernandez-Rivera, 1993). Thus, with the disappearance of the fallow system and encroachment onto grazing lands, the quantities of organic fertilizer required to attain even moderate levels of the basic soil nutrients could not be achieved. At present, manure also often replaces wood as a cooking fuel. While manure can be managed more effectively by improved corralling techniques (Powell and Williams, 1993) and covering the compost heap, the overall increase in terms of essential soil nutrients (nitrogen, phosphorus, and potassium) is small (see chapter 3). Manure is only complementary to inorganic fertilizer and is not a viable substitute (Sanders, 1989; McIntire, Bourzat, and Pingali, 1992).

Another complementary role of livestock in mixed farming is animal traction. Animal traction has historically been promoted in Sub-Saharan Africa as a means to expand area under cultivation, hence to increase productivity by saving labor. Pingali, Bigot, and Binswanger (1987) have examined the conditions under which animal traction has been successfully introduced in Sub-Saharan Africa. These include the need to intensify the farming system and improve tillage of heavy soil types, a sufficiently long crop season to use the full capacity of animal traction, and good access to markets. Where rainfall, soil, and market conditions are conducive, the use of animal traction can decrease labor costs and increase yields, thereby promoting further crop and livestock integration. The most rapid rates of adoption of animal traction in West Africa are occurring primarily in the northern areas of the Sudano-Guinean zone (wet savanna), where trypanosomiasis is not a major constraint (Adesina, 1992; Matlon and Adesina, 1991; Matlon, 1987; Panin, 1987). Here, higher-value crops with complementary purchased inputs such as seed and fertilizer are highly profitable, and resulting peak periods of labor demand create a role for animal traction.[9]

The conditions for intensified crop production that require use of animal traction are more difficult to meet in the semiarid region, since the rainfall is lower and more variable and soils are fragile and often of low fertility. The introduction of fertilizer, improved cultivars, and water retention techniques could, nonetheless, lead to the use of animal traction (oxen, donkeys, horses) in mixed farming in relatively wetter areas of the semiarid region in the Sudanian zone. Increased crop densities due to fertilizer use results in increased labor demand for some operations, such as weeding, thus making seasonal labor constraining.[10] Animal traction can then make weeding, as well as land preparation, more timely. Labor savings in weeding operations makes labor available for other activities. Moreover, more timely operations often increase crop yields. The future growth of animal traction in the semiarid region, therefore, will occur principally where crop production has been successfully intensified with increased purchased inputs, such as fertilizer and improved seed (Fussell et al., 1986; also see chapter 2).[11]

## Improving Livestock Where Crop Intensification Is Possible

More potential for improvement and intensification of livestock activities exists in the mixed systems in the subhumid than in the semiarid region.[12] The obvious qualification is the constraint that trypanosomiasis puts on the movement of livestock into higher-rainfall areas. More intensive human settlement, cutting the brush, and the introduction of trypano-tolerant breeds create ecological conditions that reduce the effects of the tsetse fly. In the relatively higher-rainfall, land-scarce areas of the semiarid region where potential for crop intensification also exists, an important policy issue is which strategy will increase farmers' incomes more, further integration of livestock with crops without purchased inputs or promoting intensification of crop and livestock activities with purchased inputs? Presently, in southern Mali farmers are using higher chemical inputs on cotton and maize and are beginning to use them on their sorghum. For livestock, *Dolichos lablab* and *Stylosanthes spp.*, both legumes, are being introduced, as well as improved management and storage of crop residues and cowpea hay.

In the semiarid region, animal feed is the major constraint to increasing livestock production. Low and variable rainfall and poor soil fertility cause limited and variable plant growth. These conditions result in high seasonal variability of traditional sources of animal feed, mainly natural pasture and crop residues. While intensified feeding occurs readily in specialized operations such as peri-urban dairying and finishing operations for meat prior to sale, improved residue management and intensified forage production for on-farm fattening have yet to take place in mixed systems in semiarid areas.[13] Improved residue management involves cutting, transporting, and storing crop residues for dry-season feeding (McIntire, Bourzat, and Pingali, 1992).

Peri-urban finishing operations, meanwhile, stimulate intensification of on-farm feed production for sale as cash crops. For instance, finishing operations at Niamey, Niger, have created demand for cowpea hay from farmers as far as 100 kilometers from this urban market. Even under traditional low-input crop technology at Libore, sales of cowpea hay accounted for 27 percent of expected total rain-fed crop income from 1984 to 1988 and substantially more of cash crop income (table 11-1). Under intensified production practices that include improved cultivars, moderate levels of fertilizer, and insecticide on the cowpeas, the share of cowpea hay in expected rain-fed crop income increases to 37%. Sixty-two percent of the income increase comes from the sale of cowpea hay.

Strategic fattening of small ruminants to meet the demand created by holidays and traditional religious and cultural practices is already an important economic activity in semiarid areas. There are well-developed markets throughout Sub-Saharan Africa for small ruminants strategically fattened. In anticipation of periods when special occasions will temporarily increase demand and hence prices, farmers will fatten a few animals for sale, depending on available feed resources. This supplemental feed presently consists primarily of stored crop residues and leftovers from household consumption. After varying periods of on-farm feeding, animals are finished in or near urban areas for holidays and feasts.

Small ruminant production, unless intensified, is not likely to be a source of increased incomes here due to the competition for land with more profitable intensified crops, including the cowpea hay.[14] Present small-ruminant activities were found to be less profitable than investment in phosphorus fertilizer alone with the improved cultivars.[15] Intensifying strategic fattening activities will require sown forages and purchase of prepared concentrates. With the falling opportunity costs for labor relative to land due to land degradation, continuing high population growth, and slow growth of nonfarm employment, these more labor-intensive types of livestock production will become more attractive. Growing cowpea hay as a cash crop at Libore with pesticides and fertilizer, meanwhile, provides a good example of the type of intensifica-

Table 11-1. Importance of Sales of Cowpea Hay, with Traditional and New Technologies, to Crop Income at Libore, Niamey Region, Niger

| | Millet/cowpea Income (US$) | Cowpea Hay Income (US$) | Total Crop Income (US$) | Cowpea Hay Share of Total Income |
|---|---|---|---|---|
| Traditional practices (millet/cowpea intercrop) | 326 | 120 | 446 | 27% |
| New technologies[a] | 396 | 232 | 628 | 37% |
| Change in income due to new technologies | 21% | 93% | 41% | |

*Source:* Calculated from farm model results, Shapiro (1990, p. 98, and appendix C, pp. 190–201).
*Note:* Exchange rate is CFA299/US$ (1990 base).
[a] New technologies here refer to improved short-cycle cultivars of millet and cowpeas with phosphorus fertilizer plus insecticide on the cowpeas.

tion that is occurring in the semiarid region of West Africa. These farmers presently specialize in this activity rather than feeding the cowpea hay to their own small ruminants.[16]

## Improving Livestock Where Crop Intensification Is Not Possible

Expansion and specialization in livestock production may be more appropriate than further efforts with crops in semiarid areas where more-intensified crop production is not economically viable. In more northerly, drier areas of the Sahelo-Sudanian zone for instance, population density and rainfall are lower than in much of the rest of the semiarid region. At Kouka, Niger, which is distant from the Niger River and urban centers, the model results show that there is limited potential for inorganic fertilizer adoption (see chapter 5). Rain-fed crop production practices are extensive, and animal herds are large. Since land is more abundant than at Libore, Niger, where rainfall is higher and land more constrained, the average number of small ruminants held are greater in number at Kouka: eight goats and three sheep, compared with two goats and one sheep at Libore.

Specialization in and expansion of livestock activities raises income risk, since specializing in animal production reduces the diversification effects of mixed farming. Furthermore, the returns to livestock vary from year to year.

Table 11-2 compares the role of livestock activities (small ruminants) in the income and risk-diversification strategies of farm households at the two sites in the Sahelo-Sudanian region. At Kouka, livestock income accounted for 37 percent of expected total annual income from 1984 to 1988, with a coefficient of variation (CV) of 89 percent. At Libore, the relatively land-scarce site, small-ruminant enterprise accounted for only 14 percent of total income, with a CV of 75 percent. This higher livestock income variability for livestock production than for mixed crop activities, due to price fluctuations and losses resulting from reproductive problems, other diseases, and theft, contradicts the frequent assertion that livestock production involves little income risk.[17]

Expansion of livestock activities through investment in small ruminants was chosen over intensified crop production at Kouka in the model results (see chapter 5).[18] Evidence from the field confirms that sheep and goats are often purchased when there is extra cash available, such as when men return from off-farm employment at the end of the dry season (Sutter, 1979, 1984; Shapiro, 1990). Small ruminants and their offspring are then fattened and sold at feast and holiday times or when cash is needed to meet household consumption requirements. The expected annual return on investment from raising one goat plus offspring at Kouka in 1984–88 was 40 percent. For sheep, meanwhile, the rate of return was 55 percent.[19] Farmers keep both species, since goats survive better in low-rainfall years and demand for them is often greater.

Key to the ability to expand and specialize in livestock production involv-

Table 11-2. Role of Livestock in Income and Variability at Relative Land Surplus and Land-Constrained Sites in the Sahelo-Sudanian Zone

| Income Source | Land-Constrained Site (Libore) | | Land-Surplus Site (Kouka) | |
|---|---|---|---|---|
| | Income (%) | CV (%) | Income (%) | CV (%) |
| Rainfed crops | 55 | 52 | 60 | 49 |
| Livestock | 14 | 75 | 37 | 89 |
| Salaried labor | 4 | 45 | 3 | 62 |
| Irrigated rice | 27 | 8 | | |
| Total income | 100 | 40 | 100 | 63 |

*Source:* Shapiro (1990, p. 119).
*Note:* These activity incomes are from the model results for these sites. Current practices are reflected here without introduction of new technologies.

ing both small and large ruminants is expanded marketing opportunities. Sut-ter (1979, 1984) has provided empirical evidence that presently Nigerien farmers sell most livestock during the soudure, or hungry period, before the end of the crop season, to buy food. Expanded marketing opportunities create flexibility in the timing of sales and thus the ability to sell where and when prices are higher. Increased marketing opportunities are made possible by access to more markets and occur through the development of roads, trans-port, and better price information. As shown in table 11-3, increased flexibil-ity in the timing of sales results in 24 percent higher livestock income and lowers livestock income variability from a CV of 89 percent to a CV of 75 percent.[20] The income change, however, is still very low, only US$44 per annum. Although the rates of return to investment in small livestock are higher than those of crops in relatively drier, semiarid areas such as Kouka, the increased returns due to improved marketing opportunities are not very large in absolute terms, and the income variability is still considerable.

Improved feed production practices would enable the expansion of special-ized livestock activities not only to meet the local demand peaks created by feasts and holidays but also to supply expanding markets, such as those in coastal areas. Possibilities for improved, but low-cash-input, livestock activi-ties include crop rotations or intercropping with forages, resulting in better

Table 11-3. Potential Income Change and Variability Due to Expanded Livestock-Marketing Opportunities at Land Surplus Site in the Sahelo-Sudanian Zone

| Income Source | Traditional Technologies | | Expanded Marketing Opportunities | | Income Change | % |
|---|---|---|---|---|---|---|
| | Income (US$) | CV (%) | Income (US$) | CV (%) | | |
| Crops | 301 | 49 | 409 | 39 | 108 | +36 |
| Livestock | 186 | 89 | 230 | 75 | 44 | +24 |
| Salaried labor | 16 | 62 | 14 | 14 | −2 | −13 |
| Total income | 503 | 63 | 653 | 54 | 150 | +30 |
| per capita income | 58 | | 76 | | | |

Source: Shapiro (1990, p. 125).
Note: Variability is measured with the coefficient of variation. Expanded livestock market-ing opportunities result in increased flexibility in the timing of sales, so higher prices can be realized.

feeding of animals, and improved soil fertility management. Such low-cash-input systems that include legumes would reduce but not eliminate the need for purchased inputs. Such innovations could raise livestock income, since more animals could be fed and sent to market, thus increasing offtake rates. More intensive legume production and ley rotations would require additional applied phosphorus fertilizer and often micronutrients.

Improved livestock activities that can substantially increase farmer incomes require replacement of crops with livestock activities and eventual consolidation of landholdings to enable improved, but extensive, animal production. Over time, population is likely to decline further. Migration of most men is already occurring seasonally (Painter, 1986; Shapiro, 1990).

## Livestock Production in the Grazing Region: The Sahelian Agroecological Zone

The Sahelian zone of West Africa has little potential for development of crop production.[21] This region has traditionally been the home of transhumant pastoralists (such as the Fulani). These herders move their stock in accordance with seasonal rainfall patterns and spend the drier part of the year in the higher-rainfall agroecological zones. Some subsistence production of millet and cowpeas is practiced in the Sahelian zone, but the principal activity is herd management. As permanent farming settlement has increased farther south in the higher-rainfall zones around traditional water sources, transhumance has become more difficult. Conflicts over property rights between these traditional herders and crop farmers are increasing. Due to the loss of animals during the recent droughts, some of the Fulani are now moving south and becoming settled agropastoralists in the relatively higher-rainfall regions (Sudano-Guinean), although they maintain much larger herds than traditional crop farmers.[22]

Moreover, with population pressure and soil degradation farther south, crop farmers have been moving north, adding to the serious land use competition in the Sahelian zone (Sanders et al., 1987). The small areas with irrigation potential are the preferred areas for agriculture. The leguminous trees in these areas provide a critical forage for the cattle, sheep, goats, and camels at the end of the dry season. The farmers cut down these trees for firewood and to extend the crop area. If some land use regulations are not implemented, one essential component of the traditional grazing system will be eliminated.

Economic changes, including the 1994 devaluations of the CFA, and increasing population pressure lead to more regional specialization. These changes are expected to bring about an expansion of livestock trade from pastoral and agropastoral operations in the Sahelian countries (where there is a comparative advantage for livestock production, especially cow-calf or breeding systems) to markets mainly found in the humid zone along the coast. As transhumance disappears, regional livestock specialization will ultimately become more important, with cow-calf or stocker operations in the Sahelian and drier parts of the Sahelo-Sudanian regions and fattening and finishing farther south, where there are more agricultural by-products, especially in the Sudanian and Sudano-Guinean regions. Barriers to trade between countries will have to be eliminated to achieve these trade gains from structural adjustment. Trade barriers between the Sahelian countries and the coastal markets include frequent checkpoints, each potentially requiring payments (Stryker, 1994; Metzel and Cook, 1993).

An important question is whether the changes in policy and transhumance would create conditions conducive to the improvement of these stocker systems in the Sahelian zone. If higher prices result from increased demand for Sahelian livestock previously met by cheap imports from Europe, herders would first attempt to expand their herds, since this would increase incomes. If this were not possible, they would still have an increased demand for low-cash-input production technologies to increase the availability of improved forages. These improvements, however, would be even more difficult than in the Sahelo-Sudanian zone, due to the very low rainfall, so the potential to introduce these improved technologies in this region is expected to be very low. With present knowledge and techniques, we would not expect the introduction of improved forages in the Sahelian zone. Hence, even the improved product prices from devaluation and increased trade with the coastal countries are not expected to lead to significant technological change in the Sahelian agroecological zone.

## Conclusion

Specialized dairying and finishing of beef cattle and small ruminants follow the same basic principles of the intensification strategy advocated in this book for increasing crop production. These operations require higher levels of inputs, usually purchased (see table 11-4). Breeding efforts raise the genetic potential of animals so they can respond to the complementary increased inputs. Meanwhile, the critical developmental aspect of such specialized activi-

Table 11-4. Potential for Intensification and Improvement of Livestock Production in Semiarid Sub-Saharan Africa

| Livestock Operation | Production System | Intensification Activity | Sahel (<350mm) | Sahelo-Sudanian (350–600mm) | Sudanian (600–800mm) | Sudano-Guinean (800–1,100mm) |
|---|---|---|---|---|---|---|
| Cow-calf | Sedentary (open range); agropastoral | Sown pasture and forages; leguminous trees | low — low | medium medium medium | — — — | — — — |
| Fattening | Sedentary; agropastoral; crop-livestock | Sown forages; leguminous trees; improved crop residues; fodder banks; by-products | — — — — — | low low low low — | medium medium medium medium low | high high medium medium medium |
| Traction | Crop-livestock | Cultivation; planting; weeding | — — — | low low low | medium medium medium | high high high |
| Strategic small ruminant fattening | Agropastoral; crop-livestock | Sown forages; improved crop residues; fodder bank; by-products | — — — — | low low low low | medium medium medium medium | high high high high |
| Finishing | Stall feeding | By-products; purchased hay | — — | medium medium | medium high | high high |

| | | low | medium | medium | medium |
|---|---|---|---|---|---|
| Peri-urban dairying | Sown pasture and | low | medium | medium | medium |
| | forages; | — | medium | medium | high |
| | improved crop residues; | — | medium | medium | high |
| Crop-livestock; stall feeding | leguminous trees; [a] | low | medium | medium | high |
| | fodder banks; | — | low | medium | high |
| | by-products; | low | medium | medium | high |
| | purchased hay | low | medium | high | high |

*Note:* Potential for change is the long-run comparative advantage rather than probability of adoption in the short or medium run.

[a] Also includes leguminous shrubs as windbreaks and live fences.

ties is that they are driven by increasing demand due to urban population and income growth. Peri-urban dairying and finishing present opportunities for only a relatively small number of producers in close proximity to urban areas.

In the Sahelo-Sudanian zone, potential for improved crop and livestock integration was shown to be limited. Improving livestock production in semi-arid areas will mainly require intensification involving higher levels of purchased inputs. Potential for intensification of livestock production in mixed farming exists in the Sudano-Guinean (subhumid) zone and in the Sudanian and wetter portions of the Sahelo-Sudanian (semiarid) zone. Opportunities for intensification and improving interactions in these mixed systems include fattening small and large ruminants, strategic fattening of small ruminants to meet demand peaks, animal traction, better use of manure, and intensified milk production with crossed or improved breeds.

The key development in livestock production in the semiarid region is the shift to planted forages, but this is occurring only in the intensive, specialized production activities in West Africa and in the wealthier Sudano-Guinean zone. This transition to planted forages begun in the wetter zones will be a major innovation of the next decade in these mixed systems in the relatively higher-rainfall areas. It is a sequential change after the increased crop productivity and will require similar techniques to increase soil fertility and to introduce new cultivars and planted forages into mixed farming.

Although finishing operations create demand for livestock from pastoral and agropastoral systems and for feed from mixed farming, they do not presently stimulate intensified livestock production on farm in the relatively higher-rainfall areas of the semiarid region of West Africa (Sudanian and Sahelo-Sudanian). However, as the opportunity cost of labor falls sufficiently relative to land and the price of meat rises relative to cereals, technological change through intensification of forage production will take place on farm. Over time, fodder banks can also be expected to play an increasing role on farms in these semiarid zones. Higher levels of inputs for improved forage and hay production can then also be expected for on-farm fattening as well as for sale to the specialized finishing and peri-urban dairy operations (see appendix to this chapter and table 11-4).

In the relatively drier areas, as in the northern part of the Sahelo-Sudanian zone where little potential for intensifying crops exists, concentrating mainly on livestock production is one development possibility. Some marginal improvements with drought-tolerant cultivars and some improved health control techniques are feasible but will have minor effects on income or production. Recent currency devaluation will result in increased income for local livestock, but income from marketed stock will be highly variable. Future research on livestock production will need to consider ways in which livestock losses can be stabilized in drought years.

The advantage that the relatively drier areas of the semiarid region have had of less disease and more nutritive grasses is disappearing with advances in the control of trypanosomiasis, pushing back the brush, and improved forage production in wetter zones. There appears to be limited potential for raising incomes from livestock improvements for the smallholder farmers in mixed farming or for herders in the traditional grazing systems in the drier parts of the Sahelo-Sudanian zone. Migration out of these marginally profitable mixed systems will ultimately lead to the introduction of larger, more-extensive livestock operations using improved livestock-forage activities. Grazing activities appear most relevant for the Sahelian region. Property rights conflicts will have to be resolved over the next ten years, or development of these areas will be hindered.

Structural changes taking place in the economies of Sub-Saharan Africa can be expected to bring about technological change in cattle production over the next five to ten years. Key among the factors pushing for shifts to more-intensive, specialized production activities are the breakdown of transhumance and recent currency devaluations and price liberalization. The price ratio of meat to cereals can be expected to rise over time, and beef production will become more regionally stratified, as has occured in other developing and developed countries. These stages include cow-calf and stocker operations in open-range systems in the arid and semiarid regions, fattening on farm and at collection or assembly points in the semiarid and subhumid regions, and finishing near urban markets in all agroclimatic zones. The main increases in purchased inputs for cow-calf operations are expected to be veterinary supplies. Fattening and finishing are expected to develop in relatively higher-rainfall areas, creating demand for forage, straw, hay, and residues grown on farm (see table 11-4). To encourage these changes, increased regional integration is needed between the Sahelian and the coastal countries through the elimination of barriers to trade such as quotas and border taxes. Such policy changes to promote regional integration will also be required in other parts of Sub-Saharan Africa.

Despite agroclimatic constraints, there are still substantial possibilities for development of animal agriculture in semiarid Sub-Saharan Africa, as shown in table 11-4. Moreover, particular opportunities for development are bolstered by access to markets around population centers. These developments will primarily involve intensification, achieved through greater levels of purchased inputs, except in the Sahelian and drier portions of the Sahelo-Sudanian zones. Moreover, throughout all the semiarid zones, increased specialization can be expected over time. As the competition between crops and livestock activities increases under structural reform leading to market development, changing land use patterns will occur through growing population pressure in the wetter regions and especially near the urban industrial centers. Population will be drawn from drier areas, making conditions in the Sahelian and drier Sahelo-Sudanian regions conducive to improved, but specialized, extensive livestock systems by larger operators.

# Appendix: Dairy Intensification in Kenya and Other Sites in Sub-Saharan Africa

Peri-urban dairying relies on high levels of inputs and thus provides an example of the intensification strategy proposed by this book as it applies to livestock development.[23] The expenses of smallholder peri-urban dairying in Kenya has been one of the major development success stories occurring in Sub-Saharan Africa. Although dairy consumption in Kenya during the period from 1977 to 1988 grew at a rate of nearly 8 percent annually, production increases kept pace with demand. Kenya's import dependency remained negligible at 0.4 percent (Shapouri and Rosen, 1992). Smallholder dairying in Kenya has long offered higher financial returns than other agricultural activities in peri-urban areas (Danida, 1991). At present, milk and milk products provide approximately 16 percent of total farm income (Mbogoh, 1987; Shapiro, Jesse, and Foltz, 1992). Smallholders in Kenya produce 80 percent of all milk (Sellen et al., 1990) and own most of the grade and purebred dairy cattle (mainly crossbreeds); one out of six smallholders owns crossbred cattle (Mbogoh, 1987).

Since independence, the success of dairying in the Kenya highlands has been based on smallholder dairy producers, many of whom use relatively intensive stall-feeding technology in zero or semizero grazing operations.[24] Stall-feeding generally involves grade dairy cattle, using farm-grown fodder and purchased supplemental feeds. Zero or semizero grazing is necessary due to population pressure and land scarcity in the Kenya highlands. Herds in zero and semizero units comprise two lactating cows on about 1.5 hectares (Sellen et al., 1990). Both zero and semizero grazing farms typically include small areas of cash crops as well as coffee or tea and sweet potatoes, with natural pasture of napier (elephant grass) for cut-and-carry stall-feeding.[25]

In semizero units, green fodder (usually napier) is the primary feed, because concentrated dairy meal is expensive (concentrate-to-milk price ratio of 2:3) given relative factor costs (land and labor to capital). Fodder is usually grown, rather than purchased, and supplemented with roadside clippings or roadside grazing. In the more intensive dairy systems, food crops such as maize are purchased, rather than grown, and available manure is applied to fodder crops. Open-grazing units also exist in less populated areas, where larger landholdings (about seventeen hectares on average) and herds (typically eight lactating cows) are viable due to resource conditions. On these larger operations, the labor-intensive napier is not grown due to the ample availability of natural pasture.[26]

Public policy has played a large role in the successful development of dairying in Kenya. The introduction of grade dairy cattle into the smallholder subsector can be attributed to government policies and support activities, including the provision of veterinary and artificial insemination services (which are now being privatized) as well as infrastructure (Mbogoh, 1987). In developing the smallholder sector, Kenya has been able to take advantage of the support infrastructure that served the large-scale producers, who predominated before independence, as well as breeding stock and skills provided by the big producers.

In the highlands of Ethiopia in and around Addis Ababa, specialized peri-urban dairying has been developing rapidly since the change in government in May 1991. A peri-urban dairy producer group with over seven thousand members has sprung up in Addis Ababa and has been organizing its own input supply and services system. Dairy production is highly profitable, since demand for fresh milk is strong and milk prices have been liberalized. The price paid by the large collection, processing, and marketing parastatal, the Dairy Development Enterprise (DDE), has doubled.[27]

Specialized dairying enterprises have also been growing rapidly around some of the larger towns of semiarid West Africa. Intensified peri-urban dairying around Bamako, Mali, for instance, has grown rapidly in spite of the inhospitable conditions normally associated with the semiarid zone. Taking place in an area where agropastoral systems predominate, this type of specialization rarely involves crossbred stock, but commercial feeds, vaccines, and preventive health measures are often used. Although a marketing parastatal is active, 45 percent of milk sold is reported to be marketed directly to consumers by herders, while itinerant traders handle another 20 percent (Achuonji and Debrah, 1992).

The relative insensitivity of peri-urban dairying to agroecological conditions and farming systems is further supported by its success in the area surrounding Accra, Ghana, in the subhumid zone. On the Accra plains, large dairy herds of zebu crosses supply the Accra markets. Some of these dairy operations are vertically integrated with processing and marketing. These large-scale operations specialize in milk production, with milk yields per cow two to three times higher than in traditional cattle herds. Due to supplementing grazing on native pastures with purchased feeds such as concentrates and fodder, the use of vaccines, and preventive health measures, smaller-scale stall-feeding operations, employing both zero and semizero grazing with grade cattle, exist closer to the urban area and are growing in number with the recent liberalization of the Ghanaian economy.

# V

## Conclusion

# 12

# Implications for Research and Development Policy

**D**ESPITE ALL THE PROBLEMS confronting Sub-Saharan Africa during the last two decades, the prospects for agricultural technology development and diffusion are not as bleak and gloomy as is often reported. A closer inspection of African agriculture shows some notable successes in the sub-humid agricultural region. Development potential is greater in the Sudano-Guinean zone than in the semiarid region because of higher rainfall and previous investments in research and infrastructure. However, soil degradation and natural resource deterioration are presently accelerating in the Sudano-Guinean zone with the increasing in-migration from the drier regions. Hence, it is becoming critical to develop new technology systems to increase agricultural productivity and to preserve the natural resource base throughout the semiarid and subhumid regions.

Introduction of new technology has been more difficult in the semiarid regions because of their harsher environments and some of the worst poverty conditions in the world (Anderson and Dillon, 1992, p. 7). The combination of lack of natural resources and the propensity of poor people to avoid risky innovations has often resulted in little public policy emphasis on agricultural development or even on agricultural research for the semiarid zone. Nevertheless, even in the less endowed regions, there have been some gains, and there is potential for increased production through more rapid technology introduction. The negative prognosis for future development does not stand up to closer scrutiny. Development of technology in the semiarid region would reduce the cereal import requirements and the out-migration from this region, thereby enabling the Sudano-Guinean zone to specialize more in export crops and preserve its own natural resources.

Some common threads connect the successes in the semiarid and subhumid zones and thus lead to a strategy of agricultural technology development. Essentially, the strategy we propose in this book consists of the combined introduction of several technology components to bring about yield-increasing technological change. The yield-increasing technologies for Sub-Saharan African agriculture that we propose require adaptive research, increased input purchases by farmers, and increased allocation of foreign exchange for chemical inputs. These intensive technologies require expenditures by farmers. The positive aspect is that farmers throughout the region are already shifting to more labor-intensive, lower-yielding variations of the strategy that we propose, such as the zaï and bunds combined with manure.

From our evaluation of the successes and potential successes, we have identified some patterns and guidelines. These are consistent with changes already observed in the region and follow the same principles of innovations resulting in gains made in other regions by applying science to agriculture. Greater emphasis in the semiarid region needs to be placed on a series of agronomic innovations to respond to the principal constraints of soil fertility and water availability.[1] The recommended technologies need to be adapted for agroecological, soil, and economic differences.

African governments will have to improve their support for agricultural research and extension institutions. Farmers need a better economic environment. Reliance on donor funding for critical research investments is increasingly risky, because donors often have short time horizons and can make quick changes in priorities and funding, whereas institutional research development requires long-term investments.

A number of other areas still need to be addressed:

- the differences between diffusing best-farmer practices and introducing new technologies
- some basic elements of research strategies for the subhumid and semiarid regions
- barriers to increasing fertilizer imports
- the development of input markets
- better collaboration in technology development between the international agricultural research centers (IARCs) and the national agricultural research systems (NARs)
- some principal concerns with the introduction of intensive technologies—risk, sustainability, and the impact on women
- land area expansion and mixed-crop–livestock systems
- high- and low-potential regions

### Movement Beyond Best-Farmer Practices

A new type of economic nationalism is hindering the introduction of rapid technological change in many Sub-Saharan countries. For example, Burkina Faso takes great pride in its indigenous village movements and has improved health systems and literacy by building programs around these movements (Smale and Ruttan, 1994). Applying these concepts to agriculture has meant identifying best-farmer practices and local inputs. Unfortunately, the zaï and the use of rock phosphate and manure cannot substitute for the types of yield increases possible with tied ridges, inorganic fertilizers, and animal traction implements.[2] Village-level innovations and a dependence on local inputs will not give Burkina rapid agricultural output growth (Ruttan, 1991).

The problem with building a development strategy on best-farmer diffusion is that farmers are not able to conceptualize major shifts in output made possible by the application of science to agriculture. Hybrid vigor, disease resistance in new cultivars, and the multiplicative effects of various inputs used simultaneously are all available from experiment stations. These are innovations resulting from a substantial accumulation of scientific knowledge and experience of agricultural scientists. Their introduction onto farms needs to be the focus of technology development programs, since diffusion of best-farmer practices gives only marginal improvements.

To identify innovations to bring about significant technological change, we need to move beyond the analysis of observed farmer innovations. Farm-level modeling based on data from field studies, experimental and regional trials, and expert opinions of agricultural scientists enables us to identify new technologies that can make possible major increases in output. A principal component of this book has been this modeling, and it is found in most chapters (chapters 3 to 11). Without considering substantial changes in agricultural technologies, the 3.5 to 5 percent growth in food output necessary to respond to population and economic growth and to gradually eliminate present nutritional inadequacies will not be forthcoming.

### Strategies for Technology Development with More Water Available: The Subhumid Zone and Irrigated Regions

The Sudano-Guinean zone and the irrigated regions have been the principal success stories recorded in this book. These areas not only have higher levels of water availability but also were the areas of concentration of past colonial research and infrastructure development. After independence from colonial rule, several parastatals and the development programs of the international agencies concentrated their activities here. Besides the successful breeding programs for cotton and maize, there have been substantial increases in the application of inorganic fertilizers.

In the Sudano-Guinean zone, the further introduction of new cultivars and higher levels of inorganic fertilizers and other chemicals can continue to increase yields. As continuous cropping and inorganic fertilization have increased, levels of organic matter in the soil have been declining. There is awareness among researchers that even though inorganic fertilization will need to increase further, it will have to be combined with organic fertilizers (Lynam and Blackie, 1994, pp. 116, 117). Presently, in countries such as Burkina Faso, there is ongoing adaptive research on introducing a legume into the cereal rotation and on other alternatives to increase levels of organic matter in the soil. There have been some dramatic successes in improving the quality and quantity of manure in Mali (chapter 3).

In the Sudano-Guinean zone, increasing migration and higher population densities are leading to greater conflicts between herders and farmers. In response, governments are exploring means of encouraging herders to establish permanent livestock-agriculture operations. Regional specialization in livestock is being concentrated in the Sudano-Guinean zone, as the clearing of the bush has pushed back the tsetse fly (Bourn and Wint, 1994, pp. 13, 14). Intensive livestock operations (fattening or finishing) use high-quality inputs, including farm by-products and cereals when grain prices fall.

Environmental problems in the Sudano-Guinean zone are increasing. Previously, population densities in this subhumid zone were relatively low due to the pressure of diseases (human and animal) and the difficulties of access to and clearing of land. As infrastructure and health conditions there have improved, in-migration from the Sudanian and Sahelo-Sudanian zones has accelerated. In these semiarid donor regions, the environment has already been degraded by population concentration, resulting in gradual disappearance of the fallow system, the pushing of crops into more marginal grazing lands, and the cutting of the forests for firewood (Gorse and Steeds, 1987). With in-migration to the Sudano-Guinean zone has come the same exploitation of land and environment as seen in the semiarid regions, including more conflict between migrants and local inhabitants, especially over cutting of the woodlands.

The forests, streams, and soil of the subhumid zone need to be better preserved, especially as the incidence of diseases is reduced, since this exposes these zones to the high population densities and accompanying exploitive environmental practices. Unfortunately, in most societies, environmental amenities are a high-income elasticity good most appreciated by people in wealthy countries. Poor people continue to need firewood and land to farm, so they put a low value on future environmental benefits.

## Strategies of Technology Development and Some Explanations for Their Slow Introduction into the Semiarid Zone

In chapters 4 through 6, we report a variety of technological responses to the dual constraints of soil fertility and water availability. In the ferruginous soils of the Sudanian zone of Burkina Faso, soil crusting is a critical problem because it leads to high runoff, so water retention generally needs to be given priority. On the sandy dune soils found in the Sahelo-Sudanian zone of Niger, the permeability of the soil to water is high. Thus, the water drains rapidly through the soil, making it difficult to retain water for plant growth. Various measures to increase soil fertility, including inorganic fertilizer and higher plant densities, also increase water use efficiency. On the vertisols of the Sudan, the natural cracking of the soil when dry gives some water retention capability. However, once wet, vertisols swell and form sticky crusts, impeding more water absorption. Hence, fertilization is effective by itself, but there is a small additional yield effect from water retention techniques that reduce runoff. Moisture management thus varies substantially between the crusting soils, where water retention techniques are the critical first step for infiltration, and the sandy dune soils, where the water needs to be held in the soil so that plants have access to it at the critical times. The vertisols are an intermediate case, since they provide their own water management by cracking when dry and their sticky clays hold onto water.

If the development of intensive technology is relatively simple and if most soil fertility and water retention techniques have been available in Sub-Saharan Africa for at least two decades, why has their introduction in the semiarid zones been so slow? We suggest a four-part answer:

1. Historically in the semiarid regions, Africans could practice "shifting agriculture" by moving into new lands after they exhausted the soil. Or they could adopt extensive technologies, such as animal traction, and expand the area to be cultivated. Recently, farmers in many areas have been exhausting the frontier and depleting the soil. As the frontier closes, the fallow system breaks down, and the implicit cost of land increases. Shifting from extensive to intensive technologies then becomes economically appropriate, especially

if product prices also rise to improve profitability. These shifts from extensive to intensive technologies are presently occurring and are documented throughout this book.[3]

2. We have emphasized the necessity of responding simultaneously to the dual constraints of water availability and soil fertility. In two of the three cases evaluated in chapters 4 to 6, better management with fertilizer alone would be viable and profitable.[4] Only in the case of the crusting on the Sudanian ferruginous soils would the simultaneous use of the two types of inputs be required. In all the cases considered in these chapters, increased inorganic fertilization is necessary. The response to fertilization will be considerably greater for new cultivars than for the traditional ones. Traditional cultivars are selected by farmers over long periods of time for yield stability under adverse conditions. In contrast, one predominant selection criterion for new cultivars is their ability to respond to moderate or high levels of inputs.

Most water retention measures require high levels of labor inputs or new implements for animal or mechanical traction. The appropriate measures for the largest effects on yields require construction of water retention devices during one of the periods of the crop season when most farmers are already faced with seasonal labor shortages. Hence, to adopt the practice, most farmers would have to mechanize some of their operations. An example is the construction of tied ridges at first weeding.

For many farmers, successful technology introduction requires the simultaneous adoption of up to four different technology components (see chapter 4). Four simultaneous input changes are difficult for researchers to study, for extension agents to promote, and for farmers to undertake. Farmers tend to adopt new technologies with gradual changes, one input change at a time (Byerlee and Hesse de Polanco, 1986; Matlon and Spencer, 1984, p. 675). But conditions in the semiarid regions are so harsh and difficult that responding to just one constraint or adopting only one technology component often has little effect. Researchers often report that as a consequence, these one-input changes have little impact on profitability. (Matlon and Spencer, 1984, p. 624, review fertilizer response without concern for water availability; also see chapters 3 to 6). Farmers prefer simple, one-input, and gradual changes, but they will not introduce them unless they have noticeable effects. In the semiarid regions, frequently more than one change is needed to make a noticeable impact.

We have never argued that introducing these combined changes will be easy; we have only shown that many of these combined changes would be economically viable and adopted by farmers, according to model results. We have also presented substantial field observations of farmers in all the regions studied who adopted similar but often simpler innovations in response to the two constraints of soil fertility and water availability. The simpler changes, such as the dikes constructed outside the crop season and the zaï in Burkina and the teras system in the Sudan, are easier for farmers to make. The more complex changes with more components have larger yield effects. The gradual process of first adopting simpler technologies has begun, as documented in chapters 2 through 6.

3. Historically, government policies have led to a neglect of agriculture. Generally, there has been insufficient public investment in infrastructure and services for agriculture. Investments in the agricultural sector have often come from the donors as African governments concentrated on industrialization and orienting economic policies to benefit urban workers and themselves.[5] The parastatals for agricultural product and factor marketing have generally been more concerned with providing employment, keeping urban food prices low, and extracting a surplus for investing outside of agriculture than with maintaining high incentives for farmers to invest and to produce (Bates, 1981; World Bank, 1986).

With structural adjustment, the stage is set for agriculture to become more profitable as exchange rate overvaluation is reduced and parastatals are replaced by private sector firms. The downside is that subsidies on fertilizer and credit will be reduced or eliminated. Moreover, it will be difficult for these governments to eliminate one of the primary factors discouraging the introduction of new technologies. This is the collapse of cereal prices in good rainfall years. Most countries in Sub-Saharan Africa have official programs to maintain cereal prices that they are not able to implement. Developed countries do not let the prices of major food commodities collapse.

Various programs to expand demand for the cereals are an alternative approach to price supports. At lower prices, food grains become feed grains. With changes in milling technologies, sorghum and millet could partially substitute for wheat in the flour mills. Some sorghum producers, such as the Sudan, need to be investing in the contacts and the quality requirements to expand their participation in the world export market. To increase price stability between years, programs for demand expansion should be implemented when countries are introducing new agricultural technologies.

4. In the foreign exchange rationing undertaken by most African countries, inorganic fertilizer imports have received a low priority. Historically,

exchange rates have been distorted, favoring imported rather than domestically produced cereals. Food and oil imports to maintain low prices for politically explosive urban workers and luxury goods for high-level bureaucrats and other influential people have often pushed inorganic fertilizer imports off the list for foreign exchange entitlements. Twenty countries in Sub-Saharan Africa have been entirely dependent on donor aid for fertilizer imports (Bumb, 1991).

Governmental failure in Sub-Saharan Africa to develop a fertilizer policy or to place inorganic fertilizer near the top of the list for foreign exchange entitlement is partially due to the lack of concern by governments and input-marketing parastatals with farmer incentives and the profitability of agriculture. This also appears to be a case in which foreign technical advice has contributed negatively to the problem. Technicians in bilateral and multilateral programs, without evaluating the viability and economics of the alternatives to inorganic fertilizer, often pick up one or more of the arguments against using inorganic fertilizer.[6] The technicians then reinforce the propensity of national government officials to put imported fertilizer at the bottom of the foreign exchange rationing list.

As the devaluations of the structural adjustment programs reduce the rationing requirements and ultimately make them unnecessary, importation problems will be simplified. Nevertheless, even with some structural adjustment, import and foreign exchange regulations are still making it difficult to import inorganic fertilizers in many countries. African governments will need to encourage private firms to import and market fertilizer. There needs to be sufficient competition in the input-marketing sector to keep fertilizer prices down so that farmers can make money as a result of using fertilizer.

High transportation costs are a fundamental problem for many isolated countries long distances from ports, such as Malawi and the Sahelian countries. Nevertheless, these countries use inorganic fertilizer on their export crops, such as tobacco in Malawi and cotton and maize in the Sahel. Hence, the fundamental problem is with food crop price levels and price stability. Agricultural development requires that farmers make money, and governments need to support this farmer objective in the food crop sector by avoiding policies to subsidize the prices of imported cereals.

Many factors slowing the introduction of technological change in the semi-arid region are now changing. Increased population pressure, slow growth of the nonfarm demand for labor, and increasing demand for food are all encouraging a shift from extensive to intensive production practices. The implementation of structural reforms with devaluations and a shift from parastatals to private firms can make agriculture more profitable and encourage investment. The national agricultural research institutions are maturing, gaining more confidence, and noticing the farmers' shifts to more-intensive technologies. All of these factors should accelerate the introduction of these intensive technologies. On the negative side, the elimination of input subsidies, especially on fertilizer, will adversely affect adoption of new technologies in the dry savannas. Higher food prices ultimately will reduce the real cost of fertilizer as long as governments do not continue to subsidize urban food prices through imports. There may be a case for renewing fertilizer subsidies in some semi-arid regions, especially when water retention techniques and new cultivars are also introduced.

Moreover, public policy intervention to avoid the price collapses of the cereals in normal or good rainfall years and to shift outward the demand for the traditional cereals with new alternative uses both seem to be appropriate if not urgent policy measures to combine with technology development and diffusion of the yield-increasing technologies. Both encouraging fattening programs and increasing use of the traditional cereals in bread when domestic cereal prices decline because of good weather or technological change are expected to be more cost-efficient and viable than the expensive and generally unsuccessful price support and storage programs.

There still is resistance in many developing countries of Sub-Saharan Africa to increased adaptive research on inorganic fertilizer and to importation of inorganic fertilizers. The recent natural resources emphasis of donors is contributing to this problem, as is the economic nationalism previously discussed. The dangers of inorganic fertilizers in the environment of Sub-Saharan agriculture are very different from those in other regions that have attained high agricultural yields with high levels of inorganic fertilizers.

## Input Markets and Agricultural Technology

In the agricultural development process, the functioning of input markets, especially for land, seed, and fertilizer, will become increasingly important (see chapters 6 and 8). The role of direct state participation in the market is being reduced all over Sub-Saharan Africa. However, there is need for caution in this shift. In Sudan, when the price for the new sorghum hybrid collapsed in the mid-eighties, the two public agencies continued seed production while the private firms left the industry (chapter 6). Now that diffusion of the hybrid sorghum is accelerating again, the public sector has had difficulty responding to rapidly increasing demand for quality seed and fertilizers. The private sector has reentered the market. The effective functioning of the public sector will often be necessary in the risky environment of technology development and introduction in Sub-Saharan Africa. The difficult problem is knowing when to phase down and eliminate some public sector activities. Strategies based on private sector investment often neglect the small-farm sector (Lynam and Blackie, 1994, p. 109).[7] The public sector can help offset some of the disadvantages of the smallholder sector in dealing with the private sector by organizing cooperatives and providing investments in transportation and communications.

This evolution of the private sector is a secondary constraint that becomes important only after the process of technological change is underway. When profitable technologies are extended to farmers, the markets for cash inputs, such as seed and fertilizer, will develop. The public sector will need to create a stable policy environment so that the private sector can profitably take over the purchased-input industries. A key means of accelerating the entrance and competition of private firms in input and product marketing in agriculture is substantially increased public investment in roads and other infrastructure, including communications. Donor involvement will undoubtedly be necessary for investments to improve the infrastructure supporting agriculture, including research.

## Implications for International Agricultural Research

The research system consists of the international agricultural research centers (IARCs); the national agricultural research systems (NARSs); the multilateral organizations, especially the World Bank; the bilateral or developed-country donors; and the country governments. The first two are the implementors of research. The last three are the funders of research and other agricultural development programs.

The Green Revolution successes began to be well documented in the late sixties. From this period to the early eighties, the international and developed-country donors operated on the paradigm that agricultural technology introduction was the engine of growth for agriculture and for the whole economy in most of the lower-income developing countries. African governments were too concerned with immediately visible projects to adequately finance agricultural research. In economic terms, the rate of time discount of developing countries was too high. Agricultural research, especially building up the institutional and human capital capacities of research institutions, is a long-term investment. It has high payoffs, but most of the returns are subtle and not immediately obvious to policymakers. For example, cereal research produces new cultivars and associated technologies that enable food prices to decline and farmers to reduce their production costs. Usually, diffusion is gradual, and the price declines are small. Compare the visibility of these gains with the enormous cathedral built by the former president of the Côte d'Ivoire in his home village. Clearly, with the historic large policy distortions against the agricultural sector in most Sub-Saharan countries, it has been even harder to appreciate the gains from new technologies.

Support for the IARC model has been based on the following rationale: agricultural research requires a narrow definition of priorities, well-trained multidisciplinary teams of scientists, and long-term time commitments (Ruttan, 1982, pp. 116–46). The donors generally concluded that the IARCs could be isolated successfully from short-run political pressures and provided sufficient financial incentives and infrastructure to put together and motivate multidisciplinary teams of scientists over long periods of time, five to ten years. The NARSs, as agencies of their governments, have had to respond to continually changing objectives of their governments and often of donors. Hence, the NARSs were unable to be isolated from these political pressures or to maintain size and continuity in their commodity research programs. Moreover, in the last two decades, the NARSs still needed to build up their human capital capacity.

The response of the international donor community was to expand the system of the IARCs. The big expansion of the IARCs started in the second half of the sixties and continued through the seventies and can be attributed to the successes of the new rice and wheat cultivars in Asia, especially in the Indian subcontinent. IRRI (International Rice Research Institute) and CIMMYT (International Maize and Wheat Improvement Center) were already in existence in the sixties but were funded largely by foundations. With the well-publicized successes of the Green Revolution, developed countries and the World Bank substantially expanded their financing and the number of the IARCs (now, in 1994, there are eighteen IARCs in the CGIAR—Consultative Group on International Agricultural Research—cosponsored by the World Bank, the FAO, and the UNDP, with thirty-nine contributing donor members. See CGIAR, 1994, p. 51). Donor support was also provided to the NARSs. Human capital formation for the NARSs has been an ongoing investment for at least two decades by the developed countries and since 1979 by the World Bank (Lynam and Blackie, 1994, p. 121).

The IARC structures became the institutional model for most of the NARS;

so it is not surprising that plant breeding became the dominant discipline in the NARSs, as it already was in the IARCs.[8] The principal function of the other disciplines in the IARCs was to support the breeding activities. The IARCs had worldwide objectives for their specific commodities. The NARSs' role as seen initially by the IARCs was to take the new cultivars and select what was most useful for their specific environments and to do agronomic and other research that was region-specific, hence outside the mandate of the IARCs (Lynam and Blackie, 1994, p. 116). As the NARSs developed, they assumed more breeding-research functions. Moreover, they pushed for a larger share of international resources. For much of the seventies there was a useful creative tension, as well as some collaboration, between the IARCs and the NARSs.

In the eighties, life became more difficult in the technology development system. From the early eighties to the present, there has been a shift in the predominant paradigm in development to "Get the prices right." This implied structural adjustment with devaluations and shifts from parastatals to an emphasis on developing a private sector and stressing exports rather than achieving food self-sufficiency (see chapter 1). With the forced economic readjustments of structural adjustment and the extraction of capital to repay the loans of the previous decade, the decade of the eighties and the first half of the nineties were very difficult for most developing countries and especially for the low-income sectors.[9] Many of these changes from structural adjustment will be good for the agricultural sector in the long run. However, with the shift of the paradigm, there has been a leveling off of donor funding for the agricultural research system. The competition for these donor funds became more intense and acrimonious in the eighties and nineties due to the struggles of both the IARCs and NARSs to sustain their research budgets.

During the eighties and nineties, many of the NARSs were successful in building up their institutional and human capital capacities. Some successes in technology adaptation and diffusion were also achieved, as documented in chapters 3 through 6. The IARCs matured and had more difficulty attracting the best scientists in the eighties and the nineties, but they have remained the principal institutional development success story for international agricultural development since World War II. The eighties were a decade of substantial institutional evolution and development for both the NARSs and the IARCs, despite the rising conflict levels and the inability of the agricultural research system to replicate the earlier dramatic successes of the miracle rice and wheat varieties.

Presently, with institutional evolution and maturity in the IARCs and the

NARSs, both are looking for some redefinition of their roles. The IARCs have been attempting to move into more basic research to support their applied research goals of introducing new cultivars. In the early nineties, there was another expansion of the IARC system, with five new centers allowed into the CGIAR system. The expansion of the system in the nineties sought to better address natural resource issues and to respond to some other food and input market considerations. Unfortunately, without the political support of a new Green Revolution there was no funding expansion to support these new centers. As a result, in the mid-nineties many of the mature IARCs are in crisis, attempting to respond to the large budget cuts resulting from an expanded CGIAR system (eighteen IARCs) and having to address new issues without a commensurate increase in funding.

Many NARSs want to take over much more of the breeding and other applied research being done in the IARCs. Generally, the NARSs are still dominated by breeders, and they still fail to invest sufficiently in agronomic research. This underinvestment in resource management issues is also a serious problem in the regional commodity networks, which are presently the main connecting link between the IARCs and the NARSs (Lynam and Blackie, 1994, p. 124). One of the main policy implications of this book is the need for the NARSs to concentrate much more on increasing the quantity and quality of their agronomic research. Lynam and Blackie (1994, p. 124) argue that the NARSs should take the leadership in the international research system in crop husbandry and soil management research rather than become small-scale replications of the IARCs with a similar concentration on breeding activities. The NARSs will probably also need some help from the IARCs in undertaking the more basic work on soils and water and in getting more agronomists trained and adequately supported in the NARS system.

A recent CIMMYT-Michigan State study (Maredia, Byerlee, and Eicher, 1994, p. 45) indicates that the NARSs are overinvesting in wheat-breeding research and that there are economies of scale to doing breeding research in institutions such as CIMMYT. The natural evolution of the international research system appears to be for the IARCs to specialize more in breeding and to increasingly turn over the other resource management activities to the NARSs, while still giving the NARSs some intellectual backstopping in the more basic research of this resource management type.

This evolution implies that the NARSs would have their own breeders but that the multiscientist interdisciplinary teams would stay concentrated in the IARCs, enabling the NARSs to specialize more in region-specific research and reduce their breeding activities. Much of the socioeconomic and institution-building activities presently being done in the IARCs could also go into the NARSs. The conservation and management of natural resources should probably stay in the IARCs, as this is long-term, difficult and expensive research with more support from donors than from national governments in the developing countries (see CGIAR, 1994, p. 52 for most of this categorical breakdown of IARCs' activities).

The other natural evolution of the system is for the NARSs to increasingly utilize the talents of a wider number of developed-country scientists. The returned Ph.D.s of the NARSs know how to plug into the international scientific networks and obtain materials, information, and collaboration. On the developed-country side, programs such as INTSORMIL support U.S. scientists to become more involved with sorghum and millet researchers in Africa. These programs need to be better tied to the African research networks.

In the short run, pending the arrival of another world food crisis, donor enthusiasm for agricultural research is unlikely to return, as the probability of having new Green Revolutions is low. We have shown in chapter 3 how continuing agricultural research has resulted in gradual but substantial gains in productivity of cotton, maize, and organic fertilizer. These same types of gains are also occurring in other commodities supported by IARC (and NARS) research, such as field beans, potatoes, and cassava. Similar gains were also shown to be possible even in the more difficult semiarid environments examined in this book (see chapters 4 to 6).

Unfortunately, these smaller gains and potential gains from agricultural research are not as widely publicized as the original Green Revolution. Presently, there is increasing donor fatigue with agricultural research. Donors have now been funding the international agricultural research system for almost three decades. Continuing agricultural technology development and diffusion will increasingly depend on support to the NARSs from their own governments.

## Risk, Sustainability, and the Impact on Women

We have spent several chapters showing that the intensive technologies respond to risk and sustainability concerns and, with some supporting policy measures, could also make women better off (chapters 7 through 9). All three of these issues are important concerns for the international development community.

After the introduction of moderate levels of inorganic fertilizer and new cultivars, second-generation technologies will increase risk levels, making risk-reduction policies more important (see chapter 7). Fortunately, the first-generation technologies are characterized by risk reduction or only moderate increases in risk.

In the fragile soils of marginal agricultural areas, poverty presses farmers into extremely exploitative resource-depleting practices. Farming more intensively in the best agricultural regions can enable some withdrawal from marginal agricultural areas. Also, as the subhumid region becomes more accessible to in-migration, preventing the introduction of the worst environmental practices there is an important environmental goal.

Neither poor people nor policymakers in poor countries will be much concerned with environmental amenities or biological diversity until two things happen:

- a higher proportion of their population is able to satisfy their basic needs;
- their economic systems develop the capacity to respond to the rapidly increasing demands for food products. [10]

So the critical first-generation problem is to get these intensive technologies moving through NARS and onto farmers' fields. Then, policymakers in developing countries will have more flexibility to respond to sustainability concerns.

Both sustainability and the impact on women generate substantial heat in the developmental discussion. Clearly, women are adversely affected by a number of economic and social policies in Sub-Saharan Africa. Moreover, men have been able to obtain control of most of the new agricultural technologies being introduced. However, we were unable to find empirical documentation for the common assertion that women's welfare was reduced with the introduction of these new intensive technologies (see chapter 9). Rather, our results and those of the empirical studies cited show that women were made better off by the introduction of the new intensive technologies. Moreover, we presented some evidence that the welfare of women and of the household as a whole would be increased more by the introduction of improved household technologies and by improvements in off-farm work opportunities than by aiming agricultural technologies specifically at women.

We are referring here to women in households headed by men. Much of African agricultural production comes from households headed by women. New cultivars, inorganic fertilizers, extension, and credit need to be made as available to these female-headed households as to those headed by men. Equal access to agricultural services often requires special policy efforts.

Progress is being made on this in Sub-Saharan Africa, as in Malawi, where a high proportion of the small farms are headed by females. One critical issue for women in households headed by men is to free up more of their time from the drudgery of labor-intensive household chores. For example, household technologies already exist to facilitate cereal processing and enhance fuel use efficiency, thereby reducing the need to gather firewood. With more free time, women can engage in additional income-earning activities, have more time to care for their children, or even enjoy some leisure time (see Lawrence, 1993, for a more comprehensive examination of these issues).

Much more attention of researchers and policymakers should therefore be devoted to the issues of risk, sustainability, and the impact of various technologies on women. However, these issues should not be barriers to financial and policy efforts to support the introduction of intensive technologies, since the introduction of new intensive technologies will help resolve these other problems. The low-income developing countries need to accelerate the pace of food-output increases. Once they have improved their capacity to more adequately feed their people and to decrease nutritional deficiencies, these countries will be positioned to put more attention on the issues of risk, sustainability, and income distribution within families.[11]

## Expansion of Land Area and Improvement of Traditional Systems

The introduction of intensive technologies requires large-scale investments in human capital, construction of experimental sites, regional and farm testing, investment in extension, and support of economic policies. Hence, it is appropriate for governments to search for and evaluate possible lower-cost alternatives to intensive technologies. We considered two alternatives in some detail: opening up new land areas through disease control (chapter 10) and improvements in the present mixed crop-livestock systems (chapter 11).[12]

We found that if disease control programs are not combined with adequate programs of intensive technologies, after a decade incomes fall to approximately half of initial incomes, and better farmers migrate to other frontier areas. In contrast, an adequate research base leads to continuing income increases and in-migration. It appears that the development of intensive technologies and the disease control programs are complementary investments (see chapter 11).

The livestock issue[13] is more complicated than the disease control issue.

- The most rapid expansion of livestock production is occurring in new intensive systems that produce milk, meat, or eggs. In their use of inputs, these systems are similar to the intensive crop systems we recommend. Confined feeding is done either with improved, cut forages or purchased feeds, or a combination of the two. Moreover, improved breeds are generally introduced.

- Once cereal production is increased with intensive technologies, the introduction of a legume in the rotation is a logical next step for both subhumid and semiarid regions. Increased cowpea or other legume productivity can benefit both human and animal nutrition. The intensive technology system for the cereals then becomes the model for forage production.

- In marginal crop areas, as in the northern Sahelo-Sudanian and all of the Sahelian zones, we recommend replacement of the mixed system with livestock and agroforestry, since the incomes of mixed systems are expected to be too low to support the present crop farmers. These new agricultural systems become viable alternatives after substantial out-migration. Similarly, we do not foresee much improvement in traditional herding systems until there is a shift from transhumance to regional specialization in livestock production.

In summary, the type of analysis used here for the appropriate technologies to be introduced in crop production also applies to the cases of the successful, rapidly developing livestock systems. In the subhumid and semiarid regions, there appears to be a necessary sequence of introducing intensive technologies into the crop system before doing so in the livestock sector. Higher incomes will lead to the increased demand for further improvement of forages and eventually to increased use of cereals as feedgrains, at least in years of good rainfall. Intensive technological change is already occurring in the specialized intensive systems of dairy production and, to a lesser extent, in cattle finishing.

In the subhumid region, pushing back the tsetse fly and ending transhumance are giving the region a greater concentration of feeding and finishing operations in both mixed and specialized systems. This is a high-priority area, as income gains would be large and farmers add value to their cereals through feeding. Moreover, the demand for animal products is expected to increase substantially over the next two decades. Governments can facilitate this process with applied research, infrastructure construction, and establishment of a regulatory environment for the successful emergence of a private sector for input and product marketing.

## High- and Low-Potential Regions

Accelerated adoption of intensive crop technologies in the subhumid tropics helps resolve the food and environmental problems of the whole semiarid zone. Greater output from the agricultural regions with the highest potential can result in environmental improvement or less degradation by encouraging the withdrawal of crops from more marginal regions. The subhumid and irrigated regions are expected to be the principal regions in which countries in Sub-Saharan Africa concentrate their agricultural research and extension activities. We are assuming that the principal objective of Sub-Saharan African governments will be to maximize the efficiency of the use of scarce research resources rather than equity, environmental, or other objectives that could encourage them to spread the resources around equally or to use them where population densities are highest or where the people are poorest.

Nevertheless, much of the semiarid zones have high population densities and the potential for much more rapid technological change. These regions have often been considered marginal or low potential. With increased availability of water, they have substantial potential, as there are fewer plant-disease problems all over the world in drier environments. One major point of this book is that the semiarid zone can increase crop and forage yields. Many technologies to provide more water are being practiced in various parts of the world. We have considered the variations in response to water retention techniques for three different soil types and in four different agroecological zones (chapters 3 to 6).

Technological change in agriculture is not complicated. It will be necessary to undertake adaptive research, introduce good extension programs offering several new inputs at one time, and create a more profitable environment for farmers, especially moderating the price collapse of the basic food crops in good years. The development of a private sector to efficiently provide increasing quantities of quality seeds and fertilizer and to improve product marketing will quickly become important, as the case of HD-1 in Sudan has indicated. These are viable strategies. They increase output and improve the welfare of both consumers and producers in semiarid zones. It is time to shift much of the semiarid zone from a low-potential to a high-potential crop production region in the perspectives of policymakers in Sub-Saharan Africa and donors to the region.

We consider two policy recommendations to be critical to the success of technology development and introduction in the semiarid zone during the next decade. First, fertilizer subsidies appear to be a necessary policy support while the complicated combinations of new inputs are becoming easier for farmers to manage. Inorganic fertilizer is the critical input without any viable substitutes in the short run. So governments need to provide these subsidies until the learning costs of the new input combinations are reduced with farmer experience. In both Zimbabwe and Namibia, inorganic fertilizer subsidies are being successfully employed presently to accompany the introduction of new sorghum and millet cultivars by small farmers (John Sanders, unpublished data).

There is a danger of a subsidized input being rationed and provided principally to wealthy or influential farmers. However, the alternatives to a fertilizer subsidy of large-scale transportation and infrastructure investment are too expensive and long run. African governments presently have a unique moment of high prices of domestic, relative to imported, cereals as a result of structural adjustment. However, they need to rapidly increase domestic food productivity or there will be strong urban pressures to again subsidize imported foods. Hence, the risks of increased income inequality due to rationed, subsidized inputs need to be taken.

The second critical measure is to find methods to raise the salaries and the research support to the newly returned, highly trained human capital in the NARSs. These Ph.D. scientists often have alternatives in the private sector and in the international labor markets. The churning process that results from these scientists leaving the research system is very inefficient and threatens the potential of the NARSs to become sustainable institutions able to respond to future agricultural research challenges.

Both the international donor community and the African governments need to commit strongly to support agricultural research institutions, the NARSs and the IARCs, so that in collaboration they turn out a continuing flow of new agricultural technologies for the semiarid and subhumid regions. Agricultural technology is still the engine of growth for the agricultural sector and for the whole economy for many of these countries. Progress has been made. A strategy is proposed here. The national institutions (NARSs) have made substantial progress in building up their human capital. It is time to be more optimistic about future agricultural technology development and introduction in semiarid and subhumid Sub-Saharan Africa.

# Notes

## Introduction

1. For example, in 1985–87, 43 percent of the maize research budget of the international agricultural research centers (IARCs) was spent in Africa (Byerlee et al., 1994, p. 4). The highest proportional share of funds from the CGIAR (Consultative Group on International Agricultural Research—all the IARCs are included in this group) in the nineties were spent on Africa (Lynam and Blackie, 1994, pp. 111, 123).

2. Twenty percent of the population of Sub-Saharan Africa lives in the humid zone, 15 percent in the highlands, and 10 percent in the arid zone (Winrock International, 1992, p. 14).

3. Rootcrops, fruits and vegetables, and tree crops are also very important in the subhumid region.

4. The historic estimate from the 1930s is that women provided 60 to 80 percent of the agricultural labor in Sub-Saharan Africa (Boserup, 1970). For more recent estimates and a more comprehensive analysis of the impact of new technologies on women, see chapter 9. Given the predominance of women farmers cultivating food crops in many Sub-Saharan African countries, the question of how new agricultural technologies affect them is not only relevant from an equity standpoint but also has bearing on long-term growth of the agricultural sector (Lele, 1986b).

## Chapter 1 Economic and Agricultural Stagnation in Sub-Saharan Africa

We are grateful for research assistance from Usha Ganesan and Ousmane Coulibaly on this chapter. Phil Abbott, Jock Anderson, John Dillon, Will Masters, Kevin McNamara, David Sammons, Wallace Tyner, Art Westneat, John Yohe, and an anonymous reviewer for the publisher provided useful comments and editorial suggestions.

1. Per capita declines in cereal availability are not all related to weather or natural resources. During the Zambian food riots in late 1986, neighboring Zimbabwe struggled to finance its "maize mountain," which was equivalent to two years of domestic consumption. The disparity between Zimbabwe's maize mountain and Zambia's empty harvest cannot be blamed solely on weather, because both countries produce the same staple food, maize, in the same agroecology and under the same general rainfall patterns (Eicher, 1988; for a summary of the Zimbabwe policies to support their maize sector, see World Bank, 1989a, p. 106; for the Zambian maize story, see Howard, 1994).

2. Fosu (1992) argues that political instability (PI)—defined as instability of governments, regimes, and communities within a nation—affects economic growth ad-

versely. Using data on successful coups d'état, attempted coups, and coup plots, he constructed an index of PI for thirty-one Sub-Saharan African countries over a thirty-year period (1956–85). The direct effect of being a high-PI country (about half the countries in the sample fell into this category) was estimated as a 1.1 percent reduction, on average, in the annual growth of GDP for the years 1960–86.

3. Structural adjustment is defined as "reforms of policies and institutions: microeconomic (such as taxes), macroeconomic (such as fiscal imbalance), and institutional (public sector inefficiencies). These changes improve resource allocation, increase economic efficiency, expand growth potential, and increase resilience to future shocks" (World Bank, 1988, p. 11).

4. For example, U.S. House of Representatives report of July 8, 1992, noted that "proponents of increased assistance to southern Africa fear the current political climate is not conducive to increasing foreign aid even to fund emergency food aid and disaster assistance." Memorandum from R. R. Randlett, 1992.

5. The decline of Chad is associated with its civil war. Niger and Senegal have to look at policy and management factors as well as the collapse during the 1980s of uranium and peanut exports, respectively.

6. These reports were the U.S. Department of Agriculture study (1981) and the Berg report (World Bank, 1981). The Lagos conference and these reports identified a series of problems, which were then acted upon in the eighties.

7. Later in this chapter we consider the argument that the agricultural environment in semiarid Sub-Saharan Africa is so harsh that more emphasis needs to be put on labor-intensive manufacturing for export and domestic consumption. With the rates of investment in the two regions and their large labor pool, Asia will probably dominate labor-intensive manufacturing to developed countries for another decade. Nevertheless, there should be some specialty niches for Sub-Saharan Africa. For example, within the agricultural sector, several Sahelian countries export string beans to France from irrigation projects.

Why is Asian growth and investment so much greater than that in Sub-Saharan Africa? There are many hypotheses that need to be considered in future sources of growth analysis: the greater levels of human capital investment, including women in Asia; higher levels of investment in infrastructure; improved public administration and the ability of the public sector in Asia to encourage private sector development; the greater concern in much of Asia with policies to increase the profitability of agriculture; the earlier switch in Asia to more-open economies; and the political economic factor of greater access of certain Asian countries to American markets.

8. The Okhawa equation relating population and income growth to demand growth indicates potentially high requirements for future food demand in the Sahel:

$$\dot{C} = \dot{P} + a\dot{E},$$

where

$\dot{C}$ = food demand growth,
$\dot{P}$ = population growth,
$a$ = income elasticity of demand for food, and
$\dot{E}$ = per capita income growth.

The income elasticity for food was assumed to be 0.6—that is, 60 percent of the increase in income would be spent on food. In two recent reviews of income elasticities of demand for calories, this 0.6 was a midpoint (Bouis, 1994, pp. 14, 15; Bouis and Haddad, 1992, pp. 336, 337). Bouis argues that the real values are lower than this.

However, there is another factor to raise the demand projection further: the need to improve incomes or access to food of the undernourished so as to eradicate malnutrition. This is Sen's (1981, 1990) emphasis on entitlements, and it is not adequately reflected in demand growth estimates.

9. In the Sahel, the attainment of food self-sufficiency is an important national objective, because most of these governments do not want to be dependent on imports for their basic food staples (World Bank, 1990). However, a more critical objective is to be able to produce or purchase sufficient food to eliminate malnutrition and to respond to the demand of a country's population.

10. These measures of price differences utilized official exchange rates. Including an adjustment for overvalued exchanges rates would further increase the spreads between domestic and world prices, as most Sub-Saharan African countries had overvalued their currencies in the seventies and early eighties. For food crops or import substitutes, these distortions were often offset by other policy measures (see Byerlee and Sain, 1986; M. Ahmed, Masters, and Sanders, 1995).

11. The food-demand situation is more complicated than this, since the income effects of these shifts have dominated the price effects (see Delgado, 1991; Delgado and Reardon, 1992; Reardon, 1993; Savodogo and Brandt, 1988). Price effect differences can result partially or entirely from the price distortions of economic policy and can be eliminated. In the demand studies cited, the income variables tended to be much more significant than the price variables, indicating that tastes and the increasing opportunity costs of women's time, rather than price distortions, were largely responsible for these demand shifts.

12. Imported and domestically produced consumer goods came from the urban areas. Frequently, transportation and marketing systems were rudimentary and expensive. The availability of imported consumer goods was reduced by foreign exchange rationing necessary to maintain overvalued exchange rates and the governmental emphasis on imports to facilitate industrial and urban development. It has been much more difficult for the rural sector than for the urban sector to benefit from the reduced import prices resulting from the overvalued exchange rates. In some countries, some of the rural sector did benefit from direct and indirect subsidies on imported fertilizers and farm machinery (see M. Ahmed et al., 1995). Rationing to more wealthy or influential farmers generally accompanied subsidized inputs for the agricultural sector (see chapter 6).

13. Since Prebisch (for a summary of his work, see Prebisch, 1984) wrote in 1949, there has been concern in developing countries about a long-run deterioration in the barter terms of trade of countries specializing in primary export products. The terms of trade in Sub-Saharan Africa have evolved differently for different country groups, and recent declines should be viewed in relation to long-term trends. There has been a 30 percent decline in the region's terms of trade for the period 1981–87, but this has to be contrasted with a 70 percent rise from 1972 to 1981 (World Bank and UNDP, 1989, p. 11). The region benefited from income gains since the seventies and into the

eighties. However, gains were primarily concentrated in the five oil-exporting countries.

Since the 1970s, the share of Sub-Saharan Africa's exports in total developing countries' exports declined from 13.8 percent (in 1970) to 5.7 percent (in 1987) (Svedberg, 1991, p. 551). Oil is the only major export product from the region that has performed positively since 1970. In 1970, oil accounted for a little less than 10 percent of total exports, but in 1985 it was more than 50 percent. In nonoil products, Sub-Saharan Africa held its position in the world markets up to the mid-seventies, and after that its share fell. In 1985, the Sub-Saharan African share of world exports was 0.9 percent, about one-third of what it was a decade earlier (Svedberg, 1991, p. 551). Had the region maintained its share of the world markets for all nonoil primary products, export revenues in 1985 would have been about one-third, or $10 billion, larger than they actually were (Svedberg, 1991, p. 551).

Over the decades there has been limited change in export structure. Most of the diversification was into new primary products. One principal problem with a heavy reliance on primary products to generate export revenues is that these commodities are subject to substantial price variability over time.

14. Countries such as Brazil, Taiwan, or South Korea that have successfully industrialized generally developed a prosperous agricultural sector first, which enabled them to generate more domestic capital and markets for the industrial sector. Generating this agricultural surplus may be a prerequisite to successful economic diversification.

15. In Sub-Saharan Africa, agriculture fell from 43 to 33 percent of GDP over the period. Other industry besides manufacturing did grow, from 10 to 17 percent. Five percent of this growth came from petroleum-related industrial production (World Bank, 1989a, p. 19).

16. The traditional trade argument is that food self-sufficiency is not an appropriate national objective if it implies producing all one's own food. Presently, most African governments are committed to food self-sufficiency, as they tend to be very sensitive to political pressures from urban areas when food prices increase (see Stewart, Lall, and Wangwe, 1992, p. 11; Bates, 1990). While food self-sufficiency continues to be debated, most food staples are low-value products with high transportation costs. Hence, a reasonably efficient agricultural sector is expected to be able to compete with foreign imports for the production of most food staples in the absence of domestic disincentives to produce and incentives to import. Unfortunately, previous policies have provided price signals pushing farmers to retreat to subsistence.

17. The internal and external hypotheses are complementary, rather than competing, explanations for the agricultural stagnation. Many internal adjustment programs also contain provisions to reduce the debt-service costs. The policy response of the nineties to the terms-of-trade problem is export diversification, rather than import substitution. But this diversification has been especially difficult for most of the African economies.

18. Gasoline and spare machinery parts have multiplier effects impacting transportation and many other sectors of the economy.

19. The balance of trade is exports minus imports. The current account is foreign exchange receipts minus foreign exchange expenditures. Besides exports and imports it includes interest payments, profits on overseas investments, and tourist and other

service expenditures. Deficits on the current account have to be offset by capital movements or transfers of accumulated reserves.

20. To foster macroeconomic and sector-level reforms while providing countries with the foreign exchange to implement these reforms, the World Bank developed new loan instruments: the structural adjustment loan and structural adjustment credit. Collectively they were called SALs and, after 1983, the sectoral adjustment loans (SECALs). Although not aimed only at agricultural policies, the agriculture sector did feature prominently in the early SALs. Agricultural SECALs, however, included conditions related solely to the agricultural sector and generally followed measures for macroeconomic stabilization (Knudsen and Nash, 1991).

21. A more relevant evaluation of structural adjustment would be to compare countries with and without structural adjustment programs. When this was done for African countries, there were substantial increases in agricultural output growth and savings rates for the countries with structural adjustment. If those countries not experiencing strong economic shocks were deleted, there also were substantial increases in GDP growth with structural adjustment (World Bank and UNDP, 1989, p. 30; Lancaster, 1991, pp. 14, 15).

22. Note that the definition of current account is exports minus imports plus unrequited transfers. Unrequited transfers include foreign aid—grants and technical and food aid (World Bank, 1992, pp. 294, 295). Hence, the positive effect of the structural reform on the current account needs to be separated into the effect of increased aid of the donors and the favorable economic effects resulting from different relative prices. One apparent positive effect of structural adjustment has been the increase of nonoil export volume of almost 10 percent in 1985–87 in Sub-Saharan Africa (World Bank, 1989a, p. 35).

23. "The CFA commonly refers to both the Communaute Financiere de l'Afrique de l'Ouest and the Communaute Financiere de l'Afrique Central" (IMF, 1994b, p. 60). The CFA is the name of the currency for fourteen countries in West and Central Africa, which were formerly French colonies. The CFA was pegged to the French franc at fifty CFA to one French franc. In January 1994, the first devaluation since 1948 took place. This devaluation was generally considered by donors to be long overdue, as the overvalued exchange rate has had deleterious effects on the agricultural sector and the foreign exchange position of the countries in this monetary union over at least the past decade (ibid.).

24. Note that in the fifties, when the World Bank had been concentrating on infrastructure investments, most of Sub-Saharan Africa were still European colonies. These infrastructure investments had not been a developmental priority for many colonial governments.

25. The modifications of structural adjustment in short-run economic policy have been easier than institutionalizing them will be, since these policy changes shift the distribution of income between sectors of the population. Shifts in economic power usually imply changes in political power, a sensitive area for international agencies or for bilateral donors. Consumers will benefit substantially in the long run from a prosperous agricultural sector, so the urban areas will also benefit from structural adjustment. Ultimately, urban areas will politically support policies beneficial to the agricultural sector as urban areas do in developed countries.

26. The long-run effects of falling prices for agricultural products with increased growth in agricultural output are a universal phenomenon. This process will benefit consumers and help ease the malnutrition problem. These falling prices also result in falling farm incomes for the later adopters of new technologies. However, this is a secondary problem in comparison with the declines in per capita agricultural production during the last three decades in Sub-Saharan Africa and the very high potential demand growth for agricultural products as per capita economic growth increases again in the nineties.

## Chapter 2  A Strategy of Agricultural Technology Development for the Semiarid and Subhumid Regions of Sub-Saharan Africa

For critical comments and suggestions on this chapter, we are especially grateful to John Dillon, David Sammons, Tim Kelley, David Rohrbach, and John Yohe.

1. An opposing view is that colonial powers and many newly independent governments promoted tractors and large farmers, neglecting animal traction and small farmers until the late seventies (Pingali, Bigot, and Binswanger, 1987).

2. The price distortions of overvaluation favored imported foodstuffs and served as a strong disincentive to agricultural investment and even to the development of research support for domestic food crops.

3. Yield increases in Sub-Saharan Africa were minimal for most food crops, although there have been dramatic successes in East Africa with maize and with export crops and irrigated crops all over the continent (World Bank, 1989a, p. 99). Maize successes of hybrids and open-pollinated varieties are impressive in Malawi, Kenya, Zambia, and Zimbabwe and more recently in West and Central Africa (Byerlee and Heisey, 1993, p. 33; for East and southern Africa, see World Bank, 1989a, p. 106; for West and Central Africa, see chapter 4).

4. Biotechnology may become very important in the next century for developed and developing countries (World Bank, 1989a, p. 99). However, there still is substantial potential to use much higher input levels in Sub-Saharan African agriculture and to take advantage of the more conventional sources of output growth by borrowing following the adapted science model.

5. Where labor has been more limiting than land, as in the United States, there was concentration on mechanical technologies to substitute for labor. The historic Japanese case was the opposite, with land scarcity; hence, in Japan there was a concentration on inputs to raise yields, thereby substituting for land (Hayami and Ruttan, 1985, pp. 73–84).

6. Boserup developed a theory to explain the interactions between population growth, land settlement, and technological change (Boserup, 1965, 1981). One component of this theory explains why higher-quality soils are cultivated later in the settlement process than lower-quality soils. This counterintuitive result apparently occurs because the higher-quality soils, as in the low-lying, mucky areas, or the vertisols are too difficult to work by hand. They require animal or other traction, and farmers adopt this later in the development process. This shift to the better soils later was observed in the Sahel (see chapter 9 for a further development of the theory and the empirical analysis).

7. Toposequence refers to the position on the slope of the fields. In the undulating

slopes of West Africa, the bottom soils accumulate water and soil deposits from farther up on the slopes. For further details, see Van Stavereen and Stoop (1985) and Stoop (1986).

8. In delta areas, these low-lying soils are associated with higher risks. In Bangladesh, farmers obtain high yields in normal years on the delta and have flooding in the high-rainfall years.

9. The explanation of Jaeger and Matlon (1990) for the failure to introduce animal traction more rapidly into West Africa is that the high payoffs depend on mechanizing both the land preparation and the weeding operations. There is a delay in farmers' mastery of the techniques of plowing and cultivating. Moreover, the associated investment costs for several pieces of equipment and the animal are high; hence, nonadoption results from farmers being unable to attain the full potential from animal traction. With only one operation mechanized, costs are frequently too high and crop prices too low for the operation to be more than marginally profitable (Jaeger, 1987, pp. 118, 119). This explanation is also consistent with the concentration of mechanization in the higher-rainfall zones where there are high-value cash crops, such as cotton and peanuts, and the crop season is sufficiently long for the additional time for land preparation (Matlon and Adesina, 1991, p. 374). Here the value of production is much higher, and the probability of both operations being mechanized is greater.

10. The tsetse fly historically limited the expansion of animal traction. In higher densities of population, cutting the brush destroys the habitat of the fly. The reduced disease and insect problems of the semiarid zone historically gave it a comparative advantage in livestock production over the higher-rainfall regions, including a greater capacity for higher rates of animal traction. However, that advantage is now shifting with the rapid agricultural output growth in the subhumid zone and this pushing back of the tsetse fly.

11. This section is adapted from Sanders (1989).

12. In India, new millet and sorghum cultivars have been rapidly introduced on the better-endowed regions corresponding to the wet savannas and the heavier-soil regions (Jansen, Walker, and Barker, 1990). In the harsher environments with lower rainfall and sandier soils, few new cultivars were introduced. (We are indebted to Tim Kelley for this observation.) The absolute yields in India with these new cultivars are still very low. So it is clear that these agronomic improvements are now necessary. Otherwise, the new cultivars will mine the soil of required nutrients, and yields will fall. The new cultivars are not a sustainable strategy without soil fertility amendments.

13. This section is adapted from Sanders, Nagy, and Ramaswamy (1990). Ruthenberg (1980) emphasizes soil fertility and seasonal labor scarcity as the principal constraints for the semiarid zone. We agree that these are two critical constraints but argue that the lack of water is the primary factor to consider to understand the response to fertilizer in this zone and when seasonal labor becomes constraining. We return to this discussion of the contribution from Ruthenberg in the conclusion, once our empirical results have been presented.

14. In some regions, such as southern Mali, and in regions of southern Africa (D. Rohrbach, personal correspondence), the increased population pressure led to improved methods of using manure and other residues (also see chapter 3). So whether the objective is to construct water retention techniques or to improve soil fertility or both, the shift has been to very labor-intensive techniques.

15. This is a rotation rather than a shift out of the isoquant, since not all the farm area is degraded (fig. 2-1).

16. Absolute out-migration from agriculture and from the Sahel has been very large. For example, for Burkina Faso, long-distance migration, especially to Côte d'Ivoire, has had an important effect on the labor supply. An estimated 25 percent of the potential labor force of Burkina Faso works outside the country (Jaeger, 1987; Zachariah and Conde, 1981).

17. Clearly, this is a testable hypothesis, and we would need to measure changes in labor productivity *(Y/L)* in degraded regions. Casual empiricism indicates significant declines, but this needs to be done more systematically.

18. As depicted graphically, the labor use $(L_2)$ is unchanged from the previous isoquant *ACD* and the new isocost line (III). This constant $L_2$ with the new technology is not a necessary feature of the technological change. Labor use with the new technologies could be greater or less than $L_2$ but larger than $L_1$.

19. In a study of coarse grains in India, the same two interacting constraints were identified in econometric analysis. Soil-by-rainfall-interaction variables were consistently found to be highly significant in explaining diffusion ceilings for the expansion of new millet and sorghum cultivars in India (see Jansen, Walker, and Barker, 1990).

20. For some regions, some of the costs for these earth and stone dikes and for transporting the stones were paid by the public sector to get the farmers organized. Once farmers saw the results, diffusion accelerated even without the subsidies.

21. There has been a debate on the introduction of new cultivars. Matlon (1987) estimates that only 5 percent of the area of millet and sorghum is in new cultivars. In low-input–high-risk agriculture, farmers plant a mix of cultivars with different maturity periods to respond to weather risk. Farmers diffused shorter-season cultivars of millet and sorghum more rapidly among themselves in recent years, (Vierich and Stoop, 1990). Some shorter-season sorghum and millet cultivars from the experiment stations also were introduced (Shapiro et al., 1993). The new sorghum and millet cultivars introduced from the experiment station have generally been selections of improved farmer cultivars. In sorghum, E-35 came from Gambella in Ethiopia, and Framida, which was introduced in Ghana, was from southern Africa. In millet, CIVT, NKP, and P3 Kolo were all selections from improved farmer materials, rather than crosses. All were introduced in Niger. The accelerated diffusion of improved farmer materials from other regions is an important contribution of breeders' activities. Moreover, there have been numerous introductions of new cowpea cultivars from breeders in the Sahel (see Sanders, Bezuneh, and Schroeder, 1994, pp. 25, 26).

22. Similarly, in the Maradi region of Niger where soils are better and fertilizer from Nigeria is cheaper, the introduction of both new millet cultivars and chemical fertilizers has been more rapid than in the Niamey region analyzed in chapter 5 (Lowenberg-DeBoer, conversation, 1993).

## Chapter 3  Success Stories: New Crop Technologies in the Sudano-Guinean Zone of Burkina Faso and Mali

Ousmane Coulibaly and Rao V. Nagubadi provided substantial input into the data collection for this chapter. We are also indebted to Jess Lowenberg-DeBoer, Tim

Kelley, and Thomas Reardon for excellent critical comments and suggestions on this chapter.

1. This pattern of a shift in emphasis in breeding from yields to lint quality is consistent with the U.S. experience. In the United States, there were substantial cotton yield gains from 1960 to 1968. After that, the breeding emphasis shifted to improvements in lint quality, and lint yields experienced a decline over the 1969 to 1981 period (Meredith and Bridge, 1984, p. 76).

2. The compound fertilizer in Burkina is known as cotton fertilizer and has a chemical composition of 14 percent, 23 percent, and 15 percent of nitrogen, phosphorus, and potassium, respectively. Similarly, in the Malian cotton zone, farmers increased average consumption of NPK from under 50 kilograms per hectare in the seventies to over 150 kilograms per hectare in the late eighties (van der Pol, 1992, p. 11). In a more detailed field study in Burkina Faso by ICRISAT with a focus on accurate measurement, especially of land, cotton yields and fertilization were lower. Savadogo, Reardon, and Pietola (1994) report average cotton yields over the 1981–85 period of 703 and 1,009 kilograms per hectare for farms relying on human and animal power, respectively. For fertilizer use, this was 109 to 113 kilograms per hectare of cotton fertilizer over the same period for these two groups. The ICRISAT area data were undoubtedly more accurate, but the representativeness of the two villages sampled is unknown.

3. "The CFDT approach has led to the development and extension of technology and assured the availability of inputs, marketing, and processing facilities. In particular, it has ensured adequate financing of the cotton sector, making possible, among other things, timely payments to farmers. . . . In the anglophone countries, faulty mechanisms and procedures for paying producer prices and ensuring input supplies have seriously undermined their potential impact, and the cotton subsectors lag behind" (Lele, van de Walle, and Gbetibouou, 1989).

4. The French research agency Institut de Recherches du Coton et des Textiles Exotiques (IRCT) was established in 1946 to coordinate French colonial research and historically has worked closely with CFDT (Lele, van de Walle, and Gbetibouou, 1989, p. 27). With independence, national research agencies and cotton parastatals took over, but both the IRCT and the CFDT maintained technical contacts with cotton operations in the former French colonies by sending short-term and long-term consultants. CFDT also has had financial participation in these national cotton parastatals.

5. In the semiarid zone of Burkina Faso, maize is raised as a vegetable next to the house, where the household refuse and tethered animals augment soil fertility and water-holding capacity, making possible the substitution of maize for sorghum in this small area. Without these soil improvements in the dry savanna, maize is too susceptible to drought to be grown in most years (see chapter 4).

6. Maize is the principal staple in the subhumid regions. In the semiarid zone, it has a very important role in household consumption, since it matures before the other cereals during the "hungry season," when family cereal supplies are running out before the next harvest. The semiarid regions customarily import large quantities of maize (Reardon, 1993).

7. Besides earliness, new cultivars have also been introduced with higher-yielding characteristics and resistance to insects and diseases.

8. Maize is a much more important crop in the coastal countries of West Africa, where most of the crop area is subhumid or humid. In Benin, Cameroon, Côte d'Ivoire, Ghana, and Togo, maize is the principal cereal by area planted. In West Africa, maize provides 10 percent of the calories, while in eastern and southern Africa, maize accounts for 50 percent of the calories and 80 percent in Malawi and Zambia (Byerlee, 1994, pp. 1, 2). In West and Central Africa, 50 percent of the maize is produced in the wet savanna and 20 percent in the dry savanna (SAFGRAD, 1991, p. 10). In West and Central Africa, in the Sudano-Guinean zone, and the rest of the wet savanna, maize is rapidly becoming a more important cereal, adding to the displacement of millet and sorghum by rice and wheat in the consumption habits of urban dwellers. However, only 15 percent of the maize in the continent comes from West and Central Africa. Maize is the predominant cereal in eastern and southern Africa. Maize's share of cereal production in Sub-Saharan Africa has been increasing, from 25 percent in the fifties to 36 percent in the late eighties (Byerlee and Heisey, 1993, p. 31; SAFGRAD, 1991, p. 10).

9. Approximately 75 percent of Africa's maize production takes place in relatively favorable environments, including the wet savanna and approximately half of the Sudanian zone (Byerlee and Heisey, 1993, p. 31). The estimate given in note 8 was that 70 percent of maize production was from the savannas, with only 50 percent of this being from the wet savanna and another 30 percent from outside the two savannas.

In the Ghanian extension program, the fertilizer recommendation varied with crop history and soil type. With the newly cultivated areas, farmers were able to use the original soil fertility without fertilization for the first three years. After three years of cultivation, fertilizer use became pervasive (Marfo and Tripp, 1992, p. 62; Byerlee and Heisey, 1993, p. 40).

10. The other traditional investment of these farmers is to increase the number of wives. As with cattle, more wives raise prestige and also provide a larger workforce.

11. Another advantage for the semiarid zone is that the grasses have a higher nutritive value than in the subhumid region as the water content is considerably lower. Unfortunately, the lower rainfall also implies much less development of the grasses (see Breman and de Wit, 1983, p. 1,346).

12. This includes milk, poultry, egg, and fattening operations. See chapter 11 for a more systematic discussion of these intensive livestock operations.

13. One economic factor discouraging increased livestock sales was overvalued exchange rates in the French monetary zone, including these coastal countries. The effect was to make it much cheaper to import meat from Argentina, Brazil, and Europe. In the seventies and eighties, these imports increasingly displaced Sahelian livestock production in the coastal cities. The devaluation of 1994 should help the herders and others in the Sahelian countries recover these coastal city markets.

14. Mali-Sud extends into the Sudanian zone and does not include all of the Sudano-Guinean zone of Mali, but the main cotton and maize production zones are in the Sudano-Guinean region of Mali-Sud.

15. This potassium deficiency comes from the lower levels of this nutrient in the compound fertilizer, since initial levels of potassium are not constraining. The level of this nutrient in manure is often high. The decline of cereal yields in long-term experimentation in Burkina Faso, when only compound fertilizer is applied, is appar-

ently explained by potassium deficiency, given the high requirements of continuous cereals for this nutrient. This hypothesis is supported by foliar analysis in the cotton zone, with the application of the traditional compound fertilizer showing potassium deficiency during the standard rotation of cotton followed by two years of sorghum (Dureau, Traore, and Ballo, 1994, p. 31).

16. One recommended application technique of manure was to put approximately 1 kilogram at the side of each seed pocket. With 15,000 seed pockets per hectare of millet and 1 kilogram of manure per pocket, this implies that 15 metric tons per hectare was recommended for application every other year. But with improvements in quality, agronomists on the experiment station in southern Mali were seeking to reduce this recommendation to 5.0 or 7.5 metric tons per hectare. There was even discussion of reducing the application level to 3.0 metric tons per hectare.

17. In the Sudanian zone of Mali, the use of organic fertilizer on the sorghum has also increased rapidly but without the simultaneous introduction of chemical fertilizer. In Mali, farmers with animal traction have traditionally constructed ridges on the contour, and these have been shown to have practically the same effects as tied ridges, especially on the light and intermediate soils.

18. This section expands on Deuson and Sanders, 1990.

19. Assuming that domestically produced millet, sorghum, maize, and rice are substitutes for the imported rice and wheat. Some processing investments by the private and public sectors may be necessary to facilitate this process.

20. Deuson and Sanders (1990, p. 197). More sophisticated work on increasing nutrient availability is also being done in international centers and developing countries (Lynam and Herdt, 1989). This would include work on biological nitrogen fixation and mycorrhizae to increase the availability of phosphorus.

21. "There are data available from IRCT (French organization for cotton research) in Burkina showing a decline in organic-matter content of soils (below 1%) and an increase in soil acidity as nitrogen fertilizer applications continue for 15 to 20 years. This contrasts with the U.S. experience where continuous maize cultivation at high inorganic-fertilizer levels has resulted in increased organic-matter levels. Some of the maize residues are incorporated in the U.S., whereas the sorghum/millet residues are generally grazed and burned in the Sahel. Soil nutrient export can be reduced by up to 50% if these residues are returned to the soil (Vlek, Mokwunye, and Mudahar, 1987, p. 47)."

22. There were improvements in management, including better spacing and timing. Some farmers also used water retention techniques. The principal innovations, however, were new cultivars and increased chemical use.

## Chapter 4   Combining Water and Soil Improvements: The Sudanian Region of Burkina Faso

For a thorough critique of this chapter, we are indebted to Tim Kelley and to Jess Lowenberg-DeBoer for useful suggestions.

1. Much of the next two sections of this chapter are adapted from Sanders, Nagy, and Ramaswamy (1990). The section on the shift from extensive to intensive technologies is a revised version of Ramaswamy and Sanders (1992).

2. The analysis of the Central Plateau farming systems throughout this article draws heavily on Jaeger (1987) and Roth et al. (1986).

3. For an excellent analysis of farmers' responses to topographical differences and the impact of soil quality deterioration over time on cropping patterns, see Vierich and Stoop (1990), Van Stavereen and Stoop (1985), and Stoop (1986).

4. The yield data are a summary of farm trial information over the period 1982–84 in Nagy, Ames, and Ohm (1985) and from table 4-2. In econometric analysis of the constraints to crop area expansion, only the millet area had a significant statistical relationship with the family labor supply (Cantrell et al., 1983).

5. Sixty percent of the farmers organized by the principal promoter of these technologies in Yatenga in the 1980s combined the organic fertilizers with these dikes (Wright, 1985). For a detailed description of the farming systems in Yatenga prior to the introduction of the dikes, see Hammond (1966).

6. In the earliest stages of this introduction, Oxfam, a nongovernmental organization (NGO), developed the contour-measuring device and provided technical assistance. In the initial steps, public subsidies encouraged collaborative efforts by farmers and paid for transporting the stone. However, once this process started, there was widespread diffusion even among farmers not receiving subsidies.

7. At a sorghum price of CFA45 per kilogram, the internal rate of return to the dikes and organic fertilizer was 12 percent on degraded soils and 20 percent on undegraded. At a sorghum price of CFA55 per kilogram, these internal rates of return were 21 percent (degraded) and 33 percent (undegraded) (Sanders et al., 1987). All the rates of return were calculated with the estimated opportunity cost of agricultural labor of CFA50 an hour (wage rate in the early and mid-eighties; see note 12). This is an estimate of the average agricultural wage during the crop season. In the peak periods of demand for labor, especially at first weeding and planting, the opportunity cost of labor would be much higher, according to programming results and field information about the availability of agricultural labor for the critical operations during the crop season. In the out-of-crop-season period, the opportunity cost for agricultural labor in the region is expected to be substantially below CFA50 an hour. Mining is a new activity that is increasing the out-of-season opportunity costs in some regions.

8. Improved land preparation combined with tied ridging would have an even larger effect on cereal yields. However, the use of a moldboard plow to fifteen centimeters, as recommended, can accelerate erosion if not properly done and is very hard on the draft animals after the long dry season. For a detailed agronomic analysis of the yield effects of various land preparation and tied ridge technologies, individually and in combination, see Nicou, Quattara, and Some (1987). This work reflects the collaboration of the French Centre National de la Recherche Scientifique et Technologique (CIRAD) and the Burkina Faso national agriculture research institution, INERA.

There has been some introduction of tied ridges in various regions of Sub-Saharan Africa, including Tanzania, northern Nigeria, and presently among maize producers in the Sudano-Guinean region of Burkina Faso (McIntire, personal communication, 1994). However the rapid introduction of these tied ridges is apparently dependent on the successful introduction of one of the animal traction implements for this ridging, due to the very large labor requirements for this activity.

9. The yield data for sorghum are summarized in Nagy, Ames, and Ohm (1985,

pp. 9, 32, 33) and in table 4-2. Inorganic fertilization is recommended, in spite of the long-term soil fertility experiments showing yield declines after ten years of inorganic fertilization of sorghum on the Central Plateau (Pichot et al., 1981). There were two major problems with these-long term experiments. First, they did not consider the induced deficiency of potassium from continuing cereal production even when potassium is applied. See the discussion on this in chapter 3. Second, this Institut des Recherches d'Agriculture Tropicale/Institut National d'Investigation Agricole (IRAT/ INIA) experiment assumed that in spite of the increases in sorghum yield from inorganic fertilizer, farmers would not change their cultural practices and begin to incorporate some of the increased crop residues. Farmers presently use almost all of these residues for grazing and then burn what is left. However, with increased yields, they could use part of the residues and leave the rest to decompose for the next crop year. It would be necessary to keep animals from grazing these residuals and to find a method of incorporating them into the soil with animal traction.

Soil fertility improvement in this region must be based on inorganic fertilizers, with some supplementation from organic fertilizers. Organic fertilizers and other substitutes for inorganic fertilizer either are very inelastic in supply (mulch, manure) or have technical difficulties limiting their effectiveness or profitability on the farm (solubility of rock phosphate, inoculation) (Sanders, 1989; Nagy, Sanders, and Ohm, 1988; Lal, 1987).

10. The farm-level testing of the yield effects from 1982–84 for tied ridges and fertilization for maize and millet is reported in three annual reports for the Semi-Arid Food Grain Research and Development (SAFGRAD) Program of the Purdue Farming Systems Unit (Cantrell et al., 1983; Lang, Ohm, and Cantrell, 1984; Ohm, Nagy, and Pardy, 1985).

11. The most complete documentation of this model is available in Roth et al. (1986). Other extensions and modifications of the model are found in Sanders, Nagy and Ramaswamy (1990), Nagy, Ames, and Ohm (1985), and in Nagy and Ames (1986). The 1987 prices and yield and labor use adjustments for the new activities were incorporated into this model from two field trips of Sanders to Burkina Faso in 1987 and 1988.

There is a methodological sequence in analyzing farm trials, from analysis of variance comparison of yields to budgeting, then to linear programming, and then to more complicated programming. Once technologies pass the simpler methodological approach, the greater rigor and data demands of the more sophisticated methodologies can be justified (Sanders and Lynam, 1982). This linear programming analysis concentrated on the income effects of various technology combinations, the level of adoption of various new technologies, and the shadow prices of those factors apparently constraining higher adoption levels Unfortunately, much of the analysis of the results of farm trials in developing countries never gets past the analysis of variance of yield differences.

12. In Burkina Faso, French agricultural research historically concentrated on cotton and developed a compound fertilizer of nitrogen, phosphorus, and potassium with percentage contributions of 14, 23, and 15 of pure nutrients, respectively. This compound fertilizer is popularly known as cotton fertilizer. Cereals require a higher nitrogen level than cotton. After a series of experiments, the on-farm trials of 1982–84

generally included two fertilizer levels of zero and of the combined application of 100 kilograms per hectare of cotton fertilizer applied in the seed pocket at planting, supplemented with 50 kilograms per hectare of urea side-dressed at first weeding. By putting the fertilizer in the seed pocket and having two fertilizer applications, increased labor application is partially substituted for higher expenditures on fertilizers. The combined nutrient levels of N, P, and K are then, respectively, 37, 23, and 15 percent pure nutrients; labor requirements are large. Combined with water retention, these fertilizer levels were consistently profitable for farmers, across sites and over the three years. (See table 4-2; Nagy, Sanders, and Ohm, 1988; Cantrell et al., 1983; Lang, Ohm, and Cantrell, 1984; Ohm, Nagy, and Pardy, 1985).

13. For data on cereal sales in various villages of Burkina Faso, see Cantrell et al. (1983, pp. 9–11). Jaeger (1987, p. 137) reports from farm interviews a daily wage of CFA300 a day for a six-hour day in the Sudanian region of Burkina Faso. According to 1987 interviews of farmers in the same region (Sanders et al., 1987), the same agricultural wage still prevailed. Jaeger also reports that during the peak labor demand (the first weeding period) agricultural wages increased to CFA500 a day.

14. We use the 1987 sorghum-millet price of CFA45 per kilogram in the above calculations. From 1982 to 1985, the farm-level sorghum price ranged from CFA65 to 95 per kilogram and then fell to as low as CFA25 per kilogram in 1986. In addition to the adequate rainfall in these two years (1985 and 1986), large-scale food aid continued through most of this period.

15. In Texas, tied ridges are called furrow dikes, and there were an estimated 2 to 3 million acres of them on the southern Great Plains in the mid-eighties ("Soil and Water," 1984, pp. 26, 27). Substantial fieldwork in Burkina has been done on an animal traction implement to tie the ridges. A similar implement is used on tractors to construct furrow dikes in Texas. On the lighter soils in Burkina, this animal traction tied-ridger works well. It still needs some engineering adaptation for heavier soils, however. See Nagy et al. (1988, pp. 26–33) for an economic analysis. When the ridger was included in the model, it further reduced labor requirements from sixty to twenty man-hours and increased annual machinery costs by CFA5,840. With the ridger in the model, the sorghum area in tied ridges and fertilization increased only slightly, to 0.83 hectare. Similarly, substantial increases in the sorghum price, still including the tied-ridger, created a shift to sorghum and cowpeas on the bush-fallow land, rather than a further increase in the tied ridging and fertilization operation on the sorghum land. Thus, in the present economic environment in which farmers can still expand onto the low-quality, bush-fallow land, there is still a preference for extensive development. As soil fertility and land availability continue to decline, this preference for extensive expansion is expected to gradually change to more intensive land use due to the falling returns to extensification.

16. The model developed by Nagy, Ames, and Ohm (1985) uses animal traction introduction with and without the ridger to extend the tied ridging, and in their model farmers substantially increased the area in tied ridges. However, they use a much higher sorghum price of CFA92 per kilogram. In our model and in most field observations, farmers who have animal traction expand the cultivated area, rather than increase tied ridges. In our model (chapter 4), the sorghum price is CFA45 per kilogram. The farmer has a completely elastic supply of bush-fallow land, but the other higher-

quality lands have an inelastic supply. However, as previously mentioned, the returns to the extensive choices have been decreasing as land access has been reduced even for the lower-quality bush-fallow land. As donkeys are not sufficiently powerful for this ridging operation in heavier soils, the tied-ridger is expected to require oxen traction in the Sudanian region.

17. With the adoption of yield-increasing technologies, there is an increased demand for animal traction to overcome the seasonal labor constraint. This shift in demand for animal traction is reflected in our model results, giving some support to our conceptual discussion in chapter 2 of the expected impacts of animal traction being the largest and animal traction utilization highest where the yield-increasing inputs are being rapidly introduced. Again, these results for animal traction occur when it becomes more expensive or impossible to further extend the cultivated area.

18. It is probably not realistic to attempt to breed cultivars that could overcome all these soil and water constraints. Rather, these agronomic improvements in water availability and soil fertility are expected to be a prerequisite for successful introduction of new cultivars. On these improved areas, there will be a better response from the new cultivars than from traditional ones. Traditional cultivars have been selected over long time periods for their stable response to stress conditions and are not expected to respond well to improved availability of water and increased soil fertility.

In the third edition of his classic work, Ruthenberg (1980, pp. 100, 357–66) anticipates many of these dynamic aspects of technological change in the Sudanian climatic zone. Nevertheless, he emphasizes the labor constraint and soil fertility, rather than the interaction of soil moisture and soil fertility.

19. The complementarity effects of combined inputs are well known to agricultural researchers, but these effects make their traditional experimental design and statistical analysis substantially more complicated. In the harsh environment of the Sahel, analyzing one factor at a time is expected to waste public money and have little payoff when yields are low and inputs have interactive effects. For an indication that agronomists have known about this problem for a long time, note the following quote from an article on British wheat yields in the 1920s: "No aphorism is more frequently repeated in connection with field trials than that we must ask Nature few questions, or, ideally, one question at a time. The writer is convinced that this view is wholly mistaken. Nature, he suggests, will best respond to a logical and carefully thought-out questionnaire. Indeed, if we ask her for a single question, she will often refuse to answer until some other topic has been discussed." R. A. Fisher (1926). This citation was taken from Dillon (1977, p. xiii).

20. In India, the situation was different. The introduction of new sorghum and millet cultivars produced moderate yield increases generally without supporting agronomic improvements for increased water availability or soil fertility amendments (Andrews, 1986). The introduction of hybrid sorghums increased national yields from 0.4 to 0.7 metric tons per hectare (Hosenay, Andrews, and Clark, 1987, p. 398). The extent of diffusion of these new cultivars is dramatic, from 1.1 percent and 0.5 percent of the area in 1966–67 to 32.5 percent and 49 percent of the area in 1984–85 for sorghum and pearl millet, respectively. This was over 5 million hectares for each of the two crops (Jansen, Walker, and Barker, 1990, p. 654).

Two hypotheses explain these greater successes of the breeding activity in India:

1. There was more population pressure on the land, hence a greater supply inelasticity for extending the land area. The pressure on the available land area results in a greater demand for yield-increasing technologies, such as these new cultivars. Many regions of Sub-Saharan Africa are now reaching this stage of land-supply inelasticity.

2. India has more trained scientists and more developed research institutions. These increases of sorghum and millet in India are still small, and the next round of breeding improvements will undoubtedly require improvements in the agronomic environment. Jansen and colleagues (1990, pp. 695–62) emphasize the region-specific requirements of agroclimatic and edaphic variation but still place principal emphasis on breeding. A recent review by the developer of the new millet cultivars that have been so successful in India and a collaborator emphasizes the complementary nature of breeding and agronomic improvements: "The potential for improving yields of sorghum and pearl millet in Africa through breeding and the use of better agronomic practices is large and will increase as food demand rises" (Andrews and Bramel-Cox, 1994, p. 119)

21. The yields used in the model were based on Cantrell et al. (1983), Lang, Ohm, and Cantrell (1984), Ohm, Nagy, and Pardy (1985), Roth et al. (1986), and Jaeger (1987). Initially, the yields were taken to be constant at different land supply elasticities. However, population pressure implies soil degradation, reducing potential cereal yields. Thus, the model explicitly considers two situations: the undegraded and the degraded cases (see fig. 4-2).

## Chapter 5   The Same Principle, a More Difficult Environment: The Sahelo-Sudanian Region of Niger

1. By 1984, there were approximately 10,000 hectares under full control or partial-control irrigation along the Niger River. This is approximately 0.5 percent of the average cultivated land area of Niger. Potential irrigable land, meanwhile, is estimated to be between 180,000 and 240,000 hectares. The proposed Kandadji Dam would substantially increase irrigated area. Currently, in the water control irrigation perimeters administered by ONAHA (the Niger's government's irrigation agency), over 20,000 farm households benefit from participating in the schemes. The irrigated area in these government schemes totals approximately seven thousand hectares (Simmons, 1984).

2. The labor of women and male and female children was weighted to arrive at equivalent male adults (Norman, Newman, and Ouedraogo, 1981). Adult women and female children between ten and fifteen years assist with planting and harvest in the Niamey region. The work capacity of one adult woman is assumed to equal that of 0.75 men. Male and female children between ten and fifteen years assist with all crop production operations and are assumed to equal 0.50 men. Children below the age of ten years are not included in this measure.

3. In the same agroecological zone, Swinton and Mamane report farm size to be 2 to 4 hectares but average family size to be only three equivalent adults with 2.4 active agricultural workers (Swinton and Mamane, 1986; their survey was done in the Maradi region). Differences in population density can result from differences in proximity to a large urban market, availability of irrigated parcels, and ethnic makeup, and these differences may explain this variation in land-to-labor ratios.

4. Hired labor is available in the area along the Niger River for rain-fed activities except during planting. Labor bottlenecks exist during weeding periods, and wages increase substantially. Wages also vary according to rain-fall conditions, being lower in worse rainfall years when weeds are less of a problem. In good rainfall years, seasonal labor is less available and is paid more, as farmers first take care of the higher labor demands on their own farms.

5. Farmers respond to prevailing rainfall conditions by varying the area under cultivation. In better, earlier-rainfall years, they plant less and concentrate their efforts on their better fields. In worse years, when the rains arrive late, they extensify. This is an adaptive strategy for a production system where inputs other than labor are low.

6. The United States Agency for International Development (USAID) estimates this investment in irrigation to have been US$116 million between 1965 and 1984 (at the 1990 official exchange rate for the CFA franc to develop approximately nine thousand hectares, at an average cost of $13,000 per hectare (Morris, Thom, and Norman, 1984). The CFA is the common currency in the entire French monetary zone, which includes fourteen French-speaking countries in West and Central Africa. See chapter 1, note 23.

7. The irrigated rice cultivars come from the International Rice Research Institute in the Philippines. STB 26 is a short-stature, high-yielding variety that originated in China.

8. The discussion of the Libore site in the following three sections is adapted from Shapiro et al. (1993).

9. Matlon (1990) lists the improved shorter-cycle cultivars of sorghum and millet adopted, including Sauna III (millet) widely grown in Senegal, the recent release of ICRISAT-improved millet varieties IBV8001 and IBV8004 in Senegal, CIVT and P3 Kolo in Niger, and Ex-Bornu in Nigeria. Matlon fails to list HKP, which is preferred by farmers over P3 Kolo in Niger and whose use has been more widespread (Shapiro, 1990). In Burkina Faso, improved sorghum cultivars recently released are also reportedly being adopted by farmers due to their substantially reduced maturity periods (the IRAT variety, IR204) and due to enhanced resistance to the parasite Striga combined with earliness (the ICRISAT varieties Framida and ICSV1002).

10. In utilizing the coefficient of variation (CV) as a measure of risk, skewness is not taken into consideration. The CV only includes the first two moments. Short-cycle varieties increase yields in low rainfall years, thus cutting off some of the lower tail of the income distribution.

11. The evidence from the field on adoption of higher densities varies by region. Field surveys in the study areas in the Niamey region showed that during 1985–87 farmers were beginning to plant at higher densities than those utilized in traditional practices (Shapiro, 1990). Continuing adoption was reported thereafter (Chandra Reddy, personal communication). However, in a later adoption survey at other research sites in the Maradi region, the higher crop densities were rarely adopted (Lowenberg-DeBoer, Zarafi, and Abdoulaye, 1992).

12. Fertilizer from Nigeria and the improved shorter-cycle millet cultivar CIVT developed by INRAN have been widely used on farmers' fields since 1988 in villages in the Maradi region and in the same agroclimatic zone as Libore (Lowenberg-DeBoer, Zarafi, and Abdoulaye, 1992; Shapiro et al., 1993). Widespread use of fertilizer was also reported in the Maradi region in 1991 (Lowenberg-DeBoer, Zarafi, and Abdou-

laye, 1992). Rapid adoption of inorganic fertilizer has also taken place in the Dosso region at Gobery, where ICRISAT and IFDC conducted fertilization experiments and farm trials over five years in the early 1980s (Mokwunye and Hammond, 1992, pp. 131, 132).

13. The sandy clay loam soils have approximately 20 percent clay, 20 percent silt, and 60 percent sand. Available phosphorus is often much higher than on rain-fed sandy soils (around thirteen to fifteen as opposed to five, parts per million), as are extractable cations (affecting the availability of calcium, magnesium, and potassium). Soil moisture-holding capacity is also much higher for the sandy clay loam soils than for the sandy dune soils (Lal, 1984).

14. According to the FAO soil classification, the sandy dune soils are arenesols and regesols (see introduction) (FAO, 1986a).

15. The physiological mechanism is not entirely understood. Apparently, the increased plant matter and root density enable use of more of the available water. The increased organic material would also be expected to slow the passage of the rainfall through the soil, increasing the water available to the plants.

16. Initial levels of four to five parts per million of phosphorus in these soils are common. Nitrogen is also deficient, but initial levels are difficult to measure.

17. The International Fertilizer Development Center (IFDC) and, more recently, the National Agricultural Research Center of Niger (INRAN) on-farm trials include treatments with phosphorus alone, as well as treatments with both phosphorus and nitrogen. Their publications maintain that the use of phosphorus is viable without nitrogen in the short run (ICRISAT, 1988, p. 82; IFDC, 1988; Reddy and Samba 1989, p. 8).

18. This rain-fed crop technology was developed and field-tested in the region by INRAN, ICRISAT, IFDC, and FAO (Mahamane et al., 1987; Maliki et al., 1988; Krause et al., 1987). Based on the research results of these agencies, the technologies recommended to increase farmers' incomes in this region have been:

1. improved shorter-cycle varieties of millet (HKP) and cowpeas (TN 578), with between 5,000 and 10,000 pockets of millet planted per hectare and the cowpeas planted at twice farmers' current practices, a medium density of between 4,000 and 5,000 pockets per hectare;

2. improved shorter-cycle varieties of millet (HKP), planted at 5,000 to 10,000 pockets per hectare, and cowpeas (TN 578), planted at high density (about 18,000 pockets per hectare); and

3. the second treatment above (2), plus 100 kilos of phosphorus fertilizer (SSP, simple superphosphate), applied before planting by the broadcast and incorporation method, and 50 kilos of nitrogen fertilizer (urea), applied in a split application after first and second weedings in early and normal rainfall onset years, with none in late rainfall onset years.

All the technologies reflect the adaptive strategies used by these farmers. The three technology combinations have the potential to respond to different types of rainfall years.

19. Another explanation for the failure of fertilizer diffusion in rain-fed agriculture is that more profitable activities than combined nitrogen and phosphorus fertilization are available to farmers, such as investment in small ruminants (Sutter, 1979, 1984; Painter, 1986, 1987; Clough, 1981; Raynaut, 1976). When the new technologies are

compared to the current crop activities available to the farm household, without the option to invest in livestock, the fertilizer technology is adopted. Combined nitrogen and phosphorus fertilizer is applied before planting to almost 2.5 of the 3.9 hectares of rain-fed land. This result is consistent with the findings of previous studies evaluating fertilizer introduction (Adesina and Sanders, 1991), which do not consider alternative investments but emphasize the constraint of availability of cash to purchase inputs in the Maradi region of Niger (Deuson and Sanders, 1990).

20. Since 1987, INRAN has been conducting on-farm testing of the preplant application of phosphorus without later nitrogen application. There are two years of on-farm results for this strategy.

21. The use of phosphorus fertilizer alone is more profitable than raising small ruminants and replaces investment in this activity. The increase in income variability is not substantial. Furthermore, the carryover effect into the next year, associated with phosphorus use, limits the financial risk.

22. The field trials at Gobery confirmed the experiment station results of an impressive response to phosphorus fertilizer on millet. Phosphorus fertilizer was introduced first on farmers' fields, later followed by combined nitrogen and phosphorus fertilizers. Thus, a step-by-step or sequential adoption strategy was used at Gobery, while the recommendation promoted at Libore was combined nitrogen and phosphorus. Since farners tend to adopt the components of a technology package one at a time (Byerlee and Hesse de Polanco, 1986), the strategy followed at Libore may in part explain the lack of adoption, given the model results.

23. To reduce the risk of the cereal price collapse in good rainfall years, Sanders (1989) suggests a price support of CFA50 to guard against price collapse. The probability of the price going below CFA50 this close to the urban market of Niamey is effectively zero. A price support at CFA50 has relevance in 10 percent of years in areas farther away from the Niger River.

24. The border had been closed since 1986, but substantial amounts of inorganic fertilizer were smuggled into Niger. The fertilizer made available through the reopening of the border with Nigeria in 1988 was implicitly subsidized by the overvalued CFA franc. The increased use of inorganic fertilizer in the Maradi region substantiates the model results of the potential effect of a subsidy on fertilizer use.

25. The cost of SSP, the recommended source of $P_2O_5$, was CFA50 per kilogram in Niger in 1988, and the price of urea (nitrogen) was CFA65 per kilogram. A fertilizer subsidy has been successfully used with cash crops to encourage adoption in Niger and in other regions of the Sahel. As early as 1987, private merchants were selling fertilizer at sites along the Niger River in the Niamey region, such as Libore. Some of this fertilizer was observed to be coming from Nigeria, thus implicitly subsidized by the overvalued CFA. The merchants, however, were not selling at the implicitly subsidized price but at the same price as fertilizer distributed by the government for rice production. Lack of market development results in limited competition and monopoly practices. The merchants thus capture economic rents by making imported fertilizer available at the same price as the government fertilizer, and farmers use it only on irrigated rice.

26. Even a 50 percent subsidy on fertilizer use at the other site in Kouka would not result in adoption, according to model results (see table 5-2).

27. Better rotations or intercropping with cowpeas to provide nitrogen fixation and

phosphorus from chemical fertilizer can be an important alternative as long as there is sufficient nitrogen fixation and farmers can manage this system (J. Lowenberg-DeBoer, personal conversation). However, due to leaching in these sandy soils and the harvest practices of these farmers, little additional nitrogen becomes available from intercropping with a legume. Moreover, the available nitrogen and organic matter in the next crop season is reduced by the farmers' practice of removing all the cowpea plant when harvesting, including the roots.

28. This estimated yield increase with improved longer-cycle cultivars is conservative, because the yield increase with improved shorter-cycle cultivars in better rainfall years was about 100 percent over traditional cultivars in farmer-managed on-farm trials.

29. Sutter has shown that at present farmers make most sales and purchases of livestock before the onset of the rains at the beginning of the crop season (Sutter, 1979).

30. The use of cash inputs, other than hired labor, is currently negligible in the two dryland systems, and the use of hired labor is almost the same on a per hectare basis.

31. The rest is due to price-yield interaction. The formula used to decompose the difference in gross revenues per hectare under millet-cowpea intercrop is:

$$\Sigma P_{iR}Y_{iR} - \Sigma P_{iD}Y_{iD} = \Sigma(P_{iR}-P_{iD})Y_{iD} + \Sigma(Y_{iR}-Y_{iD})P_{iD} + \Sigma(P_{iR}-P_{iD})(Y_{iR}-Y_{iD}),$$

where $P_{iR}$ is the price for crop $i$ (millet, cowpea grain, and cowpea hay) in Libore, $P_{iD}$ is the price for crop $i$ in Kouka, $Y_{iR}$ is the yield for crop $i$ in Libore, and $Y_{iD}$ is the yield for crop $i$ in Kouka.

32. The minimum grain consumption needs of the family during the year were determined from farm interviews. In the modeling, the farmer can meet the needs from cereal stocks by borrowing millet and then repaying in grain (at 25 percent interest) or with millet purchases. Allowing the farmer to purchase the grain gives him more flexibility in farm decisions in the model. The initial grain stocks include the carryover from a normal year. Sensitivity analysis of the available initial grain stocks does make an impact on the farmer's investment decisions (Shapiro, 1990, pp. 76, 77).

33. Including a measure of income risk in the objective function of the models had no effect on the results. Analysis of the income variability associated with the possible alternative activities showed that there was little difference in their effect on income variability. Hence, the trade-off between income and risk in the choice of new technologies is not a significant problem. The new cultivars result in a reduction of risk by eliminating some of the downside yield risk (see chapter 7 for further conceptual and empirical analyses of the risk associated with new technology introduction in the semi-arid region).

## Chapter 6  A New Sorghum Hybrid in Low-Input and High-Input Environments: The Mechanized Rain-fed Zone and the Gezira of Sudan

We are grateful for the data collection and fieldwork of Mohamed Habash, Tennassie Nichola, and Ali A. A. Salih and for the comments and suggestions of F. L. Bein, William A. Masters, Tennassie Nichola, David Rohrbach, and John Yohe.

1. In India and in the Ethiopian highlands, animal power is used successfully on

the vertisols. There is a management problem of adequately feeding the animals for the intensive soil preparation after a dry season of poor nutrition. Work animals in a weakened condition can die if pushed too hard.

2. All the demarcated land is regulated by the government, and the land rent is referred to as a tax. The undemarcated land refers to the landholdings outside the control of the MFC. The MFC is a governmental agency that regulates land use on the mechanized drylands. Officially, there is no private landownership here, only leasing and public landholding.

Producers can lose their leases if they do not follow MFC regulations. In practice, there is minimal enforcement of MFC regulations. Principally, the MFC has been encouraging longer fallows and crop rotations. Unfortunately for the MFC, there has been little experimentation on these dryland vertisols on which to base recommendations (see Habash, 1990).

3. This model was implemented with various cropping systems practiced on the vertisols. These systems were principally different types of fallow systems with sorghum or with sorghum and sesame. Unfortunately, the fallow variations observed on these vertisols affected cereal yields only marginally for one or two years, according to simulation results; the systems were too short to have much effect on fertility restoration (Salih, 1993; M. Ahmed, 1994).

4. In the historic rotation, 25 percent of the farm is allocated to cotton, 25 percent to wheat, 25 percent to fallow, and 25 percent to either sorghum or peanuts or both. Farmers usually grow more sorghum than peanuts. Some additional area outside the rotation is grown mostly in sorghum. Also, some of the area to be grown in wheat and cotton, according to the rotation sequence, may be bypassed, usually for agronomic reasons or because of irrigation and drainage problems.

5. The standard fertilizer recommendation for sorghum at that time was 2N and 1P. 2N is eighty pounds of nitrogen/feddan and 1P is forty pounds of $P_2O_5$/feddan. This translates to 184 kilograms per hectare of urea (46 percent nitrogen) and 98 kilograms per hectare of triple superphosphate (43 percent). These yield increases were averages for eighteen irrigated and nine rain-fed trials over four years (Ejeta, 1988, p. 32). The female parent of Hageen Dura-1, TX-623, came from the sorghum-breeding program of Dr. Fred Miller of Texas A&M University. This Texas research program was partially supported by INTSORMIL (the international sorghum-millet research program). The male parent was a Karper line also from Texas. These parents were selected by Dr. Gebisa Ejeta from the ICRISAT germ plasm collection at Wad Medani, Sudan. Dr. Ejeta was employed by ICRISAT, supported by UNDP funds, and worked with the Agricultural Research Corporation of Sudan.

6. The demand for HD-1 seeds and fertilizer may reach up to 600 and 16,000 metric tons, respectively, by the year 2000 if diffusion reaches 50 percent of the Gezira area crop at the higher fertilizer level. The critical unresolved problem is the ability of hybrid seed companies, public and private, to expand. Moreover, the importation of chemical fertilizer needs to be increased, and its distribution improved. This is a required transformation of the input markets to facilitate the continued rapid diffusion of HD-1. Improvements in product marketing, especially the development of alternative markets including a partial substitute for bread, livestock feed, and exports, will also become more important to maintain profitability in good rainfall years.

7. In 1991–92, Pioneer sold 62 metric tons of HD-1 seed in the mechanized rain-fed sector in the Damazin area. This seed sale represents 8,860 hectares of sorghum area under HD-1 (Tennassie Nichola, unpublished field data). The long-term average rainfall (1975–92) in Damazin approximates 600 millimeters a year (MFC, 1984, p. 71; Sudan, 1993).

8. This section and the table 6.4 are adapted from INTSORMIL (1994).

9. There is a very inelastic demand curve with respect to price. The various policy measures suggested in the rest of this paragraph in the text would increase the elasticity of the demand function and shift it outward.

10. The Erosion Productivity Impact Calculator (EPIC) considers soil-water-plant relationships and can simulate yields, soil nutrients, and water stress over time. The model does not include biotic factors, such as increased Striga, insects, and disease over time with monoculture. Moreover, other nutrients would ultimately become limiting. However, the model does indicate a high-return strategy of introducing a new cultivar and moderate levels of chemical fertilizer. This strategy apparently results in substantial yield gains for sorghum production in the drylands. This is a low level of fertilizer for a substantial yield gain, but initial soil fertility and rainfall are higher here than in the northern Gedaref region.

11. Within the larger bunds holding water in the field, smaller three-sided bunds with walls up to 0.5 meter and with 2 meters between them are constructed. These dimensions vary with the topography. Similar bund systems are also found in Somalia, Niger, and Kenya (Van Dijk and Hassan Ahmed, 1993, pp. 7–9). Sorghum is planted in the depression. Excessive water accumulation in high-rainfall years is avoided by breaking the ridges.

## Chapter 7  Risk and Intensive Technology Introduction

Jock R. Anderson and John L. Dillon made very useful suggestions and comments, which we attempted to incorporate.

1. These generalizations are based on field observations and on model results of chapters 3 to 6. Higher levels of input use will facilitate the introduction of new cultivars, as traditional varieties generally do not respond well to higher input levels. Moreover, without higher input levels in these harsh conditions, breeders are generally unable to introduce cultivars that respond better to the multiple stresses, as farmers have done with natural selection. Where new varieties alone have been introduced, the income increase will be temporary or nonsustainable, as nutrients taken out of the soil ultimately have to be replaced. When the agronomic environment is improved with water and more purchased inputs, larger payoffs to breeding over long time periods should be forthcoming.

2. Where there has been public or private support to the price, as with maize in Zambia and Mali, the diffusion process of new cultivars has often been very rapid (Howard, 1994, pp. 29, 30; Boughton and de Frahan, 1994). Unfortunately, these high prices were not sustainable by the public sector in either Zambia or Mali, and once policies shifted and prices declined, there were abrupt decreases in both profitability and diffusion of the new technologies.

3. For a review of the incorporation of risk into farm-level decision analysis, see

Anderson, Dillon, and Hardaker (1977), Barry (1984), Robison and Barry (1987), and Anderson and Dillon (1992). Meyer's technique (1977) makes stochastic dominance a more efficient tool while maintaining generalized utility functions.

4. All possible, mutually exclusive states of nature need to be represented to fulfill the basic probability law ($\Sigma P_i = 1$). Hence, some subjective estimates by technical people or farmers are sometimes required.

5. These results, however, are consistent with other studies in which there was little difference in crop mixes or income levels with variations in risk-aversion levels, unless substantial changes were made, as investments in animals or high levels of input purchases (Anderson and Hazell, 1994, p. 323).

6. In the case of new cultivars, the shorter-season varieties provide more drought escape. Since these are new technologies, some of the estimates of yield distribution for various states of nature have been based on experiment station and farm-level experiments, scientists' judgments, and other subjective estimates.

## Chapter 8   Sustainability, New Intensive Technologies, and Land Market Evolution in West Africa

Jock R. Anderson, John L. Dillon, and Stephen B. Lovejoy made useful critical comments and suggestions.

1. Another useful definition is a "production system that indefinitely meets demand for food and fiber at socially acceptable economic and environmental costs" (Crosson and Anderson, 1994, p. 1). Economic costs are market prices, and environmental costs are unknown and maybe unknowable, except in the long run. However, these environmental costs would be determined in the political process of choice of government. Thus, this definition covers everything but is ambiguous, as desired. This definition, like ours, emphasizes the satisfaction of the human demands for agricultural output and then considers a natural resources management strategy as a natural complement to guarantee the responsiveness of the agricultural production environment over time.

2. There are two qualifications here. First, countries could increase exports of other goods and increase agricultural imports, thereby diminishing the pressure on their agricultural resources at higher output levels. However, as previously noted in chapter 1, during the eighties industrial growth was stagnant in most of Sub-Saharan Africa. Secondly, we acknowledge that malnutrition and famine have both food supply and food demand aspects. In this book, we focus on the necessity for increasing food supply and reducing its costs. It will also be necessary to increase the purchasing power ("entitlement") of the poor and, in the case of famine, of the vulnerable. In market systems, the ability of the poor and the vulnerable to maintain or increase their food purchases is generally a more important determinant of malnutrition and even famine than fluctuations in food supply (see Sen, 1981, pp. 154–66). A critical component of a sustainability strategy is then an adequate entitlement program so that the poor and the vulnerable can obtain minimum nutritional goals (Lynam and Herdt, 1989, p. 391).

3. This summary comes from the Brundtland Commission and the policy statement of the international agricultural research centers (see Ruttan, 1991, pp. 24, 25). A full

definition of sustainability would include waste management, equity between generations, and new institutions to internalize to polluters the costs they impose on society.

4. This section is adapted from Ramaswamy and Sanders (1992).

5. During the early eighties, in the Senegalese groundnut basin, Gambia, and the
Central (Mossi) Plateau of Burkina Faso, 24 percent of the population lived on 2
percent of the area, at an average rural population density of forty-five persons per
square kilometer. For the entire Sudanian and Sahelo-Sudanian zones across the Sahel,
the population density was nineteen to twenty persons per square kilometer (Gorse and
Steeds, 1987, pp. 2, 8).

6. There is a minor exception to this assertion. Fulani systems with large herds
and small crop areas produce enough manure to maintain soil fertility. Moreover, the
Fulani often sell some of their manure. (See chapter 11 for an expanded treatment of
the availability of manure.)

7. Integrated pest management has been defined as "the optimization of pest control measures in an economically and ecologically sound manner accomplished by the
coordinated use of multiple tactics to assure stable crop production and to maintain
pest damage below the economic injury level while minimizing hazards to animals,
plants, and the environment" (Edwards, Thurston, and Janke, 1991, p. 110).

## Chapter 9  Technological Change in Agriculture and the Welfare of Sahelian Women

For critical comments on this chapter, we are indebted to Rekha Mehra, who was
especially helpful with our interpretation of the conclusions and implications.

1. The size and location of the private fields is decided by the household head.
The system of land rights in the Sahel is different from that typically found in the
Western world. Land is rarely owned, in the Western sense of exclusive inalienable
rights vested in one individual in exchange for cash. The land is communally owned
in the village, with long-term use rights given to household heads. These conditions
vary according to the individual's lineage, but even use rights given to outsiders are
generally considered as long-term rights. Men gain land through lineage systems, and
women obtain access to land through marriage. Technically, neither owns land; they
acquire only use rights. Lineage rights result from rank among male siblings, status in
a community, and family size. For more details on various land rights in the Sahel,
see Davison (1988, pp. 1–32) and Saunders (1980).

2. Boserup characterized female systems as rotation or slash-and-burn, communal
land ownership, and use of the hoe. In a 1977 study on agricultural labor force participation, 46 percent of the labor force were women (Gladwin and McMillan, 1989,
p. 348).

3. A useful approach to improving the welfare of women is increased efficiency in
household activities. Examples of labor-saving changes are new types of stoves requiring less wood and the substitution of rice and wheat for millet and sorghum. In the
wealthier households, there is some job specialization in tasks by rank (and age) of
the wives (Kumar, 1987, p. 138; Obbo, 1980, p. 218).

4. Among pastoralists, women are excluded from livestock care. Some pastoral

groups then allow women to farm. See Buvinic and Mehra (1990, p. 292).

5. After Ester Boserup's pathbreaking book in 1970, researchers hypothesized that agricultural technological change would increase women's workload, displace women wage earners, reduce women's incomes, and lower family nutritional status (as women curtailed breastfeeding and other health care activities crucial in preventing child malnutrition). Most studies with these types of conclusions rely primarily on qualitative analysis. Only six of the twenty-one studies reviewed analyze the impact of technological change on the income and welfare of women with quantitative data (Buvinic and Mehra, 1990). Buvinic and Mehra, in their review of these six studies, show no cases where seed-fertilizer or intensive technologies made women worse off. Rather, in the cases they cite, the welfare of women was increased by intensive technological change. In contrast, the welfare of poor women was reduced by mechanization in some of the cases cited (Buvinic and Mehra, 1990, pp. 299, 300).

6. For example, in western Nigeria, as women were employed to harvest cocoa, their self-subsistence in food production was reduced from 70–80 percent to 32 percent. Nevertheless, family food security improved with higher cash income from cocoa and with increased food purchases (Buvinic and Mehra, 1990, p. 300; Kumar, 1987).

7. In another field study, when new cash crops were introduced, Yoruba cash crop farmers in Nigeria initially compensated their wives with gifts and later in cash for their labor in cash crop production (Afonja, 1988).

8. In African cultures, women are generally socially subordinate to men (Kumar, 1987, p. 135). The relevant question is whether the social system will be modified by economic growth, or whether men will continue to use this dominance to extract all or most of the gains from the introduction of new technologies.

9. In the traditional system in Burkina Faso, women are not paid for their labor on the communal land but "were paid via a complex, intrafamilial reciprocal arrangement of gift-giving" (Gladwin and McMillan, 1989, p. 354). This is an example of the theory of generalized reciprocity, in which kinship groups provide insurance systems for each other through mutual exchange. Whether women are paid in wages, food, or gifts is immaterial to the general argument that their welfare would be increased with technological change.

10. A review of the labor market behavior of African women characterized the critical relationships:

"(1) Marriage recruits women as unfree laborers;

"(2) Husband's rights to the wife's labor (and vice versa) are not open-ended, and work is often remunerated in some form;

"(3) Agricultural intensification places increased demands on women's unfree labor and is a source of conflict between the sexes" (Whitehead, cited in Kumar, 1987, p. 140).

11. Cooperation-conflicts, according to Sen (1990b, pp. 123–49) and McElroy and Horney (1981), are a general class of intrahousehold problems of which the "bargaining problems" are a special subclass. Cooperative-conflict situations do not arise solely between the sexes but also between age groups and groups of different social status within the farm (Savanè, 1986).

12. In Burkina Faso, there is no landless labor class (as typically found in South

Asia), and local farmers have to attract other farmers or their relatives to leave their own farms for short time periods. There is also a tradition of labor exchange in these systems, but this is generally for labor-intensive projects outside the main seasonal agricultural activities. Workers also have the option of migrating to nearby Côte d'Ivoire or other coastal countries to obtain higher wages for longer time periods.

13. The relevant test of these three theories is empirical. More field studies in regions of rapid technological change of income and welfare distribution within the family over time are necessary.

14. Much of the description of the regions and the farming systems come from Burkina Faso (1989); Savadogo, Sanders, and McMillan, 1989; and Savadogo, 1990.

15. For further details on the model, see Ramaswamy and Sanders (1992). The values used for prices, yields, and farm sizes were based on reports of the Ministere de L'Agriculture (Burkina Faso, 1989) and a study done by Savadogo, Sanders, and McMillan (1989) and adapted to this southwestern region from a similar model for the Central Plateau developed by Roth et al., 1986. Also see Sanders, Nagy, and Ramaswamy (1990).

16. Three collective land types are included: (1) higher-quality, intrinsically more fertile land on which sorghum, maize, and cotton are customarily planted (1.5 to 3.5 hectares); (2) low-quality land on which white and red sorghum is planted and often intercropped with cowpeas (1.0 to 1.6 hectares); and (3) poorer-quality marginal land on which millet and peanuts are planted (1.7 to 2.4 hectares). The range in area of different land types principally reflects the differences in area cultivated by different power sources.

17. Seven hours of on-farm work is the maximum allowed. The number of working days in the agricultural season is assumed to be 112 days (Jaeger, 1987; Singh and Morey, 1987). Weighting was done for work capacity, given the importance of adult labor equivalents in overcoming seasonal labor shortages, in influencing area cultivated, and for choice of technological adoption.

| Age groups | Male | Female |
|---|---|---|
| 16–55 | 1.0 | 0.75 |
| 12–15 and 56–65 | 0.5 | 0.25 |
| All others | 0 | 0 |

See Savadogo, Sanders, and McMillan, 1989.

18. The new technologies principally improve cotton yields via new cultivars, improved agronomy, and fertilization. The fertilization is also used on maize, and the land is rotated with sorghum, so cereal yields are increased. In table 9-2, the results for only one woman are presented. The household had one head and six adult workers, all with private plots. Per capita income in the household needs to be divided by seven. Animal traction had previously been introduced and was included in table 9-2 as traditional technology. The market wage rate utilized in the model was $0.24 per hour (CFA273/US$; IMF, *International Financial Statistics*, 1990) and was a weighted average of estimates provided by Jaeger (1987) and Savadogo, Sanders, and McMillan, (1989). $S$ was set at nine cents per hour and $s$ was set initially at five cents per hour.

19. Efficient wood stoves, hand pumps to deliver water, and less time-consuming methods to process cereals have substantial effects on female welfare by reducing the large time requirements of household labor activities. A new method of parboiling sorghum (called *sori*) gives it the cooking characteristics and consistency of rice. This is a substantial breakthrough in increasing the quality of the sorghum product and reducing the differences in cooking time between traditional and imported cereals. (For further details on various household technologies, see Lawrence, 1993).

20. West Africa is ethnically heterogeneous, so caution must be exercised when making generalizations on the basis of individual case studies (Hill, 1986, pp. 78–82). Nevertheless, empirical studies reviewed here, including this combination of fieldwork and modeling, indicate that women's lot is improved with technological change, even if men control it.

21. Nash's solution is based on the following four axioms: joint rationality, independence of irrelevant alternatives, linear invariance, and symmetry of players (Nash, 1953). The Nash solution as a bargaining rule divides the surplus equally among the players. This rule was chosen for its analytical simplicity. Field studies support the cooperation-conflict approach of this rule. Alternative bargaining rules and plausible outcomes are discussed in Ramaswamy (1991).

## Chapter 10   Disease Control, New Settlement, and Technological Change

We are grateful for comments of Bruno Barbier on this chapter. This chapter draws on a recent survey of settlement experience, including case-study research at sixteen sites in four of the eleven countries (Burkina, Ghana, Mali, Togo) covered by the OCP (Onchocerciasis Control Programme) and a review of the existing literature on settlement trends in the other seven. The research was funded by the UNDP (United Nations Development Programme) and executed by the World Bank through the Institute for Development Anthropology (for a summary of the results, see McMillan et al., 1992).

1. In the 1990s, with higher cropping intensities from increased population pressure and more-intensive technologies, the bush has been cut back, removing the habitat for the fly. Also simple traps, screens, dips, trypano-tolerant breeds, and increasing tolerance to weakened infection levels by traditional cattle breeds such as the Zebu have all reduced the effectiveness of the tsetse barrier in increasing livestock production in the subhumid region (Crosson and Anderson, 1994, p. 9: Bourn and Wint, 1994, pp. 13, 14) Aerial photography has now reported substantial livestock concentrations much further south in Nigeria into the subhumid zone, the traditional area where, in the wet season, trypanosomiasis was a principal constraint to livestock production (Bourn and Wint, 1994).

2. Onchocerciasis is caused by the threadlike worm *onchocerca volvulus*. The adult worms have an estimated life of fourteen years in the human body, where they inhabit the subcutaneous tissues of the skin, causing raised nodules. Each female worm produces millions of microscopic microfilaria that live for about two years. These microfilaria migrate in the epidermis and cause itching, skin depigmentation and, eventually, eye lesions that can result in blindness. The disease is carried between

humans by the bites of a female black fly of the *simulium* genus. The flies can breed only in fast-flowing streams or rivers. As a result, the highest incidence of onchocerciasis occurs among people who live in river valleys (hence the name "river blindness").

3. Since 1988, the drug ivermectin has been used to complement the OCP's vector control operations. Ivermectin is the first drug available for the treatment of onchocerciasis that can safely be used on a large scale in rural areas. It is an effective, single-dose microfilaricide that will clear almost all microfilariae from the skin within forty-eight hours and most of those from the eyes within a few weeks (Duke, 1990).

Unfortunately, treatment has to be repeated every six to twelve months. Furthermore, the current restriction criteria on ivermectin forbids its use in pregnant women, women breastfeeding a child under three months of age, children under five years old, patients with severe disease of the heart, liver, kidney, or central nervous system, and any individual or population at high risk of diseases that might compromise the blood-brain barrier. When these exclusion criteria are applied and are coupled with the proportion of the population that is absent on treatment days or refuses treatment, the best coverage that can be obtained is no more than 65 percent of microfilariae carriers and 80 percent of the total microfilarial reservoir (Duke, 1990, p. 83).

4. See McMillan, Painter, and Scudder, 1992; OCP, 1986; Hunting, 1988; Van Raay and Hilhorst, 1981; Weitz and Applebaum, 1978; Angel, 1985; Remy, 1968, 1973, 1975; Becker, 1985; Bharain, 1981; Couty et al., 1979; Dollfus, 1981; Raison, 1979, 1981, 1985; Nicolai and Laserre, 1981.

5. The AVV uses a system of labor equivalents to determine the amount of land a household receives and a similar system to determine the distribution of supplementary food aid during the first year. The Adult Labor Equivalent (ALE) is measured by a labor index that assigns weights to persons according to sex and age. Since an adult male is considered to have the work capacity most readily transferred to a variety of tasks, this is the standard unit and is assigned a value of one. Women and children are assigned lesser values (0.75 for adult women, 0.50 for teenage boys, and 0.25 for females over fifty-five).

6. Interviews with extension agents and settlers indicated that average fertilizer use on cotton fields was substantially below the recommended 150 kilograms per hectare of the standard cotton fertilizer with components of 14, 23, and 15 percent for nitrogen, phosphorus, and potassium, respectively. This recommended fertilization is a low level of total nutrients but is still a risky strategy for a marginal rainfall area in the absence of effective water-capturing techniques.

7. Eight hundred kilograms per hectare in 1988 versus 1,000 kilograms per hectare in 1979 for cotton, and 1,000 kilograms per hectare in 1988 versus 800 kilograms per hectare in 1979 for sorghum.

8. The principal reasons for this real per capita income decrease were: (1) a switch was made from cotton to cereals, which have a lower median price but also lower labor demands; (2) higher input prices were not entirely offset by the increase in the output prices to farmers; (3) sorghum had a lower median selling price (adjusted for inflation); (4) settlers' main crop activities were restricted to the ten- to twenty-hectares project farms, which restricted the area they could clear and farm; and (5) the average family size increased.

Average prices used to calculate the value of agricultural production in the Statistical Service Survey research in 1979 were based on a two-year study of local markets. The prices used for the 1988–89 restudy were based on the median prices that farmers received for their products based on reported crop sales over one calendar year. Both 1979 and 1988 were considered good agricultural years (Savadogo, Sanders, and McMillan, 1989; Murphy and Sprey, 1980).

The consumer price index was based on costs of purchases of a typical urban household in Burkina (IMF, *International Financial Statistics*, 1989; World Bank, 1989a). We attempted to develop inflation indicators specific to Mossi farms in the AVV by comparing prices on key products purchased in 1979 and 1989.

9. The study showed substantial differences between net crop revenues for farmers at different levels of technology (table 10-2). Animal traction in Solenzo was associated with crop income levels 2.7 to 3.3 times that of manual traction. There was another big jump in productivity per worker (ALE) between animal-traction and motorized-tractor farmers. Even deducting the substantial costs of mechanized cultivation (estimated at 650,000 CFA per family per year) and high costs of fertilizer, net crop income for the tractor farmers was three times that of animal traction, reflecting their larger cultivated areas and higher productivity in growing maize and cotton.

Yields obtained by farmers with tractor technology tend to be slightly higher than those recorded for animal-traction farmers after an initial learning period (CRPA, 1989; Jaeger and Matlon, 1990). It was not possible to separate the sources of the yield differences between regions or farm types into factors, such as land-quality differences, technologies, and management. At Solenzo, 51 percent of the collectively worked fields at a new settlement were created after 1974, and 23 percent of the fields at an older settlement, which first started to expand in the early 1960s, had been farmed for six years or less, as compared with the AVV, where all the collective project fields had been farmed for ten years or more (McMillan, Nana, and Savadogo, 1990).

10. Since this chapter was written, the use of organic fertilizers has increased very rapidly in the Sudano-Guinean and the Sudanian regions of Mali, as we report in chapter 3. Given the similarities in crops, soils, and rainfall distribution, we expect that the use of manure has also expanded in the greater Solenzo region.

## Chapter 11  Livestock Development through Intensification or Improvement of Mixed Farming Systems?

This chapter gained substantially from the useful comments of Hank Fitzhugh, Ralph von Kaufmann, Sarah Gavian, Peter de Leeuw, Timothy Williams, and Bernard Rey of ILRI, John McIntire and Jock Anderson of the World Bank, and John Dillon of the University of New England, Australia.

1. Improvements in mixed farming systems here refer to increased integration of crops and livestock through more and better use of manure, increased livestock numbers, and use of animal traction.

2. Peri-urban dairy is defined as dairy production and marketing occurring in the milkshed of an urban area. The critical development aspect of peri-urban dairying is that its location is demand driven rather than determined mainly by agroecological factors (Staal and Shapiro, 1994).

3. Poultry and swine operations are not discussed here, since the development possibilities are mainly industrial in nature and as such have little potential in smallholder mixed farming systems. They are, however, also good examples of the intensification strategies discussed in the book and in this chapter, since they are dependent on high levels of purchased inputs.

4. Competitiveness refers to the relative profitability of two activities at current market prices. Comparative advantage refers to the potential profitability of alternative activities at socially optimal prices (prices unbiased by policy intervention).

The inability to control trypanosomiasis is the prinicpal factor keeping livestock production risky and costs high in the areas with more rainfall. This is changing presently, with increased population densities as the brush (the habitat of the tsetse fly) is cut (Bourn and Wint, 1994, pp. 13, 14).

5. As reported in chapter 3, the recent increase in the relative price of inorganic to organic fertilizer, due both to the elimination of input subsidies and currency devaluations, has resulted in the expansion of manure use and the adoption of techniques for improving manure quality. Manure use, thus, has partially replaced inorganic fertilizer recently. However, the limited ability to expand the supply of organic fertilizer means the potential expansion of this substitution strategy is very limited in the future.

6. Livestock functions as a savings account or a walking bank because of the lack of alternative formal banking or credit institutions in rural areas (Graham et al., 1987). The interest rates on bank savings are very low in Niger and in most other Sub-Saharan African countries. Farmers in Niger clearly see livestock as an investment that provides a high rate of return on capital, usually in the range of 40 to 50 percent (Painter, 1986; Shapiro, 1990). Furthermore, livestock prices have kept pace with inflation and devaluation. Savings accounts often do not hold their value in such circumstances.

7. The model results reported in chapter 5 show that without livestock as an investment option, farmers would adopt combined use of improved seed with both nitrogen and phosphorus fertilizers. The adoption of combined fertilizers and new cultivars did not occur because livestock activities are a more profitable investment, not because of a lack of capital (Shapiro, 1990). However, phosphorus alone or phosphorus with new cultivars was a preferred investment by farmers over livestock in model results, and farmers have been observed in Niger to be adopting this activity.

8. Cowpeas, the predominant legume in the Sahelo-Sudanian region of Niger, are normally grown in association with millet. Farmers uproot the entire plant when harvesting, including the roots, due to its high market value as animal feed (Shapiro, 1990). Moreover, little nitrogen is made available to plants through fixation. There is severe leaching in the sandy soils.

9. For a comparison of the potential of animal traction and tractors, see Pingali, Bigot, and Binswanger (1987), as well as the discussion in chapter 2.

10. The successful use of animal traction during crop intensification under semi-arid conditions will also depend on whether there are combined yield effects with purchased input use, as well as labor savings. There can be yield effects associated with animal traction from more timely operations, especially weeding, and when mechanized operations, especially plowing, increase water use efficiency or improve stand establishment from higher seedling rates (Jaeger and Matlon, 1990).

11. O'Neil (1988) evaluated the combination of animal traction and intensified rain-fed crop activities that included improved seed and moderate levels of fertilizer on sandy soils at Ndunga near Libore in the Sahelo-Sudanian zone of Niger (clay content was below 7 percent). The use of animal traction without complementary agronomic inputs, especially fertilizer, had previously been shown to have a limited effect on yields in the Sahelo-Sudanian zone of Niger (Fussell et al., 1986). Animal traction with complementary inputs resulted in increased millet densities, which in turn resulted in higher yields as well as reduced weeding time compared to manual methods. Labor input with animal traction was reduced by 56 percent and 68 percent for the first and second weedings, respectively. The use of the animal traction system for shallow field cultivation resulted in an increase in net revenues of 74 percent, while ridging increased net returns 43 percent. These results are noteworthy because planting during the second year of the on-farm trials was late due to a late onset of the rainy season.

12. This relative regional advantage for livestock development can be explained by the more rapid intensification of crops in the subhumid zone than in the semiarid zone. A more rapid increase in animal traction in mixed systems has been documented in the Sudano-Guinean zone relative to the Sudanian zone in Mali (Coulibaly, 1995; Matlon and Adesina, 1991).

13. Livestock development constraints in mixed systems in the highlands or cool tropics are similar to those in the semiarid region, but the potential for livestock intensification is greater. Disease pressure in the highlands is relatively low, and seasonal availability of feed is not as constraining as long as man-to-land ratios are not too high (Jahnke, 1982). Population pressure is increasing, so competition for land between crops and livestock is growing rapidly. However, with the heavy soils and adequate rainfall, animal traction can be essential in these systems. There is good response to fertilizer, and intensification of crop production is taking place. While use of sown pasture and forages are not widespread, they have begun in some areas where improved dairy breeds have been introduced. Intensified livestock feed production is following crop intensification in these mixed highland systems (Shapiro et al., 1994).

14. The expected annual rate of return of 52 percent on investment in goats found at Libore from 1984 to 1988 was comparable to the reported return in kind from lending millet of 50 percent (Sutter, 1984). The expected annual return per goat and resulting offspring at Libore, however, was only US$10 (at the 1990 official exchange rate, CFA298/US$1), and small-ruminant production made up only 14 percent of annual household income (see table 11-1). At Libore where land is limited due to high population pressure, few livestock can be kept (two goats, one sheep, and two oxen, on average). No farmers in the survey had cattle, other than the oxen some farmers had, which could be purchased through a credit scheme for participants in the government-managed irrigated rice perimeter. These oxen are primarily used for land preparation in irrigated rice, but also for transport. They are not presently used in rainfed crop production.

15. Widespread adoption of improved short-cycle cultivars of millet and cowpeas is taking place in the study area, and the cowpeas are sprayed with insecticide when this is available. Adoption of fertilizer and improved millet cultivars is taking place in

other areas in the same agroecological zone in Niger, where phosphorus fertilizer alone has been promoted (see chapter 5; Shapiro et al., 1993; Mokwunye and Hammond, 1992).

16. Why don't these small farmers do their own fattening activities of small or large animals rather than producing the cowpea hay to sell for fattening in the urban area? This is an important question to look at in the future. Specifically, how do the new markets for finishing livestock function? Are there economies of scale? Is access to the purchasers of the animals controled in some way?

17. Some income risk can be avoided by *not* selling animals in disaster crop years (Adesina and Sanders, 1991). Forced selling at a low price occurs because of insufficient pasture or other feed (mostly residues) in drought years or the incapacity to buy the feeds made more expensive by the drought (Swinton, 1988). In semiarid regions, panic selling is avoided in areas such as Libore, where irrigated rice stabilizes farm income.

18. Cattle-raising activities were also included in the whole-farm modeling introduced in chapter 5. However, cattle were never chosen as an optimal investment strategy at either the land shortage site (Libore) or land surplus site (Kouka) in the Niamey region, according to model results. Furthermore, cattle are disappearing from land shortage sites such as Libore, and only a few mixed farmers hold cattle at the land surplus site at Kouka (Shapiro, 1990). This does not, however, mean that cattle raising as a specialized operation could not be successfully done at such sites as Kouka, if cropping were discontinued and replaced by grazing in larger production units.

19. The returns to raising goats and sheep are based on a production period of one year and include the returns from raising one adult plus resulting offspring. Although the discounts due to mortality, disease, and theft are considerable in this harsh environment and are included in the analysis, these annual returns on investment remain quite high (Shapiro, 1990).

20. Overall income variability is reduced from a CV of 63% to a CV of 54%, but this is mainly due to the short-cycle or early-maturing crop varieties in the model results.

21. Part of this section is taken from Sanders (1989). See figure 2-2 for the illustration of the Sahelian agroecological zone. Note that the rainfall isohyet at the 90 percent probability level defines this Sahelian area as being from the northern limit of crop cultivation to 350 millimeters of rainfall, so this is an extremely marginal area for crop production. In chapter 5, the northern part of the Sahelo-Sudanian zone was also shown to be a marginal zone for crop cultivation, as with any feasible changes in policies or technologies, inorganic fertilizer use was still unprofitable.

22. Agropastoralists raise crops during the rainy season like traditional crop farmers but maintain much larger herds. These herds are fed mainly on crop residues early in the dry season and return to more northern pasture areas during the rainy season, in the care of transhumant herders.

23. Much of this section is taken from Staal and Shapiro (1994).

24. Zero grazing depends solely on stall-feeding of near-grade or grade dairy cattle, using farm-grown fodder and purchased supplemental feeds. Semizero grazing also uses stall-feeding combined with grazing of natural and sown pastures and roadsides (Sellen et al., 1990).

25. Development of a peri-urban system using a semizero grazing technology has also been taking place in coastal areas along the Indian Ocean near Mombasa, Kenya. These farms typically include small areas of maize and coconuts, with plots of napier used for cut-and-carry feeding for the dairy cows.

26. Open grazing does not use stall-feeding management and relies mainly on grazing of pastures. A limited amount of purchased supplementation is also used (Sellen et al., 1990).

27. The response of $F_1$ (first generation) 50 percent crossbred cows to supplementation with locally available concentrates, such as those including *noug* (niger seed) oil cake and wheat bran, is one kilogram of milk to one kilogram of concentrates when they are fed adequate dry matter. This is generally the response of cows grazed on pasture or roughage, but this is dependent on dairy merit. The concentrate-to-milk ratio was reported to be between 1:4 and 1:3 in virtually all Sub-Saharan Africa countries in 1991, indicating the profitability of feeding concentrate to crossbred cows (Walshe et al., 1991).

## Chapter 12   Implications for Research and Development Policy

We are grateful to Lowell S. Hardin and John L. Dillon for suggestions and comments on this chapter.

1. Ruthenberg (1980) in the third version of his classic work on farming systems in the tropics emphasized the importance of soil fertility and the seasonal labor constraint for semi-arid regions rather than the interaction of soil fertility and water availability as in this book.

We have pointed out that in West Africa animal traction has now become pervasive, except in the driest or poorest agricultural regions (chapter 2). So there has been a farmer response to the labor scarcity constraint identified by Ruthenberg. We have shown that in two of the three soil types analyzed, the water retention technique was not necessary to obtain an effect from fertilization. So we agree with Ruthenberg that the principal constraint in the semiarid zone is soil fertility. However, we still argue that the explicit consideration of both water availability and soil fertility is critical in analyzing technology development for the semiarid region. Without this attention, fertilizer field trials are easily misinterpreted. And inorganic fertilizer is the key input into the yield increasing process. Finally, once the yield-increasing technologies are introduced, an increased demand for the animal traction technologies to substitute for the increasingly scarce seasonal labor will occur.

Lynam and Blackie (1994, p. 113), while agreeing on the emphasis on soil moisture and fertility, consider a third factor, controlling biotic stress, also of major importance. They are certainly correct for legumes and vegetables, and they may also be correct for the cereals and root crops. We should have emphasized this third factor more in the book. Nevertheless, we believe that the IARCs have made substantial progress in disease and insect resistance in their breeding programs. Both the IARCs and the NARSs have apparently underinvested in other nonvarietal control measures. Hence the argument about more investment being necessary on nonvarietal pest control measures for biotic stress is analogous to our other arguments for more investments in moisture control and soil fertility improvements.

2. Actually, there is nothing fundamentally different between the zaï and the tied ridges, except that the former are done by hand and animal traction is often used for the latter. The techniques of holding water in the field are essentially identical. Soil-fertility improvements are slightly different. Unfortunately, at the low levels of soil fertility on the central plateau, organic fertilizer is not an effective substitute for inorganic fertilizer.

3. Extensive technologies increase labor productivity and are most appropriate when there is abundant land relative to labor. Intensive technologies substitute for land and principally increase the productivity of land (see Hayami and Ruttan, 1985; Ramaswamy and Sanders, 1992). The shift from extensive to intensive technologies is just beginning in the semiarid zone. In the subhumid regions, as in Burkina Faso and Mali, this shift has been going on for two decades (chapter 3). However, this shift is easier in the subhumid than in the semiarid regions, since adequate rainfall in most years makes the soil fertility improvements less risky. Also in the subhumid zone, there has been much more public support for technology introduction through investment in research, infrastructure, extension, and credit. In the semiarid region, more simultaneous changes are needed in new intensive technology components than in the subhumid zone. Moreover, there has been much less public support for this major shift from extensive to intensive practices in semiarid regions.

4. Management would include higher densities to take advantage of the increased soil fertility. Other changes often include more appropriate planting time depending on the length of season of the new cultivar and sometimes more timely control of weeds.

5. Several Sub-Saharan African countries were recently shown to depend on donor financing for 60 to 70 percent of their expenditures to support their national agricultural research agency (Sanders, Bezuneh, and Schroeder, 1994).

6. Proponents of farming systems have long argued that there are viable substitutes for inorganic fertilizer imports, such as improving the quality and use of manure and crop residues, rotations or intercropping of cereals and legumes, better integration of livestock-crop systems, and even the local rock phosphates. Agricultural scientists have frequently suggested to research institutes and officials that substitutes for inorganic fertilizer may soon become available. The most prevalent claim is for new cultivars that will have one of the following traits: drought resistance, tolerance to low levels of nitrogen or phosphorus, or tolerance to high levels of pH or aluminum. Other high-technology innovations, such as inoculation for nitrogen fixation, mycorrhizae, and even biotechnology, are argued by some scientists as alternatives that may soon become viable for farmer introduction and thereby reduce the need for increased, imported input purchases (see chapters 3 to 5 for more discussion of these soil fertility issues).

7. Similarly there is an important risk in a program to make agriculture more profitable. In many Sub-Saharan countries there is discussion of moving to free land markets rather than the communal land holding system. An open land market and more profitable agriculture could create a dual agricultural sector as in Lain America. There a small sector of large influential farmers gets most of the benefits of agricultural policy especially the access to subsidized inputs while the majority of the small farmers are left in subsistence production until they can become urban migrants. This results in an unstable social system, extremely high rural-urban migration. and slow

agricultural productivity growth. Hopefully, Sub-Saharan Africa will avoid the Latin American model. Unfortunately, there is some evidence of an imitation of the Latin American model such as the recent attempt in Zimbabwe to accomplish land reform for a few large and influential operators. In Malawi, land has been taken away from the communal producers and given to larger producers of tobacco. In Mali and Burkina, there has been discussion of programs to make it possible for civil servants to acquire agricultural land.

8. Most IARCs became essentially breeding institutions, with the other disciplines playing supporting roles. The developers (Peter Jennings and Norman Borlaug) of the most successful new cultivars in IARC history, the dwarf rice and wheat cultivars, were both trained as pathologists. But as with many other agricultural scientists in the IARCs, they worked principally as breeders in their IARC careers. Since the IARCs defined their objectives as turning out new cultivars with wide-ranging adaptation to respond to the principal constraints of the developing-country producers, it is logical that the breeders would dominate the early research process in the IARCs.

9. A few developing countries did very well in the eighties, principally the Asian "tigers" (Taiwan, South Korea, Singapore, Hong Kong, and later Thailand, and the provinces of China adjacent to Hong Kong).

10. We are not arguing for food or agricultural self-sufficiency. Clearly, some countries can increase their nonagricultural exports and pay for more food imports. However, most Sub-Saharan countries will need to substantially develop the productivity of their agricultural sector to benefit their large agricultural population and to make their governments less vulnerable to the political pressures of being dependent on food aid or food imports. The political consequences of rapid increases in urban food prices are well known to most Sub-Saharan governments (Bates, 1981).

11. We recognize that nutritional deficiencies are largely determined by inadequate purchasing power of the poor rather than by shortages in available food supplies (Sen, 1981, 1990a). However, a high proportion of the poor in these countries are in agriculture, so that production improvements and food price declines should benefit them (Weber et al., 1988). Moreover, declining food prices have been shown to benefit low-income consumers more than the rest of society (Scobie and Posada, 1978).

12. We discussed only the benefits of disease control and livestock improvements. Governmental policymakers would want some estimates of the costs and expected probability of success of different strategies. This would be the logical next step of governmental decisions on public investment strategies. Estimating costs and success probabilities would require consultations with another series of specialists in both areas.

13. In traditional mixed crop-livestock farming, improvement of the integration of livestock is a proxy for a series of other small adjustments. These gradual improvements include practices borrowed from best-farmer practices and other on-farm technology improvements. We have discussed elsewhere, in chapter 2, that these innovations can lead to only very slow growth rates, at best. Science-based changes can lead to higher growth rates (Ruttan, 1991, p. 17).

# References

Achuonji, P., and S. Debrah. 1992. "Efficiency of Fresh Milk Marketing in the Bamako Area of Mali." In Ray F. Brokken and Senait Seyoum, eds., *Dairy Marketing in Sub-Saharan Africa*. Addis Ababa, Ethiopia: ILCA (International
Livestock Center for Africa).

Adam, Farah Hassan, El Tayeb El Amin Mohammed, and Kamil Ibrahim Hassan.
1981. "Problems of Mechanized Agriculture in Developing Countries: The Case
of the Central Rainlands of the Sudan." *Development and Peace* 2:87–103.

Adesina, Akinwumi A. 1988. "Farmer Behavior and New Agricultural Technologies
in the Rainfed Agriculture of Southern Niger: A Stochastic Programming Analysis." Ph.D. diss., Purdue University.

———. 1992. "Oxen Cultivation in Semi-Arid West Africa: Profitability Analysis in
Mali." *Agricultural Systems* 38:131–47.

Adesina, Akinwumi A., and J. H. Sanders. 1991. "Peasant Farmer Behavior and
Cereal Technologies: Stochastic Programming in Niger." *Agricultural Economics* 5:21–38.

Afonja, Simi. 1988. "Changing Modes of Production and the Sexual Division of Labor
among the Yoruba." In Eleanor Leacock and Helen I. Safa, eds., *Women's
Work*. South Hadley, Mass.: Bergin and Garvey.

"African Debt: Borrowed Time." 1993. *Economist* 327(May 22): 52.

Agrotechnik. 1990. *Etude de développement régional dans le bassin versant de la
Kompienga: Rapport diagnostic*. Frankfurt: Agrotechnik.

Ahmed, Abdelmoneim Taha. 1984. "A Linear Programming Model to Examine Decision Making by Farmers in the Gezira Scheme of Sudan." Master's thesis,
Purdue University.

Ames, L. 1986. "A Preliminary Report on the Evaluation of New Technologies in
Burkina Faso." Dept. of Agricultural Economics, Purdue University, West Lafayette, Ind.

Ancey, G. 1974. "Facteurs et systèmes de production dans la société mossi d'au-
jourd'hui: migrations, travail, terre, capital." In *Enquête sur les Mouvements
de Population à Partir du Pays Mossi*, vol. 2. Ouagadougou, Burkina Faso:
Office de la Recherche Scientifique et Technique Outre-Mer (ORSTOM).

Anderson, Jock R., and John L. Dillon. 1992. *Risk Analysis in Dryland Farming
Systems*. Rome: Food and Agriculture Organization of the United Nations
(FAO).

Anderson, Jock. R., J. L. Dillon, and J. B. Hardaker. 1977. *Agricultural Decision
Analysis*. Ames: Iowa State University Press.

———. 1986. "Farmers and Risk." *Agriculture in a Turbulent World Economy*.
Brookfield, Vt: Gower Publishing.

Anderson, Jock R., and Peter B. R. Hazell. 1994. "Risk Consideration in the Design and Transfer of Agricultural Technology." In Jock R. Anderson, ed., *Agricultural Technology Policy Issues for the International Community*. Cambridge: Cambridge University Press.

Andrews, D. J. 1986. "Current Results and Prospects in Sorghum and Pearl Millet Breeding." In T. J. Davis, ed., *Sixth Agricultural Sector Symposium: Development of Rainfed Agriculture under Arid and Semi-Arid Conditions*. Washington, D.C.: World Bank.

Andrews, David, and Paula Bramel-Cox. 1994. "Breeding Cultivars for Sustainable Crop Production in Low Input Dryland Agriculture in the Tropics." In D. A. Buxton, ed., *International Crop Science I*. Madison, Wis.: Crop Science Society of America.

Angel, S. 1985. "Spontaneous Land Settlement on Rural Frontiers: An Agenda for Global Action." Paper presented at International Seminar on Planning for Settlements in Rural Regions: The Case of Spontaneous Settlements, Nov. 11–20, Nairobi, Kenya.

AVV (Aménagement des Vallées des Volta). 1985. *L'impact socioéconomique du programme de lutte contre l'onchocerose au Burkina (1974–1984)*. Ouagadougou, Burkina Faso: AVV.

Ayittey, G. B. N. 1992. "How Africa Ruined Itself." *Wall Street Journal*, Dec. 9.

Azcarate, L. D. 1986. "The World Bank in Adjustment and Economic Growth in Africa." In G. K. Helleiner, ed., *Africa and the International Monetary Fund*. Washington, D.C.: International Monetary Fund.

Balcet, Jean-Claude, and Wilfred Candler. 1982. "Farm Technology Adoption in Northern Nigeria." Dept. of West African Projects, Agricultural Division 1 (WAPAl). World Bank, Washington, D.C.

Barghouti, S., and D. Lallement. 1988. "Water Management: Problems and Potentials in the Sahelian and Sudanian Zones." In F. Falloux and A. Mukendi, eds., *Desertification Control and Renewable Resource Management in the Sahelian and Sudanian Zones of West Africa*. Technical Paper 70. Washington, D.C.: World Bank.

Barry, Peter J., ed. 1984. *Risk Management in Agriculture*. Ames: Iowa State University Press.

Bates, Robert H. 1981. *Markets and States in Tropical Africa: The Political Basis of Agricultural Policies*. Berkeley: University of California Press.

———. 1990. "The Political Framework for Agricultural Policy Decisions." In Carl K. Eicher and John M. Staatz, eds., *Agricultural Development in the Third World*. Baltimore: Johns Hopkins University Press.

Batie, S. 1989. "Sustainable Development: Challenges to the Agricultural Economics Profession." *American Journal of Agricultural Economics* 71(5): 1083–101.

Bationo, A., M. P. Sedogo, E. O. Uyovbisere, and A. U. Mokwunye. 1993. *"Recent Achievements on Soil Fertility Management in the West African Semiarid Tropics."* Paper presented at Conference on Integrated Soil Fertility Management, Ouagadougou, Burkina Faso.

Becker, B. K. 1985. "Spontaneous/Induced Rural Settlements in Brazilian Amazonia." Paper presented at International Seminar on Planning for Settlements in Rural Regions: The Case of Spontaneous Settlements, Nov. 11–20, Nairobi, Kenya.

Becker, G. S. 1973. "A Theory of Marriage: Part I." *Journal of Political Economy* 81(4): 813–46.

———. 1981. *A Treatise on the Family*. Cambridge: Harvard University Press.

Bein, Frederick L. 1980. "Response to Drought in the Sahel." *Journal of Soil and Water Conservation* 35(3): 121–24.

Berg, E., J. Bisilliat, M. Burer, H. Graetz, R. Melville, V. Volyvan, J. Park, R.C. Savadogo, H. Sederlof, and K. van der Meer. 1978. "Onchocerciasis Control Programme: OCP Economic Review Mission." Report presented to the OCP.

Berthé, A. B., A. Blokland, S. Bouaré, B. Diallo, M. M. Diarra, C. Geerling, F. Mariko, H. N'Djim, and B. Sanogo. 1991. *Profil d'environment Mali-Sud: Etat des ressources naturelles et potentialites de developpement*. Bamako, Mali: Institut d'Economie Rurale.

Berthélemy, J. C., and C. Morrison. 1989. *Agricultural Development in Africa and the Supply of Manufactured Goods*. Paris: Development Center of the Organization for Economic Cooperation and Development (OECD).

Bharain, T. S. 1981. "Review and Evaluation of Attempts to Direct Migrants to Frontier Areas through Land Colonization Schemes." In *Population Distribution Policies in Development Planning*. Population Studies 75. New York: United Nations Dept. of International Economic and Social Affairs.

Bilsborrow, R. E. 1987. "Population Pressure and Agricultural Development in Developing Countries: A Conceptual Framework and Recent Evidence." *World Development* 15(2): 183–203.

Binswanger, H. P. 1980. "Attitudes toward Risk: Experimental Measurement in Rural India." *American Journal of Agricultural Economics* 62:395–407.

Binswanger, H. P., and J. McIntire. 1987. "Behavioral and Material Determinants of Production Relations in Land-Abundant Tropical Agriculture." *Economic Development and Cultural Change* 36:73–99.

Binswanger, Hans P., and Vernon W. Ruttan, with Uri Ben-Zion, Alain de Janvry, Robert E. Evenson, Yujiro Hayami, Terry L. Roe, John H. Sanders, William W. Wade, Adolf Weber, and Patrick Yeung. 1978. *Induced Innovation: Technology, Institutions, and Development*. Baltimore: Johns Hopkins University Press.

Block, A., and P. Timmer. 1992. *Agricultural Transformation in Sub-Saharan Africa: A Progress Report*. Agricultural Policy Analysis Project, Phase 2, Collaborative Research Report 342. Bethesda, Md.: ABT Associates.

Boserup, Ester. 1965. *The Conditions of Agricultural Growth: The Economics of Agrarian Change under Population Pressure*. New York: Aldine Publishing.

———. 1970. *Women's Role in Economic Development*. New York: St. Martin's Press.

———. 1981. *Population and Technological Change: A Study of Long-Term Trends*. Chicago: University of Chicago Press.

Boughton, Duncan, and Bruno Henry de Frahan. 1994. "Agricultural Research Impact Assessment: The Case of Maize Technology Adoption in Southern Mali." International Development Working Paper 41. Dept. of Agricultural Economics, Michigan State University, East Lansing.

Bouis, Howarth E. 1994. "The Effect of Income on Demand for Food in Poor Countries: Are Our Food Consumption Databases Giving Us Reliable Estimates?" *Journal of Development Economics* 44:1–28.

Bouis, Howarth E., and Lawrence J. Haddad. 1992. "Are Estimates of Calorie-Income Elasticities Too High? A Recalibration of the Plausible Range." *Journal of Development Economics* 39:333–64.

Bourn, D., and W. Wint. 1994. "Livestock, Land Use, and Agricultural Intensification in Sub-Saharan Africa." Pastoral Development Network discussion paper, Overseas Development Institute, London.

Breman, H., and C. T. de Wit. 1983. "Rangeland Productivity and Exploitation in the Sahel." *Science* 221(4618): 1341–47.

Broekhuyse, J. T., and A. M. Allen. 1988. "Farming Systems Research." *Human Organization* 47(4): 330–42.

Bromley, D. W., and J. P. Chavas. 1989. "On Risk, Transactions, and Economic Development in the Semi-Arid Tropics." *Economic Development and Cultural Change* 37(4): 719–36.

Brons, J., S. Diarra, I. Dembele, S. Bagayoko, and H. Djouara. 1994. *Diversité de gestion de l'exploitation agricole: Etude sur les facteurs d'intensification agricole au Mali Sud.* Document 94/33. Equipe Systemes de Production et Gestion des Ressources Naturelles. Sikasso, Mali.: Institute of Rural Economics.

Bryson, J. 1981. "Women and Agriculture in Sub-Saharan Africa: Implications for Development." In N. Nelson, ed., *African Women in the Development Process.* Totowa, N.J.: Cass.

Bumb, B. L. 1991. "Trends in Fertilizer Use and Production in Sub-Saharan Africa, 1970–1995: An Overview." *Fertilizer Research* 28:41–48.

Burkina Faso. 1989. *Rapport d'activités, 1988–1989.* Ouagadougou: Ministry of Agriculture.

Buvinic, M., and R. Mehra. 1990. "Women in Agricultural Development." In C. K. Eicher and J. M. Staatz, eds., *Agricultural Development in the Third World.* 2d ed. Baltimore: Johns Hopkins University Press.

Byerlee, Derek. 1993. "Modern Varieties, Productivity, and Sustainability: Recent Experience and Emerging Challenges." Paper presented at American Agricultural Economics Association preconference workshop, Post-Green Revolution Agricultural Development Strategies: What Next? Orlando, Fla.

Byerlee, Derek, with Alpha Diallo, Bantayu Gelaw, Paul Heisey, Wilfred Mwangi, Melinda Smale, Robert Tripp, and Steve Waddington. 1994. *Maize Research in Sub-Saharan Africa: An Overview of Past Impacts and Future Prospects.* Working Paper 94–03. Mexico City: CIMMYT.

Byerlee, Derek, and Paul Heisey. 1993. "Strategies for Technical Change in Small-Farm Agriculture, With Particular Reference to Sub-Saharan Africa." In Nathan C. Russell and Christopher R. Dowswell, eds., *Policy Options for Agricultural Development in Sub-Saharan Africa.* Mexico City: CASIN (Centre for Applied Studies in International Negotiations)/SAA (Sasakawa Africa Association)/Global 2000.

Byerlee, Derek, and Edith Hesse de Polanco. 1986. "Farmers' Stepwise Adoption of Technological Packages: Evidence from the Mexican Altiplano." *American Journal of Agricultural Economics* 68:519–27.

Byerlee, Derek, and G. Sain. 1986. "Food Pricing Policy in Developing Countries:

Bias against Agriculture or for Urban Consumers?" *American Journal of Agricultural Economics* 68(4): 961–69.

Cantrell, R., M. Lang, G. Swanson, W. K. Jaeger, S. Sawadogo, and J. Perrier. 1983. *1982 Annual Report*. Semi-Arid Food Grain Research and Development Program (SAFGRAD), Farming Systems Research Unit. West Lafayette, Ind.: Purdue University, International Programs in Agriculture.

Capron, J., and J. M. Kohler. 1975. "Environnement Sociologique des Migrations Agricoles." In *Enquête sur les Mouvements de Population à Partir du Pays Mossi,* vol. 1. Ouagadougou, Burkina Faso: ORSTOM.

Carr, Stephen J. 1989. *Technology for Small-Scale Farmers in Sub-Saharan Africa: Experience with Food Crop Production in Five Major Ecological Zones.* Technical Paper 109. Washington, D.C.: World Bank.

CFDT (Compagnie Française pour le Développement des Fibres Textiles). 1992. *Annual Report.* Paris: CFDT.

CGIAR (Consultative Group on International Agricultural Research). 1994. *CGIAR Annual Report.* Washington, D.C.: CGIAR Secretariat.

Cheru, Fantu. 1992. "Structural Adjustment, Primary Resource Trade, and Sustainable Development in Sub-Saharan Africa." *World Development* 20(4): 497–512.

Chisholm, Michael. 1967. *Rural Settlements and Land Use: An Essay in Location.* New York: Science Editions.

Chopra, K., and C. H. H. Rao. 1991. "The Links between Sustainable Agricultural Growth and Poverty." In Stephen Vosti, Thomas Reardon, and Winfried von Urff, eds., *Agricultural Sustainability, Growth, and Poverty Alleviation: Issues and Policies.* Feldafing, Germany: Food and Agriculture Development Center.

Christensen, Cheryl, and Larry Witucki. 1982. "Food Problems and Emerging Policy Responses in Sub-Saharan Africa." *American Journal of Agricultural Economics* 64:889–96.

CIMMYT. 1990. *1989/1990 CIMMYT World Maize Facts and Trends: Realizing the Potential of Maize in Sub-Saharan Africa.* Mexico City: CIMMYT.

Cleaver, Kevin, and W. Graeme Donovan. 1994. "Recent Agricultural Developments in Sub-Saharan Africa." Paper presented at Annual Meeting of the American Association of Agricultural Economics, San Diego.

Clough, Paul. 1981. "Farmers and Traders in Hausaland." *Development and Change* 12:273–92.

Cocks, K. D. 1968. "Discrete Stochastic Programming." *Management Science* 15(1): 72–79.

Cohen, John. 1980. "Land Tenure and Rural Development in Africa." In R. Bates and M. Lofchie, eds., *Agricultural Development in Africa.* New York: Praeger.

Collion, M. J. 1982. "Colonial Rule and Changing Peasant Economy in Damagherim, Niger Republic." Ph.D. diss., Cornell University.

Conde, J. 1978. *Migration in Upper Volta.* Washington, D.C.: World Bank.

Coulibaly, Ousmane N. 1987. "Factors Affecting Adoption of Agricultural Technologies by Small Farmers in Sub-Saharan Africa: The Case of New Varieties of Cowpeas around the Agricultural Research Station of Cinzana, Mali." Master's thesis, Michigan State University.

———. 1995. "Farm-Level Potential of Improved Crop Varieties, Soil Fertilization, and Water-Retention Techniques in Sustaining Sorghum-Based Cropping Systems in Mali." Ph.D. diss., Purdue University.

Couty, P., J. Y. Marchal, P. Pélissier, M. Poussi, G. Savonnet, and A. Schwartz, eds. 1979. *Maîtrise de l'espace agraire et développement en Afrique tropicale: Logique paysanne et rationalité technique.* Paris: ORSTOM.

Crosson, Pierre, and Jock Anderson. 1994. "Achieving a Sustainable Agricultural System in Sub-Saharan Africa." Technical paper (in preparation), World Bank, Washington, D.C.

CRPA (Centre Régional de Promotion Agro-Pastorale de la Boucle du Mouhoun). 1988. *Rapport d'achèvement de projet: Projet de développement agricole de la Boucle du Mouhoun (ex-Volta Noire).* Dedougou, Burkina Faso: CRPA du Mouhoun.

————. 1989. *Rapport d'achèvement de projet: Projet de développement agricole de la Boucle du Mouhoun (ex-Volta Noire).* Dedougou, Burkina Faso: CRPA du Mouhoun.

Dakurah, A. H., A. A. Dankyi, K. A. Marfo, T. J. Von , P. B. Allou, and G. Aflakpui. 1992. "Farmers' Preference for Maize/Sorghum Varieties in Northern Ghana: Results from a Formal Survey." Ghana Grains Development Project/ Nyankpala Agricultural Experiment Station, Accra, Ghana.

Danida (Danish International Development Agency). 1991. "Kenya Dairy Master Plan." Report prepared by Carl Bro. International, with Ministry of Livestock Development, Nairobi, Kenya.

Darity, W. A. 1980. "The Boserup Theory of Agricultural Growth: A Model for Anthropological Economics." *Journal of Development Economics* 7:137–57.

Davison, Jean. 1988. "Land and Women's Agricultural Production." In Jean Davison, ed., *Agriculture, Women, and Land.* Boulder, Co.: Westview Press.

Debrah, S. K. 1993. "Sorghum in West Africa." In D. E. Byth, ed., *Sorghum and Millets Commodity and Research Environments.* Patancheru, Andhra Pradesh, India: ICRISAT.

DeCosse, P. J. 1992. "Structural Change in Gambian Agriculture: Stagnation or Silent Transformation?" Banjul, Gambia.

Delgado, Christopher L. 1991. "Cereals Protection and Agricultural Development Strategy in the Sahel." *Food Policy* 16(2): 105–11.

Delgado, Christopher, and Chandrashekhar G. Ranade. 1987. "Technological Changes and Agricultural Labor Use." In John W. Mellor, Christopher L. Delgado, and Malcolm J. Blackie, eds., *Accelerating Food Producion in Sub-Saharan Africa.* Baltimore: Johns Hopkins University Press.

Delgado, Christopher, and Thomas Reardon. 1992. "Cereal Consumption Shifts and Policy Changes in Developing Countries: General Trends and Case Studies from the West African Semi-Arid Tropics." In Timothy T. Schilling and Dottie Stoner, eds., *Proceedings, International Sorghum and Millet CRSP Conference.* Lincoln, Nebr.: INTSORMIL Management Entity Office.

Deuson, Robert R., and John H. Sanders. 1990. "Cereal Technology Development in the Sahel: Burkina Faso and Niger." *Land Use Policy* 7(3): 195–97.

Dillon, J. L. 1977. *The Analysis of Response in Crop and Livestock Production.* 2d ed. New York: Pergamon.

Dillon, J. L., and P. L. Scandizzo. 1978. "Risk Attitudes of Subsistence Farmers in Northeast Brazil: A Sampling Approach." *American Journal of Agricultural Economics* 60:425–35.

Dioné, Josué. 1989. "Informing Food Security Policy in Mali: Interactions between Technology, Institutions, and Market Reforms." Ph.D. diss., Michigan State University.

Dollfus, O. 1981. "Phénomènes pionniers et problèmes de frontières: Quelques remarques en guise de conclusion." *Les Phénomènes de "Frontière" dans les pays tropicaux: Travaux et Mémoires de l'Institut des Hautes Etudes de l'Amérique Latine* 32:445–48.

Doran, M. H., A. R. C. Low, and R. L. Kemp. 1979. "Cattle As a Store of Wealth in Swaziland: Implications for Livestock Development and Overgrazing in Eastern and Southern Africa." *American Journal of Agricultural Economics* 61(1): 41–47.

Dornbusch, R. 1988. "Debt Problems and the World Macroeconomy." In J. D. Sachs, ed., *Developing Country Debt and the World Economy*. Chicago: University of Chicago Press.

Drèze, Jean, and Amartya Sen. 1989. *Hunger and Public Action*. New York: Oxford University Press.

D'Silva, B. C. 1986. *Sudan's Irrigated Subsector: Issues for Policy Analysis*. Washington, D.C.: U.S. Dept. of Agriculture, International Economics Research Service.

Dudal, R., and H. Eswaran. 1988. "Distribution and Classification of the Vertisols." In Larry P. Wilding and Ruben Puentes, eds., *Vertisols: Their Distribution Properties, Classification and Management*. College Station: Texas A&M University Press.

Due, Jean, and Christina Gladwin. 1991. "Impacts of Structural Adjustment Programs on African Women Farmers and Female-Headed Households." *American Journal of Agricultural Economics* 73(5): 1431–39.

Duke, B. 1990. "Onchocerciasis (River Blindness)—Can It Be Eradicated? *Parasitology Today* 6(3): 82–84.

Dupire, M. 1960. "Planteurs autochtones et étrangers en basse Côte d'Ivoire orientale." *Etudes Eburneennes* 8:7–327.

Dureau, D., B. Traore, and D. Ballo. 1994. "Evolution de la fertilité des sols en culture continue dans la zone Mali-Sud: Système de culture à base de cotonnier." N'Tarla Experiment Station, Mali-Sud, Mali.

Edwards, Clive A., H. David Thurston, and Rhonda Janke. 1991. "Integrated Pest Management for Sustainability in Developing Countries." In National Research Council, ed., *Toward Sustainability: A Plan for Collaborative Research on Agriculture and Natural Resource Management*. Washington, D.C.: National Academy Press.

Edwards, Sebastian. 1989. "Structural Adjustment Policies in Highly Indebted Countries." In Jeffrey D. Sachs, ed., *Developing Country Debt and the World Economy*. Chicago: University of Chicago Press.

Eicher, Carl K. 1988. "Food Security Battles in Sub-Saharan Africa." Plenary address, 7th World Congress for Rural Sociology, June 26-July 2, Bologna, Italy.

Eicher, Carl K., 1992. "African Agricultural Development Strategies." In Frances Stewart, Sanjaya Lall, and Samuel Wangwe, eds., *Alternative Development Strategies in Sub-Saharan Africa*. New York: St. Martin's Press.

Ejeta, Gebisa. 1988. "Development and Spread of Hageen Dura-1, the First Commercial Sorghum Hybrid in the Sudan." *Applied Agricultural Research* 3:29–35.

Elbadawi, I. 1989. "The Extent and Consequence of Direct and Indirect Taxation of Sudanese Agriculture." Report for U.S. Agency for International Development (USAID), Khartoum, Sudan.

Faini, Riccardo. 1993. "Infrastructure, Relative Prices, and Agricultural Adjustment." In Ian Goldin and Alan Winters, eds., *Open Economies, Structural Adjustment, and Agriculture*. Cambridge.: Cambridge University Press.

Faini, Riccardo, and Jaime de Melo. 1990. "Adjustment, Investment, and the Real Exchange Rate in Developing Countries." *Economic Policy* 5(2): 491–519.

Fajemisin, J. M. 1992. "Maize Production in West and Central Africa: Trends and Research and Orientation." Bulletin, IITA/SAFRAD, Ouagadougou, Burkina Faso.

Fakki, H. 1982. "Economics and Management of Irrigation in the Sudan Gezira Scheme." Ph.D. diss., University of Hohenheim, Hohenheim, Germany.

FAO (Food and Agricultural Organization of the United Nations). 1986 to 1993. *FAO Production Year Book*. Rome: FAO.

———. 1986. *African Agriculture: The Next 25 Years*. 6 vols. Rome: FAO.

———. 1987. *World Crop and Livestock Statistics*. Rome: FAO.

———. Various years. *Trade Year Book*. Rome: FAO.

FAO and WHO (World Health Organization). 1992. *Nutrition and Development—A Global Assessment*. Rev. ed. Rome: FAO and WHO.

Feder, Gershon, and Raymond Noronha. 1987. "Land Rights Systems and Agricultural Development in Sub-Saharan Africa." *World Bank Research Observer* 2(2): 143–69.

FEWS (Famine Early Warning System). 1994. "Bulletin." SH-11, Nov. 30, USAID/FEWS Project, Tulane/Pragma Group, Arlington, Va.

Folbre, Nancy. 1986. "Cleaning House: New Perspectives on Households and Economic Development." *Journal of Development Economics* 22(1): 5–41.

Fosu, Augustin K. 1992. "Political Instability and Economic Growth: Evidence from Sub-Saharan Africa." *Economic Development and Cultural Change* 40(4): 829–41.

Fussell, L. K., and P. G. Serafini. 1985. "Crop Associations in the Semi-arid Tropics of West Africa: Research Strategies Past and Future." In H. W. Ohm and J. G. Nagy, eds., *Appropriate Technologies for Farmers in Semi-Arid West Africa*. West Lafayette, Ind.: Purdue University, International Programs in Agriculture.

Fussell, L. K., P. G. Serafini, A. Bationo, and M. C. Klaij. 1986. "Management Practices To Increase Yield and Yield Stability of Pearl Millet in Africa." In *Proceedings of the International Pearl Millet Workshop*. Patancheru, Andhra Pradesh, India: ICRISAT Animal Traction Center.

Gerard, C. J. 1985. *Furrow Diking and Subsoiling Studies in the Rolling Plains*.

Report B-1585. College Station: Texas Agricultural Experiment Station.

Girdis, Dean P. 1993. "The Role of Cotton in Agricultural Change, Land Degradation, and Sustainability in Southern Mali." Royal Tropical Institute, Amsterdam, The Netherlands.

Gladwin, C. H., and D. McMillan. 1989. "Is a Turnaround in Africa Possible without Helping African Women to Farm?" *Economic Development and Cultural Change* 37(2): 345–70.

Glantz, Michael H. 1987. "Drought and Economic Development in Sub-Saharan Africa." In Michael H. Glantz, ed., *Drought and Hunger in Africa: Denying Famine a Future*. New York: Cambridge University Press.

Goering, T. J. 1978. *Agricultural Land Settlement*. Washington, D.C.: World Bank.

Goodwin, Joseph, John H. Sanders, and Antonio Diaz de Hollanda. 1980. "Ex-Ante Appraisal of New Technology: Sorghum in Northeast Brazil." *American Journal of Agricultural Economics* 62(4): 737–41.

Gorse, J. E., and D. R. Steeds. 1987. *Desertification in the Sahelian and Sudanian Zones of West Africa*. Technical Paper 61. Washington, D.C.: World Bank.

Graham, D. H., C. E. Cuevas, K. Negash, and M. Masini. 1987. "Rural Finance in Niger: A Critical Appraisal and Recommendations for Change." Report to the USAID Mission in Niamey, Niger, Dept. of Agricultural Economics, Ohio State University, Columbus.

Guyer, J. K. 1986. "Women's Role in Development." In R. J. Berg and J. S. Whitaker, eds., *Strategies for African Development*. Berkeley: University of California Press.

Hafkin, N., and E. Bay. 1976. *Women in Africa*. Stanford: Stanford University Press.

Habash, M. K. 1990. "Potential Returns and Constraints to the Adoption of New Technologies in the Mechanized Rainfed Region (Eastern Vertisols) of the Sudan." Ph.D. diss., Purdue University.

Hamal, K. B., and J. B. Anderson. 1982. "A Note on Decreasing Absolute Risk Aversion among Farmers in Nepal." *Australian Journal of Agricultural Economics* 26(3): 220–25.

Hammond, P. B. 1966. *Technology and Culture of a West African Kingdom: Yatenga*. New York: Free Press.

Hayami, Yujiro, and Vernon W. Ruttan. 1985. *Agricultural Development: An International Perspective*. Baltimore: Johns Hopkins University Press.

Heathcote, R. G. 1974. "The Use of Fertilizers in the Maintenance of Soil Fertility under Intensive Cropping in Northern Nigeria." In *Potassium in Tropical Crops and Soils*. Berne, Switzerland: Der Bunde.

Helleiner, G. K. 1986. "The Question of Conditionality." In Carol Lancaster and John Williamson, eds., *African Debt and Financing*. Special Report 5. Washington, D.C.: Institute for International Economics.

Helmers, F. Leslie C. H. 1988. "The Real Exchange Rate." In Rudiger Dornbusch and F. Leslie C. H. Helmers, eds., *The Open Economy: Tools for Policymakers in Developing Countries*. New York: Oxford University Press.

Hervouet, J. P. Clanet, F. Paris, and H. Some. 1984. "Settlement of the Valleys Protected from Onchocerciasis after Ten Years of Vector Control in Burkina." OCP/GVA/84.5. Ouagadougou, Burkina Faso.

Hill, P. 1986. *Development Economics on Trial.* Cambridge: Cambridge Univ. Press.

Holdcroft, Lane E. 1989. "The Sudan Today: An Economy and Its Agriculture in Crisis." Field Staff Report 14, 1988–89, Africa/Middle East, USAID, Washington, D.C.

Holtzman, John J., John A. Lichte, James F. Tefft, Bagotigui Bagayoko, and Fanta Mantchiny Diarra. 1991. "Expanding Coarse Grain Utilization in Mali: Current Situation, Constraints, Opportunities, and Program Options." USAID Agricultural Marketing Improvement Strategies project paper, ABT Associates, Bethesda, Md.

Hopkins, J., and P. Berry. 1994. "Determinants of Land and Labor Productivity in Crop Production in Niger." Report to USAID, Niamey, Niger.

Hoseney, R. C., D. G. Andrews, and H. Clark. 1987. "Sorghum and Pearl Millet," in *Nutritional Quality of Cereal Grains: Genetic and Agronomic Improvement.* Agronomy Monograph 28. American Society of Agronomy, Madison, Wis.

Howard, J. A. 1994. "Improved Maize in Zambia: A Qualified Success Story." Paper prepared for symposium, Recent Technological Successes in Sub-Saharan Agriculture, American Agricultural Economics Association, Aug., San Diego.

Hunting Technical Services Limited. 1988. *Socio-Economic Development Studies in the Onchocerciasis Control Programme Area.* 4 vols. Hemel Hempstead, England: Hunting Technical Services Ltd.

ICRISAT (International Crops Research Institute for the Semi-Arid Tropics). 1985. *ICRISAT Sahelian Center Annual Report, 1984.* Niamey, Niger: ICRISAT.

———. 1986. *ICRISAT Sahelian Center Annual Report, 1985.* Niamey, Niger: ICRISAT.

———. 1987. *ICRISAT Sahelian Center Annual Report, 1986.* Niamey, Niger: ICRISAT.

———. 1988. *ICRISAT Sahelian Center Annual Report, 1987.* Niamey, Niger: ICRISAT.

IFDC (International Fertilizer Development Corporation). 1988. *IFDC/Niger Annual Report, 1987.* Niamey, Niger: IFDC.

IITA (International Institute of Tropical Agriculture). 1987. *IITA Annual Report and Research Highlights.* Ibadan, Nigeria: IITA.

ILO (International Labour Office). 1975. *Growth, Employment, and Equity: A Comprehensive Strategy for the Sudan.* Report of the ILO/UNDP Employment Strategy Mission. Geneva: ILO.

IMF (International Monetary Fund). Various years. *International Financial Statistics.* Washington, D.C.: IMF.

———. 1992. *World Economic Outlook, May 1992.* Washington, D.C.: IMF.

———. 1994. *World Economic Outlook, May 1994.* Washington, D.C.: IMF.

INTSORMIL (International Sorghum and Millet Improvement Program). 1994. *Annual Report, 1994.* University of Nebraska, Lincoln.

Jaeger, W. K. 1987. *Agricultural Mechanization.* Boulder, Co.: Westview Press.

Jaeger, W. K., and Peter J. Matlon. 1990. "Utilization, Profitability, and the Adoption of Animal Draft Power in West Africa." *American Journal of Agricultural Economics* 72(1): 35–48.

Jahnke, Hans E. 1982. *Livestock Production and Livestock Development in Tropical Africa.* Munich: Weltforum Verlag.

Jansen, Hans G. P., Thomas S. Walker, and Randolph Barker. 1990. "Adoption Ceilings and Modern Coarse Cereal Cultivars in India." *American Journal of Agricultural Economics* 72(3): 653–63.

Jayne, Thomas S., John C. Day, and Harold E. Dregne. 1989. *Technology and Agricultural Productivity in the Sahel*. USDA/Economic and Research Service, Agricultural Economic Report 612. Washington, D.C.: U.S. Government Printing Office.

Jomini, P. A. 1990. "The Economic Viability of Phosphorous Fertilizer in Southwestern Niger: A Dynamic Approach Incorporating Agronomic Principles." Ph.D. diss., Purdue University.

Jones, C. 1983. "The Mobilization of Women's Labor for Cash Crop Production: A Game Theoretic Approach." *American Journal of Agricultural Economics* 15(5): 1049–56.

———. 1986. "Intra-Household Bargaining in Response to the Introduction of New Crops: A Case Study from North Cameroon." In Joyce L. Moock, ed., *Understanding Africa's Rural Households and Farming Systems*. Boulder, Co.: Westview Press.

Karanja, Daniel. 1990. "The Rate of Return to Maize Research in Kenya, 1955–1988." Master's thesis, Michigan State University.

Kelly, V., B. Diagana, T. Reardon, M. Gaye, and E. Crawford. 1995. "Cash Crop and Foodgrain Productivity in Senegal: Historic View, New Survey Evidence, and Policy Implication." Staff Paper 95, Dept. of Agricultural Economics, Michigan State University, East Lansing.

Knudsen, Odin, and John Nash. 1991. "Agricultural Policy." In Vinod Thomas, Ajay Chibber, Mansoor Dailami, and Jaime de Melo, eds., *Restructuring Economies in Distress—Policy Reform and the World Bank*. New York: Oxford University Press.

Krause, M. A., R. R. Deuson, T. G. Baker, P. V. Preckel, J. Lowenberg-DeBoer, K. C. Reddy, and K. Maliki. 1990. "Risk Sharing versus Low-Cost Credit Systems for International Development." *American Journal of Agricultural Economics* 72(4): 911–22.

Krause, M. A., K. Maliki, K. C. Reddy, R. R. Deuson, and M. Issa. 1987. "Labor Management Effects on the Relative Profitability of Alternative Millet/Cowpea Intercrop Systems in Niger." Paper presented at the Annual Farming Systems Research Symposium, Oct., University of Arkansas, Fayetteville.

Krishna, J. H., G. F. Arkin, J. R. Williams, and J. R. Mulkey. 1987. "Simulating Furrow-Dike Impacts on Runoff and Sorghum Yields." *American Society of Agricultural Engineers* 30(1): 143–47.

Kumar, Shubh K. 1987. "Women's Role and Agricultural Technology," in John W. Mellor, Christopher L. Delgado, and Malcolm J. Blackie, eds., *Accelerating Food Production in Sub-Saharan Africa*. Baltimore, Md.: Johns Hopkins University Press.

Lall, Sanjaya. 1992. "Structural Problems of African Industry in Sub-Saharan Africa," in Francis Stewart, Sanjaya Lall, and Samuel Wangwe, eds. *Alternative Development Strategies in Sub-Saharan Africa*. New York: St. Martin's Press.

Lang, M., R. P. Cantrell, and J. H. Sanders. 1984. "Identifying Farm-Level Constraints and Evaluating New Technology in the Purdue Farming-Systems Project in Upper Volta." In C. B. Flora, ed., *Animals in the Farming System.* Manhattan, Kans.: Kansas State University.

Lang, M., H. W. Ohm, and R. Cantrell. 1984. *1983 Annual Report.* SAFGRAD, Farming Systems Research Unit. West Lafayette, Ind.: Purdue University, International Programs in Agriculture.

Lawrence, Pareena G. 1993. "Household Decision Making and Introduction of New Agricultural and Household Technologies in the Solenzo Region of Burkina Faso." Ph.D. diss., Purdue University.

Leaphart, Stephanie. 1994. "Impact of the Millet and Sorghum Improvement Programs in Senegal." Natural Resource Research Program of Oregon State University, Dakar, Senegal. Corvallis, Ore., mimeo.

Lele, Uma. 1981. "Rural Africa: Modernization, Equity, and Long-Term Development." *Science* 211: 547–53.

———. 1986a. "Comparative Advantage and Structural Transformation: A Review of Africa's Economic Development Experience." In Gustav Ranis and T. Paul Schultz, eds., *The State of Development Economics.* London: Basil Blackwell.

———. 1986b. "Women and Structural Transformation." *Economic Development and Cultural Change* 34(2): 195–221.

———. 1991. Introduction to Uma Lele, ed., *Aid to African Agriculture.* Baltimore: Johns Hopkins University Press.

Lele, Uma, Robert E. Christiansen, and Kindhavi Kadiresan. 1989. *Fertilizer Policy in Africa: Lessons from Development Programs and Adjustment Lending, 1970–1987,* Managing Agricultural Development in Africa MADIA Discussion Paper 5. Washington, D.C.: World Bank.

Lele, Uma, Nicolas van de Walle, and Mathurin Gbetibouou. 1989. *Cotton in Africa: An Analysis of Differences in Performance.* Managing Agricultural Development in Africa Discussion Paper 7. Washington, D.C.: World Bank.

Liese, B. H., P. S. Sachdeva, and D. G. Cochrane. 1992. *Organizing and Managing Tropical Disease Control Programs.* Technical Paper 167. Washington, D.C.: World Bank.

Lofchie, Michael F. 1987. "The Decline of African Agriculture: An Internalist Perspective." In Michael H. Glantz, ed., *Drought and Hunger in Africa: Denying Famine a Future.* New York: Press Syndicate of the University of Cambridge.

Lopez-Pereira, Miguel. 1990. "Economics of Sorghum and Soil Erosion Control Technologies for Small Hillside Farms in Southern Honduras." Ph.D. diss., Purdue University.

Low, A. R. C., M. H. Doran, and R. L. Kemp. 1980. "Cattle Wealth and Cash Needs in Swaziland: Price Response and Rural Development Implications." *Journal of Agricultural Economics* 31(2): 225–35.

Lowenberg-DeBoer, J., Hadiza Zarafi, and Mohamed Abdoulaye. 1992. "Enquête sur l'adoption des technologies Mil-Nièbe à Kouka, Maiguero, Rigial et Kandamo." Publication 26F, Programme de Recherche Sur Les Systèmes de Production Agricole. Departement de Recherches en Economie Rurale, Ministère de l'Agriculture, Niamey, Niger.

Lynam, John K., and Malcolm J. Blackie. 1994. "Building Effective Agricultural Research Capacity: The African Challenge." In Jock R. Anderson, ed., *Agricul-*

*tural Technology: Policy Issues for the International Community.* Cambridge: Cambridge University Press.

Lynam, John K., and R. W. Herdt. 1989. "Seeds and Sustainability: Sustainability as an Objective in International Agricultural Research." *Agricultural Economics* 3(4): 381–97.

Magar, W. Y. 1986. "Farms in the Gezira." In A. B. Zahlan and W. Y. Magar, eds., *The Agricultural Sector of Sudan: Policy and System Studies.* London: Ithaca Press.

Mahamane, Issa, M. Kadi, A. Beirada, R. R. Deuson, G. Ibro, M. Krause, G. Numa, K. C. Reddy, and B. I. Shapiro. 1987. *Evaluation des essais en milieu reel sur les cultures associees Mil-Niebe: Resultat de la campagne de 1986.* Document 17F. Niamey, Niger: INRAN/DECOR.

M. Ahmed, Mohamed. 1990. "Economic Evaluation of New Sorghum Production Technologies and Policy Implications for the Northern Gedaref Region of Eastern Sudan." Master's thesis, Purdue University.

———. 1994. "Introducing New Technologies on the Vertisols of Eastern Sudan." Ph.D. diss., Purdue University.

M. Ahmed, Mohamed, William A. Masters, and J. H. Sanders. 1995. "Returns from Research in Economies with Distortions: Hybrid Sorghum in Sudan." Dept. of Agricultural Economics, Purdue University, West Lafayette, Ind.

M. Ahmed, Mohamed, and John H. Sanders. 1992. "The Economic Impacts of Hageen Dura-1 in the Gezira Scheme, Sudan." In Timothy T. Schilling and Dottie Stoner, eds., *Proceedings, International Sorghum and Millet CRSP Conference,* Lincoln, Nebr.: INTSORMIL Management Entity Office.

Maiga, Alpha S., Ousmane M. Sanogo, Youssouf M. Diarra, Dramane Mariko. 1994. *Etude de l'Impact de la Station de Recherche Agronomique de Cinzana in Milieu Paysan.* Bamako, Mali: Institut d'Economie Rurale.

Maliki, Kadi, M. Issa, G. Ibro, H. Zarafi, G. Numa, and K. C. Reddy. 1988. *Synthèse des résultats de cinq années d'activités: 1983–1987.* Document 18F. Niamey, Niger: INRAN/DECOR.

Maredia, Mywish K., Derek Byerlee, and Carl K. Eicher. 1994. "The Efficiency of Global Wheat Research Investments: Implications for Research Evaluation, Research Managers, and Donors." Staff Paper 94–7. Dept. of Agricultural Economics, Michigan State University, East Lansing.

Marfo, Kofi, and Robert Tripp. 1992. "A Study of Maize Technology Diffusion in Ghana: Some Preliminary Results." In Nathan C. Russell, R. Dowswell, and R. Christopher, eds., *Africa's Agricultural Development in the 1990s: Can It Be Sustained?* Mexico City: CASIN/SAA/Global 2000.

Matlon, Peter J. 1987. "The West African Semi-Arid Tropics." In J. W. Mellor, C. L. Delgado, and M. J. Blackie, eds., *Accelerating Food Production in Sub-Saharan Africa.* Baltimore: Johns Hopkins University Press.

———. 1990. "Improving Productivity in Sorghum and Pearl Millet in Semi-Arid Africa." *Food Research Institute Studies* 22(1): 1–44.

———. 1991. "Indigenous Land Use Systems and Investments in Soil Fertility in Burkina Faso." Bouake, Côte d'Ivoire: West African Rice Development Association (WARDA).

Matlon, Peter J., and Akinwumi Adesina. 1991. "Prospects for Sustainable Improvements in Sorghum and Millet Productivity in West Africa." In Stephen Vosti, Thomas Reardon, and Winfried von Urff, eds., *Agricultural Sustainability, Growth, and Poverty Alleviation: Issues and Policies*. Feldafing, Germany: Food and Agriculture Development Center.

Matlon, Peter J., and Patricia Kristjanson. 1988. "Farmers' Strategies to Manage Crop Risk in the West African Semi-arid Tropics." Paper presented at Annual Meeting of American Agricultural Economic Association, July 29-Aug. 3, Knoxville, Tenn.

Matlon, Peter J., and Dunstan S. Spencer. 1984. "Increasing Food Production in Sub-Saharan Africa: Environmental Problems and Inadequate Technological Solutions." *American Journal of Agricultural Economics* 66(5): 671–76.

Mbogoh, Stephen G. 1987. "Review and Analysis of Organizational Aspects and Socio-Economic Effects of Dairy Development Schemes in Ethiopia and Kenya." In *IFPRI Workshop on the Economics and Dairy Development in Selected Countries and Policy Implications*. Washington, D.C.: International Food Policy Research Institute.

McElroy, M. B., and M. J. Horney. 1981. "Nash-Bargained Household Decisions: Toward a Generalization of the Theory of Demand." *International Economic Review* 22(2): 333–49.

McIntire, J., D. Bourzat, and P. Pingali. 1992. *Crop-Livestock Interaction in Sub-Saharan Africa*. Washington, D.C.: World Bank.

McMillan, Della E. 1983. "A Resettlement Project in Upper Volta." Ph.D. diss., Northwestern University.

———. 1986. "Distribution of Resources and Products in Mossi Households." In A. Hansen and Della E. McMillan, eds., *Food in Sub-Saharan Africa*. Boulder, Co.: Lynne Rienner Publishers.

———. 1987a. "Monitoring the Evolution of Household Economic Systems Over Time in Farming Systems Research." *Development and Change* 18: 295–314.

———. 1987b. "The Social Impacts of Planned Settlements in Burkina Faso." In Michael H. Glantz, ed., *Drought and Hunger in Africa: Denying Famine a Future*. New York: Cambridge University Press.

———. 1993. "Diversification and Sustainable Development in the River Blindness Control Zone of West Africa." *Human Organization* 52(3): 269–82.

McMillan, Della E., J. B. Nana, and K. Savadogo. 1993. *Onchocerciasis Control Programme. Land Settlement Review Case Study: Burkina Faso*. Technical Paper 200. Washington, D.C.: World Bank.

McMillan, Della E., T. Painter, and T. Scudder. 1992. *Settlement and Development in the River Blindness Control Zone*. Technical Paper 192. Washington, D.C.: World Bank.

McNamara, Robert S. 1985. *The Challenges for Sub-Saharan Africa*. Sir John Crawford Memorial Lecture, Nov. 1, Washington, D.C.

Mellor, J. W. 1988. "The Intertwining of Environmental Problems and Poverty." *Environment* 30(9): 8–13, 28–29.

Mellor, J. W. and S. Gavian. 1987. "Famine: Causes, Prevention, and Relief." *Science* 235: 539–45.

Meredith, William R., Jr., and Robert R. Bridge. 1984. "Genetic Contributions to

Yield Changes in Upland Cotton." In W. R. Fehr, ed., *Genetic Contributions to Yield Gains of Five Major Crop Plants*. Madison, Wis.: Crop Science Society of America and American Society of Agronomy.

Merghani, Faisal. 1993. "Sorghum Production Statistics." Agricultural Research Corporation, Wad Medani, Sudan.

Metzel, J., and A. Cook. 1993. "Economic Comparative Advantage and Incentives in Livestock Production and Trade in West Africa's Central Corridor, Volume I." Draft report, Associates for International Research and Development, Cambridge, Mass.

Meyer, J. 1977. "Choice among Distributions." *Journal of Economic Theory* 14: 326–36.

MFC (Mechanized Farming Corporation). 1984. "Agricultural Statistics." Bulletin 3. MFC, Khartoum, Sudan.

Migot-Adholla, Shem, Peter Hazell, Benoit Blarel, and Frank Place. 1991. "Indigenous Land Rights Systems in Sub-Saharan Africa: A Constraint on Productivity?" *World Bank Economic Review* 5(1): 155–75.

Miller, Frederick R., and Yilma Kebede. 1984. "Genetic Contributions to Yield Gains in Sorghum, 1950 to 1980." In W. R. Fehr, ed., *Genetic Contributions to Yield Gains of Five Major Crop Plants*. Madison, Wis.: Crop Science Society of America and American Society of Agronomy.

Miller, Louis H. 1992. "The Challenge of Malaria." *Science* 257(July 3, 1992): 36–37.

Mokwunye, A. Uzo, and L. L. Hammond. 1992. "Myths and Science of Fertilizer Use in the Tropics." In R. Lal and P. A. Sanchez, eds., *Myths and Science of Soils in the Tropics*. Madison, Wis.: Soil Science of America and American Society of Agronomy.

Morris, J. D., D. J. Thom, and R. Norman. 1984. *Prospects for Small-Scale Irrigation Development in the Sahel*. Water Management Synthesis Report, Logan: Utah State University.

Murphy J., and L. Sprey. 1980. "The Volta Valley Authority: Socio-Economic Evaluation of a Resettlement Project in Upper Volta." Dept. of Agricultural Economics, Purdue University, West Lafayette, Ind.

Nafziger, E. Wayne. 1993. *The Debt Crisis in Africa*. Baltimore: Johns Hopkins University Press.

Nagy, Joseph G., and Linda Ames. 1986. "Evaluation of New Technologies in Burkina Faso Using Whole-Farm Modeling." Paper presented at American Agricultural Economists Association meeting, Aug., Reno, Nev.

Nagy, Joseph G., L. Ames, and H. W. Ohm. 1985. "Technology Evaluation, Policy Change, and Farmer Adoption in Burkina Faso." Paper presented at Farming Systems Symposium, Oct., Kansas State University, Manhattan.

Nagy, Joseph G., H. W. Ohm, L. Ames, and L. Schraber. 1988. "An Animal-Drawn Ridge Tier for the Cereal Farming Systems of Burkina Faso." *Agricultural Mechanization in Asia, Africa, and Latin America* 19(4): 26–33.

Nagy, Joseph G., H. W. Ohm, and R. Cantrell. 1985. *1984 Annual Report*. SAFGRAD, Farming Systems Research Unit. West Lafayette, Ind.: Purdue University, International Programs in Agriculture.

Nagy, Joseph G., John H. Sanders, and H. W. Ohm. 1987. "Cereal Technology

Development—West African Semi-Arid Tropics: A Farming Systems Perspective." SAFGRAD, USAID Contract AFR-C-1472. International Programs in Agriculture, Purdue University, West Lafayette, Ind.

Nagy, Joseph G., J. H. Sanders, and H. W. Ohm. 1988. "Cereal Technology Interventions for the West African Semi-Arid Tropics." *Agricultural Economics* 2: 197–208.

Nana, J. B. 1989. *Rapport sur le site de la zone de sous-secteur de Niangoloko et de la forêt classée de Toumoussenini*. Binghamton, N.Y.: Institute for Developmental Anthropology.

Nana, J. B., and D. Kattenberg. 1979. *Etude préliminaire de la question des migrants spontanés*. Ouagadougou, Burkina Faso: DEPEC, Section Sociologie, AVV.

Nash, J. 1953. "Two-Person Cooperative Games." *Econometrica* 21(1): 128–40.

Nichola, Tennassie. 1994. "The Adoption of Hybrid Sorghum at the Farm and Regional Levels in the Gezira Irrigated Scheme of Sudan." Ph.D. diss., Purdue University.

Nicolai, H., and G. Laserre. 1981. "Les systèmes de cultures traditionnels et les phénomènes de pionniers en Afrique tropicale." In *Les Phénomènes de "Frontière" dans les pays tropicaux. Travaux et mémoires de l'Institut des Hautes Etudes de l'Amérique Latine* 32: 9–11.

Nicou, R., and C. Charreau. 1985. "Soil Tillage and Water Conservation in Semi-Arid West Africa." In Herbert W. Ohm and J. Nagy, eds., *Appropriate Technologies for Farmers in Semi-Arid West Africa*. West Lafayette, Ind.: Purdue University, International Programs in Agriculture.

Nicou, R., B. Ouattara, and L. Some. 1987. "Effets des techniques d'économie de l'eau à la parcelle sur les cultures céréalières (sorgho, mais, mil) au Burkina Faso." Institut des Etudes et des Recherches Agricoles (INERA), Ouagadougou, Burkina Faso.

Norman, D. W., Mark D. Newman, and Ismael Ouedraogo. 1981. *Farm-Level and Village-Level Production Systems in the Semi-Arid Tropics of West Africa: An Interpretive Review of Research*. Research Bulletin 1(4). Patancheru, Andhra Pradesh, India: ICRISAT.

Noronha, Raymond. 1985. "A Review of the Literature on Land Tenure Systems in Sub-Saharan Africa." Report ARV 43. World Bank. Washington, D.C.

Obbo, C. 1990. "East African Women, Work, and the Articulation of Dominance." In I. Tinker, ed., *Persistent Inequalities: Women and World Development*. New York: Oxford University Press.

OCP (Onchocerciasis Control Programme). 1977. *Socioeconomic Development Aspects of the Programme: Annual Report, 1977*. OCP/EDU77.1. Ouagadougou, Burkina Faso: OCP.

———. 1980. *Onchocerciasis Control Programme in the Volta River Basin Area: Information Paper*. OCP/74.1. Ouagadougou, Burkina Faso: OCP.

———. 1986. "Report on the Evaluation of the Socioeconomic Impact of the Onchocerciasis Control Programme." Report JPC 7.3. Joint Programme Committee, Dec. 9–12, Accra, Ghana.

Ohm, H., J. G. Nagy, and C. R. Pardy. 1985. *1984 Annual Report*. SAFGRAD, Farming Systems Research Unit. West Lafayette, Ind.: Purdue University, International Programs in Agriculture.

Oldeman, L. R. 1994. "The Global Extent of Soil Degradation." In D. J. Greenland and I. Szalbolcs, eds., *Soil Resilience and Sustainable Land Use*. Wallingford, Oxon, U.K.: CAB International.

Oldeman, L. R., R. T. A. Hakkelin, and W. G. Sombroek. 1991. *World Map of the Status of Human-Induced Soil Degradation, An Explanatory Note*, 2d ed. Wageningen, The Netherlands: International Soil Reference and Information Center; Nairobi, Kenya: United Nations Environmental Program.

O'Neil, M. K., B. I. Shapiro, R. Imboden, and I. Batoure. 1988. "Single Ox and Paired Oxen Animal Traction in Sahelian Sandy Soils." In P. W. Unger, W. R. Jordan, T. V. Sneed, and R. W. Jensen, eds., *Challenges in Dryland Agriculture: A Global Perspective*. College Station: Texas A&M University Press.

PAG (Preparatory Assistance Mission to the Governments of Dahomey, Ghana, Côte d'Ivoire, Mali, Niger, Togo, Upper Volta). 1973. "Onchocerciasis Control in the Volta River Basin Area." OCP/73.1. World Health Organization, Geneva.

Painter, Thomas M. 1986. "Peasant Migrations and Rural Transformation in Niger: A Study of Incorporation within a West African Capitalist Regional Economy, c. 1875 to 1982." Ph.D. diss., State University of New York at Binghamton.

————. 1987. "Bringing Land Back In: Changing Strategies to Improve Agricultural Production in the West African Sahel." In P. D. Little and M. M. Horowitz, eds., *Lands at Risk in the Third World: Local Level Perspectives*. Boulder, Co.: Westview Press.

Panin, A. 1987. *The Use of Bullock Traction Technology for Crop Cultivation in Northern Ghana: An Empirical Economic Analysis*. Bulletin 29. Addis Ababa, Ethiopia: International Livestock Centres for Africa (ILCA).

Peyre de Fabreques, B. 1986. "The Rangeland-Livestock Sector of Niger." Dept. of Agricultural Economics, Purdue University, West Lafayette, Ind.

Pichot, J., M. P. Sedogo, J. F. Poulain, and J. Arrivets. 1981. "Evolution de la fertilité d'un sol ferrugineux tropical sous l'influence des fumures et organiques." *Agronomie Tropicale* 36(2): 122–33.

Pingali, P. 1990. "Institutional and Environmental Constraints to Agricultural Intensification." In Geoffrey McNicoll and Mead Cain, eds., *Rural Development and Populations: Institutions and Policy*. New York: Oxford University Press.

Pingali, P., Y. Bigot, and H. Binswanger. 1987. *Agricultural Mechanization and the Evolution of Farming Systems in Sub-Saharan Africa*. Baltimore: Johns Hopkins University Press.

Place, Frank, and Peter Hazell. 1993. "Productivity Effects of Indigenous Land Tenure Systems in Sub-Saharan Africa." *American Journal of Agricultural Economics* 75(1): 10–19.

Plucknett, Donald L. 1990. "International Goals and the Role of the International Agricultural Research Centers." In Clive Edwards, Rattan Lal, Patrick Madden, Robert Miller, and Gar House, eds., *Sustainable Agricultural Systems*. Ankeny, Iowa: Soil and Water Conservation Society.

Posner, J. L., and E. Gilbert. 1991. "Sustainable Agriculture and Farming Systems Research Teams in Semiarid West Africa: A Fatal Attraction?" *Journal for Farming Systems Research-Extension* 2(1): 71–86.

Powell, J. M., and Williams, T. O. 1993. *Livestock, Nutrient Cycling, and Sustain-*

*able Agriculture in the West African Sahel,* London: International Institute for Environment and Development.

Prebisch, Raúl. 1984. "Five Stages in My Thinking on Development." In Gerald M. Meier and Dudley Seers, eds., *Pioneers in Development.* New York: Oxford University Press.

Pryor, F. L., and S. B. Maurer. 1982. "On Induced Economic Change in Pre-Capitalist Societies." *Journal of Development Economics* 10:325–53.

Rae, Allan N. 1971a. "Stochastic Programming, Utility and Sequential Decision Problems in Farm Management." *American Journal of Agricultural Economics* 53(3): 448–60.

———. 1971b. "An Empirical Application and Evaluation of Discrete Stochastic Programming in Farm Management." *American Journal of Agricultural Economics* 53(4): 625–38.

Raison, J.-P. 1979. "Les Modèles d'Intervention et leurs Objectifs." In P. Couty, J. Y. Marchal, P. Pélissier, M. Poussi, G. Savonnet, and A. Schwartz, eds., *Maîtrise de l'Espace Agraire et Développement en Afrique Tropicale: Logique Paysanne et Rationalité Technique.* Paris: ORSTOM.

———. 1981. "La colonisation des terres neuves en Afrique tropicale: Réflexions sur quelques travaux récent." In *Les Phénoménes de "Frontière" Dans les Pays Tropicaux. Travaux et Memoires de l'Institut des Hautes Etudes de l'Amérique Latine* 32:59–76.

———. 1985. "Les mouvements spontanés de migration en milieu rural dans les pays Africains Francophones: Evaluation et propositions." Paper presented at International Seminar on Planning for Settlements in Rural Regions: The Case of Spontaneous Settlements, Nov. 11–20, Nairobi, Kenya.

Ramaswamy, Sunder. 1991. "Technological Change, Land-Use Patterns, and Household Income Distributions in the Sahel." Ph.D. diss., Purdue University.

Ramaswamy, Sunder, and John H. Sanders. 1992. "Population Pressure, Land Degradation, and Sustainable Agricultural Technologies in the Sahel." *Agricultural Systems* 40: 361–78.

Randlett, R. Ray. 1992. "This Week in Congress." Information memorandum on Congressional legislation, July 20, USAID, Washington, D.C.

Rao, K., and C. H. H. Chopra. "The Links between Sustainable Agricultural Growth and Poverty." In Stephen Vosti, Thomas Reardon, and Winfried von Urff, eds., *Agricultural Sustainability, Growth, and Poverty Alleviation: Issues and Policies.* Feldafing, Germany: Food and Agriculture Development Center.

Raymond, G., G. Faure, and C. Persons. 1990. "Pratiques paysannes dans zone cotonniere face a l'augmentation de la pression fonciere (Nord Togo et Mali-Sud)." Paper presented at conference on Savanes d'Afrique Terres Fertiles, Montpelier, France. IRCT/CIRAD, Paris.

Raynaut, Claude. 1976. "Transformation du systeme de production et inegalite economique: Le cas d'un village haoussa (Niger)." *Revue Canadienne des Etudes Africaines* 10(2): 279–306.

Reardon, Thomas. 1993. "Cereals Demand in the Sahel and the Potential Impacts of Regional Cereals Protection." *World Development* 16(9): 1065–74.

Reardon, Thomas, Christopher Delgado, and Peter Matlon. 1992. "Determinants and

Effects of Income Diversification amongst Farm Households in Burkina Faso." *Journal of Development Studies* 28(2): 264–96.

Reddy, K. C. 1987. *Rapport de l'Agronomie Générale: Campagne 1986.* Kolo, Niger: INRAN/DRA.

Reddy, K. C., and Ly Samba. 1989. "Farming Systems Research: Some Suggestions for Agronomists." Paper presented at Regional Agronomists Training Workshop, Sept. 18–30, Bamako, Mali, organized by SAFGRAD/ICRISAT/USAID.

Reij, C., P. Mulder, and L. Begeman. 1988. *Water Harvesting for Plant Production.* Technical Paper 91. Washington, D.C.: World Bank.

Remy, G. 1968. "Les mouvements de population sur la rive gauche de la Volta Rouge region de Nobere." *Série Science Humaine* 2:45–66.

———. 1973. *Les migrations de travail et les mouvements de colonisation Mossi.* Paris: ORSTOM.

———. 1975. "Les migrations vers les 'Terres Neuves,' un nouveau courant migratoire." In *Enquête sur les mouvements de population à partir du pays Mossi,* vol. 1. Ouagadougou, Burkina Faso: ORSTOM.

Repetto, Robert. 1989. "Economic Incentives for Sustainable Production." In Gunter Schramm and Jeremy J. Warford, eds., *Environmental Management and Economic Development.* Baltimore: Johns Hopkins University Press.

Richards, Paul. 1985. *Indigenous Agricultural Revolution.* Boulder, Co.: Westview Press.

Robison, L. J., and P. J. Barry. 1987. *The Competitive Firm's Response to Risk.* New York.: Macmillan Publishing.

Robinson, W., and W. Schutjer. 1984. "Agricultural Development and Demographic Change: A Generalization of the Boserup Model." *Economic Development and Cultural Change* 32(2): 355–66.

Rosenzweig, M. R., and T. P. Schultz. 1982. "Market Opportunities, Genetic Endowments, and Intrafamily Resource Distribution: Child Survival in Rural India." *American Economic Review* 72(6): 803–15.

Roth, Michael, Philip Abbott, John H. Sanders, and Lance McKinzie. 1986. "An Application of Whole-Farm Modeling to New Technology Evaluation, Central Mossi Plateau, Burkina Faso." SAFGRAD, USAID Contract AFR-C-1472. International Programs in Agriculture, Purdue University, West Lafayette, Ind.

Ruthenberg, Hans. 1980. *Farming Systems in the Tropics.* New York: Oxford University Press.

Ruttan, Vernon W. 1978. "Induced Innovation and the Green Revolution." In Hans P. Binswanger and Vernon W. Ruttan, with Uri Ben-Zion, Alain de Janvry, Robert E. Evenson, Yujiro Hayami, Terry L. Roe, John H. Sanders, William W. Wade, Adolf Weber, and Patrick Yeung, *Induced Innovation: Technology, Institutions, and Development.* Baltimore: Johns Hopkins University Press.

———. 1982. *Agricultural Research Policy.* Minneapolis: University of Minnesota Press.

———. 1991. "Sustainable Growth in Agricultural Production: Poetry, Policy, and Science." In Stephen Vosti, Thomas Reardon, and Winifried von Urff, eds., *Agricultural Sustainability, Growth, and Poverty Alleviation: Issues and Policies.* Feldafing, Germany: Food and Agriculture Development Center.

Ruttan, Vernon W., Hans P. Binswanger, Yujiro Hayami, William W. Wade, and Adolf Weber. 1978. "Factor Productivity and Growth: A Historical Perspective." In Hans P. Binswanger and Vernon W. Ruttan, with Uri Ben-Zion, Alain de Janvry, Robert E. Evenson, Yujiro Hayami, Terry L. Roe, John H. Sanders, William W. Wade, Adolf Weber, and Patrick Yeung, *Induced Innovation: Technology, Institutions, and Development.* Baltimore: Johns Hopkins University Press.

Sachs, J. D. 1988. "Conditionality, Debt Relief, and the Developing Country Debt Crisis." In J. D. Sachs, ed., *Developing Country Debt and the World Economy.* Chicago: University of Chicago Press.

SAFGRAD (Semi-Arid Food Grain Research and Development). 1992. *The SAFGRAD Collaborative Research Networks: Avenues for Strengthening National Agricultural Research Systems in Sub-Saharan Africa.* Phase 2 Report, 1987–1991. Ouagadougou, Burkina Faso: OAU/STRC-SAFGRAD.

Salih, A. A. 1993. "Intensive Cropping Technologies for Sustainable Sorghum Production on the Dryland Vertisols of Sudan: A Modeling Approach Using EPIC." Ph.D. diss., Purdue University.

Salter, W. E. G. 1959. "Internal and External Balance—The Role of Price and Expenditure Effects." *Economic Record* 35(71): 226–38.

Sanders, John H. 1989. "Agricultural Research and Cereal Technology Introduction in Burkina Faso and Niger." *Agricultural Systems* 30:139–54.

———. 1994. "Economic Impact of the Commodity Research Networks of SAFGRAD." 1994. In John H. Sanders, Taye Bezuneh, and Alan C. Schroeder. *Impact Assessment of the SAFGRAD Commodity Networks.* Washington, D.C.: USAID/AFR/ARTS/FARA.

Sanders, John H., Taye Bezuneh, and Alan C. Schroeder. 1994. *Impact Assessment of the SAFGRAD Commodity Networks.* Washington, D.C.: USAID/AFR/ARTS/FARA.

Sanders, John H. and Joao Carlos Garcia. 1994. "The Economics of Stress and Technology Development in the Sahel and the 'Cerrados' of Brazil." In J. W. Maranville, V. C. Baligar, R. R. Duncan, and J. M. Yohe, eds., *Workshop on Adaptation of Plants to Soil Stresses.* Publication 94–2. Lincoln, Nebr.: INTSORMIL Management Entity Office.

Sanders, John H., and J. K. Lynam. 1982. "Evaluation of New Technology on Farms: Methodology and Some Results From Two Crop Programs at CIAT." *Agricultural Systems* 9(2): 97–112.

Sanders, John H., J. G. Nagy, and S. Ramaswamy. 1990. "Developing New Agricultural Technologies for the Sahelian Countries: The Burkina Faso Case." *Economic Development and Cultural Change* 39(1): 1–22.

Sanders, John H., P. Wright, P. Granier, and K. Savadogo. 1987. "Resource Management and New Technologies in Burkina Faso: A Stable Agricultural Development." Final report to West Africa Division of the World Bank. Dept. of Agricultural Economics, Purdue University, West Lafayette, Ind.

Saunders, M. O. 1980. "Agriculture in Upper Volta: The Institutional Framework." Farming Systems Research Unit working paper, International Programs in Agriculture, Purdue University, West Lafayette, Ind.

Savadogo, Kimseyinga. 1989a. *Analysis of Off-Farm Income*. Binghamton, N.Y.: Institute for Development Anthropology.

———. 1989b. *Factors Explaining Household Food Production Systems*. Binghamton, N.Y.: Institute for Development Anthropology.

———. 1990. "Production Systems in the Southwestern Region of Burkina Faso." Dept. of Economics, University of Ouagadougou, Ouagadougou, Burkina Faso.

Savadogo, Kimseyinga, and J. A. Brandt. 1988. "Household Food Demand in Burkina Faso: Implications for Food Policy." *Agricultural Economics* 2:345–64.

Savadogo, Kimseyinga, Thomas Reardon, and Kyosti Pietola. 1994. "Farm Productivity in Burkina Faso: Effects of Animal Traction and Nonfarm Income." *American Journal of Agricultural Economics* 76(3): 608–12.

Savadogo, Kimseyinga, John H. Sanders, and Della E. McMillan. 1989. "Farm and Female Incomes and Productivities in the River Blindness Settlement Programs of Burkina Faso." Institute for Development Anthropology, Binghamton, N.Y.

Savané, Marie-Angelique. 1986. "The Effects of Social and Economic Changes on the Role and Status of Women in Sub-Saharan Africa." In Joyce L. Moock, ed., *Understanding Africa's Rural Households and Farming Systems*. Boulder, Co.: Westview Press.

Scobie, G. M., and R. Posada. 1978. "The Impact of Technical Change on Income and Distribution: The Case of Rice in Colombia." *American Journal of Agricultural Economics* 60(11): 85–92.

Scott-Wendt, John, R. G. Chase, and L. R. Hossner. 1989. "Soil Chemical Variability in Sandy Ustalfs in Semi-Arid Niger, West Africa." *Soil Science* 145(6): 414–19.

Sedogo, M. P. 1993. "Evolution des sols ferrugineux lessivés sous culture: Influence des modes de gestion sur la fertilité." Thèse de Doctorat, Université National de Côte d'Ivoire, Abidjan, Côte d'Ivoire.

Sellen, D., G. Argwings-Kodhek, A. Chomba, Z. Francis, J. Mulinge Mukumbu, M. Nyambu, G. Okumu, S. Pagiola, K. R. Isaac, and A. Winter-Nelson. 1990. *Dairy in Kenya: Issues in Agricultural Policy*. Working Paper 8. RTAPAP (Research and Training in Agricultural Policy Analysis Project), Policy Analysis for Rural Development, Dept. of Agricultural Economics and Business Management, Egerton University, Egerton, Kenya.

Sen, Amartya K. 1981. *Poverty and Famines: An Essay on Entitlement and Deprivation*. New York: Oxford University Press.

———. 1983. "Development: Which Way Now?" *Economic Journal* 93:745–62.

———. 1990a. "Food, Economics, and Entitlements." In Carl K. Eicher and John M. Staatz, eds., *Agricultural Development in the Third World*. Baltimore: Johns Hopkins University Press.

———. 1990b. "Gender and Cooperative Conflicts." In I. Tinker, ed., *Persistent Inequalities: Women and World Development*. New York: Oxford University Press.

Serrao, Amilcar. 1988. "Farm-Level Response to Agricultural Development Strategies in the Evora Dryland Region of Portugal." Ph.D. diss., Purdue University.

SGB (Sudan Gezira Board). 1990. "The Gezira Scheme: Past, Present, and Future, 1989–1990." Wad Medani, Sudan.

Shapiro, B. I. 1990. "Potential Constraints, Policy, and New Technologies in the Niamey Region of Niger." Ph.D. diss., Purdue University.

Shapiro, B. I., Legesse Dadi, E. Zerbini, and Getachew Feleke. 1994. "Factors Affecting Adoption of Improved Feed Packages for Crossbred Cows at Selale, Ethiopia." In B. N. Mitaru, ed., *Proceedings of All-Africa Conference on Animal Agriculture*. Nairobi, Kenya: Animal Production Society of Kenya.

Shapiro, B. I., E. Jesse, and J. Foltz. 1992. "Dairy Marketing and Development in Africa." In Ray F. Brokken and Senait Seyoum, eds., *Dairy Marketing in Sub-Saharan Africa*. Addis Ababa, Ethiopia: ILCA.

Shapiro, B. I., John H. Sanders, K. C. Reddy, and T. G. Baker. 1993. "Evaluating and Adapting New Technologies in a High-Risk Agricultural System—Niger." *Agricultural Systems* 42:153–71.

Shapouri, Shahla, and Stacey Rosen. 1992. "Dairy Imports in Sub-Saharan Africa." In Ray F. Brokken and Senait Seyoum, eds., *Dairy Marketing in Sub-Saharan Africa*. Addis Ababa, Ethiopia: ILCA.

Simmons, Emmy. 1984. "The Economics of Irrigated Agricultural Development and Performance in Niger." In Glenn Anders, ed., *Niger Irrigation Subsector Assessment*. Niamey, Niger: USAID.

Simpson, I. G., and Morag C. Simpson. 1984. *Alternative Strategies for Agricultural Development in the Central Rainlands of the Sudan: With Special Reference to the Damazine Area*. Leeds, U.K.: University of Leeds.

Singh, R. D., and M. J. Morey. 1987. "The Value of Work at Home and Contributions of Wives' Household Services in Polygamous Families: Evidence from an African LDC." *Economic Development and Cultural Change* 35(4): 743–65.

Smale, Melinda, and Paul W. Heisey. 1994. "Maize Research in Malawi Revisited: An Emerging Success Story?" *Journal of International Development* 6(6): 689–706.

Smale, Melinda, and Vernon W. Ruttan. 1994. *Cultural Endowments, Institutional Renovation, and Technical Innovation: The "Groupements Naam" of Yatenga, Burkina Faso*. Bulletin 94–2. Minneapolis: Economic Development Center, University of Minnesota.

Smith, Joyotee, Anthony D. Barau, Abraham Goldman, and James H. Mareck. 1994. "The Role of Technology in Agricultural Intensification: The Evolution of Maize Production in the Northern Guinea Savanna of Nigeria." *Economic Development and Cultural Change* 42(3): 537–54.

"Soil and Water." *Crops and Soils Magazine* 37:26–27.

Southgate, D., J. H. Sanders, S. Ehui. 1990. "Resource Degradation in Africa and Latin America: Population Pressure, Policies, and Property Arrangements." *American Journal of Agricultural Economics* 72(5): 1259–63.

Staal, S. J., and B. I. Shapiro. 1994. "The Effects of Price Decontrol on Kenyan Peri-Urban Dairy: An Application of the Policy-Analysis Matrix." *Food Policy* 19(6): 533–49.

Stewart, Frances, Sanjaya Lall, and Samuel Wangwe. 1992. "Alternative Development Strategies: An Overview." In Frances Stewart, Sanjaya Lall, and Samuel Wanagwe, eds., *Alternative Development Strategies in Sub-Saharan Africa*. New York: St. Martin's Press.

Stoop, W. A. 1986. "Agronomic Management of Cereal/Cowpea Cropping Systems for Major Toposequence Land Types in the West African Savanna." *Field Crop Research* 14:301–19.

————. 1989. "Variations in Soil Properties along Three Toposequences in Burkina Faso and Implications for the Development of Improved Cropping Systems." *Agriculture, Ecosystems, and Environment* 19:241–64.

Stryker, J. Dirck. 1976. "Population Density, Agricultural Technique, and Land Utilization in a Village Economy." *American Economic Review* 66(3): 347–58.

————. 1994. "A Regional Strategy for Trade and Growth in West Africa." Associates for International Resources and Development (AIRD), Cambridge, Mass.

Sudan. 1993. *Agricultural Situation and Outlook* (in Arabic). Khartoum, Sudan: Ministry of Agriculture and Natural Resources.

Sutter, J. W. 1979. "Social Analysis of the Nigerian Rural Producer." In E. Berg, ed., *Niger Agricultural Sector Assessment,* vol. 2, part D. Niamey, Niger: USAID.

————. 1984. "Peasants, Merchant Capital, and Rural Differentiation: A Nigerian Hausa Case Study." Ph.D. diss., Cornell University.

Svedberg, Peter. 1991. "The Export Performance of Sub-Saharan Africa." *Economic Development and Cultural Change* 39(3): 549–66.

Swinton, Scott M. 1988. "Drought Survival Tactics of Subsistence Farmers in Niger." *Human Ecology* 16(2): 123–44.

Swinton, S. M., and A. Mamane. 1986. "Les exploitations agricoles dans trois villages de Madarounfa face à la sècheresse de 1984." Document 15F. Dept. of Research on Rural Economics, National Institute of Agronomic Research of Niger, Niamey, Niger.

Terrible, M. 1979. *Occupation du sol en Haute Volta: Son évolution entre 1952–1956 et 1975.* Ouagadougou, Burkina Faso: Centre Régional de Télédétection de Ouagadougou.

Tinker, I., ed. 1990. *Persistent Inequalities: Women and World Development.* New York: Oxford University Press.

Tothill, J. D. 1948. *Agriculture in the Sudan.* New York: Oxford University Press.

Uchendu, V. C. 1970. "The Impact of Agricultural Technological Change on African Land Tenure." *Journal of Developing Area* 4:477–86.

UNDP (United Nations Development Programme). 1986. *Employment and Economic Reform: Towards a Strategy for the Sudan.* Geneva: ILO.

————. 1994. *Human Development Report 1994.* New York: Oxford University Press.

USDA (United States Department of Agriculture). 1981. *Food Problems and Prospects in Sub-Saharan Africa: The Decade of the 1980s.* Foreign Agricultural Economic Report 166. Washington, D.C.: USDA, Economic Research Service.

————. 1993. *World Agriculture: Trends and Indicators.* Statistical Bulletin 861. Washington, D.C.: U.S. Dept. of Agriculture.

van der Pol, Floris. 1992. *Soil Mining: An Unseen Contributor to Farm Income in Southern Mali.* Bulletin 325. Amsterdam, The Netherlands: Royal Tropical Institute.

Van Dijk, Johan A., and Mohamed Hassan Ahmed. 1993. *Opportunities for Expanding Water Harvesting in Sub-Saharan Africa: The Case of the* Teras *of*

*Kassala*.Washington, D.C.: International Institute for Environment and Development.

Van Raay, G. T., and J. G. M. Hilhorst. 1981. "Land Settlement and Regional Development in the Tropics: Results, Prospects, and Options." Discussion paper. Institute for Social Studies Advisory Board, The Hague.

Van Stavereen, J. P., and W. A. Stoop. 1985. "Adaptation to Toposequence Land Types in West Africa of Different Sorghum Genotypes in Comparison with Local Cultivars of Sorghum, Millet, and Maize." *Field Crops Research* 11:13–35.

Vierich, H. I. D., and W. A. Stoop. 1990. "Changes in West African Savanna Agriculture in Response to Growing Population and Continuing Low Rainfall." *Agriculture, Ecosystems, and Environment* 31:115–32.

Vlek, P. L., A. U. Mokwunye, and M. S. Mudahar. 1987. "Soil Fertility Maintenance in Sub-Saharan Africa." Office of Technology Assessment, Congress of the United States, Washington, D.C.

von Braun, J. 1991. "The Links between Agricultural Growth, Environmental Degradation, and Nutrition and Health: Implications for Policy Research." In Stephen Vosti, Thomas Reardon, and Winfried von Urff, eds., *Agricultural Sustainability, Growth, and Poverty Alleviation: Issues and Policies*. Feldafing, Germany: Food and Agriculture Development Center.

von Braun, J., and P. J. R. Webb. 1989. "The Impact of New Crop Technology on the Agricultural Division of Labor in a West African Setting." *Economic Development and Cultural Change* 37(3): 512–34.

von Massow, V. H. 1989. *Dairy Imports into Sub-Saharan Africa: Problems, Policies, and Prospects*. Research Report 17. Addis Ababa, Ethiopia: ILCA.

Walshe, M. J., J. Grindle, A. Nell, and M. Bachmann. 1991. *Dairy Development in Sub-Saharan Africa: A Study of Issues and Options*. Technical Paper 135. Washington, D.C.: World Bank.

Webb, Patrick, Girma Bisrat, and Layne Coppock. 1991. "Food Security and Sustainable Growth for Pastoral Systems in Semi-Arid Africa." In Stephen Vosti, Thomas Reardon, and Winfried von Urff, eds., *Agricultural Sustainability, Growth, and Poverty Alleviation: Issues and Policies*. Feldafing, Germany: Food and Agriculture Development Center.

Weber, Michael, John M. Staatz, John S. Holtzman, Eric W. Crawford, and Richard H. Bernsten. 1988. "Informing Food Security Decisions in Africa: Empirical Analysis and Policy Dialogue." *American Journal of Agricultural Economics* 70(5): 1044–52.

Weitz, R. D. Pelley, and L. Applebaum. 1978. "Employment and Income Generation in New Settlement Projects." World Employment Paper 10, Working Paper 3. ILO, Geneva.

WHO (World Health Organization). 1985. "Ten Years of Onchocerciasis Control." OCP/GVA85.1B. WHO, Geneva.

Wicker, F. R. 1989. "Commercial Demonstration to Produce Composite Flour by Co-Milling Wheat and Sorghum." Report prepared for the Government of Sudan and the USAID Mission to Sudan. USAID, Khartoum, Sudan.

Williams, T. O., Powell, J. M. and S. Fernandez-Rivera. 1993. "Manure Utilization, Drought Cycles, and Herd Dynamics in the Sahel: Implications for Cropland Productivity." Paper presented at the Nutrient Cycling Workshop, Nov. 26–30, ILCA, Addis Ababa, Ethiopia.

Winrock International. 1992. *Assessment of Animal Agriculture in Sub-Saharan Africa*. Morrilton, Ark.: Winrock International.

World Bank. Various years. *World Development Report*. New York: Oxford University Press.

———. 1981. *Accelerated Development in Sub-Saharan Africa: An Agenda for Action*. Washington, D.C.: World Bank.

———. 1982. *World Development Report 1982*. New York: Oxford University Press.

———. 1986. *The Hesitant Recovery and Prospects for Sustained Growth, Trade, and Pricing Policies in World Agriculture*. New York: Oxford University Press.

———. 1988. *Adjustment Lending: An Evaluation of Ten Years of Experience*. Policy and Research Series 1. Washington, D.C.: World Bank.

———. 1989a. *Sub-Saharan Africa: From Crisis to Sustainable Growth*. Washington, D.C.: World Bank.

———. 1989b. *Successful Development in Africa: Case Studies of Projects, Programs, and Policies*. Washington, D.C.: World Bank.

———. 1989c. "Burkina Faso Economic Memorandum." Report 7594-BUR. World Bank, Washington, D.C.

———. 1992. *Development and the Environment*. New York: Oxford University Press.

———. 1993. *Investing in Health*. New York: Oxford University Press.

———. 1994. "The Onchocersias Control Program in West Africa." Information Brief H.02.4–94. World Bank, Washington, D.C.

World Bank and UNDP. 1989. *Africa's Adjustment and Growth in the 1980s*. Washington, D.C.: World Bank.

Wright, Peter. 1985. "Water and Soil Conservation by Farmers." In H. W. Ohm and J. G. Nagy, eds., *Appropriate Technologies for Farmers in Semi-Arid West Africa*. West Lafayette, Ind.: Purdue University, International Programs in Agriculture.

Youngblood, C. E. 1982. *The Structure of Incentives in Sudan's Rainfed Agriculture Sector*. Research Triangle Park, N.C.: Sigma One Corp.

Younger, S., and J.-B. Zongo. 1989. "West Africa: The Onchocerciasis Control Programme." In *Successful Development in Africa: Case Studies of Projects, Programs, and Policies*. Washington, D.C.: World Bank.

Yousif, O. A. F. 1989. "Pilot Project for Hybrid Sorghum Seed Production, Distribution, and Utilization, 1984–1988." Final report. National Seed Administration, Sennar, Sudan.

Zachariah, Z. C., and J. Conde. 1981. *Migration in West Africa: Demographic Aspects*. New York: Oxford University Press.

Portions of chapter 2 are taken from Sanders (1989), "Agricultural Research and Cereal Technology Introduction in Burkina Faso and Niger"; reprinted from *Agricultural Systems* 30:139–54, with kind permission from Elsevier Science Ltd., The Boulevard, Langford Lane, Kidlington OX5 1GB, U.K. The section on pp. 38–42 is adapted from Sanders, Nagy, and Ramaswamy (1990), "Developing New Agricultural Technologies for the Sahelian Countries: The Burkina Faso Case," *Economic Development and Cultural Change* 39(1): 1–22. University of Chicago. All rights reserved. 0013-0079/3901-0063. It is published with permission of the University of Chicago Press, grant number 29530.

Portions of chapter 3 are taken from Deuson and Sanders, "Cereal Technology Development in the Sahel: Burkina Faso and Niger." This article was first published in *Land Use Policy* 7(3): 195–97; one section is reproduced here with the permission of Butterworth-Heinemann, Oxford, U.K. Several paragraphs are taken from Sanders (1989), "Agricultural Research and Cereal Technology Introduction in Burkina Faso and Niger," *Agricultural Systems* 30:139–54, and are reprinted with kind permission from Elsevier Science Ltd., The Boulevard, Langford Lane, Kidlington OX5 1GB, U.K.

Portions of chapter 4 are taken from Sanders, Nagy, and Ramaswamy (1990), "Developing New Agricultural Technologies for the Sahelian Countries: The Burkina Faso Case," *Economic Development and Cultural Change* 39(1): 1–22. © University of Chicago. All rights reserved. 0013-0079/3901-0063. They are published with permission of the University of Chicago Press, grant number 29530. The section on the shift from extensive to intensive technologies is a revised version of Ramaswamy and Sanders (1992), "Population Pressure, Land Degradation, and Sustainable Agricultural Technologies in the Sahel," *Agricultural Systems* 40(4): 361–78. It is published with kind permission from Elsevier Science Ltd., The Boulevard, Langford Lane, Kidlington OX5 1GB, U.K.

Portions of chapter 5 are taken from Shapiro, Sanders, Reddy, and Baker (1993). They are reprinted from *Agricultural Systems* 42:153–71, "Evaluating and Adapting New Technologies in a High-Risk Agricultural System—Niger," with kind permission from Elsevier Science Ltd., The Boulevard, Langford Lane, Kidlington OX5 1GB, U.K.

Portions of chapter 8 are taken from Ramaswamy and Sanders (1992), "Population Pressure, Land Degradation, and Sustainable Agricultural Technologies in the Sahel," *Agricultural Systems* 40:361–78, and are reprinted with kind permission from Elsevier Science Ltd., The Boulevard, Langford Lane, Kidlington OX5 1GB, U.K.

Portions of chapter 11 are taken from Sanders (1989), "Agricultural Research and Cereal Technology Introduction in Burkina Faso and Niger"; reprinted from *Agricultural Systems* 30:139–54, with kind permission from Elsevier Science Ltd., The Boulevard, Langford Lane, Kidlington OX5 1GB, U.K. Much of the appendix is taken from Staal and Shapiro (1994), "The Effects of Price Decontrol on Kenyan Peri-Urban Dairy: An Application of the Policy Analysis Matrix," *Food Policy* 19(6): 533–49. It is reprinted by permission of the publishers, Butterworth-Heinemann Ltd. ©

# Index

Library of Congress Cataloging-in-Publication Data

Sanders, John H.
  The economics of agricultural technology in semiarid Sub-Saharan
Africa / John H. Sanders, Barry I. Shapiro, and Sunder Ramaswamy.
      p.      cm. — (Johns Hopkins studies in development)
  Includes bibliographical references and index.
  ISBN 0-8018-5139-4 (alk. paper)
  1. Agricultural innovations—Economic aspects—Africa, Sub-Saharan.  2. Agriculture—
Economic aspects—Africa, Sub-Saharan.  I. Shapiro, Barry I. (Barry Ira)  II. Ramaswamy,
Sunder.  III. Title.  IV. Series.
HD2117.S26   1996
338.1'6'0967—dc20                                                                              95-16944
                                                                                                        CIP